TEXTBOOKS
THIS IS THE PROPERTY OF
LA COLINA JR. HIGH SCHOOL, SANTA BARBARA, CALIF.

27

DATE	TEACHER	STUDENT	ROOM	PER.	COND.
9-17	Young	Karen Griffith	301	5	
	Prep. Emylich	Jon Koons	301	5	

EXPLANATION OF MARKS	A-GOOD	B-FAIR	C-POOR	D-DISCARD

Questions in
MODERN
GRAMMAR
AND COMPOSITION

David A. Conlin
George R. Herman

AMERICAN BOOK COMPANY

David A. Conlin

Professor Emeritus of English, Arizona State University. Dr. Conlin is the author of *A Modern Approach to Teaching English* and the senior author of the *Our Language Today Series.* He has written articles for the *English Journal* and for other professional journals.

George R. Herman

Associate Professor of English, Arizona State University, and a former coordinator of teacher training; previously a teacher of English in the intermediate and secondary grades. Mr. Herman has had numerous short stories, poems, and articles published in a variety of literary and professional magazines and is co-author of the *Our Language Today Series* at the junior high school level.

American Book Company

NEW YORK   CINCINNATI   ATLANTA   DALLAS   MILLBRAE

CONTENTS

2   *The English Sentence*   36

3   *Learning How Words Communicate*   62

4   *Problems of Usage*   90

Contents

Picture Credits

PART I

Grammar

Part I of Questions in Modern Grammar and Composition *begins with a brief history of grammar and a discussion of the different kinds of grammatical study that are currently being made. After a review of sentence structure and the ways in which words communicate, you will go on to the study of usage. In Chapter 5, you will try to focus on the problems of applying your knowledge of grammar to your writing. You will review the problems of punctuation and the methods for the improvement of spelling with particular emphasis on the relationship of the sounds of English to the graphic representation of those sounds.*

The photographs which open each chapter in Part I show a variety of writing systems used throughout the world. Some represent a written form no longer in use. The accompanying photographs offer a view of the cultural life of the speakers of that language. Your class will want to discuss the various linguistic communities depicted.

Chapter 1

A BRIEF
HISTORY
OF
GRAMMAR

ᎠᎦᏅ ᎬᏙᏓᎶᏅᏛᏂ ᎠᏍᎦᎬᎬ ᎠᏍᎬ ᎠᏂᏍᏇᏫᏛᎬᏘ. ᎠᏍ ᎬᏂᏔᏃ ᏂᏍᏗᏌᎢ
ᏐᏴᏌᏇᎣᎥ ᎠᏏ ᏥᏍᏗᏴᏌᏘ ᏞᏂᏪᎡᏣ ᎤᏍ ᎢᏍᏘ ᎤᏍᎦᎬᏣ ᎬᏂᏔᏍ ᏔᎬᎣᎥᏘᏛ
ᏍᎦᎲᏘ. ᎢᏟ ᏦᏞᎬ ᏃᏴ ᎦᎣᏴᏲ ᏃᏞᏍᏘ. ᎠᎠ ᎦᎣᏴ ᎤᎣᎸᏔᎦ ᏪᎥᎩᎥ
ᎤᎬᎡ ᏝᎠᏞᏍᏘ ᎠᏪᎶ ᏞᏂᏍᏞᎠᏍᏝᎣᏱ, ᎣᏓᎡ ᏂᏂᎬᏔᏍ, ᎠᏍ ᎢᎣᎠᎬ ᏤᏍᏣ
ᎠᎣᎦᏍ ᏂᏍᎢ ᏎᎧᏍᏝᎬᎢᎢ; ᎠᏍ ᎤᎠᎠᎬ ᏞᏂᏍᏞᎠᏍᏝᎣᏱ ᏟᎤᏴ ᎠᏪᎶ ᏐᏔᏐᎬ
ᎠᏪᎶ ᏁᎠᎬᏐᎨ ᎠᎠ ᎦᎣᏴ ᎤᎣᎸᏔᎬ ᏤᏂᎬᏔᏍ ᏂᏂᎡᏎ.   ᎴᎣᎶᎬᏃ ᏝᎠᏞᏍᏘ   *Cherokee*

A Look
Back
and
A Look
Forward

For two years you have studied grammar and composition in high school. Your work in written composition improved as you mastered the structural concepts that helped you develop more effective sentences. You learned to communicate more precisely as you improved your skill in the use of modifiers and observed the growth in your vocabulary. You gained in power to express yourself in writing as you succeeded in making full use of the resources of English structure.

Now you will look briefly at the development of grammar since the time of Dionysius Thrax, who lived in the first century B.C. Some knowledge of the history of grammar should help you to a better understanding of the subject as you study it in the final years of high school.

13

YOUR STUDY OF ENGLISH

By now you have learned to recognize the physical characteristics of the sentence. You have studied its basic patterns and the methods by which these basic sentences may be expanded. You have considered and used the grammatical devices of coordination, subordination, modification, substitution, and apposition. You have examined the word groups of English, the basic units of syntax and meaning. You have learned about the form and functions of words in communication—the noun, the verb, the adjective, the adverb, the function words. You have studied inflectional and derivational suffixes. You have learned something about the sounds of English and the relation of these sounds to spelling. You have considered the intonation patterns of speech and the relation of these patterns to punctuation. You have begun to think of English as an analytic language, a relatively uninflected language, one which permits functional shift and the flexible use of a great variety of forms in the fulfillment of functions within the sentence.

A NEW APPROACH TO GRAMMAR

It is time now for a new approach to the subject of grammar, a look at its development and meaning, its purpose and method. This approach will help you to understand the place of grammar in the curriculum both in high school and in college.

This chapter touches briefly on the history of grammar. It explains the variety of ways in which grammar is being developed by modern students of our language. It compares traditional and structural grammar in detail, since your study here is most directly related to the nomenclature and method of these two disciplines. It also elaborates on some of the unique characteristics of structural grammar. Among these are form classes, immediate constituents, objective criteria, and changing usage.

As you go on with your education, particularly with the study of language, you will find that grammar is not a single subject at all. It is a multiple subject. Instead of one grammar, there are four grammars. You have already studied some traditional grammar and some structural grammar. Later you may go into the study of generative grammar and perhaps even the study of the historical development of English which is the approach to historical grammar. The discussion in this chapter is designed to provide you with a background for this later study of the different kinds of grammar.

THE NATURE OF LANGUAGE

Imagine yourself in a country where you are experiencing difficulty in buying things, in ordering what you want to eat, even in finding hotel accommodations. This difficulty has grown out of your inability to ask questions that can be understood and to grasp statements that have been directed to you. Furthermore, no possibility of communication exists because there is no common medium through which you and the natives of this country can share ideas, thoughts, experience, directions. In other words, you and your listeners do not share a common language.

To a native Frenchman who does not speak English, your language is merely a set of noise sequences. To you, if you cannot speak French, his language is a set of noise sequences. To a fellow American, English is not noise at all, but a series of sound stimuli which evoke some sort of response on his part. He may simply nod his head and smile. He, in turn, may begin to use his speech organs, or he may even indulge in some form of overt behavior—shutting a window, opening a door, buying you your lunch, going with you to the movies. All of this may happen because he "understands" the sounds you are uttering. These sounds have meaning.

You and your fellow American have grown up in a speech community. You have heard the same or similar sounds arranged in the same kinds of patterns, accompanied by similar signals of stress, pitch, and juncture, reinforced at times by familiar gestures and accommodations of voice and body movement. You have watched others respond to these behavioral patterns, and you have copied these responses. You have become so sensitive to communication signals that your responses have become habitual. The great variety of action involved in speech by which you inform, ask, and demand of others constitutes your language. It is a form of human behavior, learned in a social situation.

Of the countless sounds made in the English language, about forty-five are used in communication. In the course of centuries, these sounds have been arranged into a limited number of patterns, or words—approximately 450,000, although the possibility of combination and arrangement is almost beyond comprehension. Then a small number of patterns have been developed for arranging these words into utterances, fragments of speech or sentences as the case may be.

One of the characteristics of language that you must recognize very early in your study is that the sounds of English are not exactly alike in different places in the United States, and that the variations in more widely separated parts of the English-speaking world are even greater. Actually, what is thought of as the English language is made up of a great many dialects or regional variations of sound, meaning, and even structure. What is thought of as standard English is actually the dialect of educated people. Also, each individual has his own unique way of using the language—his pronunciation, the intonation qualities of his speech, his grammatical style. This is his idiolect. This, too, may vary from day to day and from year to year.

Language is a dynamic form of social behavior. It is not a static quality of inherited human instinct; rather it is a changing form of learned behavior, changing with the individual, with the group, with the times. It is an integral part of human living and of the customs that grow from the demands of living together with others.

Since a language changes over the years, you cannot fully understand it as it is used today unless you know something of how it was used in other years. The history of a language is merely the record of its change. This is an important part of language study.

The study of language consists not only of the examination of its history, but it involves also the study of its sounds, its phonetics. It includes a consideration of the problems of meaning, its semantics, and the study of its patterns of structure, which is called *grammar*. It is the story of grammar that is of interest to you now.

THE GREEKS HAD A WORD FOR IT

In the Age of Pericles, about the fifth century B.C., the Greeks maintained a high standard of scholarship and learning. They were particularly interested in language—in its grammar, its rhetoric, and its logic. These studies represented the bases of the skills of communication, of debating, of convincing others, of using man's greatest gift, reason. So important was the "word" that the Greeks gave it the name *logos* which also meant the "truth," and the modern study of logic derives not only its name but also some of its function from the original Greek connotation. The letter, which was the written mark of language, was given the name *gramma*, and it is from this word that our modern word *grammar* is derived. The Greek word *gramma* was derived from the verb *graphein*, which means "to write."

The adjective *grammatikos* with its feminine form *grammatikē* referred to the study of letters, or literature (that which is written). So the study of grammar in ancient Greece became the scholarly study of literature much as literature is studied today in modern philology.

Aristotle (384-322 B.C.) is considered the first of the grammarians in the modern sense. He began the study of parts of speech and inflections. He discusses and defines his word classes in *De Interpretatione* and in

De Poetica. They are the noun and the verb on the first level, and the conjunction and the article on a much lower level. In his definitions Aristotle emphasizes meaning and recognizes, as do the modern structural grammarians, the fact that words such as *a, an,* and *the,* as well as words such as *and, but,* and *or* have little lexical meaning; they function in communication mainly as a means of determining syntax.

The Greek philosophers who lived during the time of Aristotle had two points of view about language. They started a controversy which has lasted through the centuries and established a belief that still colors the thinking of many people in their attitude toward grammar. The one group, the anomalists, believed that grammatical uses are developed by the people who speak the language, changing as customs change. The other group, the analogists, believed that language in its origin and growth is based on correspondence between a word and an idea, that it is eternal and unchanging. Since the idea was the ultimate reality of the universe, the word as the symbol of the idea took upon itself some of the eternal quality. This was the philosophy of Plato, whereas Aristotle, his pupil, held to the doctrines of the anomalists. The modern conflict between the descriptive grammarians, who describe the language as it is used, and the prescriptive grammarians, who devise rules to show how the language ought to be used, has its roots in the ancient philosophical debate of the anomalists and the analogists, the followers of Aristotle and Plato. The belief in "correct English" is a Platonic doctrine.

SOME EARLY GRAMMARIANS

The first grammarian to write a textbook was Dionysius Thrax in the first century B.C. It was a Greek grammar and was called the *Art of Grammar.* Since Dionysius Thrax was an analogist, his work reflected the philosophy of that school of thought. This would be of little importance now except that his work influenced later grammars. Actually, the *Art of Grammar* was used as a basic text in English public schools for the study of Greek until late in the nineteenth century. Dionysius Thrax listed and defined eight parts of speech — noun, verb, participle, article, pronoun, preposition, adverb, and conjunction. His definitions were based partly on meaning, partly on form, and partly on function. Today's definitions of the parts of speech in conventional grammar reflect this variable approach.

The most important Latin grammarians were Donatus and Priscian whose work in Rome in the fourth and fifth centuries A.D. was patterned on the Greek grammar of Dionysius Thrax. They, however, dropped the article as a part of speech, since it was not applicable to Latin, and added the interjection.

In the Middle Ages (from about 500 to 1500 A.D.), Latin was the universal language. It was the language of the universities throughout Europe. All knowledge available to scholars of that time was written in Latin, and it was necessary for them to be able to read and write Latin in order to acquire knowledge in any study and to express their own thoughts as a result of their learning. The study of grammar during the Middle Ages became the study of the Latin language and literature. In the liberal arts curriculum, grammar, rhetoric, and logic made up the trivium, or elementary division; arithmetic, geometry, astronomy, and music made up the quadrivium, or higher division. Treatises on grammar were written by St. Anselm and Duns Scotus. The most important work was the *Doctrinale puerorum* written in 1199 by Alexander de Villa-Dei and based on the work of Priscian.

The study of Latin and Greek as the basis of a liberal education persisted in England and the United States throughout the nineteenth century. The curriculum of the great English public schools was made up largely of Latin and Greek literature. Students were obliged to learn to read and write Latin fluently and even to compose poetry in Latin. The name *Latin Grammar School* describes the secondary school of both England and New England. The persistence of the term *grammar school* to our modern period reflects the early function of the school, the study of the elements of Latin grammar.

With the development of printing in England in the fifteenth century, books written in English became available and were read by educated people. The study of the vernacular language began in the elementary schools. In 1640 Ben Jonson's *English Grammar* was published. It was patterned on the Latin grammars and attempted to fit the English forms and inflections into the categories and patterns of the Latin language. Jonson used the Latin parts of speech to describe the word classes of English.

Grammars of this period were of little lasting importance. They were used primarily as an aid in the instruction of English to foreigners or as an aid in the study of Latin.

In the eighteenth century, however, a serious effort was made by a number of scholars to formalize grammar and to use it as a means of purifying the English language. The Latin grammars were invariably used as models. The most influential texts published were Robert Lowth's *A Short Introduction to English Grammar* (1762), William Ward's *A Grammar of the English Language* (1765), and Lindley Murray's *Grammar of the English Language Adapted to the Different Classes of Learners* (1795). All of these texts denied the standard usage in determining correct English and developed rules based either on the Latin grammar or on what seemed to be reasonable in cases where no Latin criterion existed. As a result of years of study of such textbooks as these, there developed in the United States an almost universal belief in the existence of absolute standards of correctness in English and the rejection of all usage which did not conform to these standards. Much of what is repudiated today as incorrect English — although it may perhaps be used by men of literary genius and high reputation as writers and students — can in no small measure be attributed to the diligence and efforts of the authoritarian grammarians of the eighteenth century.

For almost a hundred years, the work of Lowth in England and that of Murray in the United States dominated the teaching of grammar in these two English-speaking countries. Not only did Murray and Lowth effectively indoctrinate our culture with the philosophy of absolute standards of correctness, but they also brought about the major emphasis on the study of the eight parts of speech used today, with much the same standard definitions.

THE FOUNDATIONS OF MODERN GRAMMAR

Modern grammar begins with the work of Henry Sweet in the late nineteenth century, with the publication of *A New English Grammar, Logical and Historical* in 1891. He was the first of a number of language scholars who introduced the scientific spirit into the study and description of the English language. While he employed the basic approach of the study of parts of speech, he recognized the importance of all three categories of form, function, and meaning and used all three factors in his language analysis. He further recognized the fact that English was an analytic language, a relatively uninflected language. His analysis served to contrast English with Latin, a highly inflected language.

Other scholarly English grammars followed the work of Sweet. Alonzo Reed and Brainerd Kellogg published *A High School Grammar* in 1900. H. Poutsma published *A Grammar of Modern English* in 1904. Otto Jesperson published *The Philosophy of Grammar* in 1924 and *Essentials of English Grammar* in 1933. George O. Curme published his *College English Grammar* in 1925. The works of these men served as the basis for the study of grammar in high schools and colleges for the first half of the twentieth century. When we speak of traditional grammar or conventional grammar, we are referring to adaptations of the body of subject matter developed by these men or others whose work is similar. Traditional grammar has the weight of over two hundred years of study and change and is rooted deeply in our culture and thinking.

Structural Grammar

Probably the most dramatic and revolutionary movement in the history of grammar has been the work of the structural linguists beginning with the work of Leonard Bloomfield published in *Language* (1933). This was followed by Z. S. Harris' *Methods in Structural Linguistics* (1951), George L. Trager and H. L. Smith's *An Outline of English Structure* (1957), and Charles C. Fries's *Structure of English* (1952).

Very briefly now, the structural viewpoint embraces the idea that language is speech and that the proper subject matter of study in grammar is speech. Written English is derived from the spoken language. The structural method involves a rigorous analysis of speech into its component parts beginning with an utterance, breaking it into constituents, morphemes, phonemes, and finally phones, the individual speech sounds. It is fundamental to the structural approach that any statement, conclusion, generalization, observation must be verifiable by means of objective evidence. This develops the emphasis on formal characteristics, objective signals of structure as clues to meaning. These signals include word order, function words, inflections, derivational suffixes, and sound patterns. The appeal to semantic evidence (meaning) is largely ruled out.

Structural grammar, since it deals mainly with speech, gives considerable emphasis to the study of intonation, the changes in pitch and stress in oral communication, and the nature and kinds of juncture or breaks in the speech flow. Finally, structural grammar recognizes the importance of dialect in the language, the changing nature of language, and the importance of usage as the basis of what is considered to be good English.

Generative Grammar

Within the past ten years, another strong movement in the study of grammar has gained considerable prominence and respect. The new study began as "transformational grammar," but is now referred to usually as "generative grammar." The first important publication in this field was the work of Noam Chomsky, *Syntactic Structures* (1957). It was followed by the publications of Robert B. Lees, *The Grammar of English Nominalizations* (1960) and *Constituent Structure and Transformation Rules* (1961).

Generative grammar is concerned with the ways in which English sentences may be developed or generated. It is concerned with what the French would call *la langue*, the concept of a language in terms of "what may be said and how it may be said." This concept is in contrast with *la parole*, the concept of a language in terms of "what has been said and how it has been said." The structural linguist is concerned with *la parole*. He examines and analyzes the spoken utterances. The transformationalist is concerned, rather, with the language potential, with predicting all of the limited and precise methods of communication, and with expressing these methods in terms of exact formulas.

Generative grammar is developed in two stages. The first deals with the variety of simple or "kernel" sentences which may be found in English. The following would be considered kernel sentences:

> The child talks.
> The boy ate the apple.
> The girl has written a theme.

The second stage deals with the methods by which all other sentences are generated from these kernel sentences. Where in structural grammar the basic sentence pattern is considered, in generative grammar the kernel sentence is considered. In structural grammar the methods whereby the basic sentences are expanded is demonstrated. In generative grammar the formula by which the kernel sentences are transformed into other sentences is developed.

The two processes are not exactly parallel, however. Consider this kernel sentence:

> The child talks.

The sentence may generate many others:

> The child is talking.
> The child is not talking.
> The child did talk.
> Is the child talking?
> Did the child talk?
> The little child talks.
> The child talks poorly.
> When will the child talk?

Now consider some of the sentences that may be generated from:

> The boy ate the apple.

This kernel sentence may generate:

> The boy has eaten the apple.
> The boy did eat the apple.
> The boy did not eat the apple.
> Did the boy eat the apple?
> When did the boy eat the apple?
> The apple was eaten by the boy.
> The apple has been eaten by the boy.
> The apple has not been eaten by the boy.

Notice that the transformations are familiar sentence forms — negatives, questions, passives, negative passives, and so on. Modifiers may be added to generate more sentences. The process of generating other sentences from a simple kernel sentence follows limited and prescribed methods or rules that are invariable in the English language. The rules are expressed by means of symbols or formulas.

The kernel sentence *The boy ate the apple* consists of a noun phrase (NP) and a verb phrase (VP).

$$\text{Sentence} \longrightarrow \text{NP} + \text{VP} \text{ (The arrow means ``is written.'')}$$
$$\text{NP} \longrightarrow \text{T} + \text{N}$$
$$\text{VP} \longrightarrow \text{V} + \text{NP}$$

The noun phrase is written as an article (T) plus a noun. The verb phrase is written as a verb plus another noun phrase.

When this is transformed to the passive, a very definite order is followed. First, the noun phrase that follows the verb will now precede the verb. Second, a form of *to be* will be used with the past participle form of the verb. Third, the noun phrase which preceded the verb in the kernel sentence will be used in a prepositional phrase connected by the preposition *by*. The generated sentence will be:

The apple has been eaten by the boy.

The generative grammarian will express this in the formula:

$$\text{NP}_2 + \text{Aux} + \text{be} + \text{en} + \text{V} + \text{by} + \text{NP}_1$$

You may think that the grammarian is making a simple idea very complicated. Actually, he is doing the reverse. The language forms seem simple to you only because you are so used to them and so sensitive to them. You are so familiar with your language patterns (which are extremely complex) that you do not even notice them. Their use is habitual, like raising your arm — an extremely complex action involving the nervous and muscular systems of the body. The formula developed for generating a passive sentence from an active sentence is actually a simplification.

You, as a native-born American, have learned to use and work with the English language all your life. As a result, you may not see the value of the formula developed by the grammarian. However, you may appreciate its value in the teaching of English to a foreign student, together with countless other formulas yet to be defined. You may also appreciate the value of a formula to a machine equipped to produce language structures in amounts and kinds hardly imaginable to our own limited powers.

Exercise 1

1. Write a relatively brief report on some of the interesting facts about the historical period known as the Age of Pericles.

2. Discuss some of the contributions of Aristotle and Plato to Western thought.

3. How did these two scholars differ in their ideas about language?

4. Look up the etymology of the word *grammar*. Consult the *Oxford English Dictionary*, if possible.

5. How do you reconcile the ancient and the medieval meanings of *grammar* with its modern connotations?

6. Consult an encyclopedia for information about the anomalists and the analogists. In what way did these two schools of thought differ?

7. Discuss the work in language study of Dionysius Thrax, Donatus and Priscian, St. Anselm, and Duns Scotus.

8. Consult the encyclopedia for information about the great universities of Europe in the Middle Ages.

9. What were the "liberal arts"? What was their origin? What was the trivium? the quadrivium?

10. Into what three periods is the history of the English language divided? Give approximate dates. Discuss some of the important changes in each period.

11. Write a short paper on the study of classical languages in American elementary and secondary schools.

12. Discuss the work of Ben Jonson in the development of the study of grammar.

13. Discuss the work of the grammarians Robert Lowth, William Ward, and Lindley Murray in the development of the study of grammar. Gather your material from library resources.

14. Discuss the work of the modern grammarians in traditional grammar, structural grammar, and generative grammar.

15. Discuss some of the basic principles of structural grammar; of generative grammar.

SOME DISTINCTIONS BETWEEN TRADITIONAL AND STRUCTURAL GRAMMAR

Since the grammar you have studied in the *Modern Grammar and Composition* series has been largely traditional in its nomenclature but structural in its emphasis and its method, you should be aware of some of the distinctions between these two approaches to the study of grammar.

Characteristics of Traditional Grammar

1. PARTS OF SPEECH

In traditional grammar, words are classified as parts of speech. The parts of speech include the noun, the verb, the adjective, the adverb, the conjunction, the preposition, the pronoun, and the interjection. Parts of speech are defined by meaning, by function, and by what they communicate. A noun is the name of a person, place, or thing; an adjective is a word that modifies a noun; a verb is a word that expresses action, being, or state of being. Some parts of speech are inflected; others are not. The study of form is secondary. Classification is extensive and relatively important. There are adverbs of time, place, manner, and degree. There are descriptive adverbs, relative adverbs, interrogative adverbs, and conjunctive adverbs.

Parts of speech are essentially functional elements. The subject and object function are identified as noun functions. The predicate function is identified with the verb function. The modifier of a noun is an adjective function, and the modifier of a verb is an adverbial function. Prepositions and conjunctions are connectives. A pronoun takes the place of (functions as) a noun. The current dictionary classifications of words as nouns, verbs, and so on are strictly traditional functional classifications.

2. ANALYSIS OF THE SENTENCE

The parts of speech within a sentence are related to other parts of speech. Sentence analysis in traditional grammar is often what is known as *parsing*. It consists of the identification of each part of speech and the description of its relationship to other words in the sentence. It involves a detailed discussion of the word in each of its grammatical aspects. For example, a noun may be a proper noun, a common noun, a collective noun, or a concrete noun. It may be of the masculine, feminine, neuter, or common gender. It may be singular or plural. It may be in the nominative, possessive, or objective case according to its function in the sentence. Finally, it may be the subject, the direct object, the object of a preposition, or whatever function a noun may fulfill. The parsing of verbs, adjectives, and adverbs is developed in a similar manner with due regard to their peculiar characteristics and uses.

The emphasis is on the word in this kind of analysis. Further interest in the word as an important element in communication is expressed in the conjugation of verbs. Conjugation consists of a complete examination of the principal parts, the forms used in the active and passive voices, in the indicative, subjunctive, and imperative moods, as well as the forms of infinitives, gerunds, and participles.

The study of word groups involves the study of prepositional phrases, verbal phrases, and subordinate and coordinate clauses. The syntax of these word groups is described in the process of sentence analysis.

Sentence analysis is sometimes done by means of diagramming—a rather standardized procedure of relating words and word groups to each other by means of a straight-line drawing.

The hungry fox glared at the rooster that was crowing on the fence.

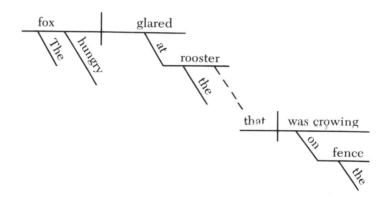

In the diagram, the subject and predicate are shown on the main line. The prepositional phrase *at the rooster* is shown as a modifier of the verb *glared*. The adjective clause *that was crowing on the fence* is shown as a modifier of *rooster*. The prepositional phrase *on the fence* is shown as a modifier of the verb *was crowing*.

3. MEANING AS A CRITERION

One of the characteristics of traditional grammar is its subjectivity, its reliance on meaning as the basis of definition and descriptive statement. For example, a sentence is usually defined as the statement of a "complete thought." An interrogative sentence is a sentence "that asks a question." The direct object of a verb may be identified because it answers the question, "What?" Adverbs may be identified because they usually answer the questions, "Where?" "When?" "Why?" and "How?" Coordinate clauses are clauses having equal value. A complex sentence is one "that contains one or more dependent clauses." A dependent clause is one "that does not make complete sense in and by itself but depends upon another clause for its full meaning."

4. PRESCRIBED USAGE

Traditional grammarians have the philosophy of the old Greek analogists who believed that language was the embodiment of the word, "the truth." This philosophy holds to the idea of the permanence of language forms, of a certain quality of universality, of a system of language absolutes. It is the basis of the belief that certain kinds of language are "correct" and other kinds are "incorrect." It is the basis of the idea of "good English" and "bad English."

In order to guarantee correct usage, rules are stated in various texts which prescribe how forms may or may not be used. For example, students are cautioned not to use a double negative, not to split an infinitive with a modifier, and not to end a sentence with a preposition. There is the rule which states that *can* is used to denote ability and *may* is used to denote permission. The word *imply* describes what a speaker or a writer communicates, and the word *infer* tells what the reader or listener understands. Another rule states that "a subject and a verb agree in number." This rule holds true in fewer than half the cases. Concord between subject and verb in modern English exists only for the third person present except for the verb *to be*, for which there is concord in the past tense and for the first person as well as the third. The exceptions to the rule tend to give it little value.

The method of the study of traditional grammar with its emphasis on definitions and rules is largely *deductive*. The student proceeds from the generalization (definition and rule) to the application. Observation comes after the principle and consists sometimes of noting the exceptions.

Exercise 2

A. *Identify the parts of speech in each of the following sentences:*

1. He ran down the street and into the police station.

2. A steel band played at their wedding.

3. Everyone on the block wants to help with the cleanup we've planned for next Saturday.

Exercise 2,

continued

4. The ship struck a hidden mine and sank quickly.

5. José always arrives when dinner is ready.

6. His brothers came with him to the party.

7. Nobody wants to wash dishes.

8. In the West, the mountains are high and the deserts are wide.

9. Ed washed cars to earn the money.

10. The rains will come soon to make the grass grow green.

11. I took my little sister to the museum yesterday.

12. The people will elect the candidate whom they prefer.

13. Fred wants to go to college, but his father would like him to help in the store.

14. Her eyes burning with tears, Cheryl tripped quickly across the stage.

15. We will begin when the orchestra is ready, and we will stop promptly at ten o'clock.

B. *Diagram each of the sentences in Exercise 2A.*

Exercise 3

Parse the nouns, verbs, adjectives, and adverbs in each of the following sentences:

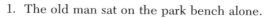

1. The old man sat on the park bench alone.

2. A small cap covered the back of his head.

3. James Baldwin speaks French fluently.

4. She left her best sweater in the school auditorium.

5. The hungry dog tipped over the garbage can.

6. The locally popular Mr. Stone is the science teacher in our new high school.

7. Skating on thin ice is dangerous.

8. Father ordered steak, but the waitress brought him chopped beef.

9. Willis always knows what he wants.

10. Father carved the chicken while Mother served the greens.

Characteristics of Structural Grammar

1. FORM CLASSES

In the study of structural grammar, the classification of words is based on formal characteristics. Nouns, verbs, adjectives, and adverbs have contrasting elements of form and are distinguished on this basis. The most important distinctive element of form is the way in which each class is inflected. Nouns are inflected for singular and plural, usually by adding *s* or *es*, or by means of an internal vowel change. Verbs are inflected for tense, for use with auxiliaries, and for use with singular subjects. Regular verbs add *-ed* to the infinitive to form the past or past participle and *-ing* to form the present participle. The singular form is developed by adding *-s* to the infinitive form. Irregular verbs (about 150 remain in the language) often have an internal vowel change when the past or past participle is formed. Adjectives are inflected for degree. The adjectives of one syllable add *-er* and *-est* to form the comparative and superlative degrees. Degree is communicated for adjectives of more than one syllable by means of intensifiers. Some adjectives, such as *good*, are inflected for degree in an irregular manner. Adverbs resemble adjectives. Some are inflected like adjectives and some cannot be inflected.

A second aspect of form consists of the characteristic prefix or suffix (mostly the suffix) which marks the form class. Noun suffixes include *-ance, -dom, -ery, -ist, -ment*, and many more. Verb suffixes include *-ize, -ate, -fy*, and *-en*. Verb prefixes include *be-, en-, em-, re-*, and others. Adjective suffixes include *-ful, -ish, -able, -ive, -ic*, and many others. The most characteristic identifying adverb suffix is *-ly* added to a noun or an adjective form. The prefix *a-* is characteristic of some adverbs.

Certain words, called *function words*, also serve as formal markers of the important communicating elements of language that are designated *form classes*. For example, words like *a, an*, and *the* go with nouns; *can, are, have*, and similar forms go with verbs; *very, more, rather, quite*, and other intensifiers go with adjectives and some adverbs.

Function words include such words as connectives, auxiliaries, determiners, and particles. Function words have little lexical (dictionary) meaning but are important for what they do in communication rather than for what they say. They make up about 7 percent of the lexicon but over 30 percent of the bulk of written language.

Stress sometimes serves as a formal identification for nouns and verbs. Words like *contract* and *permit*, for example, are spoken with contrasting stress for the noun and verb forms.

2. IMMEDIATE CONSTITUENTS

The sentence is made up of syntactic structures, words and word groups held together and separated by patterns of intonation. In structural grammar, the emphasis is mostly on the word group.

The basic sentence pattern is the chief functional unit. Within the basic sentence pattern may be modifying word groups. These may be subject-predicate word groups (a subordinate clause), a prepositional phrase, a verbal phrase. Headed word groups are those formed by modifiers clustering about a noun or a verb, or possibly an adjective or an adverb. The headword with its modifiers is called a *noun cluster*, a *verb cluster*, and so on.

Sentences may be analyzed into immediate constituents. Immediate constituents are the two parts of a structure at any level of organization. The following will serve to illustrate this type of analysis:

> The little old lady who lived in a shoe had so many children she didn't know what to do.
>
> The little old lady who lived in a shoe / had so many children she didn't know what to do.
>
> The little old lady / who lived in a shoe
>
> had so many children / she didn't know what to do.
>
> The little / old lady   who / lived in a shoe
>
> had / so many children   she / didn't know what to do.

This analysis could be continued until each structure was finally divided into morphemes, the ultimate constituents. This type of analysis reveals the syntactic units and the way in which they are related.

3. OBJECTIVE CRITERIA

Identification and description are based on objective criteria. For example, the sentence is identified by means of physical characteristics of structure — word order, intonation pattern, subject-predicate, and so on. The criteria for identifying form classes have been noted. Position is the dominant signal of function, usually reinforced by inflectional forms and function words. Descriptive statements are subject to objective verification. The method of study is observation and generalization where possible. This is the *inductive* method.

4. CHANGING USAGE

Language is considered as part of social behavior. Time brings change. As customs change, so do the needs of communication. The language habits of a scientific age will be different from those of a more leisurely agricultural age. In response to the speed and pressure of modern life, the tendency is to shorten, to clip, to abbreviate. The word *recommend* or *approve* becomes *O.K. John Fitzgerald Kennedy* becomes *J.F.K. Salted pork, roasted goose,* and *iced cream* become *salt pork, roast goose,* and *ice cream.* Most persons accept these changes without question. Who would want to talk like the characters of Chaucer's *Canterbury Tales?* Usage, then, and not rule, becomes the standard of acceptable English. The dictionary records the usage of the day from books, newspapers, magazines, and other records. This is the acceptable language of our time. Words that are used by uneducated people only are labeled as substandard or illiterate. Words that are purely regional or out-of-date are labeled as dialect or archaic. Such words are used at one's own risk since they may not communicate clearly, or they mark a speaker as ignorant and a writer as one of poor taste.

AN ADDITIONAL NOTE ON STRUCTURAL GRAMMAR. In the two preceding sections, you examined some of the contrasting characteristics of the traditional and the structural approach to the study of grammar. Structural grammar also gives added emphasis to the SEGMENTAL PHONEMES, the SUPRASEGMENTAL PHONEMES, and the MORPHEMES of the English language. For a brief discussion of these topics set within the framework of modern grammar, turn to "The Language of Grammar," which begins on page 363.

Exercise 4

1. Develop in detail some of the essential contrasts between traditional grammar and structural grammar.

2. What is meant by the "parts of speech" concept in traditional grammar?

3. In what way does the classification of parts of speech differ today from the ancient Greek? the Latin?

4. Define each of the parts of speech. Illustrate each.

5. Are the definitions of parts of speech clear in each case? Are they consistent in development? What is meant by the statement that they are largely functional concepts?

Exercise 5

1. List the principal parts of each of the following verbs: arrive, sit, grow, bring, lie, do, hang, sling, write, go.

Exercise 5,
continued

2. List all of the inflected forms of each of the following verbs:

fear	throw	bind	bet
love	begin	shoot	burst
dry	swim	hold	set
flit	know	cling	cast
skim	fly	fight	hurt

3. Conjugate each of the following verbs: hear, run, spring, watch, come, worry, forget, lie, lay.

4. Look up the definitions of the following grammatical terms in textbooks of grammar that you may find in the library, preferably those published some time ago. Then check the definitions in a recently published college dictionary.

sentence	subordinate clause	infinitive
pronoun	coordinate clause	adjunct
adverb	predicate	apposition
gerund	subject	adjective
participle	object	verb

5. Discuss the difference between a deductive study and an inductive study.

6. Look up and list five grammatical rules.

Exercise 6

1. Distinguish between *grammar* and *usage*.

2. Discuss the usage in the following sentences:
   a. He hasn't written hardly anything on his paper.
   b. There aren't but four children in the Scroggs family.
   c. Bill dove into the pond and dragged out Ella.
   d. Joe has to walk much further to school than us.
   e. Mother felt badly when she heard about Sara's illness.
   f. I cannot help but pity this child.
   g. Father immigrated from England when he was seventeen.
   h. Uncle Henry loaned Bill enough money to go to college.
   i. Mr. Parsons is the party you will have to see about the repairs.
   j. It was just too much for Frank and I to manage.
   k. We shall plan to meet you there tomorrow.
   l. This flour is the only kind that I can make good biscuits with.
   m. Harry's reason for being late was because he had to help his father fix a tire.

Exercise 6,
continued

3. What is meant by standard usage?

4. Distinguish between standard usage and correct English.

Exercise 7

1. Distinguish between "parts of speech" and "form classes."

2. List and discuss the formal characteristics of nouns, verbs, adjectives, and adverbs.

3. What is the meaning of function as applied to English grammar?

4. What is meant by the structural signals of function, or meaning?

5. What is the relation of form to function in English?

6. What is meant by the statement that English is an analytic language?

7. Write sentences to illustrate:
   a. a noun-headed word group
   b. a verb-headed word group
   c. a subject-predicate word group
   d. a prepositional phrase
   e. a verbal phrase
   f. two coordinated basic sentence patterns

8. Divide the following sentences into immediate constituents through three levels of structure:
   a. The captain of the ship warned his crew that a storm was coming.
   b. The man who teaches science has been invited to attend an institute that will be held at Harvard.
   c. The concert being given tomorrow night will feature one of the popular symphonies of Beethoven.

Exercise 8

1. Look up the approximate dates of the three important historical periods in the development of the English language — Old English, Middle English, and Modern English.

2. What great historical movements preceded the language changes involved in the first two periods?

3. List twenty common words which are derived from the Anglo-Saxon. List twenty words of Modern English which are derived from the Norman French. Do the

Exercise 8,

continued

meanings of these words reveal anything of sociological significance?

4. What language preceded the Anglo-Saxon language in the British Isles? Do we find any vestiges of this language in Modern English?

5. What were the effects of the Roman invasion on the language of the inhabitants of the British Isles?

6. How do you account for the relatively large number of Latin words in the lexicon of Modern English?

7. How do you account for the presence of many Greek words in our language today?

8. What is meant by borrowings in language development? List as many words as you can that are loanwords from other languages, languages other than the Germanic and the Latin and Greek.

9. Look up the derivation of the following words:

ooze	infringe	epigram	angle
animal	cook	democracy	havoc
wiener	tantalize	shrapnel	rhetoric

10. Many new words have come into our language in recent years as the result of scientific changes. Some of these words have become popular terms: *launching pad, lunar modules, countdown, cosmonaut, astronaut,* and *ecology.* In your notebook, develop a cumulative list of such words taken from your reading. Discuss these words occasionally in class and help to prepare a master list which may be mimeographed for general use.

11. Repeat item 10 with words derived from recent sociological changes. List words such as *hippie, The Man, slum clearance, sit-in, far right, white-collar job, commune,* and *inner city.*

12. One of the modern tendencies in English is to clip suffixes or to shorten a word by eliminating one or more syllables. Thus we have *whip cream* from *whipped cream, roast beef* from *roasted beef, prof* from *professor, exam* from *examination,* and *alums* instead of *alumni.* Look for these words in reading and in conversation. Develop a list of these words.

13. In some states, books listing place names have been published. Study these names. What do they reveal to you about the history and culture of your state?

Summary

On previous pages, you have discussed very briefly the recognition by the structural grammarians of the fact of language change. Language scholars of the past three decades have been placing more and more emphasis on the relationship between a knowledge of language change and an understanding of the present nature of language. It is felt that "it is not enough to know how to describe the English language *at a given time*."

The growing recognition of the significance of historical linguistics to the modern student of language has given impetus to the study of a variety of aspects of language change. These may include the history of sounds, the changing inflections of English words, and the changing meanings of these words, with the introduction of new meanings with the passage of time. It may include the study of word derivation with the origins of roots and affixes. Another topic may be the study of borrowings from other languages, the loanwords which are so frequent in our language. Then there is the study of dialects and changes in dialects and the related interest in place names and personal names. All of this is part of the gross phenomenon of language change and is the subject material for the growing study of what has lately come to be known as "historical grammar."

To the high school student, the thought of tackling another difficult subject with so many ramifications under the guise of "grammar" might seem of doubtful value. On the contrary, a study of language changes can be tremendously interesting to the high school English student and can give him considerable insight into the nature of the language of today.

One interesting aspect of change for

Summary,

continued

the high school student might be the study of the influence of mistakes on language change. This study could include not only research to ferret out mistakes of the past, but also the observation of the printed page of our times to find the mistakes of today. One may not need too many months to collect headlines and stories which contain errors in subject-verb agreement, pronoun reference, punctuation (principally the use of the apostrophe), spelling, and others. Speakers often make serious errors not only in the choice of a word, but also in the use of language structures, particularly on radio and television programs. Records of these lapses may be very interesting.

The study of place names in a given area may reveal some of the story of the past, the habits, the occupations, the legends of the people who lived there. Examination of dialectal words perhaps introduced by students from different sections of the United States provides a basis of study, particularly when one examines the derivation and history of some of these terms.

Another interesting project in the study of language change is the collection and study of new words. These words may be scientific terms or they may be words developed as the result of psychological or sociological change. Many of these words carry with them an interesting story.

Finally, there is always the study of the derivation and history of English words. This study can take the student back into other times with other habits of living and reveal to him the connection between his present and his past.

Майда́нов отвеча́л поэти́ческим стру́нам её души́: челове́к дово́льно холо́дный, как почти́ все сочини́-тели, он напряжённо уверя́л её, а мо́жет быть, и себя́, что он её обожа́ет, воспева́л её в несконча́емых стиха́х и чита́л их ей с каки́м-то и неесте́ственным и

Russian

Chapter 2

THE
ENGLISH
SENTENCE

A Look Back and A Look Forward

In Chapter 1, you surveyed briefly the development and meaning of grammar. In Chapter 2 and in the remaining chapters of Part I, you will be given the opportunity to renew and to reinforce your knowledge of the basic elements of grammar and syntax.

In Chapter 2, you will concentrate on the study of (1) the characteristics of the sentence; (2) the basic sentence patterns; (3) the expansion of sentences through the use of modifiers, coordination, subordination, and appositives; and (4) the immediate constitutents of the sentence.

In this chapter, you will also see how the writer's method of communication differs from that of the speaker.

37

THE IMPORTANCE OF THE SENTENCE

Much of the ability of the writer depends on how well he can construct his sentences. If he has a thorough knowledge of his subject, if he organizes his material coherently, if he has a reasonable command of words, the power and appeal of his writing will depend largely on his sentence structure.

Written communication is considerably different from speech. The writer has no voice with which to reinforce his statements. He cannot raise and lower his pitch. He cannot shout, nor can he change the tempo of his language. He cannot make gestures, use facial expressions, or repeat himself. He can only put black and white marks on paper.

Because of the limitations of his medium, the writer has to use the resources of language more extensively than the speaker. He has to think through his subject more completely before he begins to write. He has to implement the structures of language more skillfully and use words more effectively and appropriately. Above all, he must develop power and skill in the construction of sentences because the sentence is the basic unit of standard written English.

Let's look again at the English sentence, this time with even more discernment than before. Let's examine its physical characteristics and its basic patterns, investigate the importance of word order, study how the sentence works, how it is expanded, how it is transformed. All these steps are important because they are essential to the writer who wishes to develop clarity in statement and grace in style.

A good sentence has strength and beauty. The reader understands it, is affected by it, and perhaps responds to its eloquence. It not only communicates a message in the ordinary sense but also evokes feeling and arouses spirit. It provides a sense of enjoyment to the reader as he reflects upon its content.

As a student writer, you should hunt for good sentences and collect them. The following are illustrative:

In my Father's house are many mansions.   John 14:2

That man is richest whose pleasures are the cheapest.   HENRY DAVID THOREAU

As the slender spire of a New England church tells the eye and heart of its Anglo-Saxon background, so thick adobe walls and domed belltowers of the Southwest speak of the Franciscan and Indian.   RUTH KEENAN

The road from the north curved a little to the east just there, and the road from the west swung out a little to the south; so that the grave, with its tall red grass that was never mowed, was like a little island; and at twilight, under a new moon or the clear evening star, the dusty roads used to look like soft grey rivers flowing past it.   WILLA CATHER

THE PHYSICAL CHARACTERISTICS OF THE SENTENCE

There are hundreds of definitions of a sentence. Memorizing a definition, which is perhaps uncertain in meaning and difficult to understand, is no guarantee that you will use good sentences. You may glibly repeat the definition of a sentence and still use fragments, run-together sentences, and misplaced commas. Most inexperienced writers are guilty of this practice.

One thing you *can* do is observe the physical characteristics of those written structures that are called sentences. A knowledge of these characteristics (as described in the next six sections) will enable you to describe a sentence in objective terms and identify those structures that do not conform to specifications.

Punctuation

The simplest guide to sentence structure in written material is that found in punctuation. The sentence begins with a capital letter and ends with some form of punctuation—a period, a question mark, or an exclamation point. The reader is accustomed to the signals of punctuation; he separates the units of thought by means of these physical guides. It is possible to estimate the number of sentences in a paragraph of printed material merely by counting the structures contained between the capitals and the end punctuation marks. The count would not be entirely accurate because there are other standards of sentence structure besides signals of punctuation. However, over 98 percent of the structures so considered in printed material are standard English sentences.

The writer, considering this situation, must realize his responsibility. If he places a comma at a point calling for a period, or if he omits the period (as beginners often do), he provides misleading signals to his reader, slows his progress, and often confuses him.

Subject-Predicate Structure

Our world is one of persons, animals, plants, places, things, substances, qualities, ideas, actions, states. In language study these entities are called NOUNS: *John, dog, ivy, North Dakota, chair, rubber, goodness, knowledge, tension,* and so forth.

But life is not static. Ours is a dynamic universe, a universe of movement, of change. To describe experiences in such a world, therefore, another kind of word is needed. These words are called VERBS: *run, see, drive, swim.*

Our language, then, is essentially a NOUN-VERB language, or a SUB-JECT-PREDICATE language with the noun and the verb the chief actors in the little drama of communication, the sentence. A writer must never lose sight of the importance of the SUBJECT NOUN and the PREDICATE VERB. He must choose these words carefully to make his writing effective.

The second test of the sentence, then, is subject-predicate structure.

> The huge iron ball / crashed through the cement wall.
> The speed of automobiles / should have been decreased long ago for traffic safety.
> The little old lady who lives next door / cooks her own meals.

The recognition and identification of the subject and predicate within the sentence is the beginning of all grammar study. You have been accustomed to this structure since early childhood and at this stage should have little difficulty with it. The subject and the predicate provide the framework of the sentence. Modifiers, appositives, and other elements are constructed on this frame. If a structure has a subject and a predicate, it is a sentence.

Finite Verb

Sentence structure requires a finite, or main, verb. The writer has to be familiar with the form of a FINITE VERB. He must, for this reason, understand inflection and how verbs are inflected. He has to know verb forms, which are discussed briefly here and in greater detail in Chapter 3.

Some verbs have three inflected forms, some have four, some have five. The verb *to be* has eight inflected forms. The five standard verb forms are the PLAIN form, the SINGULAR form, the PAST form, the PRESENT PARTICIPLE form, and the PAST PARTICIPLE form. The verb *drive* has five forms.

PLAIN	SINGULAR	PAST	PRESENT PARTICIPLE	PAST PARTICIPLE
drive	drives	drove	driving	driven

The first three forms may be used in a sentence as finite verbs. The last two forms need auxiliary or helping verbs in order to be used as finite verbs.

> Jim and Bob drive to school every Friday.
> Once in a while Jane drives with them.
> The boys drove to the dance last evening.
> Jim has been driving since he was sixteen.
> He has driven hundreds of miles.

The sentences above illustrate the correct use of finite verbs.

When the present participle form or the past participle form is used without an auxiliary or when the past form of a four-part verb functions as a past participle without an auxiliary, the structure that results is considered a SENTENCE FRAGMENT. In order to be a sentence, a structure must have a finite verb.

> The family driving to the country.
> The Ford driven by our doctor.
> The wallet found by the janitor.

These structures are sentence fragments. Only by inserting auxiliary verbs before the verb forms can these fragments become sentences.

> The family is driving to the country.
> The Ford was driven by our doctor.
> The wallet has been found by the janitor.

The auxiliary verb used in such contexts cannot be an -*ing* form alone; nor can it be the first of a combination of auxiliaries. The resulting structures are still fragments since the verbs are not finite verbs. This principle applies only to the past participle form.

> The Model T being driven by our doctor in the Founder's Day parade.
> The wallet having been found by the janitor.

Such structures are sentence fragments. The first may be corrected by inserting *is* before the auxiliary. The second may be corrected by substituting *has* or *had* for *having*.

> The Model T is being driven by our doctor in the Founder's Day parade.
> The wallet had been found by the janitor.

The plain form of a verb is often used with the structure word *to*. The form that results is called an INFINITIVE. This form is often used as part of a verb phrase or as a verbal—either in a noun function or as a modifier. The infinitive is not a finite verb and therefore cannot function as a predicate verb. The following examples illustrate structures in which the infinitive form may be used:

> The team is scheduled to practice this afternoon.
> Most of the students want to find summer jobs.
> To learn to write effectively takes much practice.
> Maria plans to visit us over the weekend.
> The work to be studied for the review will be posted tomorrow.
> My sister has just one wish, to finish nursing school.
> Frank asked his father to increase his allowance.

The sentences above are all good English sentences. The following structures are not sentences because the verbs are not finite verbs:

The chairman to settle all disputes.
The Congress to pass needed legislation.
The boys to go to summer camp and the girls to the mountains.

Students often use such sentence fragments with end punctuation marks. Actually, these groups of words contain infinitive phrases, not finite verbs. The fragments above may be rewritten in these ways:

The chairman will settle all disputes.
The Congress will pass needed legislation.
The boys are to go to summer camp and the girls to the mountains.

Exercise 1

Separate the complete subject from the complete predicate in each sentence below. Identify the subject noun (or noun substitute) and the verb in each. Watch for compound subjects and compound predicates.

1. The mayor of Newark, New Jersey, welcomed the group of visitors from Cleveland, Ohio.

2. Ed fastened his shoe and continued to play the game.

3. The quickest student is not always the brightest.

4. The boys and their father went for a walk down Broadway.

5. The city has torn down the apartment house we used to live in to build a new housing complex.

6. This is your last chance to take the test.

7. To do this work will require much skill.

8. Singing and dancing are her great talents.

9. The man driving that new Mustang is my sister's boyfriend.

10. Uncle Martin won't eat anything but soul food.

11. The war beginning in 1914 and ending in 1918 was a struggle to end all wars.

12. The Boys Club is collecting old newspapers on this block to earn money for their new clubhouse.

Word Order

The normal word order in a sentence is SUBJECT-VERB-COMPLEMENT. This order is basic to our grammar; it is the most important determiner of meaning.

Jones knocked out Reed.
Charles cooked the fish.

Any other word arrangement either states a different fact or is nonsensical. An interchange of the subject and complement in the first sentence changes the meaning entirely, while an interchange of the order in the second produces foolishness.

> Reed knocked out Jones.
> The fish cooked Charles.

The subject of the sentence has a certain advantage in communication — the advantage of emphasis. In our language there is a device for interchanging subject and object without change in meaning — the device of transformation. The transformation in this case is to the passive voice. In this transformation, special structural signals are used.

> Reed was knocked out by Jones.
> The fish was cooked by Charles.

A second kind of transformation of sentence structure involving word order is the inversion of subject and verb to ask a question.

> Lorraine Hansberry was a great playwright.
> Was Lorraine Hansberry a great playwright?
>
> Jim has enough money to buy a car.
> Has Jim enough money to buy a car?

This simple inversion of subject and verb serves in modern English to ask a question involving the verbs *have* or *to be*. It does not serve for any other verbs. One cannot ask:

> Saw you Laurence Olivier in *Hamlet*?

Other structural signals of the question are now used in the transformed sentence.

> Did you see Laurence Olivier in *Hamlet*?
> Have you seen Laurence Olivier in *Hamlet*?

The forms of *do* and *have* as auxiliaries with the appropriate verb form in inverted word order serve to signal the question. Notice that in the inversion, the subject is placed between the auxiliary and the main verb.

The same kind of inversion of subject and verb is used in questions beginning with the function words *when, where, why, how,* and *who, whom, which,* and *what.*

> When did you go to the post office?
> Where are you going this afternoon?
> Why did you go to the movies last Friday?
> How will you spend your allowance this week?

> Whom will you ask to the party at the club?
> Which car will you buy?
> What do you want to do now?

When *who* is used in the subject noun function, there is no inversion:

> Who wants to go with us to play tennis?
> Who is knocking at the door?

Sometimes other interrogative signals such as *how* and *what* are used this way in simple questions.

> How many people are going?
> What profit is in this trade for me?
> Which books are in your desk?

Word order in the English sentence — subject-verb-complement — is a fundamental principle of English grammar. If the writer manipulates this order in any way, he changes the meaning. You have seen how questions are developed. Other effects of changed order will be discussed later.

Signal of Subordination

The connectives that serve to introduce a subordinate clause are important clues to meaning. Later in the chapter you will review subordinate clauses, but meanwhile you should become familiar with such connectives as:

because	while	how	whenever
if	since	who	wherever
although	when	whose	whatever
unless	as	whom	whoever
until	where	that	whomever
whether	why	which	whichever

A word group introduced by any of the words listed above cannot stand alone as a sentence. It must be part of a basic sentence pattern. The following subordinate structures are sentence fragments:

> If my money comes in time.
> Whatever the answer may be.
> Where the Hudson River flows into the Atlantic.
> When the work is finished next fall.

This discussion concerns standard *written* English. Structures of this kind are acceptable in conversation. They are usually replies to questions. However, you should avoid carrying these speech patterns over into your writing because in this medium they are considered fragmentary.

Structures of this kind may serve as introductory subordinate clauses in a complete sentence. For example:

If my money comes in time, I will go with you.
Whatever the answer may be, it will surely come.

The same structures may serve also as terminal subordinate clauses in a complete sentence.

New York harbor is south of the great city, where the Hudson River flows into the Atlantic.
We will go on a long vacation when the work is finished next fall.

Test Yourself

Which of these structures are complete sentences and which are subordinate clauses?

1. If it stops raining by this evening.
2. We postponed our trip because our car fell apart.
3. Bob always means exactly what he says.
4. Unless you promise to go to the movies with me.
5. Although our guests arrived on time for the theater.
6. Because we were late, we missed the train.
7. While we were in San Francisco last January.
8. The librarian asked that we return all books.
9. Whenever the boys are ready to go to the game.
10. How to go from here to Chicago.

Intonation

In speech, sentences have characteristic intonation patterns. These patterns include pitch, stress, and juncture.

Most linguists recognize four degrees of pitch: low, normal, high, and very high. These levels are designated by the phonemic symbols $/1/$, $/2/$, $/3/$, and $/4/$. There are also four degrees of stress, or loudness: zero, tertiary, secondary, and primary — as the voice moves from a soft tone to a loud tone.

Juncture describes the joining or pauses between the sounds, words, and word groups that separate speech into meaningful patterns.

The patterns of intonation can help identify the physical characteristics of a sentence, especially when you proofread orally. The ear is especially sensitive to pitch. A fall in pitch usually signals the end of a sentence; a rise in pitch usually signals a question.

Exercise 2   *Identify the sentences and sentence fragments in the following structures. Make sentences of the fragments.*

1. What a great idea, to have a block dance.

2. When Benjamin Banneker was a young man, he made a clock which kept perfect time.

3. It was an ideal vacation. Sleeping all morning and dancing most of the night.

4. Knowing what's best for all of us and wanting to do the right thing.

5. Broadway and Main Street, where the traffic is heaviest and people move about in great masses.

6. When will you be ready to begin work on this project?

7. The old man was very tired. His strength having been used up in an effort to move the lumber.

8. Harry Simpson is my cousin. His mother and my mother being sisters.

9. What an effort to shovel so much snow.

10. When the cat's away, the mice will play.

11. My aunt and her five children to visit us this summer.

12. Jumping over the whole West High team, Bill raced for the winning touchdown.

13. Harriet broke down completely. Crying and sobbing over her failure.

14. The cat's out of the bag.

15. After the movie, let's stop for a soda.

THE BASIC SENTENCE PATTERNS

Sentences as we know and read them are expanded or generated from a few basic patterns. Let's review these patterns.

1. N-V (NOUN-VERB)

$$\overset{N}{\text{Our dog}} \overset{V}{\text{howled}} \text{ all night long.}$$

$$\overset{N}{\text{The boys}} \text{ are } \overset{V}{\text{working}} \text{ in the laboratory.}$$

N   V
Sally is crying bitterly.

N   V
Football has ended for the season.

N   V
Congress adjourned yesterday.

The verb used in each of these sentences is called an INTRANSITIVE VERB since there is no complement. The communicative power of this basic sentence is limited but often powerful in a suitable context.

2. N-V-N (NOUN-VERB-NOUN)

N   V   N
Dorothy is playing the piano.

N   V   N
Webster won the game easily.

N   V   N
Debbie prefers soup to tomato juice.

N   V   N
Old Jack outwitted his buddies.

N   V   N
Father detests casseroles.

The verb used in each of these sentences is called a TRANSITIVE VERB since it has a DIRECT OBJECT. This sentence pattern is one of the most widely used in writing.

3. N-V-N-N (NOUN-VERB-NOUN-NOUN)

N   V   N   N
Mother gave the grocer a large order.

N   V N   N
Father bought Jim a secondhand car.

N   V N N
The foreman handed Al a shovel.

N   V   N   N
The teacher read the class their assignment.

Ns   V   N   N
Nobody offered Mr. Little a job. (Ns=Noun Substitute)

Each verb is a transitive verb since there is a direct object. The direct object is the outer complement. The inner complement is an INDIRECT OBJECT.

Examine these sentences in which the direct object is the inner complement:

Ns   V   N   N
They named the baby Jeff.

N   V   N   N
The citizens elected Washington president.

    N   V   N   N
The governor appointed Harrison police commissioner.

    N   V   N   N
The boys made Jim captain.

    N   V   N   N
The girls selected Alice chairman.

Each verb is a transitive verb since there is a direct object. When the direct object is the inner complement, the outer complement is called an OBJECTIVE COMPLEMENT. The objective complement refers to the direct object.

Sometimes an adjective is used with certain verbs in the objective complement function.

> The fellows made Jim angry.
> Sue considers George intelligent.
> The class thought the story boring.
> The judge held the man guilty.

4. N-LV-N (NOUN-LINKING VERB-NOUN)

    N   LV   N
Mr. Popkin is our history teacher.

         N   LV   N
The gray horse was the winner of the race.

     N   LV   N
My father has been a plumber for years.

    N   LV   N
The house on Main Street is a mansion.

   N   LV   N
Harold became a famous doctor.

The verb in each of these sentences is a LINKING VERB. The complement is a LINKING-VERB COMPLEMENT and, in this structure, is called a PREDICATE NOUN.

5. N-LV-ADJ (NOUN-LINKING VERB-ADJECTIVE)

    N   LV   ADJ
The star of the play is simply gorgeous.

         N   LV ADJ
The old gentleman is handsome.

   N   LV   ADJ
Mary looked nervous this morning.

   N   LV   ADJ
Father seems excited about his trip.

    N   LV   ADJ
The fish smells rank.

6. THE INVERTED SENTENCE

   V   N
Here is the murder weapon.

$$\overset{V}{} \qquad \overset{N}{}$$

There is the spot from which he fell.

$$\overset{V}{} \qquad \overset{N}{}$$

Here comes the guard.

As illustrated, this pattern is a statement which begins with *there* or *here*, usually (but not always) followed by some form of *to be*. Although this is the most common kind of inversion, inverted sentences are not necessarily limited to these types.

$$\overset{V}{} \qquad \overset{N}{}$$

Under the huge shade tree sat a group of picnickers.

7. THE QUESTION

Will you go to the dance with me on Saturday?
Have you a date?
Who is your date?

These are the basic sentence patterns in our language. The first five patterns are expanded by means of various grammatical devices into the structures of written English.

Exercise 3　　*Identify the basic sentence pattern in each of the following sentences. Point out the subject noun, the verb, the direct object, the indirect object, the objective complement, and the linking-verb complement.*

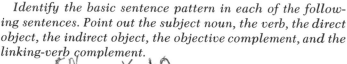

1. Harriet Tubman led slaves to freedom.

2. His boss gave Jerry his pay.

3. She finds television exciting.

4. Dionne Warwick sings beautifully.

5. Alice passed the examination easily.

6. David asked Miss Stewart a question.

7. Hillary scaled Mt. Everest in 1953.

8. Hank's brother is a sergeant in the Marines.

9. This green apple tastes sour.

10. The dogs looked miserable.

11. Ann Wilson is the oldest girl in our class.

12. Speed kills.

13. Your answer seems correct to me.

14. This is the hour for action.

Exercise 3,
continued

15. The president named a commission to study the local situation.

16. He appointed Mr. Philbrook chairman of the commission.

17. Dad gave us money for gas.

18. George felt sorry about the accident.

19. The birthday gifts made Mother happy.

20. Jim Stone is the champion of the heavyweight division.

21. Here is the story of Charles Drew's life.

22. Pablo ran as fast as he could when he heard the strange noises in the alley.

23. The two construction workers climbed to the highest point of the bridge tower.

24. Dancing is great fun.

25. Arthur Mitchell is an excellent dancer.

THE EXPANDED SENTENCE

Basic sentences are expanded by means of modifiers, by coordination, by subordination, and by apposition. These grammatical devices enable the writer to develop sentences in which he can communicate as effectively as in speech through a variety of reinforcement techniques. A good writer is able to express himself more effectively than a speaker since he will spend more time in planning *how* he will put something into words as well as *what* words he will use. The sentence structures of written English are much more highly developed and more intricately constructed than are those of the spoken language. And, of course, spoken English is replete with sentence fragments.

> It was like a peculiarly beautiful trinket to be carried unmentioned in one's trouser pocket—a rare stamp, an old coin, a few tiny gold links found trodden out of shape on the path in the park, a pebble of carnelian, a sea shell distinguishable from all others by an unusual spot or stripe—and, as if it were anyone of these, he carried around with him everywhere a warm and persistent and increasingly beautiful sense of possession.
>   CONRAD AIKEN

The writer of the sentence above has used a variety of modifiers. He has used coordination and subordination. He has used appositives. He has developed an unusually effective compound-complex sentence of 78 words—a very long sentence, much longer than the average, which has from 18 to 20 words. It is not the length of this sentence that gives it merit. It is the skill with which the writer has exploited the grammar of his language to say beautifully and forcefully what he wants to say. When this writer was faced with the need for writing such a long sentence, he had the necessary ability and word power to do so.

Modifiers

MODIFIERS are built usually around nouns and verbs. However, they are sometimes used with adjectives and adverbs. They make meaning more explicit. Word-group modifiers serve to explain and elaborate. In the developed or expanded sentence, the noun with its modifiers, or the verb with its modifiers, forms a compact unit or word group within the sentence. Noun-headed modifiers are called NOUN CLUSTERS; verb-headed modifiers are called VERB CLUSTERS.

> the little old woman who lived in a shoe
> the girl on the flying trapeze
> the candidate to be watched
> the people walking down the street
> the house that Jack built
> the frozen strawberries in the refrigerator

Each of these word groups is a noun cluster. It consists of a noun and its modifiers. The noun is called the headword. In the first example, *woman* is the headword, in the second *girl*, and so forth. The modifiers may be single-word modifiers or word-group modifiers. In the first illustration, the single-word modifiers are *little* and *old*. *The* is a determiner, a function word that signals a noun. The word-group modifier is *who lived in a shoe*. This subject-predicate word group forms an adjective clause. Other modifying word groups in the illustrations above are the prepositional phrase *on the flying trapeze*, the infinitive phrase *to be watched*, and the participial phrase *walking down the street*.

Examples of verb clusters are:

> walked hurriedly into the room
> will come if he is called
> has played to win the game
> came running down the street
> to go quickly and quietly
> driving slowly past the school

The words in color are verbs or verbals that serve as headwords around which modifiers are clustered. The modifiers are single-word modifiers or word-group modifiers. In the first example, *hurriedly* is a single-word modifier, and *into the room* is a word-group modifier, in this case a

prepositional phrase. In the second example, the word-group modifier
is *if he is called,* an adverb clause.

The following examples illustrate adjectives used as headwords with
modifiers:

> an unusually bright child
> the locally popular singer
> evidently guilty
> exceptionally beautiful

The four adjectives in color—bright, popular, guilty, and beautiful—
are modified by the words *unusually, locally, evidently*, and *exceptionally*. The adjectives themselves are the headwords; they may fulfill
either the modifying (attributive) or the predicate adjective (predicative)
function:

> Attributive: My niece is an unusually bright child.
> Predicative: My niece is unusually bright.

An adjective-headed cluster is called an ADJECTIVE CLUSTER.

The following examples illustrate adverbs used as headwords with
modifiers:

> The plane arrived early today.
> The ship slipped slowly downward.

In these examples, the adverbs in color serve as headwords. *Early*
modifies the adverb *today*, and *slowly* modifies the adverb *downward*.
An adverb-headed cluster is called an ADVERB CLUSTER.

The following sentence has been expanded with modifiers from its
basic N-V PATTERN:

> The wild animals which had escaped from the zoo were recaptured early
> today when officials from the park rounded up the last weary lion walking
> down Main Street.

Headword	Modifiers
animals	wild
	which had escaped from the zoo
were recaptured	early today
	when officials ... Main Street
had escaped	from the zoo
officials	from the park
lion	last
	weary
	walking down Main Street
walking	down Main Street

This analysis will give you some idea of the complexity developed by expanding a sentence with modifiers. It may serve also to illustrate the skill a writer must acquire in using modifiers to communicate clearly and effectively.

Exercise 4

Identify the headwords and the modifiers in the following sentences:

1. The narrow streets of the city were littered with papers which blew in circles when the wind came up.

2. The river is much too dirty for swimming.

3. The officer ran into the house where the fugitive was hidden.

4. Ray Charles, who is blind, is one of my favorite popular singers.

5. Mrs. Lyons was unusually angry when she discovered the papers that had blown over her lawn.

6. He who fights and runs away lives to fight another day.

7. When our telephone rang at 3 a.m., my mother was relieved that it was only a wrong number.

8. The laundry to be delivered is in a truck in front of the store.

9. The man who lives across the street in the house which has just been sold will move to Boston, where he will be employed in a clothing store.

10. We sold chances to everyone we knew and finally raised enough money for the class trip.

11. Diane looks especially pretty with her long black hair wrapped in heavy braids around her head.

12. The strong, handsome prince married the beautiful princess whom he had rescued from the dragon, and they lived happily ever after.

13. The old man walked along the tracks where he could easily find his way in the dark.

14. My father is a moderately successful man who has worked very hard during his lifetime.

15. Uncle Ben fell down the stairs when he stumbled over the broken step.

Exercise 4,
continued

16. The little girls jumping rope in the front of the house are the sisters of Helen's friend who lives in Brownsville.

17. Blowing its whistles cheerfully, the steamer moved into the harbor, and the crowds on the shore shouted happy greetings to the passengers.

18. The boy jumped off the woodshed roof.

19. Strictly fresh eggs are being sold for a remarkably low price in a store on Front Street.

20. Phil is working hard because he plans to go to college when he graduates from high school.

21. The man in the long robes is an ambassador from Ghana who has come to speak to us at assembly today.

22. Michelangelo's colossal *David* was carved from a block of marble which was originally 13 feet high.

23. The Countee Cullen library on 136th Street was named for a famous poet.

Exercise 5

1. Construct a N-V sentence in which the subject is the head-word of a noun cluster made up of single-word modifiers.

2. Construct a N-V-N sentence in which the direct object is the headword of a noun cluster made up of a word-group modifier.

3. Construct a sentence based on any of the first five patterns in which the predicate verb is the headword of a verb cluster made up of a single-word and a word-group modifier.

4. Construct a sentence based on any of the first five patterns in which the subject is the headword of a noun cluster made up of word-group modifiers.

5. Construct a N-LV-N sentence in which the predicate noun is the headword of a noun cluster made up of single-word and word-group modifiers.

6. Write a sentence based on any of the first five basic patterns in which both the subject and the predicate are headwords of clusters made up of a variety of modifiers.

7. Construct a N-V-N sentence in which the direct object is the headword of a noun cluster made up of a preposi-tional phrase and a participial phrase.

Exercise 5,   8. Construct a sentence in which an adverb is the headword
   continued   of a cluster made up of a single-word modifier.

9. Construct a N-LV-ADJ sentence in which the predicate
   adjective is the headword of a cluster made up of a single-
   word modifier.

10. Write a sentence expanded as fully as possible with a
    variety of modifiers.

Coordination and Subordination

Sentences are expanded by means of COORDINATION   SUBORDINA-
TION. In coordination, two basic sentence patterns are joined either with
or without a connective. In subordination, a subject-predicate word
group is included within a basic sentence pattern.

The batter struck out.
Coordination: The batter struck out, and the crowd groaned.
Subordination: When the batter struck out, the crowd groaned.

The sentence illustrating coordination is a compound sentence in
which two basic sentence patterns are joined by the connective *and.*

The sentence illustrating subordination is a complex sentence in
which the subordinate clause *When the batter struck out* is included
within the basic N-V PATTERN.

Elements within the sentence may also be coordinated, as in this
example of a compound predicate:

The pitcher fielded the ball and made an easy throw to first base.

To combine coordination and subordination requires skill on the part
of the writer. Many students use compound sentences, and many use
complex sentences. Few are able to combine the grammatical processes
of coordination and subordination effectively.

> McCovey hit a pair of homers, but his performance was overshadowed by
> that of the opposing pitcher who hurled a two-hitter, striking out the
> side four times in the last six innings.

Test Yourself

Using the process of both subordination and coordination, combine
the following sentences:

The author hopes to go abroad next summer.
He is well known to educators.
His plans depend on the success of his book.

Subordinate clauses may be modifying clauses, either ADJECTIVE CLAUSES or ADVERB CLAUSES, or they may be NOUN CLAUSES serving in the normal functions served by nouns.

An art critic is a man who expects miracles. JAMES HUNEKER
The stream that flows through Deer Valley is almost dry.
I have no words to describe to you the deep agony of soul which I experienced on that never to be forgotten morning. FREDERICK DOUGLASS

I like Americans because they are healthy and optimistic. FRANZ KAFKA
The catcher grumbled when the umpire called the runner safe at home.
If it doesn't rain today, we're going to the Dodger-Cardinal game.

What a man needs in gardening is a cast-iron back with a hinge in it.
CHARLES DUDLEY WARNER
I begin to suspect that a man's bewilderment is the measurement of his wisdom. NATHANIEL HAWTHORNE
The prediction that victory would come shortly after D Day was not borne out.

The first three sentences illustrate the use of adjective clauses; the second three, adverb clauses; and the third three, noun clauses. In all these sentences, subordination is the grammatical process used. Each subordinate clause is included within its sentence.

Exercise 6

Study the following sentences. Determine whether coordination, subordination, or both have been used. Name the coordinate clauses and the subordinate clauses. Identify the grammatical function of each subordinate clause.

1. When the rain stops, we will go fishing. (The adverb clause can be considered a sentence-modifier.)

2. Years passed, and Henry Adams became a plain middle-aged man.

3. The plane settled down easily, but many passengers were startled when the pilot brought it to a screeching stop.

4. What bothers me most is the thought that I must spend four more years in school.

5. Jones struck out because he didn't see the ball.

6. The counsellor asks that everyone be back at the fieldhouse by six o'clock.

7. The Clark boys arrived at the party at ten o'clock; then the fun began.

Exercise 6,

continued

8. Roosevelt passed the football to the quarterback, and then he was tackled and forced to the ground.

9. Cushman is the only player on the team who bats over .300.

10. The boys laughed when they saw Rita's new hairdo.

11. Frederick Douglass escaped to become a free man, but he never forgot those who were still slaves.

12. The President visited Europe as he had planned, and he was warmly welcomed by the people.

13. We will start the performance as soon as the audience settles down.

14. The fact that he is a veteran will excuse him from physical education, and then he may enroll in courses in his major field.

15. The lady who lives across the street is a friend of Aunt Martha, who lives in Boston.

16. Whenever Pete starts to play his guitar and his sister sings along, everyone on the street wants to join in, and we all sit on the porch together.

17. After the long winter had ended, the warm spring sun melted the heavy snow, and the little streams at the foot of the mountain became deep rivers.

18. The war is over, peace has come, and happiness will return once more to our people.

19. Henry picked up the books that he had been carrying and walked leisurely home.

20. Dust clouds rose over the desert as the wind blew across the dry valley, and men and horses tried to find shelter from the sudden storm.

Apposition

Apposition is used frequently in the expansion of sentences. Literally, it is a side-by-side relationship. An APPOSITIVE differs from a modifier in that it adds a word or group of words to give more information about the noun or noun substitute it follows.

> Babe Ruth, the baseball player who hit more home runs than anyone else before him, was called the "King of Swat."
> Africa, a continent peopled by highly developed cultures and by primitive tribes, is an area of wide diversity.

Jones was a ruthless man, the victim of early cruelty and needless suffering.
Williams was appointed third vice-president, a position of some importance
but little responsibility.
That was his final offer—a down payment of ten thousand dollars with a
ten-year mortgage.

Exercise 7

1. Develop a cluster of modifiers around the subject of this sentence:
    The audience cheered wildly.

2. Develop a cluster of modifiers around the verb in this sentence:
    The car horns were blowing.

3. Develop a cluster of modifiers around the direct object in this sentence:
    The starving man found a wallet.

4. Develop a cluster of modifiers around the noun in the prepositional phrase in this sentence:
    My brother keeps his new shoes under the bed.

5. Develop a cluster of modifiers around the infinitive in this sentence:
    Helen wants to drive to Buffalo.

6. Develop a cluster of modifiers around the verbal in the subject position of this sentence:
    Driving is serious.

7. Develop a cluster of modifiers around the verbal modifying the direct object in this sentence:
    We saw Henry running.

8. Develop a cluster of modifiers around the predicate adjective in this sentence:
    The school was dark.

9. Develop a cluster of modifiers around the linking-verb complement in this sentence:
    Miss Andrews is the teacher.

10. Develop a cluster of modifiers around the noun used as an appositive in this sentence:
    Ernest Hemingway, the author, was born in America.

11. Develop a cluster of modifiers around both the subject and the verb in this sentence:
    The horse jumped.

Exercise 7,
continued
12. Develop a cluster of modifiers around both the verb and
the direct object in this sentence:
Sally baked a cake.

THE IMMEDIATE CONSTITUENTS OF THE SENTENCE

Expanded English sentences may be analyzed into immediate constituents. Words in spoken English are grouped by intonation into meaningful units that are related grammatically. We may divide a sentence
into two parts. We may then divide each part into two parts, and so on.
The two components at any level of structure are called *immediate
constituents*. Immediate constituent analysis is merely a form of analysis
by which a sentence is divided into grammatical units.

> The manager of the team / removed the pitcher who had walked four men.
>> The manager / of the team
>> removed the pitcher / who had walked four men.
>> removed / the pitcher
>> who / had walked four men.
>> had walked / four men.

In this particular sentence, the first pair of immediate constituents is
the subject and predicate. The subject may be divided into the subject
noun and its modifying prepositional phrase. The predicate divides into
the verb and complement and the subordinate clause modifying the
complement. Each of these constituents may be further divided.

The immediate constituents of a sentence are not necessarily first
paired by subject and predicate. Look at the following sentences. Each
one has been divided into the immediate constituents at the highest
level.

> When the clock struck twelve / everyone went to bed.
> At a signal from the director / the cast came on stage.
> In the meantime / the prisoners were becoming restless.
> Walking slowly down Fifth Avenue / came the dapper Mr. Powell wearing
> a derby and carrying a cane.
> The lake being choppy and the night dark / we decided not to try to return
> to the village until morning.

The analysis of immediate constituents is useful because it helps you
to become sensitive to the complex layers of structure which are characteristic of our language. It may also help you avoid writing confused
or involved sentences that are impossible both to understand and to
analyze.

Exercise 8   *Analyze the following sentences into immediate constitu-ents:*

1. The girl who lives in the next apartment moved here from Akron.

2. The student returned the books to the librarian who was at the desk.

3. The nations of the world have united for the purpose of maintaining peace.

4. What creates smog in cities is believed to be the exhaust from internal combustion engines.

5. When Henry grows up, he wants to be a banker.

6. The ship from Australia put out to sea when the fog lifted.

7. The football team from Greenport won last Saturday's game when they kicked a field goal in the last minute of play.

8. The President hailed the passage of the measure as a step forward in our national economy.

9. Walking slowly down the street, the old man paused often to greet his many friends.

10. In the meantime, the boys were eating as though they were starved.

Exercise 9

1. Write a compound sentence with subject-predicate word groups connected by *but*.

2. Write a complex sentence with an adjective clause modifying the direct object.

3. Write a complex sentence with a noun clause used as a direct object.

4. Write a complex sentence with an adverb clause modifying the verb.

5. Write a complex sentence with an adjective clause introduced by the subordinator *whose* modifying the subject.

Exercise 9,
continued

6. Write a complex sentence introduced by an adverb clause.

7. Write a complex sentence with a noun clause as subject.

8. Write a complex sentence with an adjective clause introduced by the subordinator *whom* modifying the predicate noun.

9. Write a compound sentence with the conjunctive adverb *however* used as a connective.

10. Write a compound-complex sentence with an adverb clause in the second subject-predicate word group.

Summary

The sentence is the basic unit of communication in standard written English. There are a number of specific physical characteristics by which it may be recognized:

1. It begins with a capital letter and is terminated with a mark of punctuation —a period, a question mark, or an exclamation point.
2. It has a subject and a predicate.
3. It has a finite verb.
4. Its normal word order is subject-verb-complement.
5. It can begin with a signal of subordination *only* if the word group introduced by the subordinator is included within a basic sentence pattern.
6. It has a characteristic intonation pattern.

Remember that the proper arrangement of words in a sentence is highly important since an interchange of position results in a change in meaning. Subordination, too, has a direct bearing on meaning. The N-V-N PATTERN, in particular, can be expanded by word and phrase modifiers, by clause modifiers, and by appositives. The importance of word clusters cannot be overemphasized.

Muda wa kumweka mhalifu katika gereza la Chifu hauna budi kuwa mfupi kiasi cha kupata nafasi ya kumpeleka mtu yule kortini au kwenye Korti ya Kiafrika, na muda wenyewe usizidi saa 48, isipokuwa katika mambo maalum ya lazima. *Swahili*

Chapter 3

LEARNING
HOW WORDS
COMMUNICATE

A Look Back and A Look Forward

In Chapter 2, you learned that a knowledge of the physical characteristics of a sentence is basic to the development of skills in written communication. You became aware of the patterns of a sentence and how sentences can be expanded by using modifiers discriminately, by coordination and subordination, and by using appositives.

Now it's time to look a little more closely at the essential parts of the sentence—the subject and the predicate. This chapter covers the four main classes of words—nouns and verbs, adjectives and adverbs, which modify or refer to nouns and verbs.

THE STRUCTURE OF ENGLISH

Your study of grammar indicates that English is a subject-predicate language. The sentence is the basic unit of communication, and its two important structures are the subject and the predicate. This subject-predicate structure is the beginning of the whole study of grammar. It is the very basis of communication. The essential word in the subject is a noun, or a noun substitute; the essential word of the predicate is the verb. Essentially, then, English is a noun-verb language. These are the two major word classes.

As you now know, simple sentences may be expanded by means of modifiers which cluster about the nouns and the verbs. The modifiers of nouns are usually adjectives, and the modifiers of verbs are usually adverbs. Adjectives and adverbs give added power to communication; they make it more meaningful.

The four main word classes, then, are nouns, verbs, adjectives, and adverbs. These classes constitute over 90 percent of our total language. When new words are added to our lexicon, they are either nouns, verbs, adjectives, or adverbs.

All our other English words may be called FUNCTION WORDS. They are words that bind our language into coherent patterns and serve often as structural signals of meaning. For example, conjunctions connect words or join basic sentence patterns; prepositions connect word-group modifiers to a noun or a verb. DETERMINERS such as *a, an, the* serve as signals of nouns, and AUXILIARIES such as *may, would, must* serve as signals of verbs. These function words have very little lexical (dictionary) meaning in and of themselves. They take on meaning only in the context of the sentence of which they are a part.

NOUNS

Nouns communicate as subjects, as complements, as appositives, and after prepositions. The following sentences illustrate the subject function of nouns:

> The coach told the team to take a five-minute break.
> Lorraine Hansberry died at thirty-four.
> My mother serves grits every morning for breakfast.
> There was a large crowd at the rally yesterday.
> An old woman got caught in the subway doors.
> The pollution level is very high this morning.
> In two weeks the building had risen three stories.
> After the game was over, many baseball fans crowded onto the field.

The sentences that follow illustrate the function of nouns as complements. In group 1, the noun in color functions as a direct object; in group 2, as an indirect object; in group 3, as a predicate noun; and in group 4, as an objective complement.

GROUP 1

The cat ate the canary.
The guard shot his dog.
The banker gave his money to charity.
The boys pushed the car to the nearest gas station.
Rosa pays her own tuition.

GROUP 2

The man gave his son a dollar.
The teacher read the children a story.
The builder offered Father a job.
The foreman handed Ralph a shovel.
Henry bought his girl a banana split.

GROUP 3

Miss Lane is our new teacher.
Lincoln was President during the war between the states.
Mrs. Russell has been our customer for ten years.
Tracy will be class secretary.
My brother became a teacher last year.

GROUP 4

Our neighbors named the baby Jack.
The people elected Mr. White councilman.
The governor appointed his friend secretary.
The judges declared Mary Jones the winner.
The fans called the umpire a robber.

Each of the following sentences illustrates a noun used after a preposition:

The captain of the team called the boys together.
He found the money under a stone.
That novel describes the settlement of Oklahoma.
The old man divided his money among his children.
The graduating class voted to go to Washington.

Since prepositional phrases may serve as modifiers of nouns, verbs, verbals, you can easily understand the communicating power of nouns used after prepositions.

The following sentences illustrate nouns used as appositives. The sentences in group 1 illustrate nonrestrictive appositives; in group 2, restrictive appositives.

GROUP 1

Sammy Davis, a clever impressionist, did impressions of John Wayne and
   Frank Sinatra.
A young man, the leader of the group, demanded more money.
The new student, a quiet boy, made friends slowly.
The bluebonnet, the state flower of Texas, belongs to the pea family.
Jim bought a car, a 1956 Thunderbird.

GROUP 2

The impressionist Sammy Davis is very popular today.
The dancer Alvin Ailey gave a brilliant performance.
My cousin Jim owns a new Chevy.
Elizabeth the Second is Queen of England.
Ex-Dodger Roy Campanella is admired by everyone.

Restrictive appositives identify the word with which they are in
apposition and are not usually punctuated. Nonrestrictive appositives
describe rather than identify and are set off by commas.

Test Yourself

Identify the function of the italicized nouns in these sentences:

1. Bill read his *theme* aloud.

2. Tom came to *class* unprepared.

3. Joe gave his *friends* a ride home.

4. Sally, my younger *sister*, is a freshman.

5. She is *secretary* of her class.

6. Miss Clark appointed two boys *cochairmen*.

Nouns That Function as Modifiers

The modifying function is usually filled by adjectives and adverbs,
but nouns may serve as modifiers of other nouns. A noun that modifies
may be either a possessive modifier or a noun adjunct. The possessive
modifier is signaled by an apostrophe.

POSSESSIVE MODIFIER
There is a sale of ladies' coats.
Uncle Andrew sat on Grandpa's hat.
James wants to marry the boss's daughter.

NOUN ADJUNCT
The plumber repaired the kitchen sink.
Henrietta can make delicious lemon pie.
Mr. Weeks is the new science teacher.

Remember these facts about forming the possessive:

1. The possessive of singular nouns is formed by adding 's: *boy's, girl's, man's, Henry's, dog's.*

2. The apostrophe alone may indicate the possessive of singular nouns ending in s: *boss'* or *boss's; Yeats'* or *Yeats's.*

3. The possessive of plural nouns ending in s is formed by adding simply an apostrophe: *boys', girls', days', months', friends'.*

4. The possessive of plural nouns not ending in s is formed by adding 's: *men's, women's, deer's, children's.*

Exercise 1   *Identify the function of each noun in the following sentences. If it is used as a complement, classify the complement. If it is used as a modifier, identify the class of modifier.*

1. The baby is keeping the neighbors awake.

2. Of all modern poets, Langston Hughes is my favorite.

3. The mayor visited our neighborhood yesterday.

4. The doctor, a tall young man with black hair, stepped into the room.

5. This lady is my mother.

6. The players selected Bill Henry captain of the team.

7. My father's tax refund check was stolen out of our mailbox while we were all away.

8. Ruth's mother works in the cafeteria at Washington High School.

9. The gentlemen riders weighed more than the jockeys.

10. Her little sister is a big baby.

11. The soup kettle was boiling, and the smell of good food gave the boys a hearty appetite.

12. Miss Fritz appointed Mary leader of the panel.

13. Hugo Bonehead, the noted comedian, entertained the PTA.

14. King Henry the Eighth of England had many wives.

15. The name Robinson is a common one here.

16. The rancher's great horses galloped proudly down the street.

Exercise 2

1. In the following sentence, use as many different nouns as possible in the subject position:
   A huge ____ was making its way across the river.

2. Use a variety of nouns as the direct object in the following sentence:
   The skillful craftsman created a beautiful ____.

3. Use several different nouns as the objective complement in the following sentence:
   The class voted Harold the ____.

4. Use at least two different nouns as the linking-verb complement in the following sentence:
   My statement is a ____ of greater friendship between our countries.

5. Use as many different nouns as possible as the indirect object in the following sentence:
   The fellow handed his ____ my wallet.

6. Use as many different nouns as possible after the preposition in the following sentence:
   The beautiful gray horse jumped gracefully over the ____.

7. Use several different nouns as a nonrestrictive appositive in the following sentence:
   They presented the prize to Helen Crooks, the ____.

8. Use several different nouns as modifiers in this sentence:
   The young people have gone for a ____ ride.

Exercise 3

1. Write a sentence using the noun *dog* as an indirect object.

2. Write a sentence using the noun *motorcycle* as a direct object.

3. Write a sentence using the noun *acoustics* as the subject.

4. Write a sentence using the noun *author* as the objective complement.

5. Write a sentence using the noun *secretary* as a nonrestrictive appositive.

6. Write a sentence using the noun *journalist* as a restrictive appositive.

7. Write four sentences using the noun *bridge* as the object of different prepositions.

Exercise 3,
continued

8. Write a sentence using the noun *success* as a linking-verb complement.

9. Write a sentence using the noun *week* as a possessive modifier.

10. Write a sentence using the noun *cash* as a noun adjunct.

Singular and Plural Nouns

Nouns in English form their plurals in a number of ways, as illustrated in the tabulation below. What are the generalizations that apply to nouns ending in *ch, y, o,* and *f*? Which nouns in the list have internal changes when forming the plural? Which noun is the same in both singular and plural? Do all nouns have plurals? What other changes do you notice?

SINGULAR	PLURAL
cat	cats
church	churches
ally	allies
potato	potatoes
loaf	loaves
man	men
child	children
alumnus	alumni
deer	deer
tooth	teeth
information	
economics	
	pliers
people	people, peoples
mother-in-law	mothers-in-law
lieutenant general	lieutenant generals

The importance of number forms to standard English is obvious. The fact that certain nouns are used only in the singular or the plural is significant to verb usage, as you will discover later in the discussion of agreement between subject and verb.

Exercise 4

1. Write the plural of each of the following nouns:

wife	moose
jelly	goose
hero	hypothesis
auto	curriculum
tooth	man-of-war
ox	fish

Exercise 4,
continued

2. Write sentences using the plural form of each of the nouns at the bottom of page 69.

3. Write the possessive form of each of the following nouns:

James	Socrates
army	wives
children	church
boss	sister-in-law

4. Write sentences illustrating the use of the possessive forms above.

Proper Nouns

Proper nouns in English are those nouns written with a capital letter.

1.	Geographical names	New York
2.	Personal names	Donald Brown
3.	Organizations	Southern Christian Leadership Conference
4.	Names of ships	*Dublin Queen*
5.	Days, months, holidays	Monday, July, Memorial Day
6.	Institutions	Yale University
7.	Trade names	Clabber Girl Baking Powder
8.	Titles before names	Doctor Price
9.	The Deity	God, Jehovah
10.	Historical periods	the Dark Ages
11.	Geographical areas	the North, the South

Exercise 5

In the following passage, fill in the blanks with nouns appropriate to the context:

The problem of ____ is one of major ____ today. We can no longer afford to ignore the sorry ____ of our ____, ____, and ____. Not only are ____ and ____ so badly fouled that ____ can no longer use them for ____, but now the ____ they flow into shows ____ of ____. We are at a crucial ____ where drastic ____ must be taken.

In ____ throughout the ____, the ____ we breathe is now so filled with ____ that soft, black ____ often settles on ____ and ____. The ____ may come when we will be forced to wear ____ just to survive.

Probably the most obvious ____ of ____ to be seen is that on ____, where ____ and ____ litter every ____. Who stops to throw his ____ in a ____? We all must begin to, or soon we will drive ourselves off our own ____. And we have no other ____ to go.

VERBS

The reader or listener is sensitive to certain language signals that identify the verbs for him. These signals include position in the sentence, auxiliary verb forms, and inflectional endings. Communication breaks down when the reader or listener fails to recognize the verb since it is regarded as the key word in communication. The following ambiguous headlines illustrate this fact:

ARMY ORDERS CHANGE
PHILADELPHIA MISSES FIGHT
AMERICAN PLANS UPSET

The position of a verb in a sentence is fixed, as evident in the first five basic sentence patterns:

N-V
N-V-N
N-V-N-N
N-LV-N
N-LV-ADJ

The verb follows the subject noun, or it comes between the subject noun and the complement. The normal word order in English is subject-verb-complement. In questions, the word order is usually inverted.

Auxiliary verb forms include forms of *have, to be, do,* and *keep.* They also include the words *may, must, might, can, could, will, shall, would, should.*

Edward has gone to the country.
The children have been playing games.
The army may have won a great victory.
The women must have been planning this affair for weeks.
The man can speak two languages.

Regular Verbs

Most verbs in English have four forms. These are the plain form, the singular form, the past form, and the present participle. Regular verbs are verbs that form the past by adding *d* or *ed* to the plain form. The following illustrates the inflected forms of a number of regular verbs:

PLAIN	SINGULAR	PAST	PRESENT PARTICIPLE
argue	argues	argued	arguing
call	calls	called	calling
jump	jumps	jumped	jumping
play	plays	played	playing

PLAIN	SINGULAR	PAST	PRESENT PARTICIPLE
prefer	prefers	preferred	preferring
stop	stops	stopped	stopping
travel	travels	traveled	traveling
trim	trims	trimmed	trimming
try	tries	tried	trying
walk	walks	walked	walking

Irregular Verbs

Irregular verbs usually undergo an internal vowel change in forming the past inflected form instead of adding simply -*d* or -*ed*. These verbs are in the great minority of English verbs. There are fewer than 150 irregular verbs in our language.

However, irregular verbs give the speaker and writer a great deal of trouble. Many people, for example, use nonstandard forms in speech and carry these forms over into their writing. It is essential that you gain familiarity with the inflected forms of all English irregular verbs.

Five-Part Irregular Verbs

Some irregular verbs have five inflected forms, some have four inflected forms, and some have three. The verb *to be* has eight different forms (page 80). The following table lists the forms of practically all the five-part irregular verbs. These verbs present the most difficulty.

PLAIN	SINGULAR	PAST	PRESENT PARTICIPLE	PAST PARTICIPLE
bear	bears	bore	bearing	born *or* borne
begin	begins	began	beginning	begun
bite	bites	bit	biting	bitten
blow	blows	blew	blowing	blown
break	breaks	broke	breaking	broken
choose	chooses	chose	choosing	chosen
do	does	did	doing	done
draw	draws	drew	drawing	drawn
drink	drinks	drank	drinking	drunk
drive	drives	drove	driving	driven
eat	eats	ate	eating	eaten
fall	falls	fell	falling	fallen
fly	flies	flew	flying	flown
forbid	forbids	forbade *or* forbad	forbidding	forbidden
forget	forgets	forgot	forgetting	forgotten *or* forgot
forsake	forsakes	forsook	forsaking	forsaken

PLAIN	SINGULAR	PAST	PRESENT PARTICIPLE	PAST PARTICIPLE
freeze	freezes	froze	freezing	frozen
get	gets	got	getting	got *or* gotten
give	gives	gave	giving	given
go	goes	went	going	gone
grow	grows	grew	growing	grown
hide	hides	hid	hiding	hidden
know	knows	knew	knowing	known
lie	lies	lay	lying	lain
ride	rides	rode	riding	ridden
ring	rings	rang	ringing	rung
rise	rises	rose	rising	risen
see	sees	saw	seeing	seen
shake	shakes	shook	shaking	shaken
shrink	shrinks	shrank	shrinking	shrunk
sing	sings	sang	singing	sung
sink	sinks	sank	sinking	sunk
slay	slays	slew	slaying	slain
smite	smites	smote	smiting	smitten
speak	speaks	spoke	speaking	spoken
spring	springs	sprang	springing	sprung
steal	steals	stole	stealing	stolen
stink	stinks	stank	stinking	stunk
stride	strides	strode	striding	stridden
strive	strives	strove	striving	striven
swear	swears	swore	swearing	sworn
swim	swims	swam	swimming	swum
take	takes	took	taking	taken
tear	tears	tore	tearing	torn
throw	throws	threw	throwing	thrown
tread	treads	trod	treading	trodden
wear	wears	wore	wearing	worn
weave	weaves	wove	weaving	woven
write	writes	wrote	writing	written

The difficulty for some students arises in the use of the past form and the past participle of irregular verbs. The past form of a five-part verb is used only to communicate past tense, and it is *never* used with an auxiliary. The past participle is used *only* with an auxiliary verb.

> The boy wrote the composition.
> The boy has written the composition.
> The composition was written by the boy.
> The thief stole the money.
> The thief has stolen the money.
> The money was stolen by the thief.

Test Yourself

Use the correct form of the indicated verb in each of these sentences:

1. Have you ____ all your homework? (do)

2. We ____ to Maine last summer. (go)

3. Has Tom ____ to apply for a summer job? (write)

4. The boys have ____ all the chocolate cake. (eat)

5. How long have you ____ Sue? (know)

The plain form is used as part of an infinitive, with plural subjects, and with the singular personal pronoun *I*. The plain form is also used with some auxiliary verbs.

> Our canary has learned to sing.
> The boys sing in the choir.
> I sing when I feel happy.
> We must sing for our supper.

Other auxiliary verbs that can be used with the plain form of the verb include *may, can, could, should, would, will,* and *shall*. Forms of *to be* and *have* are not used with the plain form of the verb.

The singular form of the verb is used with singular subjects in the present tense. It cannot be used with any auxiliary verbs.

> The girl speaks very clearly.
> The early bird gets the worm.
> Laura knows what she wants.

Exercise 6

1. Write sentences illustrating the use of the plain form of each of the following verbs with a plural subject:

strive	weave
swim	write
tear	bear
tread	bite
wear	break

2. Write sentences illustrating the use of the plain form of each of the following verbs with a single auxiliary. Use a different auxiliary in each sentence.

begin	eat
blow	fly
choose	forget
draw	freeze
drink	give

3. Write sentences illustrating the use of the plain form of each of the following verbs as an infinitive:

go	shrink
hide	slay
lie	speak
ring	steal
see	stride

4. Write sentences illustrating the use of the singular form of each of the following verbs:

break	fall
choose	fly
do	freeze
drink	get
drive	give

5. Write sentences illustrating the use of the past form of each of the following verbs:

do	get
drive	grow
fall	know
forbid	ride
forsake	rise

6. Write sentences illustrating the use of the present participle form of the following verbs with one auxiliary in each case. Use different forms of auxiliaries.

shake	swear
hide	take
sink	throw
smite	forbid
spring	shrink

7. Write sentences illustrating the use of the present participle of the following verbs with two auxiliaries in each case. Use different combinations of auxiliaries.

tread	choose
weave	draw
write	eat
bite	drive
break	forbid

8. Write sentences illustrating the use of the past participle of the following verbs with one auxiliary verb in each case. Use as many different auxiliary forms as you can.

go	ring
grow	see
know	shake
lie	sing
speak	steal

Exercise 6, *continued*

9. Write sentences illustrating the use of the past participle of the following verbs with two or more auxiliary verbs in each case. Use as many combinations of auxiliaries as you can.

begin	ride
drink	shrink
fly	sing
forget	spring
throw	swim

Exercise 7

Fill in each blank with the appropriate form of the five-part irregular verb that best suits the context.

1. The man was ____ by the frightening experience.

2. Although we could not ____ last summer, we opened up the fire hydrant and cooled off that way.

3. Lou has ____ as many as three letters a week.

4. My grandmother and my grandfather ____ down for a nap every afternoon.

5. The witness has ____ to tell the truth.

6. The incident will be ____ in a few weeks.

7. When our class went to the Shakespeare festival, we ____ our lunches on the lawn at Stratford.

8. The shipwrecked man had ____ all the water in his canteen.

9. His clothing was ____ and his face had been ____ by mosquitoes.

10. Dad has been ____ on the couch for an hour.

11. All the bells in the city ____ when the soldiers returned home.

12. The city has ____ the heavy expense for many years.

13. The money was ____ under a board in the kitchen floor.

14. Aunt Kate ____ the scraps of yarn into a beautiful scarf.

15. The principal ____ the students to leave the school premises at lunchtime.

16. The woolen skirt ____ when it was washed.

17. The mailman ____ his feet walking in the deep snow.

Exercise 7,
continued

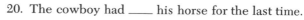

18. Three hundred soldiers were ____ in the ambush.

19. The woman ____ a picture of her father on the wall of the living room.

20. The cowboy had ____ his horse for the last time.

21. These clothes should not be ____ again until they are cleaned.

22. The boat ____ a leak and ____ quickly into the lake.

23. The trainer ____ the rope over the horse's head.

24. Henry Hicks has ____ into trouble by cutting classes.

Four-Part Irregular Verbs

There are approximately sixty irregular verbs that have only four inflected forms. Some of these verbs appear in the following table:

PLAIN	SINGULAR	PAST	PRESENT PARTICIPLE
bind	binds	bound	binding
bleed	bleeds	bled	bleeding
bring	brings	brought	bringing
build	builds	built	building
cling	clings	clung	clinging
come	comes	came	coming
feed	feeds	fed	feeding
fling	flings	flung	flinging
hold	holds	held	holding
lay	lays	laid	laying
lose	loses	lost	losing
read	reads	read	reading
run	runs	ran	running
sell	sells	sold	selling
sit	sits	sat	sitting
stand	stands	stood	standing
swing	swings	swung	swinging
win	wins	won	winning

Four-part irregular verbs do not have a special form for the past participle. These verbs use the past form in all contexts that require the past participle. The four-part verbs *come* and *run*, however, are exceptional; these words use the plain form to fill the past participle function.

The Browns won the game 42-34.
The Browns have won five out of their last six games.
Father came home early last night.
Father has come home early every night this week.

The verb *read* is a four-part verb in speech only. Although the plain form and the past form are pronounced differently, they are spelled exactly the same.

Exercise 8   1. Make up a table listing all four forms of each of the following four-part verbs:

behold	hear	sling
bend	keep	slink
beseech	lead	spend
breed	leave	spin
buy	lend	stick
catch	make	sting
creep	mean	strike
deal	meet	string
dwell	pay	sweep
feel	say	teach
fight	seek	tell
find	shine	think
flee	shoot	weep
grind	sleep	win

2. Which of the verbs above have variant forms?

3. Write sentences using the past forms of the verbs above in as many different ways as you can.

Exercise 9   *Fill in each blank with the appropriate form of the four-part irregular verb that best suits the context.*

1. The boxer's lip _____ profusely.

2. If you _____ the pass, you won't be admitted.

3. When the batter struck out, he _____ his bat across the field.

4. I _____ him my old bicycle.

5. The bank has _____ Mr. Jones the money to go in business.

6. The injured man has been _____ by a speeding car.

7. The poor old lady has been _____ to life for over a year.

8. The unfortunate man _____ his hands in utter despair.

9. The dog has _____ there for an hour waiting for its owner.

Exercise 9,
continued

10. They —— on the corner for an hour waiting for a ride.

11. Chris —— off a corner of the piece of pizza.

12. The soldier —— the grenade away.

13. The car —— around the corner and skidded to a stop.

14. George —— most of his life's savings in a bad investment.

15. He —— the roach under his heel.

16. The excited card player had been —— four aces and a king.

17. The horse had been —— for speed and not for endurance.

18. The treacherous guide —— the battalion into ambush.

19. The boys —— on hands and knees through the narrow door.

20. The tiger has —— silently away into the forest.

Three-Part Irregular Verbs

There are approximately twenty irregular verbs that have three inflected forms. Study this list:

PLAIN	SINGULAR	PRESENT PARTICIPLE
*beat	beats	beating
*bet	bets	betting
*bid	bids	bidding
*burst	bursts	bursting
cast	casts	casting
cost	costs	costing
cut	cuts	cutting
hit	hits	hitting
hurt	hurts	hurting
let	lets	letting
*quit	quits	quitting
*rid	rids	ridding
set	sets	setting
shed	sheds	shedding
shut	shuts	shutting
slit	slits	slitting
split	splits	splitting
spread	spreads	spreading
thrust	thrusts	thrusting
*wet	wets	wetting

The starred verbs—with the exception of *beat* and *bid*—have alternate
-*ed* forms for use in the past tense: *betted, bursted, quitted, ridded,* and
wetted. Beat has an alternate past participle form (*beaten*); and *bid* has
an alternate past form (*bade*) as well as two alternate past participle
forms (*bade* and *bidden*).

> Now I shut my eyes.
> Last night I shut my eyes.
> I always have shut my eyes to such things.

> Mr. Jones quit his job last week.
> The convict quit (*or* quitted) the country for good.

The verb situation is complicated by the fact that some of the regular
verbs have alternate past forms that make them four-part irregular verbs.
Such verbs are *abide, bereave, cleave, clothe, dig, dream, hang, heave,
kneel, lean, leap, learn, light, shrive, speed, spell, spill, thrive,* and *wake*.

The past form of *clothe* is normally *clothed*. However, the form *clad*
may also be used. Similarly, there is *dreamt* for *dreamed, sped* for
speeded, and *throve* for *thrived*.

Forms of the Verb To Be

The verb *to be* has eight forms.

| am | is | was | were | are | be | being | been |

Their uses are illustrated in the following sentences:

> I am the oldest member of the family.
> Anne is the most intelligent girl I know.
> The boy was the leader of the gang.
> The clouds were black and threatening.
> The girls are noisy tonight.
> The journey will be pleasant.
> The child is being good.
> The journey has been pleasant.

The verb *to be* is most commonly used in its different forms as an
auxiliary or helping verb.

> I am working at the job now.
> He has been trying to study his lessons.
> The old house was being torn down.
> We will be going to Coney Island tomorrow.
> The undertaker has been asked to come.
> I know I am being difficult.

Exercise 10 *Fill in each blank with the appropriate form of the three-part irregular verb that best suits the context.*

1. When you shouted at me, you ___ my feelings.
2. The sanitation truck ___ the street thoroughly as it swept through the gutters.
3. A pipe ___ in school and we have no classes.
4. People at auctions often ___ more than they can afford.
5. The officer had ___ the gates of the park.
6. The boys ___ the ball over the fence.
7. The lion ___ his great paw through the bars of the cage.
8. The question is ___ the group into two parts.
9. The great cloud bank ___ across the evening sky.
10. The decision may ___ our chances of winning.
11. The fisherman ___ his line far away from shore.
12. The teacher had ___ the books on the second shelf.
13. Even the mayor has ___ the city this summer.
14. The older boy ___ a bad example for his younger brother.
15. He ___ his whole week's pay on that horse.
16. The principal will ___ the students attend the play.
17. The candidate has ___ his chances for election.
18. We have ___ our house of all the insect pests.
19. The rattlesnake ___ its skin once a year.

ADJECTIVES

Adjectives communicate by serving as both modifiers of nouns and as complements — linking-verb complements or objective complements. In group 1 below, the adjectives are modifiers; in group 2, they are linking-verb complements; in group 3, they are objective complements.

GROUP 1

The angry crowd surged onto the field.
The boys drove the ancient car to school.
The matter was referred to the active members of the committee.
Mr. Means, an old gentleman of great dignity, arose in protest.
His offer of help was the kindest gesture he could have made.

GROUP 2

The crowd was angry as it swept over the field.
The boys' car was ancient.
The members of the committee soon became active.
The gentleman was old and very dignified.
Your offer of help seems kindest of all.

GROUP 3

The decision made the crowd angry.
The fellows called the car ancient.
The chairman believed the committee active.
They considered the gentleman old.
I think your offer kindest of all.

A predicate adjective is used after such linking verbs as *to be, become, seem, appear, feel, taste, smell.* An adjective used as an objective complement follows a noun or pronoun which is itself a direct object. An adjective used as a modifier almost always precedes the noun it modifies and follows determiners such as *the, an, a, this, that, many, few, several,* and so forth. Occasionally, especially in poetry, an adjective follows the noun it modifies.

This is the sword perilous.
Beware the woman scorned!
The king, angry at the insult, plotted revenge.

Test Yourself

Identify each adjective in these sentences as a modifier, a linking-verb complement, or an objective complement:

1. The terrified driver jammed on the brakes.

2. Old Mr. Black called the boy disrespectful.

3. My father was shocked at my good grades.

4. His mother considers Sam lazy.

5. Senator Brooke is a dedicated man.

6. Jean looks lovely in her new blue dress.

7. The jury believed the defendant guilty.

8. Sue was enthusiastic about our plans for the summer.

9. The growling dog frightened the messenger.

10. Mrs. Fuller's cooking seems bland to me.

Adjectives of one syllable may usually be inflected, or compared, by adding *-er* to form the comparative degree and *-est* to form the superlative degree.

young	younger	youngest
old	older	oldest
fine	finer	finest
healthy	healthier	healthiest

Some adjectives are inflected irregularly.

many	more	most
good	better	best
little	less	least
bad	worse	worst

Some adjectives of two syllables and all adjectives of three or more syllables are compared by using *more* and *most* or *less* and *least*.

musical	more musical	most musical
comfortable	less comfortable	least comfortable

When *more, most, less,* and *least* indicate degrees of comparison, they function as intensifiers.

Words like *very, really, rather,* and *quite* are often used with adjectives. They, too, are intensifiers and are said to be compatible in meaning with adjectives as well as with some adverbs.

Many adjectives have characteristic endings. These suffixes include *al, -ant, -an, -ar, -ary, -ate, -able, -ed, -ent, -en, -ful, -ic, -ish, -ive, -less, -like, -ly, -ous, -some, -y.*

His business was very personal.
The man is really pleasant.
The American citizen was given police protection.
Pete Brown is a very muscular young man.
This proposal seems revolutionary.
The boss thinks Al suitable for the job.
The ragged old man sat there eating a sandwich.
The class became more attentive after the bell had rung.

Test Yourself

Add suffixes to make adjectives from these nouns and verbs:

nation	man	danger
leaf	skill	lady
fame	luck	cheer
hero	affection	live
loathe	effect	wood
adore	depend	govern

Two or more adjectives that modify a noun may be either cumulative as in group 1 or coordinate as in group 2. Notice that a comma is used to separate coordinate adjectives.

GROUP 1
the sweet little boy
the light blue coat
a pretty German girl

GROUP 2
a pleasant, instructive experience
a careful, energetic woman
the busy, thoughtful executive

Exercise 11

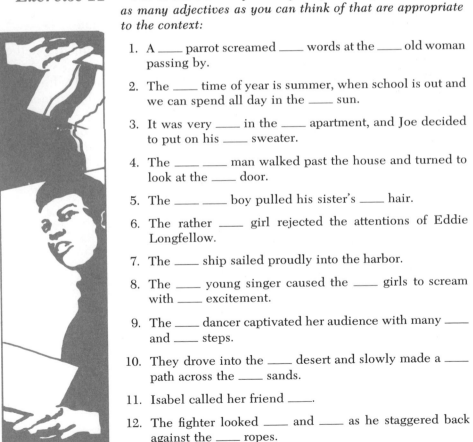

Fill in the blanks of each of the following sentences with as many adjectives as you can think of that are appropriate to the context:

1. A ____ parrot screamed ____ words at the ____ old woman passing by.

2. The ____ time of year is summer, when school is out and we can spend all day in the ____ sun.

3. It was very ____ in the ____ apartment, and Joe decided to put on his ____ sweater.

4. The ____ ____ man walked past the house and turned to look at the ____ door.

5. The ____ ____ boy pulled his sister's ____ hair.

6. The rather ____ girl rejected the attentions of Eddie Longfellow.

7. The ____ ship sailed proudly into the harbor.

8. The ____ young singer caused the ____ girls to scream with ____ excitement.

9. The ____ dancer captivated her audience with many ____ and ____ steps.

10. They drove into the ____ desert and slowly made a ____ path across the ____ sands.

11. Isabel called her friend ____.

12. The fighter looked ____ and ____ as he staggered back against the ____ ropes.

Exercise 12   1. These words are ordinarily used as nouns. Change them into adjectives by using characteristic adjective suffixes.

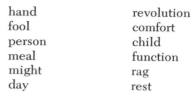

hand	revolution
fool	comfort
person	child
meal	function
might	rag
day	rest

2. These words are ordinarily used as verbs. Change them into adjectives by using characteristic adjective suffixes.

please	wonder
forget	attend
show	suit
fear	commend
perish	tire
urge	rely

3. Write sentences using the words developed above, first as adjective modifiers and then as predicate adjectives.

4. Write six sentences illustrating the use of an adjective as an objective complement. Use different adjectives and different verbs in each sentence.

5. Which pairs of adjectives need punctuation?

the silly little girl	the strong wiry athlete
the nice young man	the lovely gracious singer
the frightened dazed boxer	a happy Spanish girl
the pleasant roomy house	a vicious black dog
a cautious practical man	an old iron pot

6. Write sentences using the comparative and superlative form of each of the following adjectives:

shabby	far
cruel	little
soft	stern
good	close
bad	firm
simple	fast
sad	smart
short	rude
murky	old
young	polite

7. Write sentences using the intensifiers *very, more, most, less, least, really, rather,* and *quite* with adjectives.

ADVERBS

Many adverbs are marked by characteristic suffixes. Sometimes *-ly* is added to nouns to make adverbs.

week	weekly	year	yearly
month	monthly	hour	hourly

Many adverbs are formed by adding the suffix *-ly* to adjectives.

perfect	perfectly	honest	honestly
pure	purely	happy	happily
careless	carelessly	clear	clearly

Some adverb and adjective forms are identical.

hard	better	fast	straight
long	best	far	early
down	late	kindly	near

Some adverbs are identified by such characteristic suffixes as *-ward, -time, -way, -where, -side, -long, -wise,* and *-how.*

backward	anyway	inside	lengthwise
sometime	somewhere	headlong	anyhow

Some adverbs are formed by adding the prefix *a-.*

away	across	aboard	abreast
aground	abroad	apart	ahead

There is a large group of words used as adverbs with no characteristic formal elements for identification. The following list includes many of these words:

yesterday	never	here	forth
today	then	there	thus
tomorrow	often	north	well
soon	already	south	too
now	always	back	indeed

Finally, some of the words that we think of as prepositions (function words) are used commonly as adverbs.

in	up	beyond	between
out	through	over	throughout
down	after	under	near

In communication adverbs are ordinarily used as verb modifiers. However, they often modify adjectives and sometimes other adverbs. Occasionally words having the formal characteristics of adverbs can be used to modify nouns and as complements after linking verbs. The sentences in group 1 illustrate the use of adverbs as verb modifiers; in group 2, as modifiers of adjectives; in group 3, as modifiers of adverbs; in group 4 as modifiers of nouns; in group 5, as linking-verb complements. Some of the adverbs in group 1 can appear in several different places in the sentence. If they occur at the beginning or end of the sentence, they can be considered sentence modifiers.

GROUP 1

The regiment advanced cautiously up the hill.
The regiment advanced up the hill cautiously.
Cautiously the regiment advanced up the hill.
Our car turned slowly around.
Slowly our car turned around.
Our car turned around slowly.

GROUP 2

They went to hear the nationally popular singer.
The mother was naturally anxious about her son.

GROUP 3

The students arrived early today.
He went way down to Broadway to get a paper.

GROUP 4

The soldier advanced two steps forward.
We all enjoyed our trip abroad.

GROUP 5

The plumber will be here in the morning.
The time for decision is now.

Test Yourself

Identify each adverb in these sentences as a verb modifier, an adjective modifier, an adverb modifier, a noun modifier, or a linking-verb complement:

1. The highly regarded politician was reelected.

2. The coach spoke sharply to the members of the team.

3. It was extremely hot last Saturday afternoon.

4. The time for acting is now.

5. The picnic yesterday was a success.

6. All the actors performed magnificently.

7. Last night's thunderstorm was frighteningly close.

8. We were told to be here on time.

9. The party will be held tonight.

10. The test tomorrow should be easy.

Adverbs, too, are inflected to show the comparative and superlative degrees. Like adjectives, some adverbs are inflected by adding the *-er* and *-est* endings.

soon	sooner	soonest
early	earlier	earliest
near	nearer	nearest

Other adverbs are inflected by using the intensifiers *more* and *most* and *less* and *least*.

beautifully	more beautifully	most beautifully
viciously	less viciously	least viciously

Exercise 13

1. List five words used as adverbs formed by adding the suffix *-ly* to a noun.

2. List ten words used as adverbs formed by adding the suffix *-ly* to an adjective.

3. List as many words as possible that are used as adverbs formed with the endings *-ward, -wise, -time, -where, -way*.

4. List as many words as you can find that may be used as adverbs formed by adding the prefix *a-*.

5. Write the inflected forms of ten adverbs that are identical in form with adjectives. Use these forms in meaningful sentences and then check the sentences for ambiguity.

6. Write sentences containing the following words as adverbs: *soon, again, hurriedly, away, happily, yesterday, never, carefully, always, too*. Rewrite these sentences changing the position of the adverb used. Is the position of an adverb limited? To what extent? Is this true for each adverb used?

Exercise 14

Identify the italicized words in the following sentences as adjectives or adverbs and describe the syntax of each:

1. The salt air from the sea smelt *sweet* to us as we walked along the beach.

2. Poor Aunt Ada didn't feel *well* this afternoon.

Exercise 14,
continued

3. The basketball team played very *poorly* last night.

4. The dogs seem *unusually nervous tonight.*

5. His offer was *exceptionally* kind.

6. This rug looks too *long* for the living room floor.

7. The events in this story are *purely fictitious.*

8. The warm weather feels *good* to a native of Maine.

9. The parade *tomorrow* will be along Fifth Avenue.

10. The door slammed *shut* as the wind began to blow *hard.*

Summary

Since English is fundamentally a subject-predicate, or noun-verb, language, nouns play a major role in the construction of the sentence. In addition to their subject function, they serve as direct objects, indirect objects, objects of prepositions, linking-verb complements, objective complements, and appositives.

Verbs are identified by their position in the sentence, by auxiliaries, and by inflectional endings. Most English verbs are inflected regularly, by adding *-d* or *-ed* to the plain form to indicate action occurring in the past. Irregular verbs must be studied because of their vowel changes.

Adjectives present few problems. They serve as noun modifiers, as linking-verb complements, and as objective complements. Most adjectives, especially those of one syllable, are compared regularly by adding *-er* to form the comparative degree and *-est* to form the superlative degree. Those of more than two syllables are compared by using *more* or *most, less* or *least.*

Adverbs are often signaled by the suffix *-ly.* They serve to modify verbs, adjectives, other adverbs, nouns, and as linking-verb complements. They are inflected like adjectives.

τὸν Ἰφικράτην πολλαχόσε καὶ τῆς Ἀρκαδίας ἐμβαλόντες ἐλεηλάτουν τε καὶ
προσέβαλλον πρὸς τὰ τείχη· ἔξω γὰρ οἱ τῶν Ἀρκάδων ὁπλῖται παντάπασιν
οὐκ ἀντεξῇσαν· οὕτω τοὺς πελταστὰς ἐπεφόβηντο. τοὺς μέντοι Λακεδαιμο-
νίους οὕτως αὖ οἱ πελτασταὶ ὤκνουν ὡς ἐντὸς ἀκοντίσματος οὐ προσῇσαν
τοῖς ὁπλίταις· ἤδη γάρ ποτε καὶ ἐκ τοσούτου διώξαντες οἱ νεώτεροι τῶν
Λακεδαιμονίων ἑλόντες ἀπέκτεινάν τινας αὐτῶν. καταφρονοῦντες δ᾽ οἱ Λα-

Greek

Chapter 4

PROBLEMS

OF

USAGE

A Look Back and A Look Forward

In Chapter 2, you reviewed the structure of the English sentence; and in Chapter 3, you examined the form and function of the major word classes—nouns, verbs, adjectives, and adverbs. In Chapter 4, you will be reminded of the importance of acceptable English usage and of the sources of unacceptable usage related to the four main word classes, to pronouns, and to the subject-predicate structure of the English language.

In this chapter, you will also observe that under certain circumstances your choice of words follows certain conventions. In other words, what you write should be free of informal, dialectal, and slang expressions.

WHAT IS USAGE?

The word *usage* is a popular not a technical term, and it may be explained in a number of ways. Although it implies the ways in which English is "used," the terms *usage* and *grammar* are not synonymous.

Grammar refers to the language system or the description of the language system. You know that the normal order of sentence elements is subject, verb, complement, and you know that nouns usually form their plurals by adding *-s* or *-es*. You have studied the complicated ways in which verbs are inflected—how they change in form according to certain rules under certain conditions. This formal subject is what the modern student of language means by *grammar*.

The term *usage* in modern English study applies to the *choice* of language forms. It is bound up with conventions and sometimes with social distinctions. For example, the following statement may be presented in a number of different ways:

> He has no money.
> He hasn't any money.
> He doesn't have any money.
> He hasn't got no money.
> He ain't got no money.

Which way would you choose to communicate this fact? Here is a problem in usage. You would probably debate about the first three, rejecting the last two ways. Why? You might say that the last two are incorrect. Would you then be stating that they are not English? You would certainly have no difficulty in understanding the meaning intended.

The last two sentences conform to the language system, but they violate certain conventions. One contains a double negative, while the other includes both a double negative and the frowned-upon "ain't." Neither of these sentences is representative of conventional forms of communication among educated people.

The problems of usage for the young writer are related to the conventions of language. Certainly, in one's thinking it is difficult to separate usage from grammar; the two are closely interrelated.

Let's say that in his efforts to communicate, someone uses an ungrammatical verb form, one not part of the system. For example:

> The men drug the deer down the mountain.

The verb form used is both ungrammatical and unconventional. But suppose he said:

> The men dragged the deer down the mountain.

That verb form is both grammatical and conventional. The verb *drag* is inflected in four forms: *drag, drags, dragged,* and *dragging,* and any other form is unacceptable.

To understand the English language system so that it can be used intelligently is a major reason for the study of grammar. You take no more liberties with language conventions than with other social conventions. Those who do face rebuke, ridicule, and even ostracism. Men do not wear their hats in church, nor do boys wear overalls to school. You wouldn't think of wearing sneakers or tennis shoes to a dance, would you? Conventions are important parts of community life, and each individual must consider them seriously. You cannot take liberties with language and keep the respect of your friends and associates. You cannot use "ain't" or a double negative or incorrect verb forms and hope to maintain good social standing in an educated community. There is nothing snobbish about insistence upon the use of good English. It is merely the expression of the desire to conform to current social standards.

The young writer is faced with a number of problems. He must thoroughly understand the English system so that his usage will be *grammatical.* He must learn to distinguish between conventional forms and unconventional forms so that his usage will be *respectable.* He must be sensitive to the particular needs of written English so that his usage will be *effective.*

STANDARD WRITTEN ENGLISH

You have earlier discussed the limitations of the written language. Graphic symbolism (writing) is a secondary symbolism. The marks on paper are symbols of words (what you say), and the words are symbols of objects or ideas. So, in a sense, the writer uses symbols of symbols, and the reader has a double problem of interpretation. Besides, as you now realize, the writer does not have the benefit of reinforcement from intonation, voice qualifiers, or gestures. He has to depend solely on the power of his words and the way in which he combines these words into sentences.

Because of the difficulty of communicating in writing, there has developed in this medium a degree of standardization that is not present in spoken English. A speaker from Texas may use one dialect; a speaker from Massachusetts may use a different dialect. You can understand and respect both speakers. A writer, whether from the South, the East, or the West, uses *only one* dialect, that is, standard written English. He has to follow the conventions of spelling and sentence structure and usage so that his readers will have no difficulty in understanding his meaning. The reader can tell nothing about where he lives merely by the way he writes. Writers from all parts of the country use the same forms of language. These forms are the conventional forms of educated people. You read this language in good books and magazines, in newspapers, in textbooks. You hear it in school, in church, in public lectures, in the living rooms of educated people. This language is standard English, and this is the language that you as a student of written composition must learn to use. It is conventional; it is grammatical; it is respectable. Above all, it is acceptable to your teachers because they are trying to help you to become a member of the educated community. They are encouraging you to speak and to write the way educated people speak and write.

ACCEPTABLE ENGLISH

Standard English is language that conforms to the system of communication, the structure as we have it in this day and age. How would you criticize these sentences?

> The pencil broken is.
> These person arrived from England.
> Alice has drank her chocolate soda.
> Helen and her husband is coming to dinner.
> The students keep his books in their lockers.
> Will come you to see me tonight?
> Its a boy!

Each of these sentences in some way violates the system. The first violates English word order. The word *these* in the second sentence is an inflected form of *this*. *This* is used before singular nouns and *these* before plural nouns. In this way, the correct use of these two forms reinforces the grammatical forms of the nouns with which they are used. In the third sentence, *drunk* is the proper verb form. It is the form used with auxiliaries such as *have, has, is, was,* and so on. In the fourth sentence, the use of a singular form of the verb with a compound subject is another violation since the verb must agree with its subject. The form of the pronoun in the next sentence is incorrect. *His* refers to a singular, possessive, masculine noun. The sentence requires the use of the plural *their,* referring to *students.* The sixth sentence violates English word order. In the last sentence, the pronoun *its* is used instead of the contraction *it's.*

Each of the examples above serves to illustrate very common errors in English. Each violates the system of communication which is called the English language.

Poor usage by the writer, therefore, may result from his unfamiliarity with the grammar of English. He may be unacquainted with the inflected forms of verbs, particularly irregular verbs. He may be unaware of the requirements of concord—subject-verb agreement. He may not understand fully the use and inflection of pronouns. He may confuse adjectives and adverbs. He may even be innocent of the nuances of word order.

Because of the importance to standard usage of this grammatical knowledge, let's outline very briefly some of the sources of incorrect usage relevant to the four major word classes and to the subject-predicate structure of the English language.

Verb Usage

Problems in verb usage may develop from these sources:

1. USE OF FORM

   sprung
   The water pipes must have ~~sprang~~ a leak.
   threw
   Sandy ~~throwed~~ a perfect strike for the last pitch of the game.

2. USE OF TENSE

   walked
   Last night we ~~walk~~ out on the amusement pier to watch the fireworks.

3. SHIFT IN TENSE

   forced
   Suddenly a car cut in ahead of us and ~~forces~~ Dad into the next lane.

4. CONFUSION OF *Lie* WITH *Lay*

   lies
   Every night my cat ~~lays~~ on top of the TV set during the seven o'clock news.
   lay
   Please ~~lie~~ the coats on the bed in the front room.

Exercise 1   *Improve the following sentences:*

1. People of many different backgrounds lives on our block.

2. He lays around all day long and won't do any work.

3. My little sister cried like a baby when she dropped her tray at the cafeteria and everything breaked.

4. Bill wears his new blue sweater when he stopped at their house last evening.

Exercise 1,

continued

5. When the doorbell rang, Joe runs to answer it.

6. Yesterday Sam come to class unprepared.

7. The dance last night began at eight and closes at midnight.

8. Dad lays down for a nap every Saturday afternoon.

9. Tom walked to school, but Bob drives.

10. Have you saw the new musical comedy that opened last week?

Exercise 2

In each of the following sentences, use the standard form of the verb indicated:

1. Everyone who had eaten in the cafeteria yesterday, was ____ with food poisoning. (strike)

2. Last Friday at the "Y" we ____ the length of the pool twice. (swim)

3. The NAACP has ____ to Georgia again. (go)

4. The soda was all ____ before we got there. (drink)

5. The old lady has ____ the yarn into a beautiful sweater. (weave)

6. The batter ____ viciously at the ball but did not hit it. (swing)

7. Jim has ____ his arm for the second time. (break)

8. Jean ____ the best cartoon for the paper. (draw)

9. Bill has ____ up to be a fine young man. (grow)

10. The pitcher ____ the ball to third, and the runner was out. (throw)

11. The sun had already ____ before any of the boys woke up. (rise)

12. This material has ____ badly since it was left out in the rain. (shrink)

13. The boys have been fighting and have ____ their clothing. (tear)

14. The champ has ____ into action and has driven his opponent back to the ropes. (swing)

15. The garden hose has ____ a leak. (spring)

Exercise 2,
continued

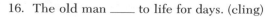

16. The old man ____ to life for days. (cling)

17. Mr. Kraft ____ each player five cards. (deal)

18. The frightened residents are ____ desperately to escape the hurricane. (flee)

19. The angry ball player ____ his bat away in disgust. (fling)

20. The teacher ____ her books quietly on the desk. (lay)

21. He ____ his blanket over one shoulder and walked quickly away. (sling)

22. The animal ____ noiselessly away into the forest. (slink)

23. The dam has ____, and all the villages in the valley are being evacuated. (burst)

24. The snakes have all ____ their skins for this year. (shed)

25. The angry man ____ his arm through the open window. (thrust)

Pronoun Usage

Problems in pronoun usage may develop from the following sources:

1. CASE

        I
My mother and ~~me~~ planted two dozen tulip bulbs last Saturday.

                         he
Our best pitchers are, in my opinion, Ed Lawson and ~~him~~.

                me
My next-door neighbor drives Sally and ~~I~~ to the bus stop every morning.

We
~~Us~~ girls are going to the convention in Washington.

           me
Let's you and ~~I~~ go bowling one of these days.

            he
You're a much stronger swimmer than ~~him~~.

2. UNCERTAIN ANTECEDENT

Bill told his cousin that he should visit him before he left for Boston.
Better: Bill told his cousin to visit him before leaving for Boston.

3. NO ANTECEDENT

Kathy is taking aspirin every four hours, which is all anyone can do for a cold.
Better: Kathy is doing all anyone can do for a cold: taking aspirin every four hours.

4. LACK OF AGREEMENT WITH ANTECEDENT

his

Nobody is to leave ~~their~~ seat until the bell rings.

5. SHIFT IN PERSON

he's

One never knows whether ~~you're~~ going to qualify for this contest or not;
the judges
~~they~~ change the rules every day.

Exercise 3

Discuss the pronoun usage in the following sentences. Make any necessary revisions.

1. Between you and I everybody must watch their English.

2. We put flowerboxes on the windowsill which were beautiful when it bloomed.

3. Rudy's sister made dinner for he and the baby.

4. This was the first time that she has gone to see her sister Kate since she broke her arm.

5. Jim joined the Navy which was a smart thing to do.

6. There was a boy with my brother waving his hand and trying to make us look at him.

7. This is a friend of Mr. Jamieson who lives in Tempe.

8. They are changing the rules so much that one never knows when you might be breaking one of them.

9. Bill is going to college which is a good idea.

10. John's father is a doctor, and I am sure that he will be rich some day.

11. Everyone should save part of their salary.

12. Every member of the team will be responsible for their own uniforms.

Adjective-Adverb Usage

Problems in adjective and adverb usage may come from the following sources:

1. ADJECTIVE-ADVERB CONFUSION

bad

I am feeling ~~badly~~ this morning.

well

Jim played so ~~good~~ that we were all proud of him.

2. USE OF THE SUPERLATIVE DEGREE

more

Which is the ~~most~~ valuable mineral, asbestos or variscite?

3. DOUBLE COMPARISON

This pot looks ~~more~~ brighter now that I've scoured it with steel wool.

4. FORM OF INTENSIFIER

really

That problem is a ~~real~~ simple one to solve.

Exercise 4 *Discuss the usage of adjectives and adverbs in the following sentences. Indicate the sentences that you would accept as standard English. Revise those that are not standard.*

1. I had such a bad headache and felt miserably.

2. He told me to drive slow and easy past the school.

3. The room seems so chilly that I am afraid that I will get a cold.

4. Henry always drives too fast on the turnpike.

5. I cannot find anything wrong with this car; it runs good and the engine sounds smooth.

6. Ann was barely in the apartment when the phone rang.

7. We felt so good that morning that we went for a swim.

8. The orchestra played well at the concert last night.

9. Diane doesn't play too badly for a beginner.

10. The piano sounded horribly, as if it were out of tune.

11. The flowers smell sweet and look prettily on the table.

12. I sure wish I could go to Boston with you.

Subject-Verb Agreement

The following complications of structure are among the most common sources of error in subject-verb agreement:

1. INTERVENING WORD GROUP

is

My mother, along with her two cousins, ~~are~~ touring Scandinavia.

was

One of our magnolia trees ~~were~~ struck by lightning.

2. INVERTED SENTENCE
> *come*
> Here ~~comes~~ the Mets.
> *were*
> There ~~was~~ several radicals among the crowd.

3. COMPOUND SUBJECT
> *have*
> Paul and John ~~has~~ already left.
> *makes*
> Cream cheese and jelly ~~make~~ a tasty sandwich. (The compound subject names a single thing.)
> *washes*
> Either Bud or his father ~~wash~~ the car every Saturday. (The compound subject is connected by *or*.)
> *was*
> Neither the choir members nor their leader ~~were~~ especially pleased with the performance. (The verb agrees with the nearer subject.)

4. SUBORDINATE CLAUSE
> *are*
> It is you who ~~is~~ wrong, not I. (The verb agrees with *you*, the antecedent of *who*.)
> *line*
> The elm and maple trees that ~~lines~~ Main Street will have to be cut down.

Exercise 5   Discuss the agreement of subject and verb in the following sentences. Make any necessary revisions.

1. Al and Dick has planned to see the Knicks play.

2. Either of the movies are all right with me.

3. Grits and eggs is not his favorite breakfast.

4. The acoustics is very bad in this auditorium.

5. Tom as well as many other students have difficulty with plane geometry.

6. Neither of the boys plan to go to college.

7. One of the players are always late for practice.

8. He is one of those people who is always looking for trouble.

9. Here comes my father and mother.

10. There has been too much argument and conflict in making this decision.

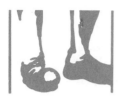

Exercise 5, *continued*

11. Neither pizza nor spaghetti satisfy my appetite.

12. Courage and stamina are the necessary qualities of a good athlete.

13. The scissors is in the drawer of my desk.

14. Neither science nor mathematics are difficult for William.

15. Debbie is the only one of the girls who are willing to help in the work.

CONVENTIONS OF USAGE

By this time you know that usage is a matter of choice of language forms. A writer may be guilty of poor usage because he uses ungrammatical language forms or because he uses inappropriate or unconventional language. He may even be guilty of poor taste in his selection of words.

The problem of usage involving the choice of appropriate language forms is part of the broader problem of diction in written composition. Anyone who uses language naïvely, who is insensitive to the limitations and needs of written English, may write poorly because he chooses words casually instead of intelligently.

The discussion of usage problems here is confined to the choice of language forms that are appropriate to the times, to the environment of the readers, and to the requirements of formality.

ARCHAIC AND OBSOLETE LANGUAGE

Archaic language is language that is old, out-of-date, seldom used, but still within the range of our reading. We find it often in poetry. In fact, the use of archaic language in poetry is one of the causes of difficulty to the casual reader. And this difficulty often creates in an indifferent reader a dislike for poetry.

Below are a few separate lines from John Keats' "La Belle Dame Sans Merci."

> Ah, what can ail thee, wretched *wight*,
>
> . . .
>
> And on thy cheek a fading rose
> Fast *withereth* too.
>
> . . .
>
> They cried—'La Belle Dame sans Merci
> Hath thee in *thrall!*'

The student who carefully looks up these words in a dictionary will get the full meaning and flavor of the poem. The word *wight* is unfamiliar to most students. The definition applied here is "a living being." The second italicized word is the old form for *withers*. The definition of *thrall* is "slavery." The poet uses these words to give his story a sense of great age or antiquity. Since the word is unfamiliar to the modern reader, it also carries to him an impact of novelty, the force of strangeness. Keats therefore used these words appropriately, even though his poem is modern, having been written in 1819.

The Bible is probably our most usual source of archaic language. The following quotation is from the 91st Psalm:

> It is good to give praise to the Lord: and to sing to *thy* name, O most High.
> To *shew* forth *thy* mercy in the morning, and *thy* truth in the night:
> Upon an instrument of ten strings, upon the *psaltery*: with a *canticle* upon the harp.

Thy is the archaic form of *your*; *shew* is an archaic form of the verb *show*; *psaltery*, the word for an ancient stringed instrument; *canticle*, the old word for "song" or "chant."

Obsolete language forms are usually ones that have completely passed from the modern scene. The use of the terms *archaic* and *obsolete* is purely relative. We could very well say that the language of Chaucer is obsolete; Middle English has changed into modern English. However, we certainly can find obsolete words in Shakespeare, in Dryden, and even in nineteenth century prose and poetry.

The following lines are from Shakespeare's *Othello*.

> And what's he, then, that says I play the villain?
> When this advice is free I give and honest,
> *Probal* to thinking and, indeed, the course
> To win the Moor again? For 'tis most easy
> The inclining Desdemona to subdue
> In any honest suit: she's fram'd as *fruitful*
> As the free elements.

The meanings of *probal* and *fruitful* as used here are now obsolete. *Probal* may be interpreted as "capable of being approved." *Fruitful* here would mean "generous" — an adjective no longer used in this sense.

Test Yourself

Search for some archaic words in one of Shakespeare's plays. Make a list of those you find and beside each word write its modern meaning. For instance, *hath* is the archaic word for *have*, and *prithee* was once used to express a wish or a request.

The problem of archaic and obsolete usage for the high school student does not focus on his writing. It is related more seriously to his reading. It is wise to develop a sensitivity to language of this kind. Take time to find definitions of archaic and obsolete words in a good dictionary and to select the definition suitable to the context of the material you are reading. In this way you will increase your word power and your reading skill. Incidentally, you will find that your reading will become much more enjoyable.

Exercise 6

Indicate which of the words in the following list are archaic or obsolete. Look up the meaning of each word. Sometimes a word may be used in a modern sense and still have an archaic or obsolete definition.

certes	fathom	grise
'sblood	cast	bootless
toged	moe	slubber
zounds	grievance	agnize
affin'd	demerits	besort
knaves	unbonneted	seel
cashiered	carack	indign
trimm'd	marry	unbitted
native	withal	weal
figure	injointed	compassing
snorting	inhibited	betimes
distempering	mountebanks	snipe

Exercise 7

The following passage is from Shakespeare's Julius Caesar. *It is a speech by Cassius in Act IV, Scene III. Identify archaic language and determine its meaning.*

Come, Antony, and young Octavius, come,
Revenge yourselves alone on Cassius,
For Cassius is aweary of the world;
Hated by one he loves; braved by his brother;
Checked like a bondman; all his faults observed,
Set in a notebook, learned, and conned by rote,
To cast into my teeth. O, I could weep
My spirit from mine eyes! There is my dagger,
And here my naked breast; within, a heart
Dearer than Plutus's mine, richer than gold.
If that thou be'st a Roman, take it forth;
I, that denied thee gold, will give my heart.

DIALECT

Dialectal differences in language are usually considered regional or geographical, although the differences may be of a social or class nature. In the United States, dialect is mostly the product of geography. Dialects differ in pronunciation, in word usage, and sometimes in structure.

In New England, *half, aunt, bath* are pronounced with a broad *a*, whereas these words in New York City are pronounced with a relatively short *a*. The word *orange* is pronounced with a short *o* sound in the Northeast, whereas in the Middle West, it is pronounced as if the first syllable were *ore*. In the East, the stressed syllable of *Nevada* is pronounced with a broad *a*, whereas in the Southwest it is pronounced with a short *a*.

You need not here be concerned with pronunciation differences in dialect, only as they might affect spelling, of course; your interest now is in vocabulary differences and in grammatical forms. Students from communities in which dialectal differences are strong may reflect the speech usage in written English. Young writers should have some knowledge of dialects and the ways in which they differ from standard English.

Three main areas of dialect are recognized by linguists in the United States. The Northern includes New England and New York. The Midland is composed of two parts, North Midland and South Midland. North Midland includes Delaware, part of Pennsylvania, New Jersey, and northern West Virginia. South Midland includes the southern part of Pennsylvania, southern West Virginia, the eastern part of Kentucky, the western parts of the Carolinas, and eastern Tennessee. The Southern includes most of Virginia and large parts of North and South Carolina, as well as the Eastern Shore of Maryland.

Of course, one may find varieties of language forms within the large dialect areas. You are perhaps familiar with the differences of dialect in Boston, the Hudson River Valley, and the Williamsburg section of Brooklyn.

The study of vocabulary differences is of great interest to the student of writing. A few examples reported by Raven I. McDavid, Jr. in *The Structure of American English* by W. Nelson Francis are cited here.

The North
pail (bucket)
swill (garbage)
clapboards (finished siding)
pit (seed)
angleworm (earthworm)
johnnycake (cornbread)
spider (frying pan)

whiffletree (whippletree)
eavestrough (gutter on roof)
brook (small stream)

The South
lightwood (kindling)
low (moo)
tote (carry)
carry (escort)
co-wench (call to cows)
hasslet (liver and lungs)
snap beans (string beans)
mouth harp (harmonica)
turn of wood (armload)

Differences in grammar include in the North the use of *dove* as the past form of *dive, clim* as the past of *climb, see* as the past of *see,* and *scairt* for *scared.* In the South may be found such forms as *it wan't me, he belongs to be careful, heern tell, gwine, outn,* and many others.

In written English students should avoid dialectal forms since they are nonstandard. Not only does the use of these forms create the possibility of misunderstanding, but it may brand the writer as naïve or provincial.

Exercise 8   *Try to find the meanings of the following dialect words and expressions:*

stoop	buttonwood	Dutch cheese
apple dowdy	batter bread	suppawn
stone boat	cuppin	olicook
smearcase	savannah	blinds
skimmerton	pinders	fatcakes
spouts	pallet	clook
grinnie	poke	clabber milk
snits	redworm	croker sack
hoppergrass	milk gap	corn house
goobers	sugar tree	groundnuts

INFORMAL USAGE

Language forms that are more appropriate to conversation than to written English are considered informal. However, professional writers often use informal terms to make material vivid. The beginning writer must understand the problem and learn to use language that is appropriate to the degree of formality required by his theme.

For example, informal English may be used appropriately and with considerable effect on the sports page of a newspaper.

Al Dark sticks to his guns.

Dark said he is "fed up with my players going up and down like a bunch of yo-yos."

Ramos gets nod over King.

Sam McDowell, the only Indian pitcher to go the route this season, tossed a four-hitter for his sixth complete game in winning, 7-2.

But even on the sports page, most writers employ standard written English. Most sports writers are college graduates, educated in departments of journalism. They write effectively because they have extensive vocabulary resources and understand and exploit fully the language structures. They use informal terms cautiously but effectively.

On the other hand, in editorials, in magazine articles, in textbooks, informal conversational English is uncommon. However, anyone searching for it will find some such usage. For example, the following appeared in a column in *The New York Times* by James Reston on May 27, 1970:

A month ago people here were satisfied to say that the country was *in a terrible mess*, but now you can't go to a dinner party without finding *some* normally sensible *character blowing off about* the "collapse" of the economy, the second American Revolution, or the fall of Rome.

Informal English is appropriate in conversation of an informal nature. If language forms used normally in spoken English to add a colorful quality are transferred to the written language, they may seem stale and trite. They usually add nothing to a theme and are poor substitutes for better English which expresses clear thinking. Examine your reading material carefully and watch for unconventional forms. Few appear in good writing, but any that you find should be evaluated in terms of suitability.

Exercise 9   *Revise the following sentences to eliminate informal usage:*

1. The class did not get what the teacher had said.

2. Our team had the jump on the South High team from the very first quarter.

3. Father decided to junk the old car and buy a Mustang.

4. The movie we saw yesterday was just great.

5. These men have been knocking about the country doing construction work.

Exercise 9,

continued

6. After a struggle, the man finally landed the huge fish.

7. The Joneses hope to see the last of their company by the end of August.

8. This year school will be let out at the end of May.

9. Jim was big enough to lick any boy in the school.

10. When we go on a picnic with the Browns, we always have loads to eat.

11. The boys read a lot of books this summer while they were on vacation.

12. The family made good time on their trip to Albuquerque.

13. He decided to stay around the place to see what was going on.

14. When his partner died, Mr. Fox was left holding the bag.

15. The men in the factory refused to play ball with the boss.

16. Tom is six feet tall and all beef.

Summary

The problem of usage may be defined very simply. It is the responsibility of the writer to use both good and clear English. Good English is language that is grammatically clear, respectable, conventional, and effective. In choosing his language forms, the writer must remember that his meaning should be clear to all, and that he must forego the use of dialectal and archaic terms. He should avoid the use of informal English unless the usage is clearly appropriate to the situation, such as a sports story or possibly in a letter to a friend. He should avoid slang entirely.

The student of writing must read widely. He should observe and study the usage of good writers in books, newspapers, and magazines. He should keep a notebook in which to record sentences and paragraphs that are skillfully written. The class should benefit from a group discussion of exceptionally fine examples, which might then be copied and posted on the board.

Disse essays, hvoraf de fleste blev skrevet i årene 1961–65, har et fælles tema. Det udspringer af mangfoldigheden og rigdommen i menneskets omfattende oplevelsesverden, i hvis spektrum man f.eks. på den ene side finder menneskets evne til ypperlig rationel tænkning, på den anden side hans irrationelle adfærds vidtrækkende perspektiver, eller hans muligheder for at leve lykkeligt og produktivt samtidig med, at han evigt drives mod fortvivlelse og nederlag. Med dette righoldige spektrum tilføres der efter min opfattelse menneskets bevidsthed visse kendetegnende karakteristika. Vi vil i denne bog beskæftige os med nogle af dem under betegnelsen »dilemma«.

Danish

Chapter 5

PUTTING

GRAMMAR

TO WORK

A Look Back and A Look Forward

The purpose of Chapter 5 is to help you apply your knowledge of the structure of English to the problems of writing. Each of the four major sections in this chapter—the theme, the paragraph, the sentence, and the word—will show the relationship of a knowledge of grammar to the problems of the writer and will provide material for practice to help direct you toward self-improvement.

109

THE THEME

Let us assume that you have chosen a suitable topic, one familiar to you as part of your own experience. You have planned your theme carefully, developed it, revised it, and handed it in. Your teacher has returned it with a grade of "C." Why didn't it rate a "B" or even an "A"? Perhaps an analysis of several student themes will help you recognize and analyze the errors that have been keeping your grades down.

An Analysis of Some Common Errors

Study the two themes that follow. Each shows some handwritten correction by the teacher. The numbers correspond to the numbered comments that follow the theme. Before reading these comments, analyze each correction and be prepared to point out areas for additional improvement.

THEME 1

Why Math Is My Subject

1. Math is one of the most important subjects ~~you can take~~ *in the curriculum*. It covers various types of problems. For instance, it starts with adding and progresses to finding the square root of a number and to many other things. The ways we study math are

2. very simple and if ~~you~~ *we* follow directions, ~~you~~ *we* will find that

3. studying math can be very easy. First, the teacher tells ~~you~~ *us*

4. what to do*;* then ~~you~~ *we* do that work, and before the class is over, he answers any questions asked. Then the work ~~you~~ *we* don't finish in class ~~you~~ *we* take home to do.

5. The real reason I like math is ~~because you~~ *that I* learn different kinds of math problems. ~~You~~ *I* learn the many different kinds and ways to work problems. The most important things are that ~~you~~ *I* learn to write numbers and read them.

   Math contributes to my education because ~~you~~ *we* work with money and numbers in ~~your~~ *our* everyday life. It helps ~~you~~ *us* to be able to give the right change when ~~you~~ *we* are working with money. It also

6. helps in <u>bookeeping</u>, everyday work such as cooking, and buying groceries. Math helps throughout ~~your~~ *our* entire life.

1. The more specific "in the curriculum" has been substituted for "you can take" to avoid the indefinite use of the personal pronoun *you.*
2. The poorest feature of this theme from a grammatical standpoint is the frequent shift in person. The topic "Why Math Is My Favorite Subject" suggests the use of the first person in relating the sequence of ideas.
3. The use of personal pronouns as subjects throughout the theme also prevents the writer from communicating more effectively with a variety of noun subjects: "First, the *teacher* explains the problems. Then the *class* works on the problems. If there are any *questions*, the *teacher* answers them. The *problems* that are not completed in class are taken home as an assignment."
4. The use of a comma between two coordinate clauses not joined by a connective is called a "comma fault," a serious breach of convention. In the absence of a connective, a semicolon substitutes for the connective and helps to signal the reader that he is reading a compound sentence.
5. The use of the subordinator *because* is confusing here since it is redundant, or repetitive. Besides, grammatically, a subordinate clause of causation should follow a verb other than a linking verb.

> He *ran* because he was late.
> She *cried* because she was sorry.

6. The misspelled word indicates a need for emphasis on spelling.

THEME 2

I Want to Live

1. During the past many years, since the first car until now,
2. there have been many, many deaths. [Most of which were caused by carelessness.] Accidents are not pleasant by any means. [Not even trying to get out of school.] One would think that after so many deaths, people would learn, but they don't.
3. They keep on doing such things as/ straddling the white line, going too far out on the shoulders, and ~~etc.~~ *others*

Not too long ago we were shown a serious movie telling
4. about some careless mistakes and what can happen, ~~some are:~~ Never try to pass a car when rounding a bend because death can be waiting at the other end. Always make sure there are no cars coming before passing. Never straddle the white line because a car could appear suddenly, and that would be your

```
         mistake for life.  Don't take your eyes off the road.  Don't
         go too far out on the shoulder, you could very easily be
         twirled over onto your side, or skid in a circle in the middle
         of the road and be hit by an on coming car.  There are many
         mistakes drivers make.
    5.      The Red Cross made tests that took many months.  This is how
         they conducted them:  They took two cars, put a cable on them,
         and made a pulley so that they would meet.  They tried many
         different speeds, and they found that by using seat belts, you
         can reduce injuries immensely.
```

1. This sentence is poorly constructed because the writer is trying to say
    too much. It might better be written, "Many deaths have been caused
    by automobile accidents."
2. The subordinator *which* followed by normal word order signals a
    subordinate clause. Since this clause is not included within a basic
    sentence pattern, it is merely a sentence fragment. The rewritten
    sentence might read, "Many of these deaths were caused by care-
    lessness." "Not even trying to get out of school" is also a sentence
    fragment. The verb is a present participle without an auxiliary to
    make it a finite verb. Since the idea is not relevant to the develop-
    ment of the subject, it may well be deleted.
3. The use of the colon after the word *as* used to function as a preposi-
    tion is unnecessary and unconventional. "They keep on doing such
    things as straddling the white line, going too far out on the shoulders,
    and others."
4. There is a comma fault here. One coordinate clause ends with
    happen. Another begins with *some.* The sentence that follows is
    illogical. The use of the colon is irregular. A period should be sub-
    stituted for the comma after *happen,* and the next sentence might
    then read, "Drivers were urged to be cautious about passing a car
    when . . . They should always make sure that no cars were coming . . .
    They should never straddle the white line . . . They should never take
    their eyes off the road or go too far out on the shoulder. The car might
    skid and crash into another car coming from the opposite direction."
5. Here is excessive coordination and therefore a lack of coherence.
    "The Red Cross conducted a number of tests to determine the effect
    of speed on damage to cars and injury to passengers. The tests were
    conducted with cables and pulleys arranged to provide some control
    on the cars used. The damage to cars was carefully checked. It was
    suggested that the use of seat belts could reduce personal injury ma-
    terially."

There are other suggestions that might be made for the improvement of the two themes under discussion. It is better, however, not to confuse the writer with too much revision. The suggestions made point, in general, to a need for consistency in the use of pronouns and a study of sentence structure, particularly of the effective use of coordination and subordination. There is a need also for a reexamination of the physical characteristics of the sentence in order to help the writer avoid sentence fragments. A review of the uses of the semicolon and the colon might also prove helpful. Apply these general comments to an analysis of one of your recent themes.

Exercise 1   *Read the following theme very carefully. Indicate the need for revision, emphasizing particularly the grammatical limitations of the work. Rewrite the theme.*

Art Is My Favorite Subject

Art has always been my favorite subject. Art covers all kinds of history, great artists, and great paintings. Art teaches you all kinds of periods like cubism, pointillism, and others, and shows you the skill in working in oil painting, water color, tempera, pastels, lettering, and many other skills.

In studying art you talk about periods in art and great artists. You can look up subjects of your particular interest. Also, art shows you how to draw only if you yourself want to learn, by not only drawing in school, but also drawing in your free time. I say that you can't learn one thing unless you really have interest in it or in what you're studying.

I happen to have a great interest in art, I like art because you never stop learning something you didn't know before, but it is always good to do things several times and get better at them.

Art will help me in many ways. I will have a better knowledge about it besides having something to talk about. Art will also keep me busy in a hobby. I am trying to be a commercial artist so a few years of art will get me a good job, and I will continue to enjoy art.

An Analysis of a Report

The theme on the next page was prepared as a report. Although the student was not familiar with the subject, he worked in the library with selected references, collecting enough material for an interesting report.

Australia

Australia is a continent as well as a country, about the
size of the United States. It has approximately 11,500,000
1. people ~~of which~~ most of ~~them~~ ʷʰᵒᵐ live along the coast or in the
urban areas. About one half of the people live in six big
cities; these are, in order, according to population: Sydney,
2,183,000; Melbourne, 1,956,000; Brisbane, 635,500; Adelaide,
593,500; Perth, 431,000; and Hobart, 119,000. The capital of
Australia is Canberra with a population of only 71,000.

More than 50 percent of the workers are union members, and
more than 25 percent of all workers are immigrants. In Australia
are immigrants from all over the world. Some are Americans,
and many are Germans and English. In 1948 about 80,000
2. immigrant bachelors found native wives. (Elaborate)
3. It is mostly a cattle-raising, sheep-raising, and wheat-
4. growing country. Wool, meat, grain, and gold still makes the
bulk of Australia's exports. One handicap is that some parts
5. of the country recieve only about twenty inches of rain.
6. Because of the light rainfall they have extended a pipeline
into the interior to supply water for the animals and crops.
An example of real wasteland is in southern Australia, where
there is not a single tree for a stretch of 328 miles.

In the back of modern Australia live the most primitive people
in the world, the Black Aborigines. They still use the
boomerang and hunt fish very primitively. Besides primitive
7. peoples, there are many rare animals here. Some of these are:
the platypus, kangaroo, koala, fairy wrens, and the kookaburra
bird.
8. Here is a summary of one of Australia's famous Gold Coasts.
The famous Gold Coast is a two-mile strip, half way down the
coast, just 500 miles north of Sydney. The Gold Coast
features a year-round mild climate, mountains, night clubs,
restaurants, and hotels. It is said to resemble Florida's
Gold Coast and Santa Monica in California. The big difference
9. is that the prices in restaurants and hotels are about half
those in America. In summer the climate along the Gold Coast
is not as muggy as it is in Florida. The weather is warm and
clear, but there are sharks; however, there has been only an
average of about five seen a year. The Gold Coast has brought
more than two million tourists to Australia since 1947.

The writer of this theme chose an interesting topic and found adequate material for a paper of this length. Her organization and development are good, on the whole. The last paragraph could have been better organized, and a concluding paragraph might have enhanced the value of the report.

Examine the theme and make some suggestions, giving consideration to the grammatical principles that were violated.

1. The "of which" phrase is awkward as well as wordy.
2. An interesting statement of this kind needs some elaboration to satisfy the reader's curiosity. This sentence might well have been used as the topic sentence of a whole paragraph.
3. A pronoun is a poor subject for the first sentence in a paragraph since it has no direct antecedent. *Australia* would be better.
4. The compound subject "Wool, meat, grain, and gold" requires the use of the plain form *make* in the interest of agreement.
5. The misspelling of *receive* indicates a difficulty with *ei* and *ie* words. A list of these words is given in Chapter 7.
6. The pronoun *they* as a subject is indefinite. The use of the passive voice here would be more effective. "Because of the light rainfall, a pipeline has been extended into the interior to supply water for the animals and crops."
7. This construction with a colon is ineffective. The previous sentence could be developed to include this information. "Besides primitive peoples, there are many rare animals here, such as the platypus, the kangaroo, the koala, the fairy wrens, and the kookaburra bird."
8. An inverted sentence beginning with "Here is" is a weak opening for a paragraph. A good strong topic sentence for the last paragraph would improve the writing greatly. "Australia's famous Gold Coast has attracted worldwide attention. It is a two-mile strip . . . ."
9. Some form of the verb *to be* was used as the predicate verb of six successive subject-predicate word groups. The verb *to be* has little communicating power. It is a linking verb which couples a subject and its complement. Many writers overuse this verb as a carryover from speech, where it is used more effectively since speech has so many means of reinforcement. Verbs of greater power are needed in writing. The verb is the most important word in the communication pattern, and the effective writer exploits this fact. The following revision is suggested for consideration: "However, food and lodging cost much less than in the United States. Warm weather and dry air, too, combine to make the climate more pleasant than that of Florida. On the other hand, sharks sometimes invade the coastal waters. It has been reported that only about five such visitors are seen each year."

The suggestions made for improvement of the preceding theme point to the need for some review of the use of relative pronouns, of agreement of subject and verb, of the spelling of *ei* and *ie* words, and additional practice in the development of effective sentence structures. Particularly important is the study of verb forms and of the use of verbs that have greater communicating power than the verb *to be* and other common ineffective verb forms.

An Analysis of Faulty Coordination and Subordination

The following theme is included in this discussion because it illustrates an extreme case of a fairly common fault—the use of the "breathless" or "runaway" sentence. The writer becomes involved in the intricacies of coordination and subordination until his sentence gets out of control.

Is Pride Good or Bad?

Pride can be good if you know when to use it and where. It can help your work and your private life, and around your friends, it is good to have a little pride because it can help you work harder at whatever your cause may be, but too much pride can be bad. It may make you lose friends, and if you really have pride and think you're too good for everybody, people may start talking behind your back, and it could get around to your employer and you could lose your job, and it could hurt your personality so bad that no one would want to be around you, and that would really make you feel bad. And just think how you would feel doing nothing for the rest of your life, and even worse, you could lose all the pride you ever had.

And that is why pride can be good or bad.

This theme cannot be made effective by merely revising sentence structure. The discussion throughout is at a high level of generalization; therefore, the writer has communicated very little. He has failed to elaborate and to support his main points with concrete illustrations. In what ways may pride help us, and in what ways may pride harm us?

The main problem, as far as sentence structure is concerned, is to break up the long sentences into shorter ones. The basic principle is to put one idea in a sentence, using coordination and subordination for related ideas. In the first sentence, the writer has violated parallel structure. The following revision is suggested:

Pride can be good if you know when and where to use it. It is valuable in your work, in your private life, and in your relationships with your friends.

The Theme

Now the writer might well give some concrete examples to support his point. After some elaboration, he might state his second point in another paragraph.

> Too much pride can be bad. It may be responsible for loss of your friends and even your job.

Here the writer might develop this idea with appropriate illustrative material. The theme could become an interesting account of human relationships.

Exercise 2

Rewrite the preceding theme. Follow the suggestions made in the discussion. Try to build human interest by introducing illustrations from your own experience. Talk about people without mentioning names or giving clues to identification. People are interesting, and most people like to hear about the experiences of others.

Exercise 3

Read the following theme carefully. Examine sentence structure and usage, and plan revision where you think it necessary. Discuss the proposed revisions with the class. Then rewrite the theme, making any other changes necessary. Discuss your revision with other members of the class.

The Story of the Trojan War

The judgment of Paris was said to be the cause of the Trojan War. The Goddess of Discord, Eris, was not invited to an important wedding. Enraged, she threw into their midst an apple engraved "For the Fairest." Everyone wanted it. Finally it was narrowed down to three. Zeus sent them to Paris, a young prince, to judge. He selected Aphrodite, who promised him the most beautiful woman. Naturally, he chose Helen, the wife of King Menelaus of Sparta.

Paris took Helen to Troy. Thus when Menelaus found her gone, the Greeks armed for war and went after her.

The war continued for ten years with neither side winning. Sickness came into the Greek camps. Many died of the sickness, many more in the war. The toll of death took many from both sides. Even the gods got into the war. Each helping the side of his or her favor, even Zeus.

Exercise 3,
continued

As the years passed the Trojans began to get the upper hand. At last the Greeks realized they must find a secret way to get inside the walls of Troy or accept defeat. The result of this determination was a wooden horse. The stratagem of the wily mind of Odysseus. So the Greeks began to build a great horse. When it was finished, one man was left to say he wanted to join the Trojans. And Odysseus with his men climbed into the horse. The rest boarded their ships and sailed out of sight, but later returned and hid.

Sinon, the one chosen to stay, was found by the Trojans. He told his story and they believed him. They asked what the big horse was for and he said it was a gift to Athena. Happy about their defeat, they pulled it inside the wall, heedless of the danger. After they had gone to bed, Odysseus and his men opened the gate and let in the men waiting outside. The Greeks flowed over the town setting fire to the buildings and killing Trojans as they came out one by one. Only a few escaped alive, all the rest were killed. The women and children were taken as slaves. When they left, Troy was in ruins.

Summary

The Theme

You can improve your written communication by applying your knowledge of the English language and how it works, by observing your themes carefully to eliminate faulty structure, and by revising for more effective expression.

1. Use standard sentence structures; eliminate all comma faults, runaway sentences, and sentence fragments.
2. Use coordination carefully; avoid excessive use of short simple sentences.
3. Use subordination for related ideas in complex sentences; avoid illogical structures and involved relationships that are obscure.
4. Avoid rambling and runaway sentences with excessive coordination and subordination; don't try to say too much in a single sentence.
5. Construct your sentences with some consideration for emphasis; remember that the subject is an important

Summary,

continued

position and that the position of modifiers is an important factor in determining meaning and emphasis.

6. Remember that the subject noun and the predicate verb are the chief actors in the drama of communication and that they must be chosen with thought and care. Excessive use of verbs like *to be, have, do,* and *keep* weakens communication.

7. Check your work carefully to insure consistency in the use of verb tenses, of the person of pronouns, of forms in parallel structure.

8. Guard against the use of the indefinite pronouns *you* and *they.* Make sure that the antecedents of all pronouns are clear. Be careful to use the proper case form, particularly in the use of relative pronouns.

9. Watch matters of agreement of subject and verb, particularly where there are intervening elements.

10. Proofread for spelling errors, being particularly careful of *ei* and *ie* words and words that are sometimes confused because of similarity of sound.

11. Check your work for punctuation. Be careful about the use of the colon and the semicolon, and the comma to separate introductory sentence elements.

12. Exercise care in the requirements of standard usage — with verb forms, plurals, adjectives, and adverbs.

If you apply your knowledge of grammar to your themes, you will find that your work will improve gradually and permanently. Of course, form is only one important part of the writing process. Substance, too, is important. You must have something knowledgeable to say, and you can communicate your message accurately by applying what you know about structure.

Exercise 4

Revise the following themes, paying particular attention to grammatical structure and referring frequently to the standards outlined in the preceding Summary. Discuss your revision with your classmates.

Communication

Communication is the basis of relationship between two people. Ever since man inhabited the earth, he has wanted to communicate with his neighbor. Since the cave man; who used many primitive ways to communicate from one person to another in such ways as grunting or pointing when he wanted something, or drew pictures for better understanding, we have now in the twentieth century been able to carry a conversation in many languages.

Speaking is more important for people than writing. It is the basis of all social relations. We usually learn how to speak by imitating what we hear other people say. A person's speech habits are formed in childhood. Once you have these habits formed you probably cannot get rid of them. This applies especially to adults. They find it hard to lose bad habits of grammar. Children are taught how to speak early in school by giving them opportunities to speak.

Writing is a way to convey a message to someone else without speaking. The study of literature will help him express himself clearly and to appreciate the beauties of language. Communication is a vital part of good relationship between two people, in a crowd of people, and among countries.

What Is Beauty?

I think that beauty comes from within. This statement is true because a person may have beautiful hair, lovely eyes, a pretty face, and a good figure, yet she may not be really beautiful. She may look pretty from the outside, but from the inside she may be a conceited snob, have a drab personality, and be no fun at all.

Quite a few people, especially teen-agers, say they wouldn't be seen in public with a "certain person" just because that person isn't a "living doll." They think being seen with a person like this will simply ruin their popularity. Well they are terribly wrong in what they are doing. No matter if a person is cute or not so cute, they can still be considered beautiful if they are sweet, fun to be with, and have a pleasing personality.

I was telling a friend of mine how beautiful I thought this "certain person" was. My friend actually looked shocked when I said this. She asked me if I needed glasses or some-

Exercise 4,
continued

thing. She said, "I don't think that girl is very cute at all." So then I told her that I never judge beauty from the outside in, but always from the inside out. This person I think of as being beautiful has a real sweet personality and never acts as if she is getting bored with what you say. She isn't very cute from just looking at her, but once you get to know her, you'd think she was beautiful too.

Well this is the way I feel about beauty coming from within, and this is the way I look at people.

THE PARAGRAPH

Examine the following paragraph by Charles B. Shaw in *The Wonderful World of Books* to learn how the author has exploited his knowledge of language structure in the interest of effective communication:

Reference books are the keys that quickly unlock the doors to the vaults of the stored knowledge and golden wisdom of our world. Billions upon billions of facts, impressions, theories, convictions, policies, and speculations are recorded in the millions upon millions of books, magazines, and pamphlets that have been published through the centuries. Not only do reference books unlock these bewilderingly vast shelved vaults, they also provide a precise map that indicates the exact location of possibly hitherto inaccessible treasures hidden in almost impenetrable mazes of texts, tables, and statistics. If we are appalled at the prospect of finding, among billions of pages of print, just where the information that we need is recorded, some reference book can be our unerring guide.

1. The repetition of *reference books* carries the thread of unity throughout the paragraph. Notice the substitution of *books, magazines, and pamphlets* for *reference books.* Also, the predication maintains the unity of the paragraph: "Reference books are the keys ...." "... reference books unlock ... vaults," "... provide a precise map," and "some reference books can be our unerring guide."
2. The author has developed his paragraph carefully, pointing out the value of reference books not only as keys that unlock doors to knowledge but also as maps of the locations of hidden treasures.
3. The writer secures emphasis in the paragraph by means of the arrangement of the ideas he presents. His topic is "Reference Books," and throughout the paragraph he gives the topic the important subject position in his sentences.

Exercise 5

Read the following paragraph from the essay "Notes of a Native Son."* Identify the topic sentence. Select the nouns which unify the paragraph, and identify relevant predication. How are transition and emphasis effected?

It seemed to me, of course, that it was a very long funeral. But it was, if anything, a rather shorter funeral than most, nor, since there were no overwhelming, uncontrollable expressions of grief, could it be called—if I dare to use the word —successful. The minister who preached my father's funeral sermon was one of the few my father had still been seeing as he neared the end. He presented to us in his sermon a man whom none of us had ever seen—a man thoughtful, patient, and forbearing, a Christian inspiration to all who knew him, and a model for his children. And no doubt the children, in their disturbed and guilty state, were almost ready to believe this; he had been remote enough to be anything and, anyway, the shock of the incontrovertible, that it was really our father lying up there in that casket, prepared the mind for anything. His sister moaned and this grief-stricken moaning was taken as corroboration. The other faces held a dark, noncommital thoughtfulness. This was not the man they had known, but they had scarcely expected to be confronted with *him;* this was, in a sense deeper than questions of fact, the man they had not known, and the man they had not known may have been the real one. The real man, whoever he had been, had suffered and now he was dead: this was all that was sure and all that mattered now. Every man in the chapel hoped that when his hour came he, too, would be eulogized, which is to say forgiven, and that all of his lapses, greeds, errors, and strayings from the truth would be invested with coherence and looked upon with charity. This was perhaps the last thing human beings could give each other and it was what they demanded, after all, of the Lord. Only the Lord saw the midnight tears, only He was present when one of His children, moaning and wringing hands, paced up and down the room. When one slapped one's child in anger the recoil in the heart reverberated through heaven and became part of the pain of the universe. And when the children were hungry and sullen and distrustful and one watched them, daily, growing wilder, and further away, and running headlong into danger, it was the Lord who knew what the charged heart endured as the strap was laid to the backside; the Lord alone who knew what one *would* have said if one had had, like the Lord, the gift of the living word.

JAMES BALDWIN, *Notes of a Native Son*

* Reprinted by permission of Beacon Press, copyright © 1955 by James Baldwin.

Maintaining Unity

The two illustrative paragraphs, from books by professional writers, demonstrate the use of technical skills which you as a student are trying to develop. You will find that the observation and study of professional writing may be very helpful in your progress toward effective written composition.

Let us examine now a paragraph written by a high school student:

> Physical education is an important subject in the high school curriculum. In P.E. we study sports and we play interesting games. Sometimes we play soccer and at other times we play handball. Each game requires teamwork, and this is a good thing to learn. P.E. keeps a person physically fit. It develops the body and helps in breathing deeply. The exercises and drills strengthen the muscles, and the running and jumping help to build up endurance. I like P.E. because I plan to become a teacher of physical education. The work that I do now will help me in my vocation. P.E. provides an opportunity to relax from the strain of study in the classroom. It gives students a chance to use up their extra energy. P.E. is one means to good health.

In this paragraph the student is discussing physical education as an important subject in the high school curriculum. He maintains unity by using the term *physical education* and *P.E.* frequently in the subject and object positions. Some of the sentences beginning with *we* and *I* could have been more effective if a better choice of subject had been made. Nouns that are related to the main idea also contribute to the unity of the paragraph. He mentions a variety of related nouns: sports, games, soccer, handball, exercises, drills, running, jumping, endurance. The predication also generally helps to develop the unity of idea.

"We *play soccer* . . . . Each game *requires teamwork* . . . . The exercises and drills *strengthen the muscles* . . . . running and jumping . . . *build up endurance.*"

Maintaining Coherence

The paragraph could be improved by the use of coordination and subordination in order to secure coherence by relating the ideas expressed. Attention to transition through the use of introductory adverbs and word groups would also improve the coherence. A suggested revision of the paragraph follows.

Physical education is an important subject in the high school
curriculum. Sports are studied and games are played which
develop recreational interests. Such games as soccer and
handball require teamwork, which is a valuable asset in group
activities. Then, too, P.E. keeps a person physically fit.
Exercises and drills strengthen the muscles, and running and
jumping help build up endurance, thus developing the body and
promoting good breathing habits. For me, physical education is
particularly important since I plan to teach in this field.
Finally, P.E. provides an opportunity to relax from the strain
of study in the classroom since it gives students a chance to
use up their extra energy. P.E. is one means to good health.

Exercise 6

Read the revised paragraph carefully. In what way is the
sentence structure more effectively developed than in the
first draft? How has the improvement been accomplished?
Make a list of the subjects of each sentence. Examine these
words carefully. How do they contribute to the unity of the
paragraph? Examine and list the predicates. In what way do
they help in the discussion of the main idea? What devices
do you find for effecting transition?

Analyzing a Paragraph

Now examine a second paragraph written by a high school student.
Observe the key words that indicate the degree of unity maintained
within the paragraph. Consider the predication as the main idea is developed. Look for transitional devices to secure coherence. Examine
the use of grammatical methods for relating ideas. The numbered comments that follow the paragraph provide a framework for your analysis.

I feel that an education is a wonderful thing. Without an
education, you would probably get no place. Usually people
without an education end up digging ditches or in some other
hard-working, low-paying job. I think that anybody who can
should get an education. With a college education, you can
probably do anything in the field of work. Any person who has
a high-paying job as a doctor or lawyer usually has a good
education.   I think it is a wonderful thing to be able to go
off to college and get an education. Usually people with an

education are brighter and better thinkers. I think that I
would probably like to have a college education and to have a
better choice of what I might do in life.

1. SUBJECTS

I	I	person	I
you	anybody	I	I
people	you	people	I

Is this student writing about the importance of an education, or is he
writing about himself and other people? The choice of subjects does not
reveal his main idea.

2. PREDICATION

... education *is a wonderful thing.*
... you *would probably get no place.*
... people *end up digging ditches . . . .*
... anybody who can *should get an education.*
... you *can probably do anything . . . .*
... it *is a wonderful thing . . . .*
... people with an education *are brighter and better thinkers.*

The writer has chosen his verbs with little thought to effective predication and without considering the development of his idea.

3. TRANSITIONAL DEVICES

Two sentences begin with the adverb *usually* and two with an introductory prepositional phrase. There is little evidence of a conscious
effort to secure transition with grammatical structures.

4. USE OF GRAMMATICAL DEVICES FOR COHERENCE

(Evaluate this factor as part of a class discussion.)

Exercise 7   *Rewrite the preceding paragraph emphasizing:*

1. Choice of nouns in key positions that will help to secure
   unity within the paragraph

2. Development of predication for maintaining unity and for
   developing the main idea

3. Use of transitional structures

4. Use of coordination and subordination to secure a coherent
   relationship of ideas

Exercise 8

Read the following paragraph carefully. Examine the choice of nouns in key positions. Study the predication. Look for transitional structures. Consider the use of coordination and subordination in securing coherence. Criticize and discuss the material in class. Then rewrite the paragraph in order to secure effective written communication.

Television and the Family

Television has a strong influence on family life. It is a great force for entertainment. It brings into the home first-rate movies, sports programs, quiz shows, and dramas. It has the advantage of being inexpensive and handy. Despite this fact, most people do not take advantage of it for their own benefit. If the better programs were watched for information rather than only entertainment, television would be a truly cultural asset. But people regard it as only entertainment, to be watched and then forgotten. They want to be able to sit down and be entertained, not to have to learn or think. The younger members of the family in particular show a preference for watching TV rather than for doing their homework. In this case television is a marked disadvantage. Besides, television often is a disturbing factor in family life. There are often heated arguments over what program should be watched. Furthermore, instead of a family being sociable and engaging in interesting conversation, they often sit silent and indifferent to each other as they lose themselves in the world of entertainment. Television has changed our lives.

Summary

The Paragraph

The unity of a paragraph is maintained through the proper choice of both noun subjects and predicate verbs. A variety of subject nouns may be used, but they must all relate to the main idea. The most effective verbs carry force.

Paragraph coherence may be developed through the use of coordination and subordination. Important also is the use of transition through the selection of adverbs and other introductory elements.

THE SENTENCE

You have devoted a great deal of time to the study of the sentence, examining its physical characteristics and its basic patterns. You have analyzed sentences in terms of units of syntax — subject-predicate word groups, word-group modifiers, noun clusters, verb clusters, and others. You have studied the grammatical devices for the expansion of basic sentence structures and have practiced the application of these devices. You have developed some degree of skill in the use of coordination and subordination in achieving coherence of expression.

You have a reasonable mastery of the concepts of English grammar. However, you have probably not yet developed a fluency in the use of written English structures equal to your facility in handling the spoken language. Your use of spoken English is easy, fluent, unstrained. You do not have to think about how you are going to phrase your thoughts. They seem "to come naturally." It will take years of practice and refinement of style in writing to develop that little "voice" within, which will speak fluently to you as you sit with pen or typewriter recording what it will have to say.

However, you can do several things to help bridge the gulf of time. One is to examine the sentences of professional writers who have developed the essential skills of structure. How do these craftsmen employ the grammar of English? Another is to practice using sentences of your own in which you, too, will make use of these effective patterns. You should be able to profit from the professional writer's years of experience.

In this chapter, you will study the sentence according to the following procedure:

1. You will examine and analyze a variety of sentences constructed by professional writers.
2. You will construct sentences with similar patterns, using ideas appropriate to your own experience.

Absolute Structure

EXAMPLE A

The man started suspiciously and peered, his head lowered as though he was about to charge, through the fog of sleep.   PAULE MARSHALL

The essential structure here is a simple N-V PATTERN followed by an absolute structure. An absolute structure serves only to elaborate and explain the statement in the main clause.

Do these sentences follow the pattern of the sample given?

The great building seemed like a gray giant, its gaunt walls rising high above into the gloomy mists of approaching night.

A sad little boy appeared with a bundle of old clothing, his dark, brooding eyes peering out from under a large cap pulled down over his long hair.

The young kindergarten teacher came into the room like a ray of sunlight, her bright red hair reflecting the glow of the morning, her eyes sparkling with good humor.

Exercise 9   *Develop three sentences using the structural pattern illustrated above—an* N-V PATTERN *followed by an absolute structure that serves to elaborate and explain or further describe what is in the basic pattern. Do you find any limitations of structure in the basic pattern? Is there any danger of ambiguity here? Discuss the effectiveness of the sentences written by various students. Make up a list of the best sentences and post it on the bulletin board.*

Compound Predicates

EXAMPLE B

The terrific acceleration of the saucer as it left Earth twisted Billy's slumbering body, distorted his face, dislodged him in time, sent him back to the war.   KURT VONNEGUT, JR.

A half-grown tortoise-shell cat leaped from the bunkhouse porch, galloped on stiff legs across the road, whirled and galloped back again.
                                                    JOHN STEINBECK

The vivid verbs that form the compound predicate in the first sentence communicate action effectively: *twisted, distorted, dislodged, sent.* In the second sentence, the strength of *leaped, galloped, whirled,* and *galloped* gives power to the compound predicate.

Are these sentences comparable to the examples above?

The slippery halfback leaped over the tackle, squirmed through opposing backs, and raced madly down the field.

The funny-looking man looked sadly at the approaching officer, jumped quickly into his stalled car, and twirled the starter noisily.

The angry tiger growled at the zookeeper, showed its long white teeth, and pawed fiercely at the bars of its cage.

Exercise 10   *Develop four sentences using the structural pattern illustrated—the use of a compound predicate made up of three or more verbs. Avoid complicating your sentences with subordinate clauses or other word-group modifiers. Do you find any limitations of structure here? Compare your sentences with those of other students. Discuss effective sentences and ineffective sentences. What are the factors involved? Make up a list of the best sentences and post it on the bulletin board.*

Loose Sentences

EXAMPLE C

The old man was sitting on a stump behind the stove, crouching over as if he were trying to hide from us.   WILLA CATHER

Here is an N-V PATTERN with modifying prepositional phrases in the predicate and a long participial phrase looking back to modify the subject. The verbal phrase includes within its structure an adverb clause. Notice how the modifiers build up at the end of the sentence, after the verb. This sentence is typical of what is called a loose sentence. A sentence of this kind can be very effective if constructed with skill.

Do these sentences follow the pattern above?

The little boy was playing on the floor with his soldiers, placing them carefully in position as though they were about to fight a real battle.

The osprey moved in great circles over the bay, gliding occasionally downward as it it were undecided about diving into the water.

The soldier leaned on his rifle in the dark, looking out into the darkness around him and listening to the distant sound of an owl hooting at regular intervals.

Exercise 11   *Develop four sentences using the structural pattern of the model illustrated above—prepositional phrases in the predicate, followed by a participial phrase that modifies the subject. In the participial phrase include an adverb clause. Do you find any limitations of structure? Is the verb in the main clause a transitive verb or an intransitive verb? Does it make any difference? Compare your sentences with those of other students. Discuss good and poor sentences. What are the significant factors involved here? Make up a list of the best sentences and post it on the bulletin board.*

Descriptive Elements Separating Subject and Predicate

EXAMPLE D

Miss Buell's face, which was old and grayish and kindly with gray stiff curls beside the cheeks and eyes that swam very brightly like little minnows behind thick glasses, wrinkled itself into a complication of amusements.   CONRAD AIKEN

This sentence is unlike any in examples A, B, or C. It has a long series of modifying elements between the subject noun and the predicate verb. The sentence is effective because it does two things: it describes Miss Buell's face, in an emphatic manner by reason of the interruption, and it uses this description to prepare for and to reinforce the final predication. The interruption between the subject and verb is not distracting because it is so relevant to the subject.

Analyze these sentences:

Miss Johnson's face, which was young and bright and lively with hair pulled into an impromptu knot and a forehead that crinkled expressively above a pair of dancing eyes, showed itself now in quiet dignity.

The old building, which had served so many youngsters in its day with its bright high-ceilinged rooms and its worn wooden stairs, like sounding boards to eager feet, trembled under the hammers of the wrecking crew.

Exercise 12   *Develop three sentences using the structural pattern of the model illustrated above. Include a series of modifying elements between the subject and the verb that will serve to describe the subject. Try to complete your sentence with predication that will be consonant to the description. What limitations of structure do you find? What factors contribute to the difficulty of your writing problem? Compare your sentences with those written by the other members of the class. Discuss and evaluate the effectiveness of the sentences. Make up a list of the best sentences and post it on the board.*

Introductory Structure

EXAMPLE E

Throughout that summer and the cool, growthless weather of the winter, when the gales blew in the river canyon and the ocean piled upon the shore, Hook was master of the sky and the hills of his range.

WALTER VAN TILBURG CLARK

This sentence has a long introductory structure consisting of preposi-tional phrases and an adverb clause which serves as descriptive elements and in a sense build up a bit of suspense. Introductory elements serve to carry along the story or description, linking what follows to what precedes.

Do these sentences follow the pattern above?

> During the long night as he waited anxiously for a final word from the doctor, Harper paced back and forth in the little back room of the cabin.

> In the second half while our team was fighting to keep the ball and struggling to move it yard by yard toward midfield, Ernie sat on the bench with his hands clenched hoping for a nod from Coach Peters.

> During that long week in July when the heat of the desert brings the living world to a complete stop in the day and only the little sounds of insects break the silence of the night, Martin searched hopefully for his partner.

Exercise 13   *Develop four sentences using the structural pattern of the model above. Each sentence should contain a long introductory structure consisting of prepositional phrases and an adverb clause, elements that would serve to carry along the narrative or description and perhaps to create a minor feeling of suspense. Compare your sentences with those of other students and evaluate their effectiveness. What factors appear to affect the clarity of this type of sentence? Make up a list of the best sentences and post it on the board.*

Periodic Sentences

EXAMPLE F

But to everybody's surprise, when Tennessee one day returned from Marysville, without his partner's wife — she having smiled and retreated with somebody else — Tennessee's partner was the first man to shake his hand and greet him with affection.   BRET HARTE

The sentence in example F illustrates what is known as a periodic sentence. In a periodic sentence, the main idea has a climactic ending. The sentence is usually long, with introductory elements and involved structures. The model sentence in example E might be considered periodic, although it does not build up to a climactic ending.

Do these sentences follow the pattern above?

> Stamping fiercely in the dust and rearing his head madly as the crowd screamed in excitement, the angry bull charged at the matador.

> With a gun clutched in his hand, with that same hard grim look in his eyes that had frightened his adversaries in life, cold and still in the rigor of death lay the battered body of the hunted gunman.

Exercise 14      *Write two or three periodic sentences. Search for sentences of this kind in your reading. Practice writing sentences which resemble those you may find. Such sentences are used sparingly by good writers, but they are extremely effective when constructed with skill.*

Expanded Sentences

Good writers and speakers have used effectively for a variety of purposes the kinds of sentences illustrated in examples E and F. There have been many kinds of adaptations of this expanded pattern—the sentence with long introductory elements. Sometimes the sentence is developed climactically as in the previous illustrations and ends with the main idea; but then the writer has an afterthought, almost an anti-climax, he wants to add. Three striking illustrations of this adaptation follow.

EXAMPLE G

Years afterward, when the open-grazing days were over, and the red grass had been plowed under and under until it had almost disappeared from the prairie; when all the fields were under fence, and the roads no longer ran about like wild things, but followed the surveyed section-lines, Mr. Shimerda's grave was still there, with a sagging wire fence around it, and an unpainted wooden cross.   WILLA CATHER

With a good conscience our only sure reward, with history the final judge of our deeds, let us go forth to lead the land we love, asking His blessing and His help, but knowing that here on earth God's work must truly be our own.   JOHN F. KENNEDY

With malice toward none; with charity for all; with firmness in the right, as God gives us to see the right, let us strive on to finish the work we are in; to bind up the nation's wounds; to care for him who shall have borne the battle, and for his widow, and his orphan—to do all which may achieve and cherish a just and lasting peace among ourselves, and with all nations.
ABRAHAM LINCOLN

You will not be asked to try to imitate this kind of prose. It is introduced to help you understand the magnificent resources at your command which, with study, practice, and skill, you may use in order to realize the power and beauty of the English sentence.

The study of the structure of expanded sentences might be very extensive, indeed. There is enough material here to illustrate the possibilities of improvement with this kind of practice. It is suggested that you continue with this type of analysis, selecting your models from good writing, not only from literature but from newspapers and magazines. Study your models; read them again and again; master their structure and their rhythm. Then use the patterns in your own writing.

Exercise 15   *Study the grammatical structure of each of the following sentences. Describe it and discuss it with the class. Develop meaningful sentences of your own with similar patterns. Evaluate the sentences by discussing their effectiveness.*

1. If the source of death is so-called natural causes, or an accident, the reaction is predictable, a feeling of impotence, humbleness, helplessness before the forces of the universe.   ELDRIDGE CLEAVER

2. Such an attitude, no matter how good-naturedly it is assumed, has the inevitable effect of making one of your arms feel shorter than the other, a hopeless handicap at this crucial juncture, where 30% of common errors occur.
   JOHN UPDIKE

3. Death, however, sat as purposefully at my father's bedside as life stirred within my mother's womb and it was harder to understand why he so lingered in that long shadow.   JAMES BALDWIN

4. In due course I shall tell the story of my own part; now it is enough to say that it was one of complete support for the president at every stage.   HAROLD MACMILLAN

5. Man is mystery to himself because he is, on the one hand, a creature of nature, and on the other hand, a free spirit who makes nature and himself his object, extends his ends beyond nature's limit.   REINHOLD NIEBUHR

6. The oldest ancestors of man, a race of upright but small-brained toolmakers that lived in East Africa about 1,750,000 years ago, have been given the official name of *Homo Habilis*.

7. Our country has surmounted great crises in the past, not because of our wealth, not because of our rhetoric, not because we had longer cars and whiter iceboxes and

Exercise 15,

continued

bigger television screens than anyone else, but because our ideas were more compelling and more penetrating and wiser and more enduring.   JOHN F. KENNEDY

8. We tie bright ribbons around their necks, and occasionally little tinkling bells, and we affect to think that they are as sweet and vapid as the coy name "kitty" by which we call them would imply.   ALAN DEVOE

9. The spider traveled down his cheek, took a station under the boy's nose, looked up into the nostrils as if to seek the brain, and then clambered softly up over the rim of the nose.   RAY BRADBURY

Summary

The Sentence

To develop a fluency in writing, you must acquire a thorough understanding of the sentence structure. To a simple sentence you may add an absolute structure, which serves to explain and elaborate. Another device which adds effectiveness is the use of vivid compound verbs. A third structural pattern is the simple sentence with prepositional modifying phrases in the predicate and a long verbal phrase modifying the subject. Still another pattern is the separation of the subject and predicate with a series of modifying elements. Then, too, a sentence may be introduced by a prepositional phrase and an adverb clause. It is also possible to construct a sentence with introductory elements and build it to a climax, thus producing a periodic sentence. Occasionally it may be necessary to expand a sentence with an afterthought, although such expanded and involved sentences are difficult to construct. You will find it helpful to examine and analyze these kinds of sentences to be found in works of professional writers.

THE WORD

When you begin to discuss "grammar and the word," you may think you are moving away from the problems of structure into the area of diction and vocabulary. Not at all. The word alone has no intrinsic value in communication. The important factor is the *function* of the word. The sentence is not the aggregate of its separate words. In its communicating power, the sentence takes on a mysterious new ingredient which grows out of the arrangement or pattern of its elements, and that new ingredient is *meaning*. Meaning develops from the way words are used.

Of course, you must know these words before you can use them. You need this word power before you can use it effectively. You must have money in your purse in order to spend it wisely.

Verb Power

As a student of grammar you know at this point that the English language is a subject-predicate language, a noun-verb structured medium of communication. This is the basic grammatical principle which must be applied in all your work if you are to make your writing effective.

While the noun is an element that functions in many positions, performing a variety of services within a sentence, the verb is the word that carries the essential burden of meaning in its work of predication. Even as a verbal, the verb form carries with it this necessary function of predication.

The following suggestions will help you make full use of the communicating power of the verb.

1. Linking verbs, especially the verb *to be*, should be used with caution.
     The function of a linking verb is to couple the subject and the complement, and its effectiveness lies not in what it communicates as a verb but in its use as a linking device.

> Mr. Jones is the chemistry teacher.
> The chemistry teacher is Mr. Jones.
>
> The boy is aggressive.
>   (the aggressive boy)
>
> The prisoner seems innocent.
>   (the innocent-seeming prisoner)

When a transitive verb is used as the predicate, it carries with it a new content of meaning which affects both the subject and the complement. You cannot then invert the order without destroying the meaning entirely.

> The gallant hunter shot the little rabbit.

Here you see the full power of a predicating verb. Obviously, you cannot interchange the subject and complement. The fact is communicated with force, with emphasis.

Then, too, the use of an intransitive verb may be more effective than the use of a linking verb.

> Anita is very intelligent.

The fact may be communicated more effectively by using a variety of verbs, often intransitive.

> Anita speaks fluently.
> Anita writes effectively.
> Anita is reading continually.
> Anita dances beautifully.

The following illustrations may serve to show how the effectiveness of material may be improved by the use of a variety of verbs to replace a linking verb, in this case *to be.*

Freedom of religion is our constitutional right.

Our Constitution guarantees religious freedom.
Our Constitution allows us to worship as we please.
Our Constitution forbids interference with individual worship.
Our Constitution secures for each of us the right to worship as we see fit.

The weather was very unpleasant.

The rain poured down on the black, wet roads.
The heavy clouds darkened the late afternoon.
The force of the wind shook the little house.
The fog concealed the traffic ahead of us.

A dictionary is a useful book.

The dictionary defines unfamiliar words.
The derivation of a word can be found in the dictionary.
Often synonyms and antonyms are suggested following the definition.
Frequent illustrations clarify the meaning of words.

Exercise 16 *Rewrite each of the following sentences in a number of different ways, with verbs other than linking verbs. Discuss the sentences that you write. In what way have you improved the effectiveness of the original sentences?*

1. The war was over.
2. Kathy is a very likeable person.
3. The game was exciting.
4. This novel looks very interesting.
5. Exercise is good for the health.
6. Johnson seems upset.
7. Tony Green is a good sport.
8. Jim Smith was hurt in the automobile accident.
9. Our car looks very dilapidated.
10. The high school play was a success.
11. Jeffrey was the captain in the game that we won last Saturday.
12. The reason for Mr. Brown's success is that he is aggressive.

2. Forms of *have, do, keep, go,* and *come* do not communicate as effectively as verbs with a more precise meaning. Be cautious in your use of verbs like these, which are at a relatively high level of generalization.

Mary has a friendly personality.

Mary has won many friends.
Mary usually smiles at her own difficulties.
Mary often sympathizes with others.

Mr. Spring keeps his yard very neat.

Mr. Spring mows his lawn every week.
Mr. Spring trims his borders and rakes up the grass.
Mr. Spring cultivates his flower beds often.

He has to do his homework.

He must solve his algebra problems.
He will write a theme.

Mother is going to Boston on Monday.

Mother will fly to Boston on Monday.
Mother will drive to Boston on Monday.
Mother will accompany Mrs. Dewitt to Boston on the 5:15.

Exercise 17   *Rewrite each of the following sentences in two or three ways. Use verbs that will communicate more clearly and precisely than those in the given sentences. Revise the sentence where necessary. Compare your sentences with those of other students. Discuss the effectiveness of the revised sentences. In what way have you improved the original sentences?*

1. Carol does very well in her new position as secretary.

2. Michael did a good job on his term paper.

3. Georgina has a new dress and it looks very attractive.

4. Mrs. Parks keeps her home very neat.

5. The boys always do the errands for their mother.

6. The old car has a very bad rattle.

7. An elephant went down the street.

8. Mr. Wild comes from a very wealthy family.

9. Jim has a plan for earning his way through college.

10. What have you done with all that money?

11. Mrs. Fernandez has a bright light in her window.

12. Mr. Spratt lets his wife keep boarders so that he can do what he likes.

3. Colorful verbs, often used in a figurative sense, add much to the communicating power of the predicate.

> The fighter elbowed his way through the cheering fans.
> Lulu mouthed her singing lesson as if it had no meaning.
> A great crowd sluiced its way through the turnstiles.
> Tender words, dripping with sentiment, flowed from the speaker's mouth.
> Brown's mighty kick propelled the ball high into the air.
> Mr. Sparks glowed with warm friendliness for his business associates.

4. Verbal phrases may be used effectively either as introductory elements or as terminal elements of the sentence.

Bowing gratefully to her audience and smiling happily with success, Lydia waited for the applause to subside.

Battered and beaten, overwhelmed with a deep sense of defeat, the champion sank to the floor.

To win his family's approval, to earn that love and respect which he felt that he had lost, this craving urged Arthur to his greatest effort.

He paused for a moment, hoping that his words had convinced his mother, fearing that they had not.

The little girl looked up at her brother, intensely pleased with herself and satisfied that she had won his admiration.

For many years Fred had been creating a vision of his future: to attend the University, to graduate with honors, to become a doctor.

Exercise 18

1. Write sentences using each of the following verbs in the predicate:

startle	frame	fume
clatter	burst	plow
rustle	bluster	pancake
shoulder	jabber	shatter
crush	bulge	creep

2. Make up a list of ten verbs that may be used in a figurative sense and write sentences using them in a colorful way.

3. Bring to class a list of five sentences in which the writer has used verbs in an especially effective manner. You may find such sentences in short stories, novels, newspapers, and textbooks.

4. Write four or five sentences using verbal phrases as introductory elements. Be careful to use parallel structure.

5. Develop several sentences with verbal phrases as terminal elements. Discuss these sentences in class. What effect have these terminal phrases on the total power of the sentence?

Nouns in Communication

Nouns exert greatest power in the subject position; they rank second in importance to the predicate verb. Therefore, the writer must choose his subject noun with great care. Select concrete and specific nouns and avoid those at a high level of generalization. Students have a tendency to begin their sentences with personal or indefinite pronouns. Be alert to this weakness.

Why are the following sentences ineffective?

I want to go to college because I want to get an education.
We get our freedom from the Bill of Rights.
You shouldn't work too hard because you might get a nervous breakdown.
You should have seen that team try to make a touchdown.
People are never satisfied with what they earn.
The birds were flying over the desert.
The new house is located on Front Street.
Our old car is in bad condition.
The road to Batsville is in need of repair.
Education is important for all young men and women.

The sentences above would be improved by a choice of a more meaningful subject.

A college education is part of the plan for my future.
The Bill of Rights guarantees us our freedom.
Hard work may cause a nervous breakdown.
The football team fought to make a touchdown.
Some workers are not satisfied with what they earn.
The turkey buzzards were circling over the desert.
Mrs. Smith's new cottage is located on Front Street.
Our old Buick shows signs of age.
The turnpike to Batsville needs repairs.
Vocational training is important for young men and women.

Sometimes the selection of the wrong noun as the subject results in the use of the passive voice.

The carriage was driven by an elegant coachman in a red-and-black uniform.
The pennant was won by the New York Mets last year.
A park on the outskirts is being developed by the city.
Many buildings were destroyed by the earthquake.

If the verb in each of the sentences above is changed to the active voice, the emphasis of the subject position will be on the word that should receive it.

An elegant coachman in a red-and-black uniform was driving the carriage.
The New York Mets won the pennant last year.
The city is developing a park on the outskirts.
The earthquake destroyed many buildings.

As you know, nouns have a variety of functions. They serve as subjects, complements, in prepositional phrases, as appositives, and even as modifiers. The nouns of English are the elements of the experience communicated to others. You are limited in your use of these important words by your knowledge of English words. You will develop power in using nouns to enrich your language as you enlarge your vocabulary through wide reading, study of words, and practice in using them.

Exercise 19   *Revise each of the following sentences to make the subject noun more effective in communication:*

1. He keeps staring at me all the time.
2. I think Nick is a great baseball player.
3. They're having a display of Gordon Parks' photographs.
4. Everyone loves a winner.
5. You never know what might happen in the course of a day.
6. Everybody is always complaining about the cafeteria.
7. I don't like algebra because it is too hard.
8. Nobody loves Henry Peabody.
9. What you don't know won't hurt you.
10. There will never be another President like Kennedy.
11. They put out the fire with chemicals.
12. The first baseball of the season was thrown by the President.
13. People love to watch television.
14. There are too many people here today.
15. A book like *The Elements of Style* is always handy.
16. One of my favorite subjects is typing.
17. He got tired of carrying the albatross all the time.

Adjectives and Adverbs

Adjectives and adverbs are treated together because both are essentially modifiers. True, adjectives are often used in the predicate position after a linking verb. However, the discussion here will relate principally to the modifying function.

Remember that adjectives and adverbs are secondary word classes in communication. Modifiers make meaning more exact, more precise.

Since modifiers are secondary words in a sentencé, use them cautiously. Too many adjectives and adverbs will tend to confuse the reader by concealing the important nouns and verbs. The flowers will be hidden by the leaves.

> The hungry, vicious old tiger paced restlessly and angrily back and forth across his cage.

A second consideration is mainly a vocabulary problem. Many student writers know relatively few adjectives, and they therefore overuse their scant supply or resort to slang. Adjectives such as *nice, good, fine, swell, old, mean,* and *poor* contribute little to effective writing.

Exercise 20   *Discuss the use of adjectives and adverbs in the following sentences. Revise the sentences to make them more effective.*

1. I though *A Separate Peace* was a swell book, but I liked *Slaughterhouse-Five* better.

2. Terry has a new dress which is really pretty.

3. His long, graceful fingers played restlessly on the typewriter keys.

4. We're tired of the same old television programs; we want to see something original and new.

5. The poor old man walked slowly across the street.

6. Henry feels bad about the whole matter.

7. Thank you for a very nice evening.

8. Your father looks better than he did last winter.

9. Peter took a bad fall down the icy steps of the school building.

10. Lennie is a fine boy, and we all know that he will make a great success of his life.

11. Barry Reed played a great game in the second half, and the coach was mighty well pleased.

12. The violinist was an incomparably gifted artist whose exquisite technique afforded the critics the opportunity for ineffable praise.

13. Allison is a sweet girl but her sister is nicer.

14. We poked our way carefully through the heap of old rubbish.

15. The Ancient Mariner had a long, gray beard and a glittering eye.

Exercise 21   *Discuss the use of nouns, verbs, adjectives, and adverbs in the following selection. What do you think the author has accomplished by his style? Do you feel that the style is unusual? Why or why not?*

The dark, he discovered, was mottled; was a luminous collage of patches of almost-color that became, as his open eyes grew at home, almost ectoplasmically bright. Objects became lunar panels let into the air that darkness had given flat substance to. Walls dull in day glowed. Yet he was not comforted by the general pallor of the dark, its unexpected transparence; rather, he lay there waiting, godlessly praying, for those visitations of positive light that were hurled, unannounced, through the windows by the headlights of automobiles pausing and passing outside. Some were slits, erect as sentinels standing guard before beginning to slide, helplessly, across a corner, diagonally warping, up onto the ceiling, accelerating, and away. Others were yellowish rectangles, scored with panes, windows themselves, but watery, streaked, the mullions dissolved, as if the apparition silently posed on a blank interior wall were being in some manner lashed from without by a golden hurricane.

JOHN UPDIKE, *The Music School*

The Word

Summary

To communicate effectively, you must not only acquire word power but understand the function of words. Since English is a subject-predicate language, you should learn to appreciate the variety of services the noun performs and the burden of meaning carried by the verb. Be cautious in your use of linking verbs and verbs that merely generalize. Remember to choose colorful and forceful verbs as well as concrete and specific nouns. Although adjectives and adverbs add to the effectiveness of a sentence, be careful to use them more or less sparingly. The inclusion of too many of these modifiers can cause confusion and obscure meaning.

נקודות המוצא לניתוח מתנדים הן התנגדות-שלילית או משוב, אך מבחינה מתימטית
אין הבדל מוגדר בין השנים ואפשר לבחון כל מתנד מסוים מכל נקודת ראות. במחולל
הידוע בשם מחולל צורת-גל בהתנגדות שלילית, קיים משוב חיובי פנימי שתפקידו
בדרכלות לאנ הקספד. שם אשר כל הנבא ארחה אנא הרחר הרקספד לארכל
המחדר הרספם. ביכל ארחל המארח הרחרטמטיא המהרמ... אברל דבנד ארחם.

Hebrew

Chapter 6

PUNCTUATION

A Look Back and A Look Forward

You already know a great deal about punctuation. This chapter serves merely to review the conventional marks used in written work to guide the reader to a full understanding of sentence and paragraph meanings. You will not be required to learn tiresome rules but only to reexamine the signals uniformly employed in English composition to help you communicate ideas without being misunderstood.

PURPOSE OF PUNCTUATION MARKS

Chapter 2 pointed out the differences between spoken English and written English. Spoken English is reinforced by sound patterns called *intonation.* These sound patterns are developed by changes in pitch and tone and by minute pauses. By separating meaningful words and word groups, intonation helps the listener to understand. The message of the speaker is communicated mostly by the patterns of sound and the arrangement of the words.

In written English, punctuation marks must substitute for the sound patterns. A period at the end of a sentence indicates a momentary pause; the voice falls. A question mark at the end of a sentence usually calls for a rise in the tone of voice. A comma within the sentence demands a very slight pause. All these punctuation marks help in grouping words into meaningful units; they add to an understanding of the relationship of words and word groups to each other. Meaning is therefore enhanced by these standard signs.

Punctuation is a guide for the reader. The writer must never forget that he punctuates, not because of a rule, but because he wants to guide his reader. Of course, there are some rules that are followed arbitrarily. Such rules are simply conventional. Also, in standard written English, punctuation practice is fairly uniform throughout the United States. It is necessary for you to become familiar with this practice.

The writer who understands the structure of his language should have little trouble with punctuation. The discussion of the practice used in composition assumes the student's knowledge of grammar. The need for punctuation is related to the structure of the sentence. You need not be concerned with a blind memorization of rules.

SEPARATING WORD GROUPS

You have learned that a compound sentence is constructed of two or more basic sentence patterns. These patterns may be joined by a coordinator. Some common coordinators are *and, but, or,* and *nor.* A comma is placed before the coordinator to separate the two groups.

> The English colonists crossed the mountains, and soon they had settled along the great Ohio Valley.
> The driver lashed the horses furiously, but the wolves continued to follow the sleigh.
> The student will have to complete the work, or he will not receive credit for the course.
> There is not much food left in the cabin, nor will there be much chance for getting through the snow to find more.

Frequently the writer omits the coordinator in a compound sentence. Then a semicolon is used to separate the basic patterns.

The game was over; the team walked wearily off the field.

Sometimes a conjunctive adverb blends the two ideas in a compound sentence. A semicolon is then used before the conjunctive adverb.

The escaped criminal is desperate; therefore, he must be recaptured immediately.
The man has been injured seriously; however, he will recover within a few months.
The child has been in school only three months; nevertheless, she has already learned to read many words.

The use of the comma after the conjuctive adverb depends on the relation of the adverb to the rest of the basic pattern.

Test Yourself

Punctuate these sentences:

1. Walter will graduate in June and he plans to get a job.
2. Charley had hoped to go to college but now his plans are uncertain.
3. Linda has worked very hard however her grades are not very good.
4. Karen doesn't want to go to college nor does she plan to be married for several years.
5. Sam will work all summer hence he will earn enough to pay for his clothes and books.

INTRODUCTORY WORD GROUPS

A sentence is often constructed with an introductory word group. Such word groups are usually prepositional phrases, adverb clauses, participial phrases, or absolute structures. The comma separates the word group from the subject of the sentence.

Before the arrival of the President, a great crowd assembled at the airport.
When the audience was seated, the conductor raised his baton as a signal to the orchestra.
The mooring ropes having been cast off, the steamer moved slowly away from the pier into the river.
Sitting quietly in her seat, the little girl watched the picture with great interest.
In the meantime, the rain stopped and the sun reappeared.

Test Yourself

Identify these introductory word groups and punctuate the sentences:

1. When the tests are over the class will be dismissed.
2. Having seen the program before Andy turned off the television.
3. The school year being almost over we don't have much time to plan.
4. After the party for Dad my brother went south.
5. If it doesn't rain on Saturday we should go play ball after lunch.

INTERNAL WORD GROUPS

If an adjective clause within the body of a sentence is purely descriptive, it is set off with commas. Such an adjective clause describes rather than identifies the word it modifies and is called a nonrestrictive clause.

> Mr. Stacks, who is our librarian, placed the book on the desk.
> The steamer, which was a beautiful new Greek ship, moved slowly toward the pier.
> The football game, which is played annually between Washington and East High, is always well attended.
> The police found the gunman, who had just committed the robbery, hiding behind the stone wall.

When the adjective clause helps to identify the word it modifies, it is called a restrictive clause and is not set off with commas.

> The hat which Aunt Sarah is wearing cost a fortune.
> The old woman who lived in a shoe had entirely too many children.
> The company that manufactures this car guarantees it for fifty thousand miles.
> The proposal which you have just outlined should be put in writing and presented to the Mayor.

When an adverb clause interrupts the normal order of sentence structure, usually coming before the verb it modifies, it is enclosed with commas.

> The city streets, after the heavy snows of winter have melted, are usually in bad condition.
> The audience, although it was deeply moved by the performance, applauded the actors with some reluctance.
> The commanding officer of the regiment, when he saw that the battle was lost, ordered his men to withdraw.

When participial phrases, prepositional phrases, or absolute structures are used as interrupting elements within a sentence, they are set off with commas.

> The senator, having delivered a powerful address, was certain of winning the support of his associates.
> The attorney, in a desperate effort to convince the jury, called witness after witness to support his client's testimony.
> This building, as a matter of fact, is poorly designed.

Test Yourself

Punctuate these sentences, explaining the reason for the need for commas. Which sentences are correct as they stand?

1. The used car that we bought last month runs perfectly.

2. The policeman having made an arrest dispersed the crowd.

3. Miss Brown who visited us in June is sailing for Europe next week.

4. The play I regret to say was poorly attended.

5. The doctor whom we called was on vacation.

TERMINAL WORD GROUPS

When a descriptive adjective clause occurs at the end of a sentence, it is preceded by a comma.

> One of my favorite authors is Ralph Ellison, who wrote *Invisible Man*.
> Next week my cousin Geraldine from Alabama is coming to New York, where she hopes to find a job.
> Henry will be stationed in Fort Bragg, which is in North Carolina and almost five hundred miles from here.

If the terminal adjective clause is restrictive (identifying), no comma is used to separate it from the rest of the sentence.

> The guards fired at the prisoner who was trying to escape.
> The company advertised for a girl who could operate a switchboard.

Adverb clauses falling at the end of a sentence are not usually punctuated. But sometimes such a clause is used to give additional information. The rest of the sentence communicates adequately without it. In this case, a comma precedes the adverb clause.

The South High team was being pushed down the field by Central, while Charley sat it out with the other boys on the bench.

Christopher Columbus is said to have discovered America, although he was not the first white man to cross the Atlantic.

The population of the United States will be almost two hundred million by 1980, if we are to believe certain estimates.

If a participial phrase at the end of a sentence refers back to the subject, it is usually set off with a comma.

Hawthorne was critical of Puritan intolerance, having been a resident of New England all his life.

Charles Drew made a great contribution to medicine, having developed a way to store blood plasma.

The quarterback was anxious to get back on the field, knowing that his team needed his support.

Exercise 1   *Use punctuation where needed in the following sentences:*

1. When darkness finally came it was still much too hot to sleep in most of the apartments.

2. During the assembly Gary recopied his entire book report and did his history homework.

3. The secretary had just gotten back to her desk when the doctor's telephone rang.

4. The taxicab raced madly down the street and frightened people dodged wildly out of its path.

5. The Post Office which was completed last month will be dedicated in July.

6. This is the boy who plays the glockenspiel in the high school band.

7. The student received a low grade on his final however he will pass the course.

8. Running and screaming through the halls of the apartment house little Frankie was the terror of the building.

9. Professor Askew is flying to Chicago where he will address the National Speech Foundation.

10. Coach Green has discovered a runner who can sprint one hundred yards in ten seconds.

11. Jim Brown paid the girl for his groceries but he forgot to pick up his change.

Exercise 1,
continued

12. The weather is very bad tonight we'll have to stay in the house.

13. The workers have been on strike for a month therefore the building will not be finished on time.

14. The new school will be located on Front Street which has just been widened and repaved.

15. This house to tell the truth was built before the Spanish American War.

16. The man who owns this property will sell it if he can find a buyer who will meet his terms.

17. The nurse having done all that she could for the patient walked slowly out of the room.

18. The attorney's request to examine the accounts of the bankrupt firm was granted by the judge.

19. The prize will be given to the student who can spell the most words.

20. On the advice of her lawyer the woman decided to settle the lawsuit out of court.

SEPARATING WORDS

A transitional adverb introducing a sentence is usually followed by a comma.

> Also, the evidence indicated that the burglar might have had an accomplice.
> Finally, the engine is assembled and placed on a block ready for installation.
> Next, the batter is poured into a well-buttered cake pan.
> Again, there is need for caution in presenting this matter to the committee.

Words in a series are separated by commas.

> The president, the secretary, and the treasurer attended the board meeting.
> He jabbed, feinted, and pranced around the ring.
> She attacked his position openly, viciously, and outrageously.
> The delicate, sensitive, emotional Miss Price swept across the stage.

A comma or commas separate a loose, or nonrestrictive, appositive from the rest of the sentence.

> Mr. Brunswick, the delegate from New Jersey, will be the chairman of the meeting.

Arthur Ashe, the noted tennis player, scored another victory.
The old man shook his cane, a battered stick of wood.
The huge airplane, a 747, descended slowly.

Close, or restrictive, appositives are not punctuated.

The old movie *A Night at the Opera* is still popular.
The comic Flip Wilson is frequently on television.
I read my little brother the book *Peter's Chair.*

The use of commas with dates and place names is illustrated in the following sentences. Note that when the dates or names are within the body of the sentence, a comma both precedes and follows the date or name.

The battle was fought on July 23, 1918, in the rugged mountains of central France.
The child was born on March 15, 1963.
The family lived in Burbank, California, for fifteen years.

When just the month and the year are given, usage varies.

His father came home in June 1970 and has stayed ever since.

Adjectives of equal value, called coordinate adjectives, are separated by commas. Usually the word *and* could replace the comma. Such adjectives could be rearranged in position.

The enemy general was a cruel, relentless leader.
The energetic, aggressive Mr. Brown has been promoted again.
The salesman needs to take a polite, friendly approach.

Adjectives not equal in value, called cumulative adjectives, are not separated by commas. The word *and* could not be inserted between such adjectives.

The Boy Scout helped the little old lady across the street.
The Smiths bought a new brick house.
This smart young man is coming to call on us.
Heavy dark clouds swept across the sky.

Notice that the following sentence includes both coordinate and cumulative adjectives:

Joanna is a serious, thoughtful little girl.

A comma is used to separate a name in direct address from the rest of the sentence. This use is important to avoid ambiguity.

Mr. Smith, the mailman is coming.
I called you, James, to ask you a question.
Will you turn the light on, Joe?

Exercise 2

Punctuate the following sentences where necessary:

1. However the rain stopped and we resumed our journey.

2. The tweed jacket one of Paul's best is hanging on a hook in the back bedroom.

3. Peter Bart is driving the newest model a specially built racing car designed by the Ford Motor Company.

4. Yesterday an airplane was hijacked to Cuba after the passengers including the noted singer William Warfield were allowed to disembark in New York.

5. The family moved to Akron Ohio where they will remain for at least a year.

6. Sir Stanley the old gorilla has been captured.

7. The sweet little boy grew up to be an ill-tempered obstinate man.

8. This year we have read books by Eldridge Cleaver Kurt Vonnegut Ernest Hemingway and Richard Wright.

9. Here comes Andrew Panatella the well-known bore from the Bronx.

10. On December 26 1969 a great blizzard swept New York and New England the city of Albany New York was burried under heavy snow.

11. He read the order slowly deliberately and clearly.

12. Miss Ashley the English teacher was born in Bangor Maine.

13. I believe Sam that I have read that book.

14. Our doctor came to this state in March 1920 when very few people lived in the Southwest.

15. Dr. Stone the noted kidney specialist is to lecture to the internes tomorrow.

16. Mr. Johnson is a quiet thoughtful young man.

17. Next the concert was given at Trenton New Jersey where it was welcomed by large crowds that packed the auditorium.

18. Did you call Sally?

19. The chairman a prominent lawyer is ill.

20. My dog is friendly gentle and playful.

CONVENTIONS OF PUNCTUATION

Quotation marks are used to enclose material that is repeated exactly. If either a period or a comma comes at the end of the statement, it must be included within the quotation marks.

> The boy replied, "I will be home early tonight."
> "You won't find me home this morning," said the rabbit, "and I will be hopping mad if you call on me when I'm not home."

In the first sentence, notice that a comma is used before the direct quotation. In the second sentence, commas are used to separate the parts of the direct quotation from the interrupting narrative.

> The lady asked the officer, "Where can I park my car?"
> The officer inquired, "How long do you expect to be here?"

Notice three things in the sentence above: the comma before the direct quotation, the capital letter beginning the first word of the quotation, and the question mark within the end quotation marks.

Quotation marks are used to enclose material quoted from a book, an article, a poem, or other published matter.

> In a Mark Twain novel, Huckleberry Finn expresses his enjoyment of life on the great river: "Yonder was the banks and the islands across the water; and maybe a spark—which was a candle in a cabin window; and sometimes on the water you could see a spark or two—on a raft or a scow, you know . . . . It's lovely to live on a raft."

Quotation marks are used to indicate the title of an article, a story, a poem, a song, or a chapter title.

> Gwendolyn Brooks is author of the poem "The Children of the Poor."
> Did you read the editorial "Another Lake, Another Dollar" in *The New York Times* last Sunday?
> The story "Should Wizard Hit Mommy?" by John Updike is part of the collection *Pigeon Feathers.*
> Of all the songs by the Beatles, "Yesterday" seems to have been recorded most often.
> "Punctuation" is the title of this chapter.

Test Yourself

Use quotation marks properly in these sentences:

1. Have you read Flying Home the story by Ralph Ellison?

2. Last week we read Naming of Parts by Henry Reed.

3. Yesterday Miss Scott said Please review this chapter for tomorrow.

4. We will have a test she added next Tuesday.

5. The band played The Star-Spangled Banner as it passed the reviewing stand.

In manuscript, italics are indicated by underlining the words to be italicized. Besides the titles of publications, it is customary to use italics to indicate the names of ships and to indicate the use of words as words, letters, and figures.

The *Queen Elizabeth II* will sail at ten o'clock tomorrow.
The noun *condition* ends with the characteristic noun suffix *-tion*.
There is an extra *t* and a missing *4* in the first line of his typed material.

The colon and the dash are conventional punctuation marks. Remember that in standard usage, the colon points forward; the dash points backward. In other words, the material following a colon is necessary to complete the explanation or elaboration of what has been stated.

In modern grammar, words are grouped into four main classes: nouns, verbs, adjectives, and adverbs.

The dash points backward at some word or statement. What follows the dash is descriptive and secondary to the main idea which has been stated.

There will be twelve hundred graduates in this year's class—the largest graduation class in the school's history.
The air was hushed and still, and not a breath was moving—the world was waiting for the storm to break.

The colon is used after the salutation in a formal letter, in Biblical references, and in numerical expressions of time.

Mr. Henry C. Friend   Mark 15:3
Yankee Publishing Company   4:25 p.m.
Reno, Nevada

Dear Mr. Friend:

The apostrophe is used to indicate the possessive case of nouns and to designate contractions.

The boy's hat is lost.
The girls' uniforms are very attractive.
The father announced proudly, "It's a boy!"
Don't tease the poor cat.
I will be home at five o'clock.

The apostrophe is used also to indicate the plurals of numbers, letters, and words used as words. There is a tendency, however, to eliminate the apostrophe in some plurals.

> There are four 5's in our new license number.
> There are two *r*'s and two *l*'s in the name *Farrell*.
> You use too many *and*'s in your story.

Test Yourself

Use apostrophes where necessary in these sentences:

1. Its too cold to go outside this afternoon.

2. Who doesnt like cold weather?

3. Marys books were found under a table in the library.

4. There are four *ss* in *Mississippi*.

5. Our vacation hinges on too many *ifs*.

Parentheses are marks of enclosure. A parenthetical statement is one that explains or describes. It is usually an interrupting element in a sentence. When the writer wishes to insure clarity, particularly if the parenthetical statement is a sentence, he uses parentheses. A comma or commas may be used instead of parentheses to set off such words, as in the third sentence below.

> Once last week (I don't remember which day) we didn't have any homework to do.
> World attention was focused on Montgomery, Alabama in 1955 and 1956 (the years of the bus boycott).
> World attention was focused on Montgomery, Alabama in 1955 and 1956, the years of the bus boycott.

Brackets, too, are marks of enclosure. They are used in quoted material when the writer wishes to insert words of his own. On page 154 is a quotation from *The Adventures of Huckleberry Finn*. A part of the quoted material is repeated here with inserted explanatory words.

> "Yonder was the banks and the islands across the water; and maybe a spark — which was a candle in a cabin window; and sometimes on the water [the Mississippi River] you could see a spark or two — on a raft or a scow, you know."

Ellipsis is used to indicate an omission. Three dots indicate an omission within a sentence, and four dots indicate that the omission coincides with the ending of a sentence. The Mark Twain quotation on page 154 is illustrative.

Exercise 3

Punctuate the following sentences where necessary:

1. Amos Markwardt wrote a poem entitled The Petunia Died.

2. Come here the old man said and I will tell you about your parents.

3. Gordon Parks the author of The Learning Tree is also a famous photographer.

4. As a child my favorite book was E. B. Whites Charlottes Web.

5. I dont believe what youre saying Sharon cried and I wont listen to another word.

6. Robert Frosts poem The Death of the Hired Man tells of the return of a homeless farm worker who is old ill and helpless.

7. Father asked Where have you been all evening

8. Theres nothing in the refrigerator said Bob and Im starving.

9. The Lusitania was sunk by the Germans during World War I.

10. It was 4:25 a.m. and the Cohens' party was in full swing.

11. The word too is often misspelled by high school students.

12. The parade will consist of four divisions the bands the brigade of infantry the civilian marchers and the high school drum corps.

13. The jury brought in a verdict of not guilty a very just decision in view of the lack of evidence.

14. The teacher replied There will be no home work over the weekend.

15. I will be home at four oclock said Julie and I would like an early supper.

16. There are three 4s in the number on your license plate.

17. The furniture in the guest room was all very attractive a spinet desk a great mahogany bed and an old-fashioned chest of drawers.

18. Why do you accuse me she asked indignantly.

19. The tornado had swept violently across the valley not a single house had survived its onrush.

Exercise 4   *Punctuate the following sentences where necessary:*

1. In Lenox Avenue Mural Langston Hughes speaks of a dream deferred.

2. I refuse to answer the defendant said on the grounds that it may tend to incriminate me.

3. Uncle Otto came home with a great basket of groceries tomato soup salami onions potatoes crackers and a large rib roast of beef.

4. The riot spread quickly through the city the police were unable to cope with the situation.

5. Mother yelled George where have you left your jacket

6. On the other hand theres no real reason why you should be drawn into this long bitter controversy.

7. There came the Queen Elizabeth a long sleek greyhound of the ocean.

8. We came to the wooded area at the foot of the mountain where we decided to stop and make camp for the night.

9. This is the house that Jack built and well sell it to you for only ten thousand dollars.

10. Mrs. Van Allen the dear old lady who lives across the street is giving a party for her daughter Joan.

11. This report according to a reputable informant describes the true situation in Cuba.

12. Johns clothes were all torn but he had no serious injury.

13. When the rain had stopped we decided to continue our trip but unfortunately we discovered that we had a flat tire.

14. Mr. Herman Smith who has a delicatessen store on Milton Avenue was born on June 27 1895.

15. Theres nobody home remarked the wise old gander perhaps someone is cooking my goose.

16. A dark shape arose before me in the twilight my blood congealed in my veins.

17. The Declaration of Independence was signed on July 4 1776 a date that will always be remembered by Americans.

18. Rocky ran as fast as he could fearing to look back at his pursuer.

19. There was Donna trim and sleek walking with her boyfriend who seemed to be entirely unaware of her.

Exercise 4,
continued

20. At exactly 225 a.m. the countdown for the space shot which is scheduled for tomorrow will begin.

Exercise 5

Punctuate the following selection*:

I spent two days just riffling uncertainly through the dictionarys pages. Id never realized so many words existed! I didnt know which words I needed to learn. Finally just to start some kind of action I began copying.

....

I believe it took me a day. Then aloud I read back to myself everything Id written on the tablet. Over and over aloud to myself I read my own handwriting.

I woke up the next morning thinking about those words immensely proud to realize that not only had I written so much at one time but Id written words that I never knew were in the world. Moreover with a little effort I also could remember what many of these words meant. I reviewed the words whose meanings I didnt remember. Funny thing from the dictionary first page right now that aardvark springs to my mind. The dictionary had a picture of it a long-tailed long-eared burrowing African mammal which lives off termites caught by sticking out its tongue as an anteater does for ants.

I was so fascinated that I went on I copied the dictionarys next page. And the same experience came when I studied that. With every succeeding page I also learned of people and places and events from history. Actually the dictionary is like a miniature encyclopedia. Finally the dictionarys A section had filled a whole tablet and I went on into the Bs. That was the way I started copying what eventually became the entire dictionary. It went a lot faster after so much practice helped me to pick up handwriting speed. Between what I wrote in my tablet and writing letters during the rest of my time in prison I would guess I wrote a million words.

I suppose it was inevitable that as my word-base broadened I could for the first time pick up a book and read and now begin to understand what the book was saying. Anyone who has read a great deal can imagine the new world that opened. Let me tell you something from then until I left that prison in every free moment I had if I was not reading in the library I was reading on my bunk. You couldnt have gotten me out of books with a wedge.

MALCOLM X, *The Autobiography of Malcolm X*

* Reprinted by permission of Grove Press, Inc. Copyright © 1964 by Alex Haley and Malcolm X. Copyright © 1965 by Alex Haley and Betty Shabazz. Also by permission of Hutchinson & Co., Ltd., London, England.

Summary

Uses of the Comma

1. Before a coordinator that joins the parts of a compound sentence
2. After a transitional word that helps to blend two ideas in a compound sentence in which a semicolon appears
3. After a prepositional or participial phrase, an adverb clause, or an absolute structure preceding the subject of a sentence
4. To set off a nonrestrictive adjective clause
5. To set off an adverb clause falling between the subject and the predicate
6. To set off a participial phrase, a prepositional phrase, or an absolute structure used as interrupting elements within a sentence
7. Before a descriptive adjective clause ending a sentence
8. Before an adverb clause ending a sentence if it provides additional information
9. Before a closing participial phrase if it refers back to the subject
10. After a transitional adverb that introduces a sentence
11. To separate words in a series
12. To set off a nonrestrictive appositive
13. To separate the day and the year in dates
14. To separate a city and a state
15. To separate adjectives of equal value
16. To set off a name in direct address

Uses of the Semicolon

1. In a compound sentence to replace a conjunction
2. In a compound sentence to separate the subject-predicate word groups if there is internal punctuation within one of the word groups

Summary,

continued

Uses of Quotation Marks
1. To enclose a statement repeated exactly
2. To enclose material quoted from a publication
3. To indicate the title of an article, a story, a poem, a song, or a chapter title

Uses of Italics
1. To indicate the title of a book, a periodical, a newspaper, or any separate publication
2. To indicate the names of ships
3. To indicate the use of a word as a word, a letter, or a figure

Uses of the Colon
1. To point forward to details that follow a statement to be elaborated
2. After the salutation of a formal letter
3. In Biblical references
4. In expressing time in numerals

Uses of the Apostrophe
1. To indicate possession of nouns
2. To designate contractions
3. To indicate the plurals of figures, letters, and words used as words

Uses of Miscellaneous Marks
1. Use a dash to indicate material that is descriptive and secondary to the preceding statement.
2. Use parentheses to enclose explanatory or descriptive material that offers further clarification.
3. Use brackets when adding explanatory words to quoted matter.
4. Use three dots to indicate an omission within a sentence and four dots if the omission follows a sentence ending with a period.

ænocclxxvii· heri cynepulf ᴣoffa ᴣefuhton ymb beneꝛinᴣ tun ᴣoffa
ᴣenam þone tun· ᴀᴎ·ꝺccl xxxiii ᴀᴎ·ꝺccl xxix
ᴎᴎ·ꝺcclxxv heri ealoꝛexe ᴣffanꝺan ᴣefuhton ·ᴀᴎ·ꝺcclxxvi· ᴎᴎ·ꝺcclx
ᴀᴎ·ꝺcclxxxvi heri cyncheaꝺo offloh cynepulfcinᴣ ᴣheþæþiᴘeanꝺof
ꝼleᴣen· ᴣl xxxvi· manna miꝺhim ᴣþaonfenᴣ þeoþheꝛie
þæꝛꝛexnaþuceꝛ· ᴣheþuxoꝺe·xvi· þinceᴘ ᴣhifliclẟ æꝛþeþham

Old Engl

Chapter 7

PHONEMES

AND

GRAPHEMES

IN ENGLISH

A Look
Back
and
A Look
Forward

In Chapters 2 through 6, you have been reviewing certain standards of usage and
punctuation that are part of effective communication. In Chapter 7, you will reexamine the
relationship between phonemes and graphemes in English. You will also work with those
complications of English that sometimes in-
terfere with accurate spelling, and you will
observe how knowledge of affixation will increase not only your reading and speaking vocabularies but also your spelling skill.

THE RELATIONSHIP BETWEEN PHONEMES
AND GRAPHEMES

By this time you are thoroughly aware that uniform spelling is as important to effective written communication as correct word order and choice of words. You know from your own experience that rapid reading depends to a large extent on the accuracy of what you are reading. If the word *hour* appears as *our,* you must go back to see what is meant, and your reading speed is slowed down.

You are also aware of the fact that standard English is a status symbol in our present-day world. You realize that well-educated people tend to be critical of those who misspell words in their letters, their job applications, their reports, their examinations, and other forms of composition.

Words do not exist on paper only. Since written language starts with the *sounds* of words, it is essential to understand the relationship between those sounds and the written symbols, or letters, which represent the sounds. To increase this understanding is the purpose of this chapter.

The Complications of English Spelling

Nearly every sound in English may be represented in more than one way, and some sounds may be spelled in as many as ten or twelve different ways. The schwa, \ə\, our most common PHONEME, or sound, is a good example. Any of these six vowel GRAPHEMES, or letters, *a, e, i, o, u,* or *y,* or almost any possible combination of them, may represent the schwa phoneme in English words.

The paragraph that follows is from Washington's "Farewell Address to the People of the United States." Read it aloud (or to yourself) and listen for the schwa vowel phoneme, which you hear in both syllables of the word *upper.* Find words in which this phoneme is spelled by the graphemes *a, e, i, o,* and *u.* How many schwa sounds are there altogether in the paragraph?

> The unity of government which constitutes you one people is also now dear to you. It is justly so; for it is a main pillar in the edifice of your real independence, the support of your tranquility at home, your peace abroad; of your safety; of your prosperity; of that very liberty which you so highly prize.

The paragraph above also illustrates the fact that a single grapheme may stand for several different phonemes. One reason this is necessary is that we have many more sounds than we have letters in our alphabet. What eight different sounds or combinations of sounds does the letter *o* spell in these words?

home	pot	women	do
none	woman	song	one

Another problem of English spelling is the presence of silent letters in such words as *glisten* and *Wednesday*. Some of these silent letters are vestiges of former pronunciations. Our spelling has not yet caught up with more recent changes in pronunciation. What letters are silent in *people* and *highly*?

Not all silent *e*'s are useless, however. Notice that silent *e* in *safety*, *prize*, and *home* signals a "long *a, i,* or *o*" sound, the phonemes \ā\, \ī\, or \ō\; and silent *e* in *peace, edifice,* and *independence* signals the "soft *c*" sound, or the phoneme \s\, rather than the "hard *c*," or \k\ phoneme, as in *picnic*.

Exercise 1

For each blank below write the word from the list that best fits the context. Underline the silent letter or letters (one word has three). The compound graphemes ck and tch and vowel combinations such as ay and eu do not include any silent letters. Use your dictionary if necessary.

balk	wrest	blight	knavery	distraught
wry	plight	writhe	rhetoric	rheumatic
caulk	wreak	ghastly	wretched	pseudonym
deign	benign	aplomb	rhapsody	playwright
ghoul	wrack	sleight	mortgage	rhododendron

1. George Gershwin's "_____ in Blue" is a piano concerto which was first performed by the composer himself in 1924.

2. With the greatest _____ the daring freshman approached the popular senior girl and inquired, "Would you _____ to dance with me?"

3. As Jim observed the girl's heavy eye makeup and pale cheeks and lips, he thought, "How _____ and _____ she must feel, to look so _____!"

4. Molière was the _____ of the seventeenth-century French _____ Jean Baptiste Poquelin, whom many critics consider the world's greatest writer of comedies.

5. Sir James Barrie put _____ whimsy into his delightful fantasy *Peter Pan*.

6. The dark deeds of a grave robber, or _____, are one of the worst forms of _____ imaginable.

Exercise 1,
continued

7. The early pioneers found it difficult to ____ a living from the land because of wild animals, insects, ____, and drought.

8. When the villain was ____ed in his plot to foreclose the ____, he lost his ____ expression and began to ____ in confusion.

9. After Edgar had started to ____ the bedroom window, he noticed the ____ of a young robin that had fallen from its nest in the tall ____.

10. On the lonely shore Jerry spied a weather-beaten ____ that appeared to be a hundred years old.

Phonemes, the Basic Units of Sound

Any sound that can make a difference in meaning is a phoneme. What are the consonant phonemes that make the difference in meaning between *bit* and *pit*? What are the vowel phonemes that make *rift* and *raft* different in meaning? If you look up the etymology of *phoneme*, you will see that it is derived from a Greek word meaning "speech sound." A phoneme, according to linguists, is one of the smallest significant units of speech-sound in a language.

All the vowel and consonant sounds are phonemes, and most of them are SIMPLE PHONEMES. A COMPOUND PHONEME, or DIPHTHONG, results from blending two simple phonemes so completely within one syllable that they seem to be only one sound. In English the diphthongs are \aù\ as in *now*, \ī\ as in *high*, and \òi\ as in *point*. By pronouncing these three words slowly to yourself, you can hear the two simple phonemes which are blended to form each compound phoneme. What are they, in each case?

Graphemes, the Basic Units of Writing

You know that the twenty-six letters of the alphabet, which are used to represent the phonemes in writing, are called graphemes. The linguistic term *grapheme* is derived from a Greek word meaning "to write." A grapheme is one of the smallest significant units of written language. Not only the letters of the alphabet, but also the punctuation marks, the figures 0-9, and other written symbols (such as $) are graphemes.

As you read this rhymed epitaph by an unknown author, listen for the simple and compound phonemes:

> Here lie the remains of Christopher Day,
> Who died maintaining his right of way.
> He was right—dead right—as he sped along,
> But he's just as dead as if he'd been wrong.

What compound phoneme, or diphthong, do you hear in three different words in the epitaph?

Now think about the graphemes that stand for the phonemes in the rhyme. A SIMPLE GRAPHEME is a single letter that represents a phoneme, whereas a COMPOUND GRAPHEME is two or more letters representing a phoneme. What simple and compound graphemes stand for the compound phoneme in the first two lines? Which two compound graphemes represent the phoneme \ā\? What compound graphemes stand for the phonemes \k\, \f\, \e\, and \i\? Find two other compound graphemes in the rhyme. Be sure that each combination you find represents a *single* phoneme, not two separate phonemes.

Which two words in the epitaph begin with a silent *w*? Which word contains silent *gh*?

Exercise 2   *After you have read the following anonymous limerick, answer the questions about the phonemes and graphemes in the rhyme.*

"There were two cats of Kilkenny;
Each thought that was one cat too many;
    So they fought and they fit,
    They scratched and they bit,
Till instead of two cats there weren't any."

1. Which two simple graphemes are used to represent the consonant phoneme \k\?

2. What three double letters are compound graphemes?

3. Which other compound grapheme stands for the same phoneme as the double vowel?

4. One compound grapheme of three letters represents the same phoneme as another compound grapheme in the rhyme. What are the two graphemes?

5. What compound grapheme stands for the phoneme \ē\ in one word and \e\ in another?

6. Find the compound grapheme that represents the same phoneme as the first grapheme in *till*.

7. Which compound grapheme stands for two different consonant phonemes in different words?

8. Two compound graphemes represent the vowel phonemes \ä\ and \ȯ\. What are they?

Different Graphemes Representing the Same Phonemes

The PHONEMIC SYMBOLS used in the dictionary to indicate the pronunciation of words have been developed by linguists over a long period of years. Each symbol, as you realize, represents only one simple or compound phoneme, such as \b\ and \òi\. Every language has its own set of phonemes and no two languages have exactly the same set, although many phonemes are used in several languages. For example, French has no phoneme \th\ as English has. The list below includes almost all the common English phonemes, but not those you hear only in foreign words that have not been anglicized.

All the phonemic symbols are alphabetic except for the schwa \ə\ and the \ŋ\. (A superior schwa, as in \'rid-ᵊl\ and \'rid-ᵊn\, indicates the lack of a vowel sound in a syllable containing a syllabic consonant.) Following the symbols are illustrative words which contain most of the simple and compound graphemes that may represent the phonemes.

Pronunciation Symbols*

Vowel Phonemes

\ə\   suppose, alone, hopeless, possible, color, physician, pageant, foreign, sturgeon, parliament, religion, does, tortoise, flood, spacious (See also \ər\.)

\a\   patch, plaid

\ā\   name, paid, gauge, display, croquet, steak, deign, they

\ä\   yacht, knot, sergeant, hearth, bazaar, reservoir

\au̇\   house, allow, sauerkraut (This diphthong is \a\ + \u̇\.)

\e\   whether, anyone, bury, aesthete, said, says, weather, heifer, leopard, friendship

\ē\   complete, gasoline, gaily, steal, sleep, perceive, people, money, achieve, aeon, quay, phoenix

\i\   invent, English, clear, cheer, tier, gym, women, busy, building

\ī\   high, rely, tied, height, buy, lye, eye, kaiser, kayak, coyote (This diphthong is actually \ä\ + \i\.)

\ō\   cone, foam, foe, indoors, shoulder, flown, chauffeur, sewing, bureau, owe

\ò\   tall, astronaut, awful, awe, off, abroad, sought

\òi\   coil, coy (This diphthong is \ò\ + \i\.)

\ü\   flute, stool, crew, maneuver, outdo, canoe, through, pursuit, clue, two, adieu, Sioux (See also \yü\.)

\u̇\   sugar, book, could, wolves, pneumatic (See also \yu\.)

---

* These symbols are used by permission of G. & C. Merriam Company, publishers of the Merriam-Webster dictionaries. For further information, see *Webster's New Students Dictionary,* © 1969 by G. & C. Merriam Company.

Pronunciation Symbols, *continued*

Consonant Phonemes

\b\	rub, rubber
\ch\	which, witch, picture, mansion, suggestion, conscience, conscientious, righteousness (This sound is actually \t\ + \sh\.)
\d\	mud, muddy, rolled
\f\	if, stiff, grapheme, tough
\g\	fog, foggy, guide (See also \gz\.)
\h\	ahead (See also \hw\.)
\j\	jewel, gypsy, exaggerate, gradual, ledge, soldier, adjoin (This sound is actually \d\ + \zh\.)
\k\	look, fact, luck, scheme, accuse, quite, physique, acquit, excellent (See also \ks\.)
\l\	talent, willing
\m\	swim, swimmer
\n\	fun, funny
\ŋ\	thing, think
\p\	zip, zipper
\r\	river, errand
\s\	mistake, miss, face, science, quartz (See also \ks\.)
\sh\	wish, relation, chivalry, delicious, ocean, surely, omniscient, session, repulsion, assure, nauseous, anxious, schwa
\t\	mat, matter, slipped
\th\	wreath
\th̲\	wreathed
\v\	sliver, flivver, of
\w\	aware, acquire, choir (See also \hw\.)
\y\	yesterday, opinion (See also \yü\, \yu̇\, \yə\.)
\z\	wizard, sizzle, rise, scissors, anxiety (See also \gz\.)
\zh\	collision, leisure, azure, rouge

Special Phonemic Combinations

\ər\	perplex, early, chauffeur, circle, shirr, work, worried, courage, curl, hurry, myrtle, myrrh
\gz\	exact
\hw\	whale
\ks\	exercise
\yü\	human, mew, ewe, beauteous, eulogy, queue, imbue
\yu̇\	curious, European
\yə\	reputation

How Graphemic Word Lists Aid in Spelling

A study of the foregoing chart of English phonemes, together with their variant graphemes, will reveal that there is a very definite relationship between sound and spelling. It is fortunate that this relationship exists, since otherwise each word would be a unique problem, as is the case in Chinese and Japanese.

One excellent method of improving your spelling power and skills is to evolve your own lists of words that employ the same grapheme to represent the same phoneme. Will all this work be worth the time it takes? Here are some benefits of such a project:

1. You will unconsciously be mastering the English phonemes, their different graphemes, and the relationship between them.
2. You will become more sensitive to the sounds of words (for example, to the \ch\ sound in *mention* versus the \sh\ sound in *action*).
3. You will learn to associate many words that have the same spelling of the same sound.
4. You will become familiar with the spelling, pronunciation, and meaning of a number of words you could not spell or seldom used before. In other words, your speaking and writing vocabularies will be increased.

You will discover, in compiling your lists, that for some phonemes there is one dominant grapheme, and for some graphemes you can find only one or two illustrations. The \v\ phoneme, for instance, is almost always spelled *v*. You may not find any common examples of *vv* and *f* aside from *flivver* and *of*.

It might help you, before you start, to consider some illustrations of the phonemic combination \yü\, spelled without the letter *y* or *i*. None of the words such as *new*, which are pronounced with or without the \y\ sound, will be listed.

u		*ew*	*eu*	*eau*
use	commute	few	eucalyptus	beauteous
fuse	compute	hew	eulogize	beautician
music	refute	mew	eulogy	beautiful
abuse	utilize	pew	euphemism	beautify
accuse	fume	skew	euphony	beauty
amuse	perfume	askew	euthanasia	
confuse	human	hewn	feud	
excuse	mule	mewl	feudal	*ue*
profuse	molecule	pewter		cue
fusion	union			hue
usual	universe			imbue
rebuke	commune			fuel
cute	impugn			refuel

In order to complete your graphemic lists for the various phonemes, you can look for appropriate words in the books you read, in newspapers and magazines, in your studying, and in the dictionary. Include some unfamiliar words, remembering to check both pronunciation and spelling with the dictionary unless you are certain of them. You may be surprised at the pronunciation of some very familiar words. Word lists could be posted on the bulletin board and new words added from day to day.

Exercise 3   *Begin by listing five or more words that illustrate each of the following graphemes:*

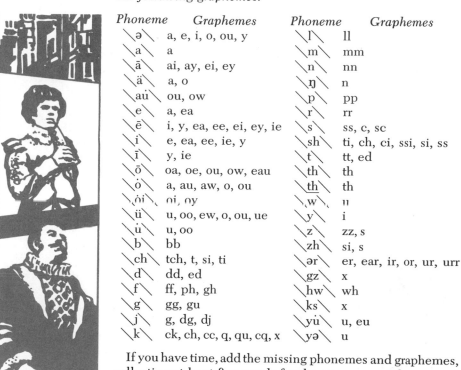

Phoneme	Graphemes	Phoneme	Graphemes
\ə\	a, e, i, o, ou, y	\l\	ll
\a\	a	\m\	mm
\ā\	ai, ay, ei, ey	\n\	nn
\ä\	a, o	\ŋ\	n
\au̇\	ou, ow	\p\	pp
\e\	a, ea	\r\	rr
\ē\	i, y, ea, ee, ei, ey, ie	\s\	ss, c, sc
\i\	e, ea, ee, ie, y	\sh\	ti, ch, ci, ssi, si, ss
\ī\	y, ie	\t\	tt, ed
\ō\	oa, oe, ou, ow, eau	\th\	th
\ȯ\	a, au, aw, o, ou	\t͟h\	th
\ȯi\	oi, oy	\w\	u
\ü\	u, oo, ew, o, ou, ue	\y\	i
\u̇\	u, oo	\z\	zz, s
\b\	bb	\zh\	si, s
\ch\	tch, t, si, ti	\ər\	er, ear, ir, or, ur, urr
\d\	dd, ed	\gz\	x
\f\	ff, ph, gh	\hw\	wh
\g\	gg, gu	\ks\	x
\j\	g, dg, dj	\yü\	u, eu
\k\	ck, ch, cc, q, qu, cq, x	\yə\	u

If you have time, add the missing phonemes and graphemes, collecting at least five words for the common graphemes and as many words as possible for the uncommon ones.

Phonemic Transcriptions

You have had so much experience in using the dictionary that you are undoubtedly familiar with the phonemic transcriptions, or respellings, which show the pronunciation of words within the diagonals. You under-

stand the use of hyphens to separate the spoken syllables, of high and
low accent marks to signal primary and secondary stress, and of parentheses to indicate a stress mark or a phoneme that is optional in the
pronunciation. You realize that many words have variant spellings, as
well as variant pronunciations.

Exercise 4   *Using your knowledge of silent letters and of the relation*
                    between phonemes and graphemes, write the accepted spell-
                    ing or spellings for the phonemic transcriptions that follow.
                    The number (2) refers to variant spellings. Check each word
                    with the dictionary and be sure you know its meaning.

\'nēl\   \'är-kən-ˌsȯ\
\'siv\   \'kü-gər, -ˌgär\
\'rōg\   \'kər-ē,'kə-rē\
\'təŋ\   \'bər-ō, 'bə-rō\
\'lərch\   \'sər-ē, 'sə-rē\
\'plāg\   \'hik-(ˌ)-əp\(2)
\'lāth\   \pər-'sep-shən\
\'trȯf\   \'jəj-mənt\(2)
\'aj-əl\   \ri-'vəl-shən\
\'kȯi-lē\   \dis-'en-chən\
\'nək-əl\   \es-'thet-ik\(2)
\'fäd-ər\   \prə-'pəl-shən\
\'kəj-əl\   \sə-'sep-tə-bəl\
\'sham-ē\   \'brōch, 'brüch\
\ri-'sēt\   \kə-'net-i-kət\
\'raŋ-gəl\   \mi-'kan-i-kəl\
\an-'tēk\   \sə-'lil-ə-kwē\
\'präf-ər\   \'rü-mə-ˌtiz-əm\
\'kərd-ᵊl\   \jim-'nā-zē-əm\
\sha-'tō\   \sə-'me-tri-kəl\
\'pī-ˌrīt\   \'plā-jə-ˌriz-əm\
\'bȯl-yən\   \'fla(ə)r, 'fle(ə)r\
\'trü-ˌsō\   \ig-'zek-(y)ət-iv\
\'pȯr-pəs\   \'slü, 'slaȯ, 'sləf\
\'bas-chən\   \mə-'lek-yə-lər\
\dī-'net\   \n(y)ȯ-'män-ik\
\pər-'sēv\   \rī-'näs-(ə-)rəs\
\'hōl-ˌsāl\   \ˌak-wə-'zish-ən\
\'kris-chən\   \və-'vā-shəs, vī-\
\'frak-shəs\   \ō-'blēk, ə-, -'blīk\

Exercise 4,
continued

\\'kərt-ē-əs\\
\\'fyü-zhən\\
\\ri-'zaŭnd\\
\\shə-'grin\\
\\ˌsil-ə-'wet\\
\\'bräŋ-kē-əl\\
\\bō-'kä, bü-\\
\\'plät, 'plat\\
\\'bräk-(ə-)lē\\
\\'zī-lə-ˌfōn\\
\\'səl-fər\\(2)
\\di-'sizh-ən\\
\\'jep-ər-ˌdīz\\
\\'tran-chənt\\
\\rō-'dī-lənd\\
\\'sint-ºl-ˌāt\\
\\pər-'nish-əs\\

\\ˌpər-myu̇-'tā-shən\\
\\'sō-bri-ˌkä, -ˌket\\
\\'pyu̇(-ə)r-əl, -ˌīl\\
\\'myü-chə-wəl, -chəl\\
\\ˌfär-mə-'süt-i-kəl\\
\\ˌsī-kō-ə-'nal-ə-səs\\
\\'käz-mə-ˌnȯt, -ˌnät\\
\\sə-'kī-ə-trəst, sī-\\
\\'klōr-ˌēn, 'klor-, -ən\\
\\'prēsh-(ē-)ən(t)s,
'presh-\\
\\'än-(ə-)rə-bəl,
'än-ər-bəl\\
\\'sər-ə-ˌgät,
'sə-rə-, -gət\\
\\ˌres-tə-rə-'tər,
-ˌrän-\\(2)

SPECIAL PROBLEMS IN SPELLING

The word lists presented in this section may or may not contain words you need to study. If you are already an accurate speller, you can prove it by your success in a series of pretests in which the words of each list are dictated in context. If, however, you encounter words of which you are not certain, you will want to employ the most efficient method for mastering them before a final test is given. Either a notebook or 3 x 5 cards will be useful, but whichever way you record your words, be sure of their pronunciation and meaning before you learn to spell them. Here are some suggestions:

1. Carefully write or print each word on a card and add a definition or a meaningful sentence containing the word. On the other side of the card copy the phonemic transcription. (In the case of homonyms, add a sentence with a blank for the word.) Carry your cards with you, and whenever you have a chance, practice spelling each word from its pronunciation, checking yourself by turning the card over.

2. Select a partner and study your words together, dictating them to each other in context. Test each other until both of you have mastered your own words.

3. Use your words whenever possible in your compositions or other written work, being careful to spell them correctly every time.

4. Study in a similar way any other words you need to learn that do not appear on the lists in this section.

Words Frequently Misspelled

In written work the majority of students misspell the common words more often than the less common ones. Words like *doesn't, you're, believe, receive,* and *separate* are among the most frequently misspelled words in the language. This first list consists of 120 such words, gleaned from students' compositions.

accommodate	custom	knowledge	racial
ache	dangerous	librarian	realize
acquainted	dealt	magazine	receive
across	decided	marriage	religious
address	decision	meant	ridiculous
all right	definite	missile	roommate
almost	disappoint	misspelled	satisfied
although	disease	mortgage	sense
analyze	divine	muscle	separate
answer	doctrine	naturally	since
arctic	doesn't	Negroes	sincerely
assist	echoes	niece	stomach
athlete	embarrass	ninety	stopped
attempt	enemies	obey	stretched
attitude	equipped	occurred	studying
beginning	especially	odor	succeed
belief	extremely	opinion	successful
believe	finally	opportunity	tendency
bus	foreign	opposite	themselves
business	forfeit	optimistic	therefore
cafeteria	generally	origin	thirties
captain	grieve	paid	thought
ceiling	guarantee	perform	together
cocoa	handkerchief	picnic	tragedy
committee	height	picnicked	truly
conscious	heroes	possess	until
considered	hypocrite	privilege	usually
control	immediately	proceed	weight
courageous	interest	pronunciation	writing
criticize	interpret	pursue	you're

Exercise 5   For each blank in the sentences below write the word from the preceding list that best fits the context.

1. One day last summer we drove into the White Mountains and ___ in the woods near Hegler Creek.

Exercise 5,
continued

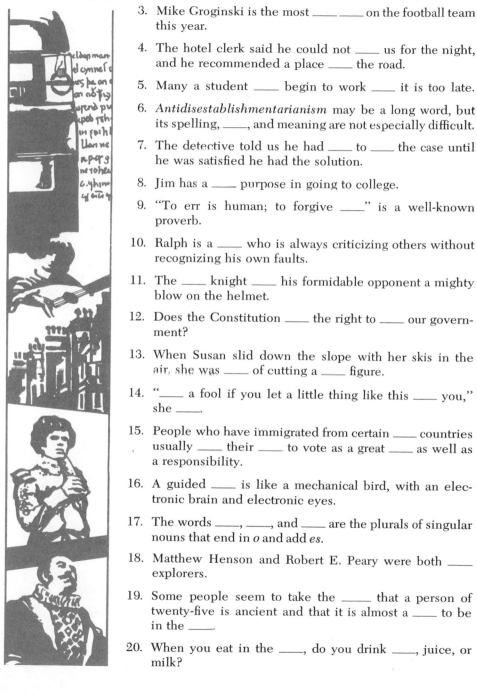

2. Yesterday on the subway, an old man sneezed five times before he took out his ____.

3. Mike Groginski is the most ____ ____ on the football team this year.

4. The hotel clerk said he could not ____ us for the night, and he recommended a place ____ the road.

5. Many a student ____ begin to work ____ it is too late.

6. *Antidisestablishmentarianism* may be a long word, but its spelling, ____, and meaning are not especially difficult.

7. The detective told us he had ____ to ____ the case until he was satisfied he had the solution.

8. Jim has a ____ purpose in going to college.

9. "To err is human; to forgive ____" is a well-known proverb.

10. Ralph is a ____ who is always criticizing others without recognizing his own faults.

11. The ____ knight ____ his formidable opponent a mighty blow on the helmet.

12. Does the Constitution ____ the right to ____ our government?

13. When Susan slid down the slope with her skis in the air, she was ____ of cutting a ____ figure.

14. "____ a fool if you let a little thing like this ____ you," she ____.

15. People who have immigrated from certain ____ countries usually ____ their ____ to vote as a great ____ as well as a responsibility.

16. A guided ____ is like a mechanical bird, with an electronic brain and electronic eyes.

17. The words ____, ____, and ____ are the plurals of singular nouns that end in *o* and add *es*.

18. Matthew Henson and Robert E. Peary were both ____ explorers.

19. Some people seem to take the ____ that a person of twenty-five is ancient and that it is almost a ____ to be in the ____.

20. When you eat in the ____, do you drink ____, juice, or milk?

Words Ending in -able and -ible

Such words as *creditable* and *credible, acceptable* and *accessible* are often confusing because the grapheme *a* or *i* represents the unaccented schwa phoneme no matter which way it is spelled. Listed below are some examples of words with the suffixes *-able* and *-ible*, both of which may have the same meaning. You will be able to gather many more such words from your reading and listening and thus to develop your vocabulary still further. The class may wish to compile additional lists and make them available to each student.

Any words you need to learn should be studied in separate groups so that you will associate the words that have the same endings. Since there are comparatively few *-ible* words, it might pay you to master those first, using the study methods outlined at the beginning of this section, or your own best method.

acceptable	desirable	manageable	reasonable
admirable	durable	miserable	receivable
advisable	enjoyable	movable	recognizable
agreeable	flammable	notable	reliable
available	formidable	noticeable	removable
avoidable	indefinable	pardonable	replaceable
believable	indispensable	payable	respectable
breakable	inevitable	peaceable	sal(e)able
capable	intolerable	perishable	serviceable
changeable	justifiable	preferable	taxable
charitable	laughable	probable	understandable
comfortable	liable	profitable	usable
conceivable	likable	pronounceable	valuable
creditable	lovable	readable	vegetable
accessible	eligible	irresistible	reversible
audible	illegible	legible	sensible
collectible	incredible	permissible	susceptible
contemptible	indefensible	possible	terrible
credible	indestructible	responsible	visible

Exercise 6   *Write the word from the preceding lists (-able and -ible) which most appropriately fills each blank below.*

1. On the back of the gasoline truck was the warning, "____."

2. From our position along the parade line, the band was ____, but the majorettes were not ____.

Exercise 6,
continued

3. Benjamin Banneker believed slavery to be ____ and wrote of his feelings to the President, Thomas Jefferson.

4. Most accidents are ____; very few are ____.

5. Marianne has so much makeup on she is hardly ____.

6. The letters in the word *rotor* are ____.

7. We thought the old brick apartment house was ____, until it was burned down.

8. When Joan tried to buy a platter to replace the one she broke, she found that the pattern was no longer ____.

9. What average do you have to have to be ____ for the football team?

10. When Jake tried to get $100 for his sixteen-year-old jalopy, he discovered it was not ____ at any price.

Words Ending in -ant *and* -ance, -ent *and* -ence

What is your method of remembering whether words like *defendant* and *dependent, resistance* and *persistence* spell the unaccented \ə\ phoneme with the *a* or the *e* grapheme? If you have a good method, you would do your classmates a favor by sharing it with them. People who visualize such words are usually at an advantage over those who do not visualize them.

Find out which, if any, of the following words you need to study, and learn them in separate groups, as you did the *-able* and *-ible* words. Be sure you know the pronunciation and meaning of each word. You can probably add a good many useful words to these lists if you look for them.

abundant	distant	lieutenant	restaurant
assistant	dominant	pleasant	servant
attendant	extravagant	redundant	significant
consonant	ignorant	relevant	tolerant
contestant	important	reliant	vigilant
defendant	incessant	resistant	warrant

abundance	attendance	extravagance	relevance
acceptance	balance	guidance	reliance
accordance	brilliance	hindrance	remittance
admittance	conveyance	ignorance	resemblance

allowance	distance	importance	resistance
annoyance	disturbance	maintenance	significance
appearance	dominance	nuisance	substance
assistance	endurance	performance	tolerance
assurance	entrance	protuberance	vigilance

ancient	different	opponent	resilient
antecedent	efficient	patient	reverent
apparent	eminent	permanent	silent
confident	equivalent	persistent	student
consistent	evident	prevalent	sufficient
convenient	excellent	proficient	superintendent
correspondent	intelligent	prominent	talent
current	magnificent	recent	translucent
decent	obedient	resident	transparent

absence	difference	magnificence	prominence
audience	eminence	obedience	reference
conference	evidence	occurrence	residence
confidence	excellence	patience	resilience
confluence	existence	permanence	reverence
conscience	experience	persistence	science
convenience	influence	preference	sentence
correspondence	intelligence	presence	silence

Exercise 7   *Use each of these words in an interesting sentence which shows that you understand the meaning of the word:*

eminent	relevance	tolerance	protuberance
warrant	incessant	prominent	antecedent
vigilance	confluence	dominance	maintenance
prevalent	redundant	translucent	permanence
defendant	resilience	conveyance	extravagant

Words Ending in -ar, -er, *and* -or

The following lists present the same type of spelling problem as the *-ant* and *-ent* words, except that there are three possible endings, all of which sound alike because of the unaccented schwa phoneme. Only by visualization or by sheer memorization can you distinguish between the *-ar, -er,* and *-or* in such words as *beggar* and *trigger, debater* and *operator, treasurer* and *juror*. These lists are but a sample of the numerous words you can glean from your reading and listening. When you have discovered which ones, if any, you need to concentrate upon, study them in three groups.

beggar	dollar	nuclear	scholar
burglar	familiar	particular	similar
calendar	grammar	peculiar	singular
circular	liar	popular	spectacular
curricular	molecular	regular	vinegar

announcer	dealer	laughter	remainder
carpenter	debater	lawyer	reporter
charter	designer	miner	soldier
container	employer	officer	timber
customer	explorer	recorder	treasurer
cylinder	fever	register	trigger

actor	conqueror	instructor	radiator
aggressor	debtor	interior	refrigerator
ambassador	dictator	janitor	sailor
ancestor	director	junior	senator
anchor	distributor	juror	senior
auditor	doctor	labor	sponsor
author	editor	legislator	superior
aviator	elevator	major	survivor
bachelor	factor	minor	tailor
behavior	favor	mirror	terror
carburetor	flavor	motor	tractor
collector	generator	odor	vapor
color	governor	operator	victor
competitor	harbor	professor	visitor

Exercise 8   Write the accepted spelling for each of these phonemic transcriptions:

\\'kəl-ər\\   \\ə-'gres-ər\\   \\'lej-ə-ˌslāt-ər\\
\\'laf-tər\\   \\fə-'mil-yər\\   \\'kär-b(y)ə-ˌrāt-ər\\
\\'skäl-ər\\   \\sər-'vī-vər\\   \\am-'bas-əd-ər\\
\\'sim-ə-lər\\   \\'sərk-yə-lər\\   \\kə-'rik-yə-lər\\
\\'gram-ər\\   \\'kaŋ-kər-ər\\   \\mə-'lek-yə-lər\\
\\'ȯd-ət-ər\\   \\prə-'fes-ər\\   \\spek-'tak-yə-lər\\
\\'sil-ən-dər\\   \\'jen-ə-ˌrāt-ər\\   \\ri-'frij-ə-ˌrāt-ər\\

Words Ending in -al, -el, and -le

Are you always sure of whether words ending with the syllabic *l* phoneme \\-ᵊl\\ or with an unaccented schwa and *l* \\-əl\\ are spelled with -*al*, -*el*, -*le*, or in some other way? The three groups of words below contain some of these words that you should know how to spell. You

can find many more if you look for them, as well as similar words end-
ing in *-il* (*pencil*), *-ile* (*facile*), *-ol* (*capitol*), and so forth. If you need to
study any of these words, learn them in groups, as you have done
previously.

actual	dismissal	internal	musical	rival
annual	economical	journal	mutual	royal
approval	electrical	legal	neutral	rural
arrival	equal	liberal	numeral	serial
bridal	fatal	local	oral	signal
capital	federal	loyal	original	skeptical
cardinal	festival	manual	ornamental	spiral
carnival	feudal	material	physical	spiritual
cereal	final	mechanical	plural	technical
chemical	formal	medal	political	terminal
continual	fundamental	medical	principal	tribal
corporal	historical	mental	removal	tropical
criminal	hospital	metal	renewal	universal
critical	individual	moral	reversal	usual

angel	chisel	funnel	marvel	shovel
apparel	colonel	gavel	model	squirrel
barrel	counsel	gravel	nickel	tinsel
bushel	cruel	kennel	panel	towel
cancel	cudgel	label	parcel	travel
channel	enamel	laurel	quarrel	tunnel
chapel	fuel	libel	sequel	vowel

ample	buckle	idle	saddle	tackle
angle	bugle	jungle	sample	temple
ankle	cable	kettle	simple	title
article	castle	knuckle	single	tremble
assemble	cattle	meddle	sparkle	tumble
battle	eagle	mettle	stable	turtle
bicycle	feeble	principle	startle	uncle
bottle	handle	resemble	struggle	whistle
bridle	humble	rifle	table	wrestle

Exercise 9   *Write the correct spelling for each transcribed word in
these sentences:*

1. My mother is very \\'skep-ti-kəl\\ about Gordon's story
of how he wrecked the new car.

Exercise 9,
continued

2. Did you ever try to read an \'ärt-i-kəl\ in a \'tek-ni-kəl\ \'jərn-ᵊl\ and wonder what it was all about?

3. If you publish something injurious to another person's reputation, you are \'lī-ə-bəl\ to be sued for \'lī-bəl\.

4. A person who \'chiz-əlz\ in an exam is violating the \'mòr-əl\ \'print-sə-pəl\ of honesty.

5. The \'kərn-əl\ \'mär-vəld\ at the spirited manner in which the old \'sad-ᵊl\ horse \'trav-əld\ down the \'brīd-ᵊl\ path.

6. As Jimmy \'res-əld\ with his \'rī-vəl\, he was thrown to the ground and his \'nək-əlz\ were slightly injured by the \'grav-əl\.

7. The Golden Gate acts as a \'fən-ᵊl\ for the cool air coming in from the Pacific.

8. "Haven't you heard that it's a \'kap-ət-ᵊl\ offense to walk on the grass?" asked the good-natured bobby of the American tourist. "Do you want to be shot as a \'krim-ən-ᵊl\ at sunrise?"

9. The \'kòr-pə-rəl\ proved his \'met-ᵊl\ in his first \'bat-ᵊl\ and was presented with a \'med-ᵊl\ for his courage.

10. "Be an \'ān-jəl\," said the youthful patient to the \'häs-ˌpit-ᵊl\ assistant, "and bring me something that tastes less like \'ken-ᵊl\ rations than this \'ē-vəl\-tasting \'sir-ē-əl\."

Homonyms and Other Words Often Confused

The final word list in this section includes homonyms (words that have the same phonemic transcription but are spelled differently, such as *ceiling* and *sealing*) and words that are similar, but not the same, in sound or spelling (such as *angel* and *angle*). The meanings are different in either case. Though you can probably distinguish between most of these pairs or groups of words already, there may be a few you will need to study further, using the methods you have found to be most efficient.

accent	breath	device	practicable
ascent	breathe	devise	practical
assent			

accept	censor	died	quiet
except	censure	dyed	quite
access	charted	eminent	respectfully
excess	chartered	imminent	respectively
advice	choose	hoard	shear
advise	chose	horde	sheer
affect	cite	ingenious	suit
effect	sight	ingenuous	suite
	site		
aisle		its	their
isle	coarse	it's	there
	course		they're
all ready		loose	
already	contemptible	lose	thorough
	contemptuous		through
all together		mantel	
altogether	decent	mantle	to
	descent		too
alumna		moral	two
alumnus	desert	morale	
	dessert		weather
alumnae		personal	whether
alumni	detract	personnel	
	distract		who's
			whose

Exercise 10

For each blank in these sentences write the word from the preceding list (or a form of it) which best fits the context.

1. If the ____ does not improve, we will have to postpone the field trip until next week.

2. The committee has visited several hotels in an effort to ____ a ____ for the spring dance.

3. Most people do not think a French ____ will ____ from one's ability to speak English.

4. All the women ____ of the high school have been asked to help serve at the reunion dinner, but the ____ men will have no work to do.

5. The whole world watched the ____ of Apollo with interest, but its ____ was less widely seen.

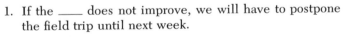

Exercise 10,
continued

6. His brother was _____ on the first string team when he was a freshman.

7. Father rented a _____ of rooms on the fifth floor of the Third Avenue Hotel.

8. The doctor ordered Uncle Ted to have a _____ physical checkup.

9. Betty and Jane were _____ to start their hike when it began to rain. They were glad they were not _____ on their way.

10. This trap is a very _____ _____ for catching mice.

11. The _____ of the company was excellent as it moved toward the fighting area.

12. The football team and the band rode to the game in _____ buses.

13. Black clouds and heavy gusts of wind warned us that a severe storm was _____.

14. The honey you spilled on the steps has attracted _____ of insects.

15. When a person has bronchitis, _____ difficult for him to _____.

16. Nearly everybody likes ice cream for _____.

17. The _____ this summer has been very hot and humid.

18. "_____ afraid of the big bad wolf?"

19. The _____-looking woman was a _____ to behold with her hair _____ a vivid red.

20. I don't know _____ or not I'll be able to go to that seven-_____ dinner on Friday night.

Affixation

Affixation, or attaching prefixes and suffixes to base words, is one of the main sources of enrichment in the English language. Although suffixes sometimes present a spelling problem (as indicated in several of the preceding sections), prefixes seldom do. However, when you learn to build other words from words you already know, you not only increase your reading and speaking vocabularies you also increase your spelling vocabulary. Note, for example, the derivatives on the next page made from the simple word *act*.

actability	acts	inactivation	reactionally
actable	coaction	inactive	reactionary
acted	counteract	inactively	reactor
acting	counteraction	inactivity	retroactive
action	counteractive	interact	retroactively
actionable	deactivate	interaction	retroactivity
activate	deactivation	interactional	self-acting
activation	deactivator	overact	self-action
active	enact	overaction	self-active
actively	enactment	overactive	self-activity
activity	enactor	react	transact
actor	inaction	reaction	transaction
actress	inactivate	reactional	transactor

Exercise 11   *Using other simple words such as* arm, like, man, move, pay, play, *and* work, *develop a list similar to the one given above for* act. *Be sure that the derivatives in any one list are derived from the same etymological root.* Dislike *and* unlike, *for example, are derived from different roots.*

Exercise 12   *For twenty-five or more of the prefixes and combining forms listed in* The Language of Grammar *under the heading* Prefixes and Combining Forms, *find at least two examples for each affix listed. Correctly write (1) each word you select, (2) the prefix and its meaning in that particular word, (3) the meaning of the root, (4) the meaning of the derivative, and (5) an interesting sentence that illustrates the meaning of the word.*

Summary   Because accurate spelling is essential to written communication and is also a symbol of education, it is important to understand the relationship between English phonemes and graphemes. Spelling problems arise from the fact that most phonemes may be represented by various graphemes; that a single grapheme may stand for several different phonemes; and that many words contain silent letters.

Summary,
continued

A phoneme is one of the smallest significant units of sound in speech. All the vowel and consonant sounds are simple phonemes except for the diphthongs \au̇\, \ī\, and \ȯi\, which are compound phonemes. Significant units of written language are called graphemes. A single letter that represents a phoneme is a simple grapheme, whereas two or more letters representing one phoneme, such as *ch* or *ai*, constitute a compound grapheme.

The pronunciation symbols listed on pages 168-169 serve to represent the vowel and consonant sounds in the phonemic transcriptions given in the dictionary. Developing graphemic word lists will help you master the various phonemes, together with their variant graphemes, and also increase your vocabulary and spelling power.

Pretests of the special lists provided in the second section of this chapter will reveal which words, if any, you need to learn to spell, as well as to pronounce and to use correctly in context. The suggested study methods may be applied to all of the lists and to any other words you need to master.

The first list comprises 120 common words that students often misspell in their written work. The lists of words ending in *-able* and *-ible, -ant* and *-ent, -ance* and *-ence, -ar, -er,* and *-or, -al, -el,* and *-le,* are apt to be confusing because of their unstressed schwa phonemes or syllabic consonants. They should be studied in groups in order to associate the words that end in the same way. The final list contains homonyms and other words that must be distinguished from each other in meaning before they can be mastered.

PART II

Composition

In the second part of this book, you will study the important area of critical thinking, with its implications for the writer. The chapter on the précis considers the techniques of summary writing as preparation for research, for note taking, and for paraphrasing. A detailed development of the library research process and of reporting research naturally follows; it will prove of great value to you as a study technique. Creative writing will be a new challenge for all, especially those who are original and imaginative. Finally, you will examine the problems involved in revision and rewriting and work with the solutions to those problems.

The theme of language communities and their writing systems is continued through the photographs in Part II. With your teacher's help, you will want to discuss the advantages of an alphabet, a syllabary, or an ideographic writing system for a particular language.

Japanese

Chapter 1

CRITICAL
THINKING

にさらに「敵も持たない」という言葉がつけ加えられる場合も多いが。

バランスのとれた人物

今世紀のはじめ、ジョセフ・ピューリツァーは、彼の新聞『ニューヨーク・ワールド』の編集者を探していた。彼は、デトロイトの『フリー・プレス』のフランク・I・コッブを推薦してきた友人に電報を送り、その中で、そのポストに必要な資質について説明している。いまから見れば古くさい言い方ながら、彼は、その中で、「コッブはアメリカ史では何を読んだか。らみれば古くさい言い方ながら、彼は、その中で、「コッブはアメリカ史では何を読んだか。憲法や成定法についてはどのような本を読んだか。彼はブックルの『文明史』を読んだこと……憲法や成定法についてはどのような本を読んだか。彼はブックルの『文明史』を読んだこととがあるか。彼の健康状態はどうか。彼の身長は。声は不快な声かそれとも気持ちのよい声であるか。……彼をディナーにつれていって、テーブル・マナー（食事作法）を観察してくれ。

A Look Back and A Look Forward

In Part I you reviewed basic grammar in the study of the English sentence, in considering how words communicate, and in punctuation. You acquired a more sophisticated approach to grammar through the brief history of grammar, the problems of usage, and the skills involved in putting grammar to work in actual writing situations.

As a prelude to your work on composition in Part II, the following chapter will help you develop the ability to think critically, an ability which is essential to good writing.

189

WRITING WITH CLARITY AND CONVICTION

To write with clarity and conviction, you must choose words that mean precisely what you have in mind. You must explain and define terms for your reader so that he cannot possibly misinterpret your meaning. Then you must be consistent in maintaining the interpretation you have given your terms.

A statement that involves judgment or opinion has little value if it is not supported by evidence. Someone who writes that Joe Namath was the best quarterback that football ever produced is making an assertion that cannot be proved. The reader may dismiss the statement or even resent it. When the advertiser makes the claim that a particular toothpaste prevents decay, his statement has no validity whatever unless accompanied by evidence sufficient to prove it.

However, care must be exercised in the selection of supporting evidence. Suppose a writer states that most teen-agers who find themselves in trouble with the law come from poor families, and then tries to support his assertion by referring to just one magazine article or by offering figures based on local situations. Won't he be open to criticism for using inadequate evidence? The advertiser who claims the superiority of a hair tonic on the basis of its use by noted athletes is even more blameworthy since his claim is deliberate and his motives clear.

Critical thinking is an important asset to the careful, mature writer. Not only does it involve the definition of terms and the limitation of their meanings, but it includes the support of assertions with valid evidence, the intelligent use of generalizations, skill in problem solving, and the recognition and avoidance of fallacies in reasoning. In this chapter you will discuss some of these concepts.

DEFINING TERMS EXACTLY

A careful definition of terms enables the writer to think clearly about the words he is using, to say precisely what he means, and to limit this meaning throughout his discussion. For example, one student wrote the following as the opening sentence in a theme about Emerson:

> Emerson said that to be great, a man must be a nonconformist.

The first problem of this writer was to determine what Emerson meant by *nonconformist*. He should then have explained the meaning in his theme. Having the meaning clearly in mind would have been helpful both to him and to his readers. This particular writer, however, failed to define the term, perhaps assuming that everyone would understand its meaning. The result was a vague and inconclusive theme.

Since written composition is a form of communication, the definition and the explanation of terms will help the reader to know exactly what the writer has in mind. It must be remembered that abstract words have many meanings. The writer who defines and limits the meaning of his terms is helping his reader to understand what he wants to convey. Suppose a student has used the term *pessimistic* to describe the attitude and outlook of Edgar Allan Poe in his poetry. He should then go on to explain that Poe was unduly preoccupied with the theme of death. He would thus help his reader to understand the attitude of the poet and the point of view of the writer.

These excerpts from student themes illustrate situations that need definition and explanation of terms:

1.

Attaining the greatest amount of equality is based primarily upon place of birth. This can be shown in the way the people of a region achieve their goals in relation to their ability.

2.

In Hawthorne's works we feel his intense belief in the presence of sin and evil in man. In a sense, Hawthorne was somewhat of a pessimist in that he saw only evil in people and completely overlooked goodness and creativity.

3.

By now, you have probably discovered that I am an atheist. I am not ashamed of it. In this great country of ours, there is supposed to be religious freedom. It seems to me that if a person has the right to believe in the religion of his choice, then he should have the right not to believe in a religion.

The first is an example of "fuzzy" writing. The statement is at a high level of generalization with such abstract terms as *equality, goals,* and *ability.* Not only does the student have a responsibility for explaining and illustrating what he means by these words, but he has to reduce the whole idea to a level of experience that will be meaningful to his readers. Frequently a student will let such a statement speak for itself and go on with his other universal concepts. There is enough in the original statements for pages of elaboration. As a matter of fact, the statements are so vague as to be almost meaningless.

In the second illustration, the student has two problems. She uses the terms *sin, evil, pessimist, goodness,* and *creativity* in a very glib manner, as if the words were sufficient unto themselves. Not only should she define these terms with reference to Hawthorne's works, she should also produce evidence in support of her assertions. If she were to examine the character of Hester Prynne in Hawthorne's *The Scarlet Letter,* for example, she might have difficulty proving her assertion.

The third writer assumes a universal understanding of such terms as *atheist* and *religious freedom*. Not only is *his* thinking somewhat confused but also that of the reader. The logic of the conclusion is somewhat questionable. This student would have helped himself a great deal by a preliminary examination of his terms and an attempt to limit their meanings. He might even have attempted to clarify his own thinking by some outside reading on the subject. In so doing, a student sometimes learns that he isn't at all prepared to write on a given subject. While he may be familiar with the sound of a word, he does not understand its meaning and implications.

The definition of terms involves some difficulties. The first obligation is to designate the object or concept being defined as belonging to a class. For example, suppose a student explained *joyriding* in these words:

> Joyriding is when people drive recklessly.

This writer has not fulfilled the first requirement of definition. He has not classified his concept. Since the term is a noun, he should use a noun in his definition:

> Joyriding is a pleasure trip often marked by reckless driving.

Again using the proper classification, a student might define *pessimism*:

> Pessimism is a belief that evil is more common than good.

The terms used in these definitions are familiar and need not be reduced to a lower level of generalization. Suppose, however, that the word *penchant* were defined as "a propensity." The word *propensity* would then have to be reduced to "a strong leaning."

A good definition limits the area of meaning attached to the word being explained. Suppose a student wishes to report on a certain author's style. He cannot use the term *style* loosely and expect his readers to understand what he means by it. He might explain it something like this:

> In literature, style is the characteristic manner in which a writer expresses himself. One author's writing is always clear and forceful, free of unnecessary clutter. Another writes in a free-flowing, graceful manner, easily recognizable to those familiar with his works. As we read, we associate a writer with his style, just as we associate a definite personality with each of our acquaintances.

To summarize, a definition should include a classification for the object or idea, it should exclude terms that need to be explained, and it should limit the meaning to an understanding of exactly what is included. A definition of the term *university* illustrates this point:

> A university is an institution of higher learning that provides opportunities for teaching and research. It has an undergraduate division, which includes various departments such as liberal arts, business, and engineering, and a graduate division, which includes professional schools such as law and medicine.

A careful examination of words and their meanings with an attempt to define and explain them is an important aspect of critical thinking. It helps the writer to understand clearly what he is trying to communicate and to express his ideas so that his readers will understand him. It helps to eliminate one of the worst faults of the beginning writer — the careless and unthinking use of words with resulting vagueness.

Exercise 1

Develop short paragraphs in which you define and explain the meanings of these terms:

public school	motel	novelist
grammar	teacher	poet
rhetoric	student	witch
athlete	curriculum	institution
optimist	photograph	stock market
history	penitentiary	earthquake
science	peace	ecology
family	diction	atmosphere
second cousin	irrigation	longitude
revolution	drama	pollution
usage	fermentation	county
psychology	autobiography	senator
city	Puritan	segregation

Exercise 2

Develop paragraphs in which you use the following statements as topic sentences. Explain the meaning of each abstract term by moving to lower levels of generalization.

1. Mr. Swanson is a person of high moral character.

2. Our landlady is a dreadful gossip.

3. Severe damage was done to our house in the recent hurricane.

4. The principal of our high school is said to be a fine administrator.

5. The treasurer of our social club is a very honest person.

Exercise 2,

continued

6. Environmental pollution is everyone's problem.

7. We cannot condone violence in the streets even for a just cause.

8. *Slaughterhouse-Five* is an antiwar novel.

9. My father just called me a little socialist.

10. Mary Lou has a charming personality.

11. Robert Modest is the most intelligent boy in our class.

12. Mark Twain helps us to understand the happiness of boyhood.

13. The policy of apartheid is practiced in the Union of South Africa.

14. The diamond is noted for its quality of hardness.

15. Elaine had a bad case of stage fright just before the play began.

16. England has a democratic form of government.

17. Merrie felt a twinge of conscience when she asked to borrow two dollars from Ed.

18. Walt's attitude toward grammar is one of massive indifference.

PROVIDING SUPPORTING EVIDENCE

Just as a word may need definition and explanation, so a statement may need elaboration or supporting evidence to make it credible and convincing. An intelligent reader does not accept an opinion, a judgment, or even what is presumably a fact unless it is accompanied by some support of its validity.

For example, a writer might state that the nation's general economic situation was deteriorating. This assertion could be supported by reference to a report in *The New York Times* of May 24, 1970 stating that "Stock prices were battered to their lowest level in seven years. The Chase Manhattan Bank calculated that the market value of all securities has dropped by more than $150-billion since the start of 1970—and by $280-billion since President Nixon took office." Additional reference could be made to charts accompanying the *Times* article comparing the Gross National Product, Unemployment, Prices, and the Dow Jones Index Closing Prices for 1969 and 1970.

Since the New York *Times* has a reputation for accurate reporting and since the Chase Manhattan Bank is a reputable, established firm, most readers will accept their authority for the preceding statement, considering it a statement of fact. The writer has established its validity.

In themes, students frequently make no attempt to validate assertions with appropriate evidence. Their statements may be true, but without supporting evidence the reader will wisely raise questions. The following statements have been taken from themes written by high school students. The fact that you may believe some of them yourself does not necessarily establish their truth.

There aren't as many job opportunities for young people as there are for adults.

As a child grows and matures, his reasoning power and mental abilities increase at a rapid pace.

It has now been ascertained that self-education is the only real education that we receive.

The question of whether all men are created equal has raised quite a bit of controversy among illiterate and bigoted persons today.

In all his writing, Nathaniel Hawthorne wrote as a moralist.

Notice that in each case there is need for evidence to support the statement. The search for evidence requires effort and frequently a great deal of research.

Acceptable evidence for statements like those above may come from a variety of sources. United States government agencies, such as the Department of Labor, publish periodic reports that are available to the public. You may be able to find them in your library. These reports may serve to provide information on a great variety of subjects—labor, education, economics, social problems, government budgets, population, and many others.

Articles appear in periodicals on many subjects of interest to the public. The interested student may find his way to these articles by using the *Readers' Guide to Periodical Literature*, which, no doubt, can be found in most high school libraries. He should, of course, do preliminary reading on any topic requiring information that cannot be drawn from personal experience. The value of the evidence collected from sources such as magazine articles depends on the status of the writer and the sources of his material. A valuable source of material is *The New York Times Index*, a guide to all material published in the *Times* since 1913.

The writer interested in literature and authors may find help in the writings of literary critics. This material may be found in periodicals or in books located through the use of the card catalog in the library. Frequently a statement about a novel or a poem is well supported by references.

Reasonable caution should be exercised in making assertions. The first illustrative statement on page 195, for example, might be related to a particular time or place.

> In Arizona in 1970, there were fewer job opportunities for young people under twenty than for adults.

In the third statement, the term *self-education* is vague in meaning and requires explanation. The original assertion might have been phrased more carefully.

> According to Professor Blank of Blank University in an article in the May issue of *Blank Magazine*, learning is a form of discovery.

This statement, of course, would have to be elaborated. Some details of the article referred to might serve to clarify it.

The fourth statement implies an unrecognized assumption of the writer. The assumption seems to be that only "illiterate and bigoted persons" argue about the heritage of equality.

The fifth statement could have been stated more advisedly.

> In many of his stories, Nathaniel Hawthorne wrote as a moralist.

Assertions about yourself or your experiences also require support. If you declare that you are a clumsy person, you must be prepared to prove this to your readers with specific examples from your life.

When a student deals with information outside his own circumscribed range of immediate experience, he makes the error of thinking that something is so "because I say it is so." Try to avoid this type of writing by doing the research necessary to support your statements. Factual and reliable evidence will convince your readers; you will not then be accused of providing them with misinformation.

Exercise 3　　　*Write paragraphs using the following statements as topic sentences. Develop each paragraph with evidence that will support the assertion made in the topic sentence.*

1. Coffee is a stimulant.

2. Censorship of books for high school students is a violation of their rights.

3. Film is a more stimulating art form than theatre.

Exercise 3,
continued

4. In 19____ more automobiles were manufactured in the United States than in any other year.

5. Automation is responsible for the loss of many jobs.

6. Public officials are concerned about high school dropouts.

7. Chicken is a less expensive form of protein food than beef.

8. The cost of living has been gradually increasing from year to year.

9. The earnings of college graduates exceed those of high school graduates.

10. Huckleberry Finn's trip down the Mississippi River was an attempt to escape from the restrictions of the adult world.

11. During the 1960's, the Beatles revolutionized the world of music.

12. Criminal activities have reached dangerous proportions in some of our large cities.

QUALIFYING GENERALIZATIONS

Exactly what is a generalization? The meaning of this commonly used term is somewhat uncertain. As used in the discussion of critical thinking, it refers to a statement applying to *all* members of a given classification. Note the presumption in each of the following statements:

Women are good cooks.
Men are smarter than women.
People who live in the suburbs are snobs.
Old people should have a hobby.
All black people can sing well.
Actresses are beautiful women.
College professors are highly intelligent.
College graduates are more successful than high school graduates.
Private schools provide better training than public schools.

Such general statements need to be qualified or expressed with greater caution. They need to be supported with evidence to make them credible and convincing:

Many women are good cooks.
Some men are smarter than some women.
Many people who live in the suburbs appear to be snobs.

Some old people should have a hobby.
Many of our great singers are black.
A great many actresses are beautiful.
Most college professors are highly intelligent.
The income of college graduates is higher on the average than that of high
    school graduates.
Private schools sometimes provide better training than some public schools.

In community life, there is a tendency to accept such group ideas and
to mouth them in ordinary conversation as platitudes. They sometimes
worm their way into written communication, particularly into the themes
of high school students. A few illustrations from high school themes
follow.

Television is a good thing because it keeps families at home.
Young people today don't realize the wisdom of thrift.
The only way to get ahead in our society is to have a fat bank roll.
Happiness is what all people want.
People today are too much concerned with money.
The strong survive and the weak perish.
Modern women have little housework to do.
Young people in their teens do not like to face reality.

Try to avoid unqualified generalizations. Most of them are of doubtful
validity, and many such commonplace statements are trite and stale.
Furthermore, the writer who uses sweeping generalizations is likely
to mark himself as intellectually naïve, leaving the reader to question
seriously the validity of whatever he is attempting to communicate.

Exercise 4   *Discuss the validity of each of the following statements:*

1. The good die young.

2. A rolling stone gathers no moss.

3. Never put off until tomorrow what you can do today.

4. Haste makes waste.

5. There's no fool like an old fool.

6. Young people are going to the dogs.

7. Students who work their way through college profit
   more from their education.

8. The causes of drug addiction are to be found in the home.

Exercise 4,
continued

9. Girls and boys drop out of high school because they lack the ability to do the work required.

10. No one over sixty-five should be licensed to drive a car.

11. The voting age should be lowered to eighteen.

12. Labor unions help the workingman.

13. Labor unions do not help the workingman.

14. Workers under seventy-two should not be forced into retirement.

15. Walking is a healthful exercise.

16. People should work eight hours, play eight hours, and sleep eight hours.

17. All work and no play makes Jack a dull boy.

18. Cats make fine pets.

SOLVING PROBLEMS

Decisions of all kinds must be made daily. These decisions may arise from quite simple situations, or they may develop from extremely complex circumstances:

Should I enlist in the Navy?
What should I wear Saturday night?
How can I earn enough money to buy a car?
How can I get along with my mother?
Should I try a cigarette?
Why can't I learn math?
What should I do after graduation?
Why aren't I popular?
How should I develop this theme topic?
How can I help stop pollution?
How can I prepare for a happy marriage?
Should I take typing or Spanish?
How can I keep my brother from dropping out of school?
Where can I find material on the effects of smoking?
Where can I get a summer job?
Which book shall I report on?

Problem solving involves critical thinking. In general, the problem must first be defined precisely. Then consideration must be given to ways of finding a solution. Finally, the conclusions reached must be tested to make sure they work.

Suppose Walter is unhappy at school; he wants more spending money. He is thinking about dropping out of school to get a job. His family and teachers ask him to give the problem more thought before he makes a decision. Exactly why does he want to leave school?

So Walter thinks about his reasons for wanting to quit. He recalls that most of his close friends have already finished school; many have jobs and have even bought cars. Walter does not know many people in his school. Most important of all, his grades are low and he believes he may fail anyway, so why not quit?

Now that Walter has outlined his problem, he must consider the two alternatives realistically. What kind of job can he get if he leaves school now? How far can he expect to advance in a job he might get, and what kind of salary can he earn? If he decides to stay in school, how can he improve his situation there? And how will staying in school affect his job and salary possibilities?

After weighing all the alternatives, Walter decides on a course of action. He will stay in school, speak to his guidance counselor about the best courses for him, and work to improve his grades. He will make an effort to develop friendships among his classmates.

How will Walter know whether he has found the right solution to his problem? Experience will be the test. If he tries to make this solution work, he should notice his own changed attitudes toward school life, and an increased satisfaction with daily experiences. However, Walter must realize that his proposed solution is merely tentative, subject to further testing and examination; he may find it necessary to seek an entirely different way to solve his problem, if this one is not satisfactory.

Exercise 5   *Consider the following problems. Define each one precisely as it applies to you. Assemble the relevant data. List possible courses of action. Test the validity of conclusions by a consideration of possible consequences and the experience of others. Qualify your conclusions. List possible subsequent courses of action. Then select one of the problems and explain in writing how you think it should be solved.*

1. You have been asked to have a conference with your guidance counselor. The purpose of the conference is to discuss your vocational plans.

2. Two boys have invited you to an important high school dance. Both boys are friendly and intelligent. However, the best-looking and most popular one has been going out regularly with your closest friend.

Exercise 5,

continued

3. You have been selected by the class to act as chairman of a panel discussion. The panel will discuss the effects of taking amphetamines.

4. As a member of the school council you have been appointed to help plan assemblies for the coming year. You are expected to plan for ten different programs with a mixture of speakers, skits, and celebrations of special events in school.

5. You have been absent from school because of illness. Upon your return you feel completely lost because you have missed a month's work.

6. You have an older sister whose grades in high school established for her a fine scholastic reputation. No matter how hard you work, your grades are only average. Your parents and teachers are constantly reminding you of your sister's record.

7. You feel a need for more spending money. Your parents cannot afford to increase your allowance. You have a Saturday job, but your earnings are insufficient to enable you to keep up with the others in your group.

8. The boy next door is in your algebra class. His grades are higher than yours, and his mother is continually reminding your mother of this fact. The truth of the matter, however, is that your neighbor cheats on almost every test, and you have proof. Now your mother threatens to take away some of your privileges if you don't raise your grades to match those of your friend next door.

9. You have been given an assignment in written composition. The assignment is the writing of a 500-word paper on the causes of drug addiction in the United States.

10. You have been asked to participate in a round-table discussion on the question: "Is *Soul on Ice* recommended for teen-agers?"

RECOGNIZING FALLACIES

Sometimes, as a result of efforts to solve a problem, unsound conclusions are reached and bad decisions made. The fault may lie with a too-limited examination of the problem, or it may be the result of some mistake in reasoning. Perhaps the conclusion did not follow from the steps taken. Perhaps a time sequence was confused with cause and effect. Perhaps assumptions were mistaken for facts. Perhaps some evidence was irrelevant to the problem. Perhaps feelings rather than logic influenced the situation. These errors in reasoning are called *fallacies in thinking*. Conclusions based on faulty reasoning are hardly valid.

One of the commonest types of error in arriving at a conclusion is the one that carries the Latin label *non sequitur,* which literally means "it does not follow." In this fallacy, the conclusion does not follow from the premises, or the steps taken in reasoning it out.

Suppose that you remark to a classmate, "The cost of living is rising year by year." He replies, "Yes, but I think we'll have rain tomorrow." The second quoted statement does not follow the first. Since the conclusion has no relation to the first remark, the reasoning is erroneous.

Conclusions are sometimes founded on assumed cause-and-effect relationships that are based on a sequence of events. This type of fallacy, too, has a Latin name: *post hoc, ergo propter hoc.* This term means literally "after this, therefore because of this." The cause is assumed to be something that occurred immediately preceding the event.

A person who becomes ill after eating a meal in a certain restaurant might blame the food and arrive at the conclusion that the restaurant serves inferior food. He decides that he will not patronize the restaurant in the future. His decision is wrong since it is uncertain that the food he ate at this particular meal caused his illness. The cause might have been fatigue or the crowded room or food consumed earlier. His conclusion to avoid the restaurant will not prevent subsequent attacks if he has not found the real cause of his illness.

Behavior based on superstition is often affected by invalid conclusions growing out of assumed cause-and-effect relationships. We hear such statements as:

> Joe failed his math test; he forgot his rabbit's foot.
> Dad anticipated an accident when that black cat ran in front of the car.
> Poor Mr. Higgins broke his leg. He had just walked under a ladder.

Sometimes conclusions lead to political decisions based on this kind of fallacy. For instance, the election of President A was followed by a depression. But the country has enjoyed prosperity ever since President B took office. If business continues to flourish, many people will vote for President B when he becomes a candidate for reelection.

Exercise 6   *Discuss the steps taken in reaching each of the following conclusions. How valid do you believe the statement to be? Discuss the reasons for your opinion.*

1. Eddie has been ill ever since he came home from camp. A change of water always has that effect.

Exercise 6,
continued

2. Senator B has great personal appeal. He will make a very strong candidate in the elections next fall.

3. Angela has a fever and has broken out in a rash. Mother is sure that she has measles.

4. Jim has done very well in his history class this term. He has a fine teacher.

5. Before World War II the French constructed the Maginot Line. They believed that it was impregnable and that it would give France security.

6. There was another bad plane crash today. I just won't travel by plane; they're so dangerous.

7. I have been trying to get some of that new Mudpack for my face. Margaret has been using it and she has a beautiful complexion.

8. Bill's parents are urging him to take a pre-med course at State College. His father was a successful doctor.

9. Don't waste your time reading novels. Read something that is practical and that will help you in your daily life.

10. This house is a wonderful buy. It will be ideal for your family. The family room is just the spot for the children while you enjoy the beauty and quiet of the living room.

11. Henry has a part-time job in the drugstore. Now he will be able to save money for college.

12. There come the Philbricks home from their vacation. She looks tired, and he looks angry. They must have had a terrible time.

13. When I go to college, I plan to study law. I've always been interested in jury trials, especially criminal cases.

14. Try to avoid Mrs. Phrynn's courses. She assigns too much homework.

15. Federal aid to education means federal control of education.

Begging the Question

Quite often people arrive at a conclusion by "begging the question." In this fallacy, the conclusion is only assumed to be true. The boy who argues that he failed Miss Parson's English test because she gives such difficult examinations is arguing in circles. He begs the question in presenting such evidence as the cause of his failure.

Suppose a politician urges that no one vote for "this discredited candidate for reelection." He is condemning his opponent without providing a reason. The legislator who states that proposed legislation is bad because "it is unconstitutional" is simply assuming, without the support of a single argument, that such legislation would be undesirable.

Irrelevant Evidence

Let us assume that Joe Murdock wants to buy a new car. The paint on his old one is chipped and the motor badly in need of repair. He realizes that he cannot afford such a purchase at the moment because of accumulating financial obligations. However, he really needs a new one. Furthermore, all his neighbors have new cars.

Joe finds many reasons to justify such a purchase. He visualizes the impression he will make on his boss and his many business associates. Then, of course, he thinks of how proud his wife would be to drive that beautiful model he saw last week in a showroom. The children, too, would be able to compete socially with their friends. Finally, and this is the clinching argument, he estimates the terrific expense of having the old car repaired. It wouldn't be worth it—and he'd still have an old car.

The evidence Joe used to arrive at the conclusion he so badly wanted to reach is largely irrelevant.

All too many conclusions are based on irrelevant evidence. One hears the statement that Mr. Crowfoot is a very fine gentleman. He dresses in good taste and uses excellent English. Who knows, he may be a veritable tyrant in the home and a great bore to his business associates. The old saw that you can't judge a book by its cover is testimony of the traditional wariness toward irrelevant evidence.

The use of irrelevant evidence in advertising is familiar to everyone. The after-shave lotion that *you* should use is the one recommended by a well-known athlete. Not for a minute is his judgment to be questioned.

Many of the familiar political slogans are devices for persuasion. They carry implied premises that are irrelevant to the conclusions desired. The famous "He kept us out of war" may have helped to reelect Woodrow Wilson. The fact that the statement was relevant to the past but not to the future became apparent when Congress, at Wilson's request, declared war on Germany in 1917.

Faulty Analogy

The careless use of analogy in reasoning is likely to introduce a fallacy, since the evidence may be only deceptively convincing. The slogan "Don't swap horses in the middle of the stream" was used in the election of Franklin Roosevelt during World War II. While this logic may be sound in dealing with horses, we must proceed with caution when applying the analogy to human affairs.

The argument that eighteen-year-olds should be allowed to vote because they are eligible for the draft is based on the incorrect assumption that the same kind of maturity is required to do both things, and thus the analogy is unsound.

Selected Evidence

Evidence that will lead to a desired conclusion is sometimes carefully presented, while unfavorable evidence is suppressed. Although the evidence selected may be sound, the picture is distorted. The statement that "Anything can be proved by statistics" reflects the fact that many different interpretations can be placed on one set of data, often depending on which part of the data is actually examined.

If you customarily read more than one newspaper, you are probably aware of some of the ways news can be slanted in the reporting, in the headlines, and in the placement of a news story. One paper may play up the strong points of a political speech and overlook its weaknesses. Another may emphasize the less important features of an opponent's talk or interpret a remark in a way that gives it an objectionable connotation. A remark quoted out of context can imply a meaning quite different from that expressed by the speaker. For example, he may have said, "I don't believe in education that fails to build an appreciation of the basic values of democracy." If he is quoted as saying, "I don't believe in education," he will lose supporters.

A slanted headline can be damaging. For example.

PRESIDENT SUFFERS ANOTHER DEFEAT IN CONGRESS

The statement may be true, but the implication to the reader is plain. Here is a President who is repeatedly defeated in his legislative program. Is he a weak President? A more objective headline might read:

FEDERAL AID FOR EDUCATION STALLED IN CONGRESS

Furthermore, if this headline is blazoned across the front page, it will catch the attention of more readers than if it appears under a one-column head on page 2. The placement of a story often determines its impact.

Exercise 7   *Discuss the validity of the conclusions expressed or implied in the following statements. What method of reasoning is used? What fallacies do you find?*

1. There are only two ways of looking at the political situation — either you are a liberal or you are a conservative.

Exercise 7,

continued

2. The number of students in colleges and universities in the United States is at an all-time high. We shall soon be the most highly educated nation in the world.

3. Henry is going to remain home for a year after his graduation from high school. He will be only seventeen—too young to be without parental supervision.

4. It's bound to be a good sunny day tomorrow. It's been raining for a week now.

5. I wouldn't vote for John Smith, a candidate for the legislature. His record is bad. When he was sixteen, he was charged with stealing a car.

6. Fran says that she doesn't plan to take mathematics when she goes to junior college because math has always been her weakest subject.

7. The weather is fine. I have two dollars. My car is in the parking lot. It's too hot to work. Let's go for a swim.

8. Secondhand cars are no good. They always give trouble.

9. Hank won't eat strawberries because they give him a rash.

10. The Dodgers have four good starting pitchers. They should win the pennant this year.

EMOTIONAL APPEALS

Emotions play an important role in our lives. Love, insecurity, fear, jealousy, ambition are poor words to describe some of the basic human drives that move us to unreasoned decisions. Poetry and fiction are filled with stories of the conflicts of men and women who struggle within the confines of instinctive behavior.

There is a wide range of unreasoned behavior, such as that expressed in physical attack. We try to avoid the extremes by exercising self-control, but our efforts are likely to be unsuccessful unless we recognize the emotions responsible for drawing us away from reason. A quarrel with worried parents, a disagreement with a good friend, a disappointment over an election—all involve emotion.

The public is continually being bombarded with words designed to point out the wisdom of following certain courses. In advertising, in politics, in everyday life, people are urged to follow one procedure or avoid another. Many of the appeals are planned to challenge feelings rather than intellects.

In advertising, there is the appeal to pride. Women must be beautiful, like the girls in the advertisements. Men must be strong and successful. Everyone is constantly on guard against offensive odor, warring with soaps, deodorants, lotions, perfumes, and sprays, which will enhance one's image.

There is the appeal to the desire for more security. Insurance advertising often stresses the importance of providing for the education of one's children. The specter of death may be the force that motivates a man to buy more and more insurance. Manufacturers of "nonfattening" foods capitalize on the fear of being unpopular, ridiculed, or rejected.

Labels that suggest and dramatize loyalties and antagonisms are often effective in shaping minds. Terms like *liberal, conservative, socialist, communist, hawk, dove, unconstitutional, Americanism,* and expressions like *lunatic fringe, radical right, grass roots movement,* and *creeping socialism* are examples of such labels. "Name calling" is an adaptation of the use of loaded language, the condemnation of a man with the magic of a word which has gained a powerful emotional appeal.

Exercise 8

1. Write a short theme about your school cafeteria, slanting your material so that your reader will be impressed with the food served, the service, and other features.

2. Write a letter to the editor of your newspaper in which you complain about the tax rates in your community. Defend your statements with valid factual evidence, but select language that will give your material emotional appeal.

3. Write a theme in which you discuss the erratic use of labels and name-calling in political statements and in editorials. Use material from newspapers to provide concrete examples for illustration.

4. Write a theme in which you discuss the use of emotional appeal in advertising. Use concrete examples to support your discussion.

5. Prepare a notebook with illustrative advertising material showing a variety of emotional appeals to the prospective buyer. Use this material for class discussions.

Summing Up

In this chapter you have discussed some of the ways to develop critical thinking. The writer who wants to express himself with clarity and conviction must be able to define terms precisely, support his statements, select relevant evidence, and qualify generalizations. He must possess skill in solving problems and learn to detect and avoid faulty reasoning. He should also guard against the deliberate misuse of language in an effort to persuade for selfish motives.

Chapter 2

PRÉCIS
WRITING

यदि बीच के बिंदुओं पर बाह्य बल P_1 और P_2 लगाये जाएँ जैसा कि चित्र में दिखाया गया है, तो फर्श के द्वारा निचले सिरे पर होने वाली प्रतिक्रिया R का मान निकालो । संख्यात्मक ग्राँकड़े इस प्रकार हैं : $P_1 = 3000$ पौंड, $P_2 = 6000$ पौंड, $a = 4$ इंच, $b = 8$ इंच, $c = 12$ इंच ।   उत्तर $R = 3500$ पौंड ।

6.   एक वर्गाकार बाही (post) एल्यूमिनियम और फौलाद के दो टुकड़ों को साथ-साथ मिलाकर बनाई गई है जैसा कि चित्र F में दिखाया गया है । यदि   *Hindi*

A Look Back and A Look Forward

In the preceding chapter, you recognized the importance of critical thinking. You now know the necessity for defining terms exactly, for supporting your statements with evidence, and for avoiding faulty reasoning.

In Chapter 2, you will learn what is meant by précis writing and how to condense lengthy material into compact form without loss of essential facts.

THE TRANSLATING PROCESS

You have probably read an article in a digest magazine, retold a story
in your own words, or been asked for a summary of something you have
read. All of these activities involve language based on other language,
or words drawn from other words, a form of translation which will be
the focus of this chapter.

Study the following statement by a fictitious Mr. Weston. Then notice
the variety of ways in which the original statement has been changed
in the process of being passed on from a second person to a third:

ORIGINAL

If we can put the snowplows on the road at daybreak tomorrow, we may
be able to make enough headway by tomorrow afternoon to permit essential
traffic to attempt the pass in convoys of from four to six vehicles. Then, if
no further snowfall occurs, regular traffic may be allowed to proceed shortly
after noon on the day after tomorrow.

VERSION 1

Mr. Weston said, "If we can put the snowplows on the road at daybreak
tomorrow, we may be able to make enough headway by tomorrow afternoon
to permit essential traffic to attempt the pass in convoys of from four to six
vehicles. Then, if no further snowfall occurs, regular traffic may be allowed
to proceed shortly after noon on the day after tomorrow."

VERSION 2

Mr. Weston said that if snowplows can be put to work at daybreak tomorrow, "essential traffic" might be permitted to attempt the pass in the
afternoon, in "convoys" of four, five, or six vehicles, with "regular traffic"
resuming about noon on the day after tomorrow, if no more snow falls.

VERSION 3

Mr. Weston was hopeful of getting snowplows into operation and "essential traffic" over the pass tomorrow afternoon, followed by "regular traffic"
around noon the next day.

VERSION 4

Mr. Weston said that essential traffic vehicles would get through the pass
tomorrow, but that regular traffic would have to wait another day.

VERSION 5

Mr. Western said something about the snowplows getting out tomorrow
or the next day by noon and maybe after that he would use a convoy during
the next snow, or something like that.

Each of the five numbered versions you have just read is a translation
of Mr. Weston's original statement. In this chapter, you will look into
the process whereby, without leaving your native tongue (English),
you translate one expression into another expression, or one statement

into another statement. You will explore and practice many different applications of this translating process, but the central object will always be identical with that of "translating" in the ordinary sense of the word (from one tongue to another); that is, you will substitute one set of words for another, without deliberately destroying, distorting, de-emphasizing, or exaggerating the original message.

This kind of translating has been given many names. In order to indicate generally what this chapter is about, the term "précis writing" has been chosen.

Exercise 1

Look up précis *in your dictionary. Then look up the definition of any synonym given for it. Finally, look up the definition of each of the synonyms of the synonym. Notice how you go around in verbal circles.*

What Did He Say?

It is apparent that long before man developed a written language, he communicated orally with a friend, who passed on his message to a third person. Likewise, before the printing press was invented, man's reports were carried by word of mouth and power of memory to places far removed from where the reports were first issued. Tape recorders and communications satellites have now been developed, but the human nervous system is probably the world's most widely used recorder and transmitter of what someone else has said or written.

How often, for example, have you found yourself involved in a conversation similar to the following in response to the simple query, "What did he say?"

"Why, he said . . ."

"Really?"

"Well, if you want his *exact* words, he said . . ., but if you ask me, it all boils down to. . . ."

"And what did *you* say?"

"Well, then I told him . . .; I said, ". . . ."

"And then . . .?"

"And then we went over to the laboratory, and I said to Mr. Willingham. . . ."

Thus you see how vitally you are involved, not only with what happens in the world around you, but also with what words are spoken or written to you, about you, or concerning you.

As suggested, man is probably the world's most widely used recorder and transmitter of language. Yet, when it comes to performing (in a human way) the tasks assigned to tape recorders, communications satellites, or cameras, human beings are not terribly efficient. A single snapshot from a small camera can reproduce a scene much better than most people could reproduce it, either verbally or graphically. And who would challenge a tape recorder to an extended test for reproducing the spoken word?

There have been people who maintained they could watch a long freight train pass and then "play back" the serial numbers of all the boxcars on the train. But most people lack either the training or the capacity for such memory recall. However, by applying your ability to write, to take notes, to devise other "shorthand" systems, it is possible to reproduce language with reasonable precision. Furthermore, when it comes to preserving the spirit of a message even when its form is changed, man is still the most versatile translating machine in the world.

You yourself are a translator, even though you may have no other language beyond your native English. You translate your teacher's words into notes in your notebook. You translate information from sources into notes for papers, speeches, and class reports. You may translate a portion of a text into some notes on a page which you will then memorize while cramming for an examination. When you relay stories, news reports, and anecdotes to others without having memorized them, it is as a result of having translated the original words into your own words. Later on, in any occupation where language is an important tool, you will be called upon to translate one statement or document into another statement or document—a mass of material, for example, into a coherent report.

Why We Translate

You may find a need for translating what is long into what is brief, what is forgettable into what is memorable, what is vague into what is clearly comprehensible. When you are able to recall the "spirit" of what has been said, but not the exact words, this translating process should work almost automatically. In general, you usually translate passages into more manageable language in terms of the particular situation at hand. This conclusion will be demonstrated in the exercises appearing throughout the chapter.

PITFALLS IN THE TRANSLATING PROCESS

Before moving on to explore further and to practice translating-within-the-language, consider how the process can backfire if it is misused, misunderstood, or misrepresented to others.

The translated version of a message must never be confused with the original message. The two are never identical; there is always change. Even when there is exact reproduction of the words of the original message, the time and circumstances are different. The words may be similar, but the second speaker or writer may have a completely different point of view and audience; in a different context, the message can take on an entirely new meaning. Letters to magazine editors often reflect the fact that an original speaker disagrees with the periodical's interpretation of his words. As we have discussed in the previous chapter, the selection of quotations can help determine the reader's interpretation of the speaker's message.

The primary concern here, however, is not with cases where there is close reproduction of the words, but with translations in which the translator is under no obligation to reproduce the original words and where, on the contrary, he may consciously avoid reproducing the original words. Clearly, here, you move from the realm of verifiable observations (fact) to the realm of human interpretations (inference).

Imagine yourself reading a passage which you know is not an original but a translation of the original. Thus you know you have a version that has been changed. But how great is the change? If you had the original so you could check the translation, you could judge for yourself how much change had been made. However, if you had the original, you probably would not need the translation. Perhaps you have chosen a translated version because it is shorter, saves you time, and frees you from having to read through material you consider irrelevant.

So there you are, reading a passage that purports to be a translation of an original but one you know is changed from the original. And the degree of change is an unknown variable in the equation; it rests upon the very subjective, very human interpretive judgment of the man in the middle — the translator! Without the original, with nothing but a translation to go on, you are at the mercy of the translator's personal evaluations.

Imagine yourself an honest translator. You want to take someone else's words and put them into expressions that are more manageable, while at the same time you have no wish to distort the original message, particularly that portion of it that is appropriate to your purpose.

Here are three ways your translations could go wrong, despite your best intentions:

1. You may fail to understand either the subject matter *or* the language in which it is presented, thereby affecting your translation.

2. Your existing attitudes, consciously or unconsciously held, might unintentionally influence your translation.

3. Your purpose may affect your translation, making it inadequate or even misleading for the use of other people in circumstances different from your own.

Failure to Understand the Content or Language of the Original

Consider the following passages and their translations:

ORIGINAL

Iago: Who steals my purse steals trash; 'tis something, nothing; 'twas mine, 'tis his, and has been slave to thousands; but he that filches from me my good name, robs me of that which not enriches him, and makes me poor indeed.   From *Othello*

TRANSLATION

"This guy is feeling put down because he has nothing but a ratty old purse or pocketbook to keep his money in." (This translator fails to realize that the main subject here is *not* a purse—trashy or otherwise—but the value of one's reputation. He misunderstands the language.)

ORIGINAL

In high-lead logging, logs are yarded in to a centrally located landing from which they can be loaded on trucks or railroad cars for shipment to the sawmills. A yarding engine stands—tied fast—at the landing and draws the logs to it on a flexible steel line which is wound around a revolving steel drum turned by power from the engine. Such an engine, called a "donkey," also furnishes the means by which the lines are returned to the place where the logs lie waiting to be yarded.

TRANSLATION

This author tells how logs are carried into the railroad yard after being hooked on a drum. After this doohickey gets the logs in, a donkey carries the whole thing back out where the logs are. (The translator here fails because he does not understand the technicalities of the subject.)

ORIGINAL

Boss (*to foreman*): Every one of the men will get a share of the bonus money. (Note that nothing has been said about the size of the shares, the size of the share the boss might get, and so forth.)

TRANSLATION

Foreman (*to some of the men*): The boss says you will share the bonus money. (The foreman suggests that this group, and no one else, will share the bonus money.)

Exercise 2   *Put into your own words the following verse from Leslie M. Collins' "Stevedore"*:

The enigmatic moon has at long last dies.
Even as the ancient Cathedral Saint Louis
Peals her lazy call
To a sleepy solemn worship,
Night's mysterious shadows reveal their secrets
And rise into nothingness
As honest day unfurls her bright banners.

° Used with permission of the author.

Translation Influenced by Personal Predisposition

Now consider the following passages and their translations:

ORIGINAL

Nancy (*to Jane*): If Leroy and I get married in June, and we will if he gets his leave from the Air Force, you can be my maid of honor if you want to, since both Mary and Carla will be visiting in the East at that time.

TRANSLATION

Jane (*to her mother*): Nancy said I could be her maid of honor. (Is Jane so eager to be the maid of honor that she cannot see all the qualifications that have been attached to the possibility? What would be the effect of adding ". . . if everything goes according to plan" to Jane's translation?)

ORIGINAL

I had just parked my car and was preparing to slide out, on the curbside, when a rending crash knocked me to the floor on all fours.

With a deliberate effort I pulled myself back to the seat, where I sat for a moment, slightly stunned.

When my eyes began to focus properly, I saw a red convertible, with one crumpled front fender and damaged grill. It was stopped at right angles to my car, blocking the street.

Then, as though having waited to be sure that I was still alive, the driver of the red convertible smiled broadly, waved at me, and drove off down the street.

TRANSLATION

This man tells about a red convertible smashing into his car while it was parked at the curb. He relates how he was knocked to the floor of his car and how, when he had pulled himself up, he saw the other car blocking the street. Then, as soon as the other driver saw that he was apparently unhurt, she gave him a big smile and took off down the street in her convertible. (Consider the possibility that this translator had a pre-existing attitude toward drivers of a certain sex and that this attitude found its way into the translation.)

Exercise 3   *Describe the following invitation to a parent without letting your great desire (predisposition) to go cause you to distort the message:*

If enough students sign up, and enough faculty sponsors volunteer, and if each student pays half his expenses and the class raises enough from the show to pay the rest of the expenses, the seniors will be able to go to Washington on their trip.

Translation Influenced by Purpose

Look for the purposes behind the following translation:

ORIGINAL
    John (*to Bill*): I see a giant, four-engine, silver jet airliner approaching from the northwest.

TRANSLATION
    Bill (*to Jim*): John says he sees a plane coming.

Is this a good translation? Has it retained the basic message of the original? Actually, the usefulness of the translation depends on the specific circumstances.

If John, Bill, and Jim are on a raft in the ocean, waiting to be spotted, then any discoverer might suffice, and the size, type, color, or function of the aircraft is nonessential, as is the direction from which it is coming.

However, if the survival of John, Bill, and Jim hinges not only on being discovered but on being picked up immediately, then the type of aircraft is vital; the boys need one that can hover over or land on water. For such circumstances the translation above would be inadequate.

If a translator's purpose is markedly different from your own, his translations may be of no help. Consider this passage and its translation:

ORIGINAL
    An examination of photography taken on Wednesday, the 17th of October, showed several other installations, with at least sixteen and possibly thirty-two missiles of over a thousand-mile range. Our military experts advised that these missiles could be in operation within a week. The next day, Thursday, estimates by our Intelligence Community places in Cuba missiles with an atomic-warhead potential of about one half the current ICBM capacity of the entire Soviet Union. The photography having indicated that the missiles were being directed at certain American cities, the estimate was that within a few minutes of their being fired eighty million Americans would be dead.
    The members of the Joint Chiefs of Staff were unanimous in calling for immediate military action.
                                          ROBERT KENNEDY, *Thirteen Days*

TRANSLATION
    The buildup of Soviet missiles in Cuba was quick and efficient. Within a week's time, the lives of eighty million Americans were threatened. In Washington the Pentagon saw military action as the only safeguard.

Imagine, now, that you need specific information about the Soviet arms strength in Cuba during the Cuban crisis. Which passage would you draw from? Would you select any material from the translation? Which parts of either passage would you use?

Sometimes a translation, validly made to suit one purpose, may be not only inadequate, but misleading to a reader with another purpose. Study the report below and one translation of it.

ORIGINAL

(Prepared by the X Mining Company)

Mine accidents in the X Mining Company in 1970 were at an all-time low. While thirty-one lost-time accidents were reported, this number considered in proportion to man hours of operation not only constituted an accident rate several points below the national average, but also represented the lowest accident rate in all the state's mining operations. The figure was below the national average for five other occupational groups as well.

The thirty-one accidents included one fatality, one total disability, three permanent partial disabilities, and eleven other cases in which more than two weeks' time was lost. The remaining fifteen cases involved time losses averaging two days per injury.

Also shown by the report . . . .

TRANSLATION

(Prepared for a study of the proportion between the more serious mining accidents and the less serious accidents in the industries of the state.)

Meanwhile, at the X Mining Company in 1970, there was a higher proportion of permanent disability to nondisabling injuries than the percentage reported in five other companies. Of thirty-one persons injured in that year, five sustained fatal or permanently disabling injuries compared to 26 who did not. This is a ratio of almost one in every six serious accident cases.

Comparing the original and the translation, one can quickly see how different they are. Yet, in terms of the stated purpose of the translator, there is no evidence of bad faith or deliberate distortion in the translation.

Nevertheless, if you were looking for information on the occupational hazards for miners, you might see the translation as evidence of hazardous mining conditions. Ironically, however, the original report from which the translation came might have supplied you with enough evidence to lead you to an *opposite* conclusion! From this it is clear that however sincere a translator may be, the validity of his translation must be measured in terms of his purpose for making it.

Thus, you can see how the translating process, a very useful communication tool, can still produce confusion, contradiction, and misinterpretation—even when employed with the very best intentions. Through (a) lack of understanding of subject matter or the expression of it, (b) influence, often unconscious, of preexisting attitudes, and (c) confusion or conflict of purpose, a translator, his reader, or both may unintentionally distort the basic message contained in an original statement.

Your best defense against being misled may be to remember that a translation is never identical with that from which it was translated. There is always change, and the degree of change has been left up to the very human judgment of the translator. With this awareness, you may then take the necessary steps to test the validity of the translations on which you must depend. As a further stay against unintentional distortion, you might take the precaution of phrasing your translation in a manner that will make it impossible for your reader to confuse the translation with the original.

None of the pitfalls in the translating process that you have been discussing are to be confused with the *deliberate* distortion of translations or their basic messages. This is a particularly insidious kind of falsehood, vastly different from the unintentional confusions described above. Such dishonesty is often called *slanting*, and it is invariably accompanied by an attempt to convince the reader that a translation is identical with its original. But before you consider slanting, explore the vast possibilities of the translating process as it may be honestly employed.

Exercise 4   *At the discretion of your teacher, make your own translation of each of the originals above, improving, when possible, on the translation supplied.*

SPECIFIC TRANSLATING ACTIVITIES

It is impossible to anticipate all the situations in which you might apply the technique for manipulating language and ideas which in this text is called "translating-within-the-language." The most common of such activities involve (a) changing the wording without concern for length, and (b) shortening the original by deletion or substitution of words.

Translating to Change the Wording (Paraphrasing)

Naturally, if you shorten or lengthen a work, you are going to change the wording somewhere. Such situations will be considered later in this chapter. But first, let's consider some occasions where it might be useful to translate something from one set of terms into another irrespective of length. The process is often called paraphrasing, and we use it to (a) show originality or avoid needless repetition, or (b) to test our understanding of the material we are paraphrasing.

If the original manuscript from which you are working was written by a good professional writer, it might be considered presumptuous to think that you can express his ideas in fresher, more original, or more appropriate language; but there seems little harm in your trying, if the situation calls for it. If, on the other hand, the original is worded in tired phrases or clichés, you have a natural opportunity to inject some freshness and life into the translated version.

Repetition in phrasing is another matter. There is no lack of virtue or effectiveness in saying the same thing twice. If repetition does not reinforce a message upon your consciousness, why do the writers of TV commercials employ it to such extent?

However, negative feelings can also be generated by continual repetition. When you want to repeat a message to reinforce it upon your reader but do not wish to risk such negative feelings, you can simply translate the message into other words. You do this quite naturally. A child does it when he is badgering a parent:

> "Mommy, may I have something to eat?"
> "Will you give me a cookie?"
> "What are we having for dinner?"
> "I'm almost starved."
> "Isn't there something I could eat?"
> "How about a nickel for a candy bar?"

In expository themes, the central idea is often stated in a sentence near the beginning and rephrased at the conclusion. This device is effective in achieving reinforcement of the idea without the negative reaction which repetition in wording might produce.

There is yet another very significant application of the process whereby one set of words is substituted for another; no other change is made. Dr. L. M. Myers describes this process in his book, *Guide to American English*. It involves translating the words of a writer or speaker into your own words as a test of your understanding of the original passage. You need follow this process only a few times, with statements which at first are incomprehensible, to demonstrate the value of the technique.

Exercise 5 **A.** *Translate each of the following into words that reflect freshness or maturity of expression, without distorting the basic message of the original. Substitute everyday expressions for the clichés. Don't worry about length.*

1. Frank piped up to say Cal was a good egg.

2. Due to insufficient funds in the treasury, the club must dispense with its annual yuletide celebration this year. However if sufficient interest is expressed, a limited seasonal observation might be considered.

Exercise 5,

continued

3. Big Jim used to be a fireballing southpaw headed for the big time, but now he's over the hill since he threw his arm away, the last time around, in the bush leagues.

4. You are hereby notified that, because neither your accomplishments in our employ nor your efforts directed toward those accomplishments have met with the standards of this organization, as those standards have repeatedly been impressed upon you by your superiors, your association with this firm is terminated, forthwith.

5. You know, he really copped out when it finally came down to the nitty-gritty work, moving all those library books to the new pad. A bunch of us — only about five — had to do all the work, and it was one tough job! Well, anyway, it took the rest of us guys a good four hours to get through that stack of books, and then we didn't get one red cent for all our trouble.

B. *Imagine that you have already used each of the following statements and wish to repeat the idea expressed without repeating the original wording. Translate each of the originals accordingly.*

1. Just as some people learn other languages in addition to their own, speakers of a single language may acquire other dialects besides the one most natural to them.

2. Because I do not agree with the principle behind this demonstration, I would like to submit my resignation to the committee.

3. I can furnish letters of recommendation that will attest to my effectiveness in looking after children, especially infants and preschoolers.

4. Our team was termed "toughest in the state" by the newspaper association probably because we held our opposition to the lowest scores, on the average, of any team in the state's history.

5. Responsible young people are numerous, but because their behavior conforms with that of society as a whole, they often go unnoticed in that society.

6. For the last three basketball seasons, our class (originally the freshman class, now the junior class) has been issued the least desirable seats in the gym, and I think that's unfair.

C. *Translate the following statements into other words to show that you understand the original. Consult your dictionary whenever necessary.*

Exercise 5, *continued*

1. A bilingual speaker should be proud of his ability to function in two separate linguistic environments.

2. While the antebellum period may have been characterized by an agrarian economy south of the Mason-Dixon Line, it is equally evident that the North was showing signs of growing industrialization.

3. In the absence of mitigating circumstances, this body is powerless to intervene in the dispute, beyond its sworn duty to exercise its authority to bring about an impartial hearing.

4. When, in the course of human events, it becomes necessary for one people to dissolve the political bands which have connected them with another, and to assume among the powers of the earth, the separate and equal station to which the laws of nature and of nature's God entitle them, a decent respect to the opinions of mankind requires that they should declare the causes which impel them to the separation. *Declaration of Independence*

5. In the civilized life of to-day the contact of men and their relations to each other fall in a few main lines of action and communication: there is, first, the physical proximity of homes and dwelling-places, the way in which neighborhoods group themselves, and the contiguity of neighborhoods. Secondly, and in our age chiefest, there are economic relations,—the methods by which individuals cooperate for earning a living, for the mutual satisfaction of wants, for the production of wealth. Next, there are the political relations, the cooperation in social control, in group government, in laying and paying the burden of taxation. In the fourth place there are the less tangible but highly important forms of intellectual contact and commerce, the interchange of ideas through conversation and conference, through periodicals and libraries; and above all, the gradual formation for each community of that curious *tertium quid* which we call public opinion. Closely allied with this come the various forms of social contact in everyday life, in travel, in theatres, in house gatherings, in marrying and giving in marriage. Finally, there are the varying forms of religious enterprise, of moral teaching and benevolent endeavor.
W. E. B. DUBOIS, *Of the Sons of Master and Man*

Translating to Shorten by Deletion

So much for the process of putting an author's words into your own — *with no other change.* This is not the commonest application of the translating-within-the-language process. Usually, when you set out to make the speech or writing of others more manageable for your purposes, you shorten the original material, no matter what your other purpose may be. This shortening is accomplished in one of many ways, and it always involves either change or deletion in the wording of the original.

In certain situations, some of the words, phrases, clauses, and sentences can be deleted, while the rest are left as they appeared in the original. Let's talk first about shortening by deletion.

Whether you shorten by (a) cutting or by (b) substituting fewer words for more words or by (c) a combination of both cutting and substituting, your primary problem is the same: What is to be retained and what is to be omitted? What is most essential to the basic message and what is least essential?

Consider the sample news item below. It represents one of the very few kinds of written material than can be effectively shortened by being pared off at one end—in this case, the bottom.

LOS ANGELES—A 58-year-old grandmother made three trips into an upstairs room of her blazing ocean-front home early today to rescue two pet cats, a bowl of goldfish, and a half-dozen parakeets.

Mrs. Evalina W___ of 9999 Seaside Blvd. was asleep in her ground-floor bedroom when the odor of smoke awakened her. Scurrying outside, the gray-haired grandmother of nine found the second story of the seven-room frame house completely ablaze.

While neighbors summoned firemen and fought futilely against the blaze, Mrs. W___ hastened to the rescue of her animals. Crawling up the stairway on hands and knees to escape the heavy smoke, the stouthearted woman located her pets. First she brought down the cats, snarling and hissing in fear. Next came the parakeets; and on the third trip, the goldfish.

Firemen arrived too late to save Mrs. W___'s home, but they were credited with preventing the fire from spreading to nearby dwellings.

Fire Chief, Roy B___, was quoted as saying the blaze seemed to have broken out in the room next to the one occupied by the animals.

The house was declared a total loss, and the loss set at $20,000.

News stories are written with a view to shortening them to fit the available space. The editors merely cut off a sentence or paragraph at a time to the desired length. Most other kinds of writing must be selectively cut, if they are to be shortened without other changes.

In shortening an expository article, the most significant ideas and statements must be left intact at the expense of lesser ideas, expendable details, and illustrative material.

Consider, for example, the following portion of a hypothetical speech. Candidate A, running for city office, has addressed a number of groups around the town. On the present occasion, he is pressed for time and must cut his speech. In doing so, he remembers that the residents in this less affluent south side of town are concerned most with issues directly affecting them. Here is a portion of the speech:

> Now that I have told you something about myself, my personal background, and the things that I feel qualify me to serve as your mayor, let me go into some detail about those issues and actions that would occupy my attention in the mayor's office.
>
> Our biggest job is educating the young, and that problem will always come first with me. A recent study undertaken under my direction indicated a need for five more elementary schools, *two on the north side, where an anticipated population increase will soon make the existing facilities inadequate, and* three on the south where the situation is critical and overcrowding has been the rule for two years.
>
> I believe we can achieve this improvement in education through sounder economic policies which can also lead to an eventual lowering of taxes. In addition, my outlined plan for bringing new industries to the city can create more jobs for all and added revenue for the city. This additional revenue must be wisely spent, lest it be wasted. You know and I know that the city should increase its service to you in this part of town. I have read your letters requesting help in improving your streets and street lighting, as well as water, trash collection, and other city services.
>
> On the subject of recreation facilities I have spoken repeatedly. *It was I who developed the proposal to buy the McBurney farm on North Dover Road and develop it into a ball park.* One of my own proposals has been for an extension of the City Public Library, the extension to be located at 16th Street on South Mercator Avenue.
>
> On the matter of health and safety, my views have been frequently expressed. The search must go on for continued improvement in our air-pollution control measures. *No part of the city can escape the effects of impure air if the causes of pollution are left unchecked as they were some years ago.*
>
> Furthermore, a project close to my heart has been *to take whatever steps are necessary* to develop pride in our city, in the hearts of all who live in it. *We can move toward this by increasing the size of our Annual Civic Day Parade.* There are many *other* ways to instill this feeling in every citizen. *My own choice involves my plan to restore to their original condition the first homes of the city's founders. These five old dwellings on North Stayton*

*Street have been falling into decay since the city acquired the property
twelve years ago.*

Once all of us take pride in our city and manifest this pride in our words
and deeds, the city itself will progress. *One outcome, I feel sure, will be
the expansion of airline facilities to larger nearby cities. These expanded
air services have always been another of my aims.*

The italicized portions of candidate A's speech indicate where 156
words can be eliminated without altering the basic message—as delivered to an audience living on the south side of town. By other means,
still more could be cut.

Stories, too, as well as other kinds of writing may be shortened by a
deletion of words that leave the rest of the original intact. As usual, the
rule to follow in making the deletions is to cut first what is least essential to the basic message, and then what is least essential of what is left,
and so forth.

Exercise 6

1. Cut an additional 100 words from the political speech
   above. Number the deletions in the order you would
   make them, beginning with the one you consider least
   essential.

2. Beginning with the original speech, indicate how you
   would delete 100–150 words and leave its basic message
   intact for a *north side* audience.

3. From your daily newspaper, clip several items, one news
   story like the one above and the others from elsewhere
   in the paper—perhaps a feature story, a column by a nationally recognized columnist, and an editorial. Try
   cutting one quarter of the total length of each—from the
   bottom. Check your results and compare the effectiveness of the remaining portion of the news item with the
   uncut portions of the other items. Then, at your teacher's
   discretion, selectively reduce one or more of the original
   features, columns, or editorials until what remains of
   each is three fourths of the original length, with its
   basic message intact.

Translating to Shorten by Substitution

Another common way to shorten the statements of others is through
changing the original wording. This is not to be confused with merely
changing words, for their own sake, as described earlier. This process
shortens as it translates, substituting shorter expressions for longer ones.

Paragraphs can be translated into sentences; sentences can be reduced to clauses or phrases; clauses can be cut to phrases or words; and phrases can be shortened to single words.

ORIGINAL	TRANSLATION
My brother once had a pigeon. Frank (that's my brother) found the pigeon when it was young. It had an injured wing and could not fly. (26)	Once my brother Frank found a young pigeon that had an injured wing and couldn't fly. (16)
Frank doctored the wing. He fastened it to the pigeon's body so that the bird could not move it. Then he fed and took care of his new-found companion. (29)	Frank cared for the pigeon and tied its injured wing fast to its body so the injury could heal. (19)
When the pigeon recovered, my brother Frank let him go. But the bird would not leave. It came to the yard every day to be fed by Frank. One day in autumn, however, the pigeon came to eat, and then rose into the air. As it climbed, it swung southward and we never saw it again after that. (58)	When the bird was recovered and freed, it came daily to be fed by Frank, until an autumn day when it swung southward into the sky, never to return. (29)

A distinct advantage of this method of shortening is that if the process is followed to the same degree with parallel units — sentences, paragraphs, and so on, the structural pattern of the original remains intact. As you can see in the translation above, while paragraphs have been translated into sentences, the three parts stand in about the same relation to each other and to the whole, in both the original and the translated versions. Note that each paragraph has been reduced by 40–50 percent.

Exercise 7

Sacrificing as little of the basic message as possible, shorten each of the following as directed:

1. Paragraphs into sentences —
   (a) She was a fiery-tempered woman. Her name was Henrietta B____. She tipped the scales at over two hundred pounds, not the least of which went into lung power. When she cut loose upon T____, the landlord, she made the windows rattle. Her words were distinct a block away, and they could be heard indistinctly, like distant thunder, for another block.

(b) There are at least three valid reasons for my reluctance to watch television these days. First, I find myself unable to tolerate the inane and insultingly juvenile subject matter of the regular series programs. Secondly I find the constantly repetitious commercial messages annoying and meretricious, a paean not to what is good in our society, but to our lust for acquisition. And finally, I am appalled by the medium's failure to represent an accurate picture of the multiple nature of our culture.

(c) Sightseeing by automobile can become somewhat boring, if one must drive for days through an area where the topography does not vary a great deal. No matter how pleasant red clay hills, for instance, appear at first to the senses, after hours in such surroundings, the eye is likely to become surfeited with the sight of them. At times like these, travel by a more rapid means, such as air, may seem vastly more desirable.

2. Sentences into subordinate clauses or phrases (or both) —
   (a) The free end of the rope used to tow the raft he tied securely to his wrist.
   (b) We walked all the way around the island.
   (c) She fell from the motorcycle, which was going very fast, and injured her arm.
   (d) We shut and locked all the doors and windows and turned off the electricity, water, and gas.
   (e) The band continued to play; its music soothed me.

3. A word or phrase substitution for the italicized words —
   (a) *Since he was now reduced to walking,* the old man was able to cover only a few miles a day.
   (b) The uncoupled boxcar, *which was now running wild,* gathered momentum down the grade.
   (c) *It's a good thing that* someone spotted the newly started fire.
   (d) *When I looked to my left,* I could see nothing but the rising, muddy water.
   (e) *As it toppled to the ground,* the dead tree struck the power lines carrying all the city's electricity.

4. A single word substitution for the italicized words —
   (a) Frank Duncan, *who was 58 years old,* stood at his cabin door.
   (b) *The rising of the sun* found him far from home.
   (c) His clothes looked *as though they might have cost a lot of money.*

Exercise 7,
continued

(d) *In a gracious manner,* the young labor leader invited us to be seated.

(e) The man *who is making all the noise* has been asked to leave the hall.

(f) *Lurching this way and that,* the injured man *made his way* to the first-aid station.

(g) I might have transported the fugitive in the back of my truck *without any knowledge, on my part, of having done so.*

(h) The cat threaded its way along the chinaware counter *without making a sound.*

(i) *Without once getting excited,* the jeweler *slowly and carefully* replaced the delicate parts of the watch.

(j) All of our efforts to free the boy from the grating were *to no avail.*

Combining Translating Techniques

You have considered two distinct ways of conveying the basic message of an original statement in a shortened translation. The first process, shortening by deletion or selective cutting, is one you might use if you had compiled a list of twenty friends to invite to your home and your mother limited you to ten.

On the other hand, if you wrote an entry for a 500-word essay contest and found your effort ran to 700 words, you might try substituting short expressions for longer ones, to reduce your entry with no risk of inadvertently cutting an important idea.

On the professional level, one or the other of these processes is sometimes employed separately. When book publishers, for instance, wish to turn out shortened versions of an original work, some will cut less essential passages, leaving the rest intact, while others will translate longer passages into shorter ones. But publishers—and most writers as well—usually combine the two processes into one and translate by both cutting *and* substituting expressions as the particular original seems to demand.

Exercise 8

By (a) eliminating nonessential words, phrases, and sentences and (b) restating the remaining ideas more concisely, produce a translated version of the following passage, reducing it to about a third of its original length:

Franklin Cooke was 39 years old and a cab driver. He lived in a small stucco house on Long Island. Mr. Cooke spent his working hours driving his cab on the expressways, the clut-

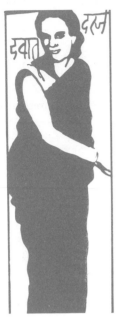

Exercise 8,
continued

tered side streets and the snarled main thoroughfares of the New York City area. He dreamed of paying off the mortgage on his house someday.

Naturally he came to know the City thoroughly from driving all over it. During the day he liked to shuttle between Manhattan Island and the airports—Kennedy, La Guardia, and sometimes Newark—and the ball parks and race tracks, too. If he drove at night, he often found himself scurrying from theatres to night clubs, or to Greenwich Village, Lincoln Center, Madison Square Garden, or wherever people wanted to get to—or from.

Mr. Cooke knew that cab drivers were sometimes victims of holdups, so he accepted it rather stoically when it happened to him. He was held up no more than the average of his co-workers, and he was never mistreated, nor was his cab taken. Only once was he cheated out of his fare. That was in his first year as a driver. The rider in that instance was a young, sweet-and-innocent looking girl who hailed him at Hunter College.

Franklin Cooke was killed in a traffic accident. It was one day in April. A fork lift came loose from a truck and Cooke was following the truck and ran into the fork lift. He was off-duty—driving his own car—on the Long Island Expressway.

TRANSLATING BY DESCRIPTIVE REFERENCE

Probably the commonest device by which all these translating techniques are applied at once is the extended reference that describes the original while it translates it. The difference here is merely one of *point of view*; the translator does not just restate the original—he tells about it.

Perhaps a difference between a translation that is simply a restatement of an original and one that represents a rephrased *description* of the original can be demonstrated. Consider first a version of "The Three Bears," retold from memory.

Once upon a time in a deep forest there lived three bears—a big papa bear, a middle-sized mama bear, and a wee little bear. The three bears lived in a house, where each had a chair and a bed. The papa bear had a big chair, the mama bear a middle-sized chair, and the baby a wee little chair. The papa bear's bed was a big bed, the mama bear's bed was a middle-sized bed, and the baby bear's bed was a wee little bed.

One morning the three bears left their bowls of porridge to cool on the table and went for a walk. While they were gone, a girl named Goldilocks came to the house; and, finding no one at home, she walked in. Being very hungry, she tasted the porridge she found on the table. "This porridge is too hot," she said, after sampling the contents of the first bowl. "This porridge is too cold," she said, tasting the porridge in the middle-sized bowl. "But this porridge is just right," she said as she ate all the porridge in the wee little bowl.

This version of the universal story probably contained words or phrases different from those you recall from childhood. The phrasing of such tales changes in their retelling, from generation to generation. The length, too, may vary greatly, depending on how many details are retained. By simple deletion from the version above, we can produce this shorter version:

> Three bears lived in a house. One morning the three went for a walk. While they were gone, a girl called Goldilocks stopped at the house. Discovering no one at home, she walked in. She found bowls of porridge on the table and sampled the porridge. "This porridge is too hot," she said, after tasting the first. "This porridge is too cold," she said, tasting that in the middle-sized bowl. "But what's in this bowl is just right," she said, after tasting the porridge in the wee little bowl, and she ate it all.

You can recognize both versions of "The Three Bears" as simple retellings of the old story. See if you can recognize a distinction between a translation through retelling and the following translation of the story:

> "The Three Bears" is a story about a girl named Goldilocks and three bears—a papa bear, a mama bear, and a baby bear. In the story the bears go for a walk, leaving their house unattended. While they were gone, so the story goes, Goldilocks walked in. Sampling two bowls of porridge on the table and remarking that the porridge in one bowl was too hot and that in the second too cold, she found a third bowl to her liking and ate its contents. Finding one chair too hard and another too soft, she settled upon the third but broke it down. . . .

Perhaps you will see the distinction better if you notice how the translator of this version works to keep himself apart from the story. He does so in several ways. Where the second version focused attention on the subject of the story, the last version reminds the reader that the writer is translating and wishes to keep his own point of view.

"The Three Bears" is a *story* about . . .
In the *story,* . . .
. . . so the *story* goes, . . .

By describing Goldilocks' remarks, rather than quoting them directly, and by compressing the story so greatly, the writer of the descriptive version keeps his own point of view distinctly separated from that of the original storyteller.

The descriptive reference is a very useful and very flexible way to translate to your own purposes what others have written or said. Its usefulness follows from the way it lends itself to any combination of translating techniques discussed here, while at the same time it clarifies the translator's role by showing him to be looking at the original from the outside.

Its flexibility follows from the freedom of the translator's point of view. Since he is talking *about* the original rather than *from inside* it, he can range quite smoothly from (a) translation of the original, to (b) judgment of the original or its author, to (c) interpretation of the original, to (d) comment on the original or its author, and so on, indefinitely. Let's demonstrate this process with "The Three Bears."

THE TRANSLATION	THE FRINGE BENEFITS
"The Three Bears" is an *old* and *highly unlikely* story about a girl and three bears—a papa bear, a mama bear, and a baby bear. These bears lived *much as people do*, in a house with beds, chairs, and food *eaten at a table*. They left their breakfast one morning to take a walk in the woods.	Comment on the original Judgment of the original Implied judgment of the original Implied judgment of the original
A girl called Goldilocks appeared. *Probably* she was lost and hungry because she *barged right into* the bears' house *without an invitation* and *helped herself* to the hospitality of the house—including the food.	Interpretation of the incidents or events or characters of the original

Since the descriptive reference permits so many personal interpretations and evaluations to be worked smoothly into the translation, it is a device to be used (or accepted from others) with caution. There may be less danger that a reader will confuse the *translation* with the *original*, but there is the added danger that a reader will fail to separate (a) the basic message translated from the original and (b) the translator's judgment of the original, its writer, and so on. To allow or to encourage a confusion is a form of *slanting*, a deliberate misuse of the translating process which will be discussed later in this chapter. While including his own opinions and evaluations, the translator is obligated to permit a distinction between *them* and the basic message of the original which must show through without deliberate distortion.

FURTHER FLEXIBILITY IN DESCRIPTIVE REFERENCES

Descriptive references may vary immensely in length, thus adding to their flexibility in use. Such a reference may contain a single word, or it may be longer than the original to which it refers.

Consider all that has been written to tell of the deeds of Achilles, in the ancient legends of love and war at Troy. (Notice how these last ten words translate that story, in a sense, just to recall it in this passing reference.)

If a storyteller wanted to tell you about Charlie Quackenbush, a fictitious character, laid low because of an injury to his heel, he might begin:

> Charlie fell like Achilles . . .

Would this beginning be an attempt to translate all that you recall about the Achilles story to the discussion of Charlie Quackenbush? The storyteller might have said:

> Charlie fell like Achilles of old, who also fell victim to his small but certain vulnerability when he . . .

If the storyteller preferred a longer reference, he might well have said:

> Charlie fell like Achilles, of old. Achilles was . . .

Do you see how the descriptive reference could be expanded until the whole story of Troy would have been required to complete it?

A worthwhile distinction might be made between very brief references and longer ones. It might be said that the briefer the references, the likelier it is that the association it hopes to evoke must come from the reader's or hearer's memory, not from information contained in the reference itself. The reference must be expanded to insure your making the association.

It can be assumed that you are familiar with:

> Charlie Brown
> The Trojan Horse
> Room 222

Or a translation of the original might be given, varying indefinitely from one word up:

> Charlie Brown, loser, . . .
> The Trojan Horse, a mammoth object, presented . . .
> Room 222, a reference to a television program, . . .

Exercise 9

1. From your own recollections, write a detailed translation of "Little Red Riding Hood" or "The Three Little Pigs," touching upon all the significant details of the story that you can remember. Begin with "Once upon a time . . . ," and tell it straight—as though you were the first person to tell the story. After you have finished this *retelling, tell about* the story in three descriptive references, one 100 words long, one 50 words, and one 25 words, telling as much of the basic message each time as space will permit.

2. Write two 200-word papers about a book or a story you have read recently. In one, confine yourself strictly to a translated version of what the author said in the book or story. In the second, combine a brief translation of what the author said with general descriptive details about the book, its author, publisher, dates, and any other information. Study the two translations so that you can discuss their differences in class.

3. By prior arrangement with your teacher, select a serious television documentary from the schedule of coming TV presentations and agree with your classmates to watch it. Then through (a) notes taken during the program, (b) a translation before class, (c) a brief translation, from memory, written in class, and (d) class discussion, demonstrate: (1) the differences between kinds of translations and (2) the difference between *restating* ideas presented on the program and making *descriptive references* to the presentation.

OTHER APPLICATIONS OF THE TRANSLATING PROCESS

In addition to the many activities already considered, three specific applications of the process under discussion should be mentioned briefly: translating to make the forgettable memorable, translating to clarify, and translating to analyze.

Translating to Make Memorable

Someone translated this basic message:

There are thirty-one days in January, March, May, July, August, October, and December, and thirty days in April, June, September, and November, while February has . . . .

And came up with this:

> Thirty days hath September,
> April, June, and November;
> All the rest have thirty-one,
> Excepting February alone, . . .

Apart from its poetic merit or lack of it, this verse serves as an aid to memory. The notes you take from lectures probably represent an even more vital translation of material into more manageable, more memorable form. This device need not always result in a second version shorter than the original. If, for example, you wanted to remember the idea embodied in the word *pessimist*, you might be able to do so by translating the single word into a longer expression: "a man wearing both belt and suspenders."

Translating to Clarify

A statement is translated both to test an understanding of it and to arrive at an understanding of a passage difficult to interpret. Interpretation involves consulting the dictionary and putting the original phrases or words into "your own words," several different ways, if necessary, until a translation is found which seems both to fit and to make sense.

Exercise 10   In a copy of Shakespeare's *Hamlet*, find the speech in Act III, Scene I in which Hamlet begins: "To be, or not to be: . . ." Read the speech straight through a time or two rather quickly. Then write a 50–100 word description of the speech, beginning: "In this speech Hamlet is talking about . . . . He says . . . ." Then translate the poem into prose sentences of words natural to you — sentence by sentence. When you finish, go back and reread your original description.

Now compare the descriptive statement with the more detailed translation. You should notice quite a difference.

Translating to Analyze

Differing somewhat from the processes described above, but of vast importance, nevertheless, is the practice of analyzing an original statement by reducing it to its central points, essential facts, or principal conclusions. Look for the thesis statement, or pull out important ideas and list them, either in order of their appearance or in order of importance. Moreover, it is possible to reduce the original to a kind of skeleton — to study the important points and at the same time to see those points

in relation to each other. Thus you analyze *structure* as well as *content.*
It goes almost without saying, however, that this analytical device will
be most useful with the kinds of writing that are most often developed
by a logical pattern, namely, *exposition* and *argumentation.*

Study this hypothetical example of one such kind of writing, a portion
of the prosecutor's closing remarks to the jury:

> Gentlemen of the jury, it has been a long trial, and I know you are anxious
> to resume the affairs that filled your lives before you took up this civic duty.
> Therefore, I will come right to the point. The defendant is guilty. He is
> guilty four times over. I did not say he is guilty of four offenses. He is guilty
> not of four offenses but of the one offense with which he is charged. I say
> "guilty four times over" because each of the principal pieces of evidence
> should be enough to convince you of his guilt, and there are four such pieces
> of evidence. In the first place, we have presented eyewitnesses to the of-
> fense. Secondly, we have the defendant's own statement. If further proof
> is needed, there is the expert testimony that has been offered regarding ex-
> hibits A, B, and C. Finally, we have shown you a photograph of the de-
> fendant in the act of breaking the law.

Now let's extract some of the ideas expressed by the prosecutor:

> . . . it has been a long trial, . . .
> . . . you are anxious to resume the affairs that filled your lives before you
> took up this civic duty.
> . . . I will come right to the point.
> . . . The defendant is guilty.
> . . . He is guilty four times over.
> . . . He is guilty not of four offenses but of the one offense with which he is
> charged.
> . . . each of the principal pieces of evidence should be enough to convince
> you of his guilt, . . .
> . . . there are four such pieces of evidence.
> . . . we have presented eyewitnesses . . .
> . . . we have the defendant's own statement.
> . . . there is the expert testimony regarding exhibits A, B, and C.
> . . . we have shown you a photograph of the defendant in the act of breaking
> the law.

Notice how one translation has already been brought about by elimi-
nation of clearly nonessential phrasing. Notice how other translations
may be made. The prosecutor's statement:

> . . . you are anxious to resume the affairs that filled your lives before you
> took up this civic duty.

can easily be translated:

> . . . you are anxious to resume your private affairs.

Likewise, all these statements can be translated into one statement:

> The defendant is guilty.
> He is guilty four times over.
> . . . each of the principal pieces of evidence should be enough to convince you of his guilt, . . .
> . . . there are four such pieces of evidence.

Such as:

> The defendant is guilty four times over, since there are four principal pieces of evidence, each one of which should be convincing.

Or:

> The defendant is guilty as proved four times by four separate kinds of evidence.

Another translation might eliminate other statements as nonessential:

> . . . it has been a long trial. (*beside the point*)
> . . . you are anxious to resume your private affairs (*beside the point; see translation above*)
> . . . I will come right to the point. (*obvious*)
> . . . He is guilty not of four offenses but of the one offense with which he is charged. (*obvious*)

There remain:

> The defendant is guilty as proved four times by four separate kinds of evidence. (*see translation above*)
> we have presented eyewitnesses   (*translated now*)
> . . . we have the defendant's own statement. (*translated now*)
> . . . there is expert testimony regarding Exhibits A, B, and C. (*translated now*)
> . . . we have a photograph of the defendant in the act of breaking the law. (*translated now*)

It will be clear to you that the first of the remaining statements (in translated form) is the thesis, or central argument, of the presentation, and that the remaining four items represent the essential points of the presentation. By the way the original portion ended, you might speculate that further supporting details are offered in subsequent paragraphs. This data could easily be translated into a *formal outline*, either a sentence or a topic outline:

SENTENCE OUTLINE:

> Central idea: The defendant is guilty.
> I. We have presented eyewitnesses.
> II. We have the defendant's own statement.
> III. We have expert testimony regarding exhibits.
> IV. We have a photograph of the defendant in the act.

TOPIC OUTLINE:

Central idea; The defendant is guilty.
  I. Eyewitnesses
  II. Defendant's statement
  III. Expert testimony
  IV. Photograph of defendant

Exercise 11   *Study the following advertising announcement; then proceed as follows:*

1. List all the statements that might be important. (In translating from the original to the list, omit those statements
   that are clearly nonessential; and combine, restate, and
   simplify the remaining statements to make the structure
   more apparent.)

2. Eliminate additional statements of lesser importance.

3. Arrange the remaining statements appropriately to show
   the relationship of each to the others, as subordinate or
   coordinate (the formal outline).

4. Reduce statements to words or phrases, where appropriate,
   to create a topical outline.

5. Translate the whole outline back into a single descriptive
   paragraph, beginning: "The advertisement for the Voomco
   Special . . ."

Voomco Special

We welcome your attention and your patronage. We want
you to come in and see the automobiles we are offering for
sale and to look over our showrooms. It is fine with us if you
want to shop around, comparing the offers that may be made
to you by other dealers.

We are confident, however, that when you have seen all
others, you will conclude that our Voomco Special is the most
attractive, most prestigious, and most powerful twelve-
cylinder sports car on the market today. If you are not convinced when you come in, our salesmen will present you with
proof that our statements are true. The final proof, however,
will be your own exhilarating test ride in the Voomco Special.

You will become startlingly aware of the Voomco's attractiveness when you see yourself, behind the wheel, in our
twelve-foot showroom mirrors. This impression will be
strengthened when you view live-action color films of the

Exercise 11, continued Voomco as its classic lines outdazzle all the more common sports cars in unrehearsed scenes captured on the French Riviera. If that isn't enough, the Voomco's Scotch-plaid exterior finish will surely awaken you to the vehicle's attractiveness.

Who could ask for an automobile with more prestige value? This is no mass-produced stereotype! The Voomco is unique; only four hundred will be manufactured. Thirty-four of these are owned by heads of state around the world, and seven others have been confiscated from deposed heads of state. Twenty of the world's wealthiest men treasure their Voomco Special above other worldly goods.

Moreover, Voomco is the *power* leader in the twelve-cylinder class. In repeated tests in the Hollowdale Salt Marshes, Voomco proved that there was no mud too deep, no hill too steep for the Voomco Special's tireless engine, nor was there any load that could be fitted into the Special's 2000-cubic inch trunk that the Voomco could not pull.

Therefore, car buyers, if power, prestige, and beauty are the qualities you want in the automobile you own, you owe yourself the unforgettable experience of a visit to Valley Voomco, the home of the remarkable, redoubtable, incomparable Voomco Special!

Slanting in Translations

When you translate the spoken and written statements of others to suit your own purposes, you assume an awesome responsibility for the integrity of the writer of the original. Unless you act in good faith, your readers may hold the original writer accountable for statements, attitudes, and opinions that are not really his, but yours, consciously or unconsciously forged into your translations. You have been put on guard against several ways a well-meaning translator can *unconsciously* distort, exaggerate, destroy, or de-emphasize the significance of the basic message he is translating. Unfortunately, there are those who deliberately undertake to do so when translating the speech and writing of others. At least, such flagrant distortions can be found that one may assume they must have been deliberately contrived. This device is called *slanting.*

Slanting can occur in original reporting as well as in translating the spoken or written statements of another person, but your concern now is solely with the latter situation.

Not only is slanting more subtle than outright falsehood, but its insidiousness is increased because the translator attributes the distortion to another person. The *effect* of the falsehood is thus increased, since the original writer may command a wider audience than the translator who produces the distortion.

There are many ways an unscrupulous person may subvert the purpose of an original passage to his own purpose. All translations beyond exact reproduction pose for the translator this question: What is to be retained and what omitted? Therefore, a common method of slanting involves retaining what works to the translator's advantage and omitting what works to his disadvantage.

ORIGINAL REPORT	TRANSLATION ·
John Z is five feet tall.	John Z is a short kid who gets de-
John Z is 14 years old.	merits in school and flunks subjects.
John Z got four demerits.	He washed out of football, and he
John Z goes to church.	eats like a pig.
John Z was "paperboy of the month."	
John Z is a bowling champion.	
John Z makes average marks in school.	
John Z failed algebra.	
John Z dropped out of football practice.	
John Z protects his sisters.	
John Z eats rapidly.	

Since the slanter wants to get his attitudes, opinions, and interpretation into what appears to be the words of another, he may translate neutral expressions from the original into expressions that reflect strong feelings. The translation cited above is illustrative.

five feet tall	*becomes*	short kid
failed	*becomes*	flunks
dropped out	*becomes*	washed out
eats rapidly	*becomes*	eats like a pig

Another common way of slanting is through quoting out of context:

ORIGINAL	TRANSLATION
"I dislike Americans who make nuisances of themselves when traveling abroad."	He says he dislikes Americans.
"I think we are going to win this year."	He says we are going to win this year.
"Of the candidates that have announced so far, there is no one for whom I would vote."	He says there is no one for whom he would vote.

The extended descriptive reference permits a person to describe a book, a speech, an article, or a story in his own words and interpret or pass judgment on the original.

> "Three Blind Mice" is a *ridiculous* [critical judgment] little nursery rhyme about three *overly brave* [interpretation] mice who *took out after* [interpretation] the farmer's wife . . .

A person who makes translations involving controversial matters, *deliberately* confusing the parts played by the original writer and the translator, is guilty of slanting.

In general, slanting is a deliberate breach of faith with the authors cited. The slanter turns *their* words to *his* purpose.

Spotting Slanted Translations

Since slanting is an act of bad faith, you might study what you read for some hint of the translator's good faith — or lack of it. The following questions might help you. Ask yourself these questions about a person who has referred you to the words of another:

1. Has he clearly acknowledged that he is citing the words of someone else?
2. Does he identify the source clearly enough for you to find it?
3. Does he act the least bit reluctant for you to know, find, or see his original source?
4. Does he identify the sources in a way to suggest that he would be flattered, or resentful, if you traced one down?
5. Does he seem to be seriously attempting to keep his own point of view completely separate from that of the author he cites?
6. Is he clear or vague about his purpose?
7. Is there any obvious discrepancy between the translator's purpose and that of the writer of the original?
8. Are expressions suggestive of opinion, judgment, or interpretation (awful, great, wonderful, lazy) used indiscriminately?
9. Are statements of opinion or judgment stated as fact, with no person (writer, translator) listed as the holder?
10. Does the translator revert to exact reproduction of the original in essential parts, or does he use exact reproduction in unimportant passages and go into his own words in critical passages?

If you *must* know whether a person is slanting the words of another, your best test is to compare the translation with the original. By studying the original and then its translation, you should be able to say whether or not the translator has kept faith — whether he has translated the basic message without deliberate distortion. If he has not, then he is not to be trusted in the future.

Exercise 12

To check your understanding of slanting in translations, follow these directions:

1. Study the data below and then write a brief, *neutral* report on the background of Martin K., high school junior, seventeen years old. Include those details you feel are essential for a candid picture that neither glorifies nor excuses Martin.

2. Using only that data which fits your purpose, write a longer report which is as strongly favorable or unfavorable to Martin as you can make it, without letting it sound implausible to one who has not seen the data sheet.

Verified Data on Activities of
Martin K., High School Junior, 17 Years Old

. . . attended public elementary school, graduated third in a class of five.

. . . attended Brockton Junior High . . . compiled perfect attendance record for two years.

. . . was voted "outstanding junior high footballer" by teammates who called him "roughneck," referring to his style of play . . . was moved from quarterback to end at mid-season for what the coach called his "superior pass-catching ability."

. . . worked three years as newspaper delivery boy, during which time he increased the number of subscribers in his area by 200 percent, making his route the largest in town when it had been the smallest . . . left this job to begin work in supermarket.

. . . was questioned four times in three days by authorities about a robbery he witnessed while a customer in a store which was held up.

. . . dropped out of scouting after attaining the rank of Eagle Scout.

. . . played minor role in the sophomore play at North High School.

. . . earned average of "C" in $2\frac{1}{2}$ years at N.H.S.

. . . failed advanced algebra . . . repeated course with grade of "A."

. . . failed plane geometry . . . repeated course with grade of "B."

. . . voted "Most Cooperative Student," by the assembled teachers of N.H.S. juniors.

. . . ran for office of Junior Class vice-president . . . was defeated by vote of 221 to 227.

Exercise 12,
continued

... withdrew from football in high school on advice of physician after developing knee trouble.

... initiated plan freeing his parents and two families of aunts and uncles for an evening out each week while he sat with young children, without compensation.

... tried out unsuccessfully for N.H.S. Junior Class play.

... was forced to leave supermarket job after two days following injury in automobile accident.

... was temporarily incapacitated, painfully but not seriously injured, when father's car, which he was driving, was involved in an accident ... was driving through school zone at legal speed when struck from the rear by a speeding car whose driver was subsequently cited for reckless driving ... saw speeding car approaching (in rear view mirror)... shouted warning to companion who fell to the floor and escaped injury, while the automobile was demolished in the crash. (Hint: In writing a slanted translation of the data above, it will increase plausibility if you insert such expressions as: ". . . school records will prove . . .," ". . . no one can deny that . . .," ". . . it is a fact that . . .," and ". . . there is documented evidence that . . . .")

Exercise 13

Find a newspaper or magazine article in which the author takes an extreme position—is strongly opinionated. Reduce the original version to a translation of about a fourth or half the original length. In your version, be sure you convey both the basic information and the author's strong feelings. But make your own role as translator so clearly separate from that of the original writer and your own function so objective that another person can read your version without knowing whether or not your own attitude agrees with that of the original writer.

ACKNOWLEDGING ORIGINAL SOURCES

One of the best ways to guard against an accusation of slanting is to demonstrate good faith in acknowledging the words, ideas, and opinions that are not original with you. The most formal devices for such acknowledgment are *footnotes* and *bibliographies*, which are treated in the study of the research paper. Your concern here, however, is with the handling of documentation in the text of what you say or write, as a gesture of your willingness to offer translations for comparison with the originals. Consider these two beginnings:

I was reading last week that . . .

I read in the latest government report on smoking that . . .

As a reader, you can only *trust* that you won't be misled by these two translators. Either one could be trying to fool you, or both may be sincerely attempting to inform you. The fact that the second offers you a starting place, in case you want to check up on him, may be taken as evidence of his good faith. If the writer were trying to mislead you, he would be reluctant to help you find the original against which his version can be checked. A third person who says, "The latest U.S. Health Department report on smoking says . . . ," offers even greater evidence of boldness and good faith.

It is not difficult to include such acknowledgment in the source of one's remarks:

In a recent article, General S___ tells . . .
The current issue of ___ magazine reveals . . .
Today's *Times* carries an article by ___, in which . . .
Stating his opinions in a speech in Portland last night, P___ said . . .

You can also show your good faith as a translator by the clarity with which you distinguish your role as translator from that of the original author.

Exact Reproduction

Once you have identified an original source, exact reproduction can be signaled (a) by enclosing the passage in quotation marks, or (b) by centering and single-spacing the reproduced words. The second method is recommended for lengthy quotations, say more than two or three lines.

When the only departure from exact reproduction is omission of portions of the original, the omissions must be signaled. It is then assumed that the basic message is not distorted as a result of the deletion. Three dots, called *ellipsis*, indicate the omitted words. For example:

". . . that we would all come to his house."

"Smith bought the . . . dog for less than nine dollars."

"We have not much farther to go . . . ," she said.   (Comma retained from original)

"The freight included harness, wire, kerosene, [and] bacon . . ."   (Word added in brackets to give appropriate expression to remaining quotation)

"The train for Worm (*sic*) Springs was late."   (Signal of error in original left uncorrected)

"The train for Worm (Warm) Springs was late."   (Signal of word added by translator to correct error in original)

Indirect Quotation

The absence of quotation marks when an original source is cited may be taken as evidence that some translation of the original expression has occurred.

ORIGINAL STATEMENT	INDIRECT QUOTATION
"You had better go home."	He told us to go home.
"You cannot go with me."	He said we couldn't go with him.
"I will not be home before sun-down."	He said he wouldn't get back till after sunset.

If unique, controversial, or crucial words are left untranslated in an indirect quotation, such words should be signaled by the use of quotation marks.

He said my hair was like "spun gold."

The governor contended that all state employees should "willfully participate" in the commemorative ceremonies.

Captain Tylor reported his sector "secured and ready for any eventuality," while Lieutenant Jones signaled that he needed reinforcements "immediately."

According to the ___ *Magazine* report, two hundred men will be "going hungry" by spring if the plant fails to resume "normal operation."

Indirect quotations like those above may convey the good faith of their users because they perform many functions in few words.

(1) They indicate quickly that another source is being consulted.

(2) They allow for any degree of identification of the original source that the user wishes.

(3) They permit any degree of translation of the *basic message*; it may be shortened little or much, or even lengthened; all, none, or some of the original words may be retained.

(4) They permit the translator to keep his own opinions and attitudes clearly distinct from those he is citing.

For effective variation in handling of indirect quotations, a wide range of terms may be called upon to describe the spoken or written expressions of another:

Tom Brown said . . .

The governor answered him, saying . . .

The doctor reported that . . .

The commandant decided . . .

Meanwhile, our teacher was of the opinion that . . .

Mayor Jones contends that . . .

He warned the crowd that . . .
It was his contention that . . .
In the lawyer's judgment, . . .
Sheriff Smith believes that . . .
The union leader was quoted as saying that . . .
We could only conclude that . . .
His statement to the press suggested that . . .
Her words were thought to indicate that . . .
The senator snapped back that . . .
In effect, his speech conveyed the impression that . . .

CONCLUSION: WHAT DOES IT SAY?

Now you are back to central questions around which this chapter has
been built. These questions, or variations of them, face you every day:

What did the doctor tell you?
What did the caller want?
What does the report say, Miss Jones?
What does the whole case boil down to?
What are the main points of the argument?
What is the general drift of the story?

Sometimes you can answer questions word for word. Usually, however, the limitations of time and memory do not permit verbatim
answers. Often a direct quotation is not even desired.

"Just fill me in, Joe; hit the high spots."
"The heart of the matter is all I want."
"Just give me the gist; what does it add up to?"
"Skip any *whereas*'s and tell me only what this case is all about."

Exercise 14 A. *Follow the directions in these translating activities:*

1. Retell in 500 words the action of a story you have read
   or heard recently.

2. Retell your first version in 300 words.

3. Retell the story in 100 words.

4. Retell it in 50 words.

B. *In such sources as those given below, find both an original
and a translation. Study the two versions carefully, and then*

Exercise 14, write a paper describing what happened to the original in
continued this particular translating process.

1. A story or an article in its original printed form and the same story or article in a nationally known "digest" magazine.

2. Any document as originally printed and an "abridgment" of the same document.

3. Several installments of a magazine serial story and an abbreviated version, or synopsis, of previous installments appearing for the benefit of those who have not read the story from the beginning.

4. An original edition of a novel and a résumé of the novel found in a collection of novel plots.

5. Any original document and an abstract of the original.

C. *(For advanced students) Look up dictionary definitions of the words below. Select several of the terms you think will prove useful to you from now on, and in a brief paper relate those words to the processes handled in this chapter.*

abridgment	digest	paraphrase	review
abstract	epitome	plot	substance
allusion	gist	précis	sum
analysis	minutes	reference	summary
condensation	outline	résumé	synopsis

Summing Up

Précis writing is a translating process used in reporting as briefly as possible the statements of others. In writing a précis, be sure to preserve the basic message. You may change the words, you may delete, you may make substitutions. But while you may make these changes to suit your purpose, you are bound in good faith to keep the basic message intact. Never distort what others say by putting your opinions and judgments in their mouths.

You translate to analyze, to simplify, to clarify, and to make memorable. You shorten the original to make it more usable. Do you want to know the story of *Helen of Troy* in a hundred thousand words? You are able to. A hundred words? All right. There will be a difference—but the *rule* involved will remain the same: You must not deliberately distort the basic message, and you must do your best to convey as much significant detail as time and space will permit.

صغار . وفي عصر انتشار السيادة الوطنية خضعت سياسة التعليم الى المثل
السياسية . لقد كافحت الدول الديمقراطية من اجل صيانة تكامل العقل الحر
السماح للتطور الفردي دون اتجاه عقائدي وقد اصبح نظام التعليم مركزياً في
الدول الدكتاتورية فخضع الى اهداف الدولة واستخدم لتنظيم التعليم الجديد *Arabic*

Chapter 3

THE
RESEARCH
PROCESS

A Look
Back
and
A Look
Forward

In Chapter 2, you learned how to translate a statement without distorting the meaning of the original. In Chapter 3, you will work with the research paper—a project in which you must first draw your material from what other people have said or written and then indicate the source of each reference you use.

In this chapter, you will also look into the various source materials provided by the library. You will reevaluate your skills in library research, in outlining, and in taking notes. You will learn how to work from your notes and how to bridge the gap between your first rough draft and your final paper.

247

EXAMINING FOUR EXCERPTS

Study the four labeled excerpts that follow, looking for a characteristic that is common to all four. Although excerpt D is by far the longest, it actually represents only a small part of the body of the paper. By studying the outline and the bibliography that accompany it, you should have a reasonable idea of what has been omitted in the interest of space.

EXCERPT A

"The superintendent says there will be a full two-week holiday."

EXCERPT B

According to the meteorologist on duty at the United States Weather Bureau office in Los Angeles, the four-day forecast for this coming weekend includes cooler daytime temperatures. Highs are expected to average 82 degrees, with little chance of precipitation in the 96-hour period.

EXCERPT C

A recent *New York Times* story reports that federal investigators meeting in Detroit, Michigan believe both cities and industries are failing to honor their pledge to stop pollution of the water flowing into Lake Erie. The goal of a clean Lake Erie by 1972 was mentioned again.

The Federal Water Quality Administration investigators noted that 78 of 110 cities and 44 of 130 industries were failing to meet their original cleanup schedules. In addition, 49 cities are more than one year behind schedule.

According to Murray Stein, assistant commissioner for enforcement, there is a possibility of court action to spur the offenders in their cleanup efforts. Among the major cities listed as polluters are Detroit, Cleveland, and Euclid, Ohio.

A NOTE ON EXCERPT D: This excerpt offers you an abbreviated view of a topic of strong national interest at the time of the writing. It is included here because it is a fine example of the research process. Do not concern yourself with the comments on the left-hand pages at this point. Later in the chapter, you will be referred back to these comments.

WHAT IS SUBLIMINAL PERCEPTION?

by

Frank McCloud

English 10-AA

Macomber High School

May 25, 19___

¶ Pages 282-283 discuss an approach to outlining. The guidelines that follow stress the formalities of outlining.

• The title is written above the body of the outline without a number.

• Note that in the outline on the facing page the main heads are numbered with Roman numerals followed by a period.

• This outline is an example of a topic outline: the heads are expressed in phrases. The first word and other words that would be capitalized in a sentence are capitalized, but there is no end punctuation.

• Subheads under a Roman numeral head are lettered A, B, C, etc., followed by a period. Note the position of each subhead: under the first letter of the first word of the main head.

• When further subdivision is necessary, numbering and lettering follow this form with all numbers or letters of the same kind coming directly under one another in a vertical line:

```
I.  _____
    A.  _____
    B.  _____
        1.  _____
        2.  _____
            a.  _____
            b.  _____
                (1)  _____
                (2)  _____
                    (a)  _____
                    (b)  _____
II.  _____
```

• An outline should never show a single subhead—an A without a B; a 1 without a 2, etc. Subheads are subdivisions; division implies two or more parts.

What Is Subliminal Perception?

◪ Pages 281-282 discuss an approach to choosing a title for a research paper. Here are some guidelines for the final form of the title:

- When the paper is typed, the title should be centered at least two inches from the top with extra space between it and the first line of the report.

- The first and last word of the title and all other important words are capitalized.

- Text page 249 shows one way of arranging the title page (or cover sheet), which precedes the outline and the first page of the report.

◪ Pages 288-289 and 293 discuss the process of footnoting. Here are some guidelines for putting footnotes into final form:

- Note the rule that separates the footnotes from the body of the report. Note, too, the generous indention of the first line in each footnote.

- Footnote 1 is an example of a periodical citation. The author's name is not inverted in footnotes but is inverted in the bibliography.

- Footnote 3 illustrates the form used for the second and succeeding citations of a source. The first time (footnote 1) the full entry is given; thereafter an abbreviated form is used.

- In footnote 4, the abbreviation *Ibid.* (from the Latin word *Ibidem*) means "in the same place" and always refers to the immediately preceding footnote.

What Is Subliminal Perception?

For several weeks, during the late summer of 1957,[1] 45,699 movie fans[2] filed in and out of a theater in Fort Lee, New Jersey. They watched the double attraction, ate popcorn, and drank soft drinks. What they did not know was that two advertising slogans, "Hungry? Eat Popcorn" and "Drink Cola," were being flashed on the screen alternately every five seconds for just one three-thousandth of a second. This exposure was much too brief to be consciously perceived by the Fort Lee patrons.[3]

But subconsciously, the 45,699 movie-goers did see the slogans, and many reacted to them — according to the tester, Mr. James M. Vicary, a New York marketing researcher and psychologist.[4] Mr. Vicary's proof: Popcorn sales went up 57.5 percent during the test, he said, while soft-drink sales picked up by 18.1 percent.[5] Vicary gave the credit for the boost to the unseen advertisement — the "phantom plug," as one critic called it, a process which

---

[1] Herbert Brean, "'Hidden Sell' Technique Is Almost Here," <u>Life</u>, vol. 44 (March 31, 1958), p. 104.
[2] Gay Talese, "Most Hidden Hidden Persuasion," <u>The New York Times Magazine</u> (January 12, 1958), p. 22.
[3] Broan, "'Hidden Sell' . . . ," p. 104.
[4] <u>Ibid</u>.
[5] Marya Mannes, "Ain't Nobody Here but Us Commercials," <u>The Reporter</u>, vol. 17 (October 17, 1957), p. 35.

- Beginning with page 2, each page of a long report should be numbered. The page number may be positioned as shown here, or it may be positioned consistently either in the upper right corner or centered at the bottom of the page. The title page, the outline, and the first page of a report are usually not numbered although practice varies.

- Note that here and in the next-to-last sentence on this page, the directly quoted material is enclosed in quotation marks and run in with the rest of the paragraph. The next page comments on an example of how to handle longer quotations.

◪ Note the following guidelines for footnoting quoted material:

- Footnote 7 documents material that is not quoted directly.

- Footnote 9 documents material that is quoted directly.

[2]

was ". . . painless, odorless, nonfattening, and very sneaky."[6]

The key word in any description of the Fort Lee test or of the techniques involved is <u>subliminal,</u> a term which comes from the Latin, <u>sub</u> (below) and <u>limen</u> (threshold).[7] Thus this apparent ability to perceive below the threshold of consciousness is called "subliminal perception," or simply "SP."[8]

One observer defined SP as "the ability to absorb sights or sounds that are too fleeting to be detected consciously but definite enough to cross the threshold of the subconscious mind."[9] Another used the analogy of sounds with too high a frequency for the conscious ear, yet proved to exist and able to penetrate some area of the human consciousness.[10] So, although the New Jersey movie-house test may have jolted the average person, it involved a principle already accepted by many psychologists:[11] "We are able to perceive or apprehend something even though we are not actually conscious of it through our physical senses."[12] This is SP.

---

[6] Talese, "Most Hidden Hidden Persuasion," p. 22.

[7] Brean, " 'Hidden Sell' . . . ," p. 102.

[8] <u>Ibid.</u>

[9] "Devilish?", <u>Newsweek,</u> vol. 50 (October 14, 1957), p. 98.

[10] Mannes, "Ain't Nobody Here . . . ," p. 36.

[11] " 'Ghost' Ads Overrated," <u>Science News Letter</u>, vol. 72 (October 26, 1957), p. 260.

[12] "Subliminal Ads Tried on TV," <u>Radio & TV News,</u> vol. 59 (February 1958), p. 143.

- A quotation longer than two lines is usually indented as shown here, is single spaced, and is not enclosed in quotation marks. Regular paragraph indention is not used here, because the quotation does not begin a paragraph in the original source.

◨ Note the following guideline for putting footnotes into final form:

- The abbreviated form of footnote 120 indicates that the book *The Hidden Persuaders* has been cited before. The first footnote for this source took this form —
    Vance Packard, *The Hidden Persuaders*, New York, David McKay Company, Inc., 1957, p. 4.

[23]

[At this point, several typewritten pages have been omitted.]

The future of subliminal perception is a highly speculative

matter. Research has led this writer to the following conclusions:

SP appears to be a physical reality. It is possible to stimulate

the unconscious areas of the human nervous system — through very

brief signals — without a person's conscious awareness of being

exposed to these signals. Whether these unseen signals can

influence a person's actions or attitudes is yet to be clearly

established, despite the Fort Lee theater test.

If SP messages can influence human behavior, then SP ads can

be widely (and perhaps unethically) employed. "We live by symbols,

not sense," said Pierre Martineau, the research and marketing

director of the Chicago Tribune.[119] Louis Cheskin, another Chicago

authority echoed this sentiment:

> Actually in the buying situation, the consumer generally acts
> emotionally and compulsively, unconsciously reacting to the
> images and designs which in the subconscious are associated
> with the product.[120]

It is doubtful if Americans have anything to fear from SP in

the foreseeable future. One of the best assurances in this regard

---

[119] "The Consumer: What Makes Him Buy?", Newsweek, vol. 50
(September 30, 1957), p. 103.
[120] Packard, The Hidden Persuaders, p. 8.

• Again, note the indention and spacing used for quoted material that runs longer than two lines.

• Note that the final footnote in this report is an abbreviated form of footnote 12.

[24]

comes in the statements reportedly issued to TV stations by their

networks and from the National Association of Radio and Television

Broadcasters:

> In essence, the networks have forbidden the use of such
> techniques, while the NARTB stated that the process should not
> be permitted on the television broadcast medium.[121]

Furthermore, while the Federal Communications Commission has

not acted to ban SP ads, sources cited in this paper indicate that

the agency <u>could</u> and <u>would</u> use its regulatory power if any threat

to the medium or to the public should arise.

What about the beneficial applications to be found for subliminal

perception? It may be too soon for speculation but, on the other

hand, who could have predicted that hypnosis — once widely

disclaimed and discredited as a sideshow gimmick — would become

in the hands of responsible men an unquestionable good in medicine

and in psychotherapy? Perhaps as much can be hoped for the

future of subliminal perception.

---

[121] "Subliminal Ads Tried on TV," p. 143.

◖ Pages 285, 288, and 293 discuss the preparation of bibliography cards. On this page and on the two left-hand pages that follow, you will find some guidelines for correct bibliography form.

- The bibliography usually begins a new typewritten page.
- Books and periodicals may be run into the same alphabet.
- Items are arranged alphabetically according to the last names of their authors. Note the alphabetical order of the first source, which was prepared by the editors of *Fortune*, a magazine.

- Note the alphabetical order of the first periodical source which appeared in the magazine *Advertising Age* without a by-line. Such anonymous items are placed alphabetically by the first word of their titles.

- If the first word is *A, An,* or *The,* the second word determines the alphabetical order.

[25]

Bibliography

BOOKS

<u>Fortune</u> Editors, <u>The Amazing Advertising Business,</u> New York, Simon & Schuster, 1957.

Packard, Vance, <u>The Hidden Persuaders,</u> New York, David McKay Company, Inc., 1957.

Sargant, William W., <u>Battle for the Mind,</u> New York, Doubleday & Company, Inc., 1957.

PERIODICALS

"Admen Flop as "Guinea Pigs" in Subliminal Test," <u>Advertising Age,</u> vol. 29 (February 17, 1958), p. 2.

"Ads You'll Never See," <u>Business Week</u> (September 21, 1957), pp. 30-31.

Bendiner, Robert, "Subliminal Persuasion," <u>New Statesman,</u> vol. 54 (November 2, 1957), p. 551.

Brean, Herbert, "'Hidden Sell' Technique Is Almost Here," <u>Life,</u> vol. 44 (March 31, 1958), pp. 102-114.

"Britt Proposes More Scientific Subliminal Test," <u>Advertising Age,</u> vol. 29 (March 31, 1958), pp. 3, 30.

"Canadians Brood Over Subject of Subliminal Pitch," <u>Advertising Age,</u> vol. 29 (January 27, 1958), pp. 3, 34.

"The Consumer: What Makes Him Buy?", <u>Newsweek,</u> vol. 50 (September 30, 1957), pp. 102-103.

Cousins, Norman, "Smudging the Subconscious," <u>Saturday Review,</u> vol. 40 (October 5, 1957), p. 20.

Curtis, K. D., "Learn While You Sleep," <u>The American Mercury,</u> vol. 82 (May 1956), p. 83.

"Devilish?", <u>Newsweek,</u> vol. 50 (October 14, 1957), p. 98.

- Note that the second line is indented so that the name of the author stands out.

- The title of the article is enclosed in quotation marks; the title of the magazine is underscored to indicate italics.

- Note the use of single and double quotation marks.

- Commas separate the parts of each item. The volume number precedes the parenthetical date of the issue cited. The number or numbers of the page on which the article appears are given last. A period at the end is optional.

[26]

"Diddling the Subconscious," <u>The Nation,</u> vol. 185 (October 5, 1957), p. 206.

DuShane, Graham, "The Invisible Word, or No Thresholds Barred," <u>Science,</u> vol. 126 (October 11, 1957), p. 681.

" 'Exaggeration of Dangers' Charged to Packard Book," <u>Advertising Age</u>, vol. 28 (December 9, 1957), p. 93.

"FCC Sets Subliminal Demonstration," <u>Advertising Age,</u> vol. 29 (January 6, 1958), p. 1.

Geller, Al, "Truth About Those 'Invisible' Ads," <u>Science Digest,</u> vol. 42 (December 1957), pp. 16-18.

" 'Ghost' Ads Overrated," <u>Science News Letter,</u> vol. 72 (October 26, 1957), p. 260.

Griswold, Wesley S., "TV's New Trick: Hidden Commercials," <u>Popular Science Monthly,</u> vol. 172 (April 1958), pp. 95-97, 252.

Hyams, Edward, "Hidden Persuaders," <u>New Statesman,</u> vol. 54 (October 26, 1957), pp. 524-526.

"If Subliminal Ad's Hypnotic, It Won't Sell; If It Sells, It's Unethical, Say Doctors," <u>Advertising Age,</u> vol. 28 (September 23, 1957), p. 2.

"Invisible Ads Are Quick as a Flash, But Not Too Quick for FCC's X-Ray Eyes," <u>Business Week</u> (November 16, 1957), p. 125.

"The Invisible Monster," <u>The Christian Century,</u> vol. 74 (October 2, 1957), p. 1157.

Johnson, Gerald W., "The Unconscious Itch," <u>New Republic,</u> vol. 137 (November 11, 1957), p. 8.

Larson, Cedric, "The Age of Manipulation," <u>The American Mercury,</u> vol. 85 (October 8, 1957), p. 146.

"Ludgin Says Ad Excess Makes All Ads Subliminal," <u>Advertising Age,</u> vol. 29 (February 17, 1958), pp. 2, 98.

Mannes, Marya, "Ain't Nobody Here but Us Commercials," <u>The Reporter,</u> vol. 17 (October 17, 1957), pp. 35-36.

- If the bibliography includes more than one source by the same author, a dash may be used in place of the author's name in all items after the first. For example, an additional source by Elmo Roper would take this form:

  —— "Learning Is Total," *Saturday Review*, vol. 41 (May 24, 1958), p. 20.

[27]

"NAB to Be Asked to Put Subliminal Ban Into TV Code," Advertising
    Age, vol. 29 (April 7, 1958), p. 70.

"Non-Coffee Using Housewife Made Fresh Coffee After Hint in
    Subliminal Radio Test," Advertising Age, vol. 29 (February 3,
    1958), pp. 3, 58.

Packard, Vance, "The Growing Power of Admen," Atlantic Monthly,
    vol. 200 (September 1957), pp. 55-59.

"Proponent of SP Deprecates Effect," Broadcasting, vol. 54 (March
    24, 1958), pp. 47-48.

Roper, Elmo, "How Powerful Are the Persuaders?", Saturday Review,
    vol. 40 (October 5, 1957), p. 19.

"Subliminal Ad Is Transmitted in Test but Scores No Popcorn Sales,"
    Advertising Age, vol. 29 (January 20, 1958), pp. 2, 94.

"Subliminal Ads Tried on TV," Radio & TV News, vol. 59 (February
    1958), p. 143.

"Supersoft Sell," Time, vol. 70 (September 9, 1957), pp. 67-68.

Talese, Gay, "Most Hidden Hidden Persuasion," The New York Times
    Magazine (January 12, 1958), pp. 22, 59-60.

"Unseen TV Gets Exposure on Both Coasts," Broadcasting, vol. 54
    (January 20, 1958), pp. 98-99.

"What Sways the Family Shopper," Business Week (November 30, 1957),
    pp. 46-49.

"Whispering Campaign," Time, vol. 71 (February 24, 1958), p. 60.

WHAT THE EXCERPTS HAVE IN COMMON

Clearly, the four excerpts you have just read differ widely. The shortest is one sentence, while the longest is several pages — actually twenty-seven pages if we visualize the complete paper. The final excerpt has two scholarly attachments (footnotes and a bibliography), not shared by the others. The first excerpt is obviously a fragment of a casual conversation, while the others suggest varying degrees of formality. The most formal, you will agree, is excerpt D, which might be called a "dress parade" of theme techniques.

Thus, whatever characteristic these selections may share, it is not a matter of length, of format, of formality, or of topic. What, then, is left? Let's look again at the shortest excerpt. The common characteristic(s) will probably be more noticeable, with so little room in which to hide.

"The superintendent says there will be a full two-week holiday."

The clue is obvious: "The superintendent says . . . ." The author (in this case, the speaker) is telling us something *he learned from someone else*, just as the other three authors are.

The authors of all four excerpts have gone beyond their own limited experience. In A and B they have added to their knowledge that of a single outside source. The author of excerpt C has extended his own experience by drawing upon a newspaper article and the report of a federal agency. Excerpt D has expanded its author's experience to include that of dozens of authorities. For all their wide differences, however, at the heart of each of the excerpts is an act common to all — the author jumps the fence surrounding his total past experience. He extends the boundaries of his knowledge by calling upon that of someone who occupies a position of authority on the subject under consideration.

ELEMENTS OF THE RESEARCH PROCESS

This appeal to authority is what is called the *research process*. The vast differences between the first excerpt and the last do not alter this basic similarity; whether seeking support from one source or many — whether with or without footnotes — both excerpts rely upon the knowledge and judgment of someone else.

With the power and skill to call upon authorities for information or expert opinion, you need never feel that you stand alone in any verbal controversy. If you can find experts to supply you with information or to back you up in your point of view, if you can make the most of the authority of those experts, you should be able to inform others and, if necessary, win them over to your views.

Without this ability to apply the experience of others to your own knowledge, you live in a world no larger than the reach of your arm or the sweep of your vision or the range of your hearing. But even with one well-chosen book, you have a record of what happened a thousand miles away — or what happened a thousand years ago. Through the research process you can add all those records of other experiences to your own.

HOW THE RESEARCH PROCESS TOUCHES OUR LIVES

Would you have called only excerpt D a research project? Many people would. They would give all the others another label, ignoring the appeal to outside authority shared by all. Certainly, the last excerpt is the only one to have all the outward features of a research project. So let us call it a *formal* presentation of research. You will probably be expected to practice these formalities yourself. But call the other excerpts, research papers, too. They represent a kind of *everyday* research which you will continue to use all the days of your life. And you will use this research process poorly or well, depending upon how you approach it now. It is not just a game you play with footnotes; it is a method for giving strength to your statements and a technique for getting help in making up your mind.

In Everyday Conversation

As a well-informed person you can cite news events. You can make historical parallels to current happenings. You can quote recent public statements of persons of prominence when such statements are appropriate. You should know what position the editors of your favorite newspaper take on the issues of the day. All this involves application of the research process.

In Religion

You apply the research process when you cite the book in which are collected the tenets of your faith. Furthermore, you may recall a pronouncement made by your minister on an issue and add his voice to your own.

In Matters of Health

When you are well, you read to learn how to avoid colds and other discomforts. When you are ill, you search for recommended remedies. What family is without some book of advice on child care or on what-to-do-till-the-doctor-arrives? What doctor does not consult his colleagues, either in person or through medical records, when he wishes to add another's wisdom to his own?

In Matters of Business

You apply the research process directly when you compare items and prices on shopping expeditions. You consult the Better Business Bureau and read magazines providing aids to consumers. You look for statistics that are the result of research often employed by advertisers.

In Citizenship

Some adults do not bother to vote, and some vote automatically without regard for the facts of the situation. But still others go outside their own experience—they listen and read and then vote upon the basis of their research.

In Homemaking

A housewife is a researcher, too. She consults the cookbook, the telephone directory, and the mail-order catalog. If her washer or mixer or any other appliance breaks down, she might go to the manufacturer's manual to try to diagnose the mechanical failure. She probably studies magazines for hints on family health, food, and clothing. Other magazines offer her advice on keeping up her home, inside and out. If she is in a position to buy a house, she consults dozens of authorities on the design and the materials, to say nothing of all the other matters upon which she feels the need for expert opinion.

Exercise 1

1. Supply three other categories of human activities, paralleling those cited above, in which information or opinions furnished by others might be helpful.

2. Try to add at least one application of the research process to each of the six fields of activity listed.

WHO IS AN AUTHORITY?

On the subject of your own unique experience, *you* are probably the world's foremost authority. Once outside the field of your unique experience, however, your claims to authority dwindle noticeably. But all human claims to authority are *somewhat* limited. In a world in motion, today's "expert" may be surpassed tomorrow by someone more in tune with the shifting pattern of human events.

Whose opinion on a matter do *you* most respect? Whose opinion does your society in general seem to respect most? These are probably your best measures of the relative value of authority. Before you accept the opinions of another person, or before you ask others to accept them, you might ask yourself some of these questions about your informant:

1. What training has he had in the subject on which he speaks? How long did he study? Where? With whom? Does any particular prestige attach to any of these answers?
2. How much experience has he had in the field in which he speaks? If he hits home runs in Shea Stadium, you might look to him for authoritative statements on baseball. However, you would question his authority to speak as an expert on manufacturing or engineering.
3. Does he hold an office which brings him recognition as an authority?
4. Does he enjoy the respect of other recognized men in his field? Is he invited to address his peers? Is he honored by them in other ways?
5. Are his views in print? If so, does any prestige attach to the publishers and editors with whom he is associated?
6. How are his published remarks received? Are his views respected (although not necessarily agreed with) by those commentators whose judgment you respect?

In short, to whatever extent an outside source of information or opinion serves to convince you of its validity, you may cite that source in seeking support for your views and in asking others to accept them.

Exercise 2   *From the list on the right, select at least four sources of information and opinion that might reasonably be thought to carry some authority on one of the topics listed at the left. Next, rank your choices from "most promising" to "least promising," and give reasons for your rankings. Your reasons should include a summary of the particular claim to authority of each source. (Personal evaluations will apply here, as they do in our lives when we must choose a doctor, a dentist, a lawyer, and so forth. Therefore, it is of little consequence if disagreements arise over the rankings; what matters is that you make a logical case to support your choice.)*

Exercise 2,

continued

Topic

1. Using nuclear power for peaceful purposes

2. Replacement of substandard housing

3. The use of hypnosis as a possible substitute for anesthetic drugs in surgery

Sources of Information and Opinion

a. Mayor of one of the ten largest U.S. cities

b. A person who has been hypnotized by a magician at a carnival sideshow

c. An expert on nuclear warheads

d. Representatives of groups of residents who would be or have already been affected by urban renewal

e. A city-wide taxpayers' group

f. The senior medical officer of a large metropolitan hospital

g. A university professor whose field is atomic physics

h. A United States Government Printing Office publication on housing standards

i. An anesthesiologist trained and experienced in both hypnosis and drug-induced anesthesia

j. The owner of a large block of rental property in proposed renewal area

k. The spokesman for a group of privately owned natural-gas and electric power companies

l. A person who has undergone a successful operation while under hypnosis

m. An expert on radioactive isotopes

n. The director of an atomic reactor

o. A medical doctor specializing in heart ailments

p. A man completing a five-year study of the nature of fissionable materials

q. The Secretary of the U.S. Dept. of Housing and Urban Development

r. The head of a drug company

DIRECT AND INDIRECT SOURCES OF AUTHORITY

If you had the means to do it, you could direct your inquiries, in person, to the ranking authorities on a subject. Sometimes that is possible. If you want to know, for instance, what percent of the citizens of your town eat peanut-butter sandwiches, you could survey the town, asking each person the vital question. Your summary would reflect the *direct* approach, and your results would be close to factual, provided you could overlook the discrepancies produced by (a) those who lied, (b) those who had stopped eating or who began to eat peanut-butter sandwiches shortly before or after responding to your question, (c) those who could not be reached, and so forth.

On other occasions you can get directly at the facts by appearing on the scene to observe and report what you see and hear. Scientists often arrange to observe the tests of their hypotheses; such observation is a vital part of their experimental method. Live telecasts of events—of sports competitions, of historic occasions, of official government pronouncements—give similar opportunities to get right to the source of information.

But no one can be everywhere at once. You cannot observe *all* that is happening even in one place. Thus, you will miss most of the events taking place in the world if you limit yourself to direct research, to direct observation of events, or to direct contact with authorities.

Luckily, you are not so limited. Through reports and opinions preserved in the written word, human experience from all recorded times and places is available. If you receive these secondhand reports shortly after they are written, they are "news." Yesterday's news is today's history. Today's news will be tomorrow's history. And the place that preserves the best reports of all these yesterdays is the library. So the library is usually the place where the research process takes us. On the next few pages, therefore, you will review certain basic library skills.

Exercise 3

1. Make a direct survey of the class on any agreed upon topic. Then prepare jointly a paper based on the results of your research.

2. Select a topic on which you might get information from a government agency to be used in a class research paper. Then choose a classmate to write a letter to an official of that agency, requesting information that would add authenticity to the research paper you are to write on the topic.

THREE CLASSES OF LIBRARY MATERIAL

Whether your school library is housed in an impressive building, in a converted army barracks, or in the corner of a room, it contains three basic kinds of source material: (1) books, (2) periodicals, and (3) reference works. These classifications are arbitrary; they have been listed merely to illustrate how you can use the material in your library to best advantage. The categories provide you with *one* of the approaches. Any search for material on a subject is incomplete if you fail to check all three of these kinds of sources. The first contains the regular *bound* volumes, both fiction and nonfiction; the second includes newspapers and magazines, as well as any other data issued *periodically*; the third includes those sources to which one is likely to *refer* for specific information.

It would not be impossible to find information in your library simply by reading all the books, magazines, and references as you come to them, knowing that sooner or later you would happen upon the particular information you seek. But what an endless task that would be! There is a much easier and faster way to approach these sources. It involves learning the system used by librarians to store information and following that system to go directly to the proper source.

Books

The most valuable guide in helping you locate bound volumes in a library is the card catalog. When a book is received by the library, a librarian prepares three—and sometimes four—cards for it: an author card, a title card, a subject card, and a cross-reference card.

The first line of the author card has the author's last and first names. The first line of the title card has the title of the book. The first line of the subject card has a topic—like Advertising or Zoology. The cross-reference card refers to a related topic if there is one. Each card has the call number in the left-hand corner. This number determines the placement of the book on the library shelves. The cards are filed alphabetically in several labeled drawers referred to as the card catalog.

Study the cards at the top of page 273. Notice that the author's last name always precedes his first name. If the title of a book includes *A*, *An*, or *The*, this word is disregarded. Note the information given on the cards.

The two main classes of books are *fiction* and *nonfiction*. Books classed as fiction are arranged alphabetically on the shelves by the last name of the author. For the arrangement of nonfiction, most libraries use the Dewey Decimal System, which divides the books into ten general classes. The call number indicates to which class each belongs.

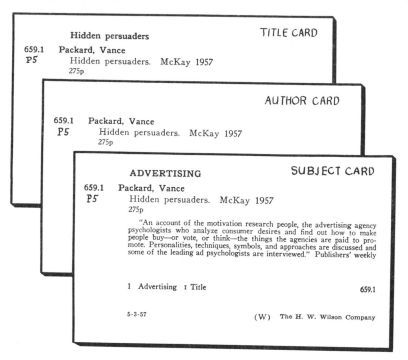

Here are the ten major classifications of the Dewey Decimal System:

000-099 General Works (including encyclopedias)
100-199 Philosophy (study of character and the mind)
200-299 Religion (including myths)
300-399 Social Sciences (races, education, government, clubs)
400-499 Language (including dictionaries)
500-599 Pure Science (mathematics, chemistry, physics, nature)
600-699 Useful Arts (health, aviation, engineering, cooking)
700-799 Fine Arts (painting, music, photography, games)
800-899 Literature (plays, poetry, essays, speeches)
900-999 History, Travel, Biography

Each major classification is subdivided into ten divisions. For instance, 900-909 is general world history, 910-919 is travel and geography, and 920-929 is collective biography. Some libraries extend a classification into decimal points (973.917), and many libraries add an author number to the Dewey Decimal number.

It is easy to see that this system is of invaluable help in finding a needed book even if you have forgotten much of the identifying details. You should be able to find the book you need as long as you can remember any *one* of these details: (a) the author's last name, (b) the first major word of the title, or (c) its general subject.

Periodicals

Days of thumbing through magazines at random could never unearth the specific information that an index to periodical literature can provide within minutes.

Periodical indexes, too, list material by author, title, and subject. Knowing just one of these things about a magazine article makes locating it possible. However, there are two points to be kept firmly in mind. First, periodical indexes are brought up-to-date at regular intervals, which means that each volume of the index lists only articles and stories appearing during the specific span of time indicated on the volume. Secondly, an index lists only those items appearing in the particular periodicals that have been regularly reviewed by that index. Therefore, if you are looking for an article in a magazine called, for instance, *Way Out*, determine first whether the index you are consulting includes *Way Out* in the listing of the magazines it examines.

An index that surveys a very broad range of general magazines is *The Readers' Guide to Periodical Literature*. This comprehensive index examines many of the general-interest magazines you see on magazine stands, and catalogs their articles and stories.

Here is the Readers' Guide entry for one of the periodicals listed in the bibliography for excerpt D.

> MANNES, Marya
> Ain't Nobody here but us commercials. Reporter
> 17:35-7 O 17 '57

For a translation of the abbreviations, examine the bibliography entry on text page 263. If you have trouble deciphering the abbreviations used in the *Readers' Guide*, use the abbreviation key in the front of the *Guide*.

Magazines whose articles are related to a particular field of interest are usually included in an index in that field. Find out if *your* library has one of these indexes to the periodical literature related to your own field(s) of interest. Here are a few such indexes:

Agricultural Index
The Art Index
Business Periodicals Index
The Education Index
Essay and General Literature Index
Industrial Arts Index
The International Index to Periodicals
The New York Times Index
Short Story Index

Reference Materials

You have only to picture a metropolitan telephone system without telephone directories to recognize what a great need there is for books in which certain information is presented in a systematic way. Once you have learned what information your telephone book contains (names, addresses, and telephone numbers) and discovered the system by which that information is presented (alphabetically by last name), you have a tremendous store of knowledge at your disposal. You are under no obligation to absorb all that information; you merely wait until the need arises to refer to just the bit you want.

Imagine how much more information is printed and waiting for your use in reference books of all kinds. No human mind could possibly absorb so much data. Yet any part of it is at your disposal if you have access to such references and know generally (a) what kind of information the reference contains and (b) by what system that information is arranged.

Here are some commonly used reference works. Find out which of them *your* library has available and study them until you know what is in them, generally, and how to find information in specific instances.

ENCYCLOPEDIAS
Collier's Encyclopedia
The Columbia Encyclopedia
Compton's Encyclopedia
Encyclopædia Britannica
Encyclopedia Americana
New International Encyclopedia
World Book Encyclopedia

OTHER REFERENCES
Dictionary of American Biography
Information Please Almanac
The N.Y. Times Encyclopedic Almanac
Webster's Biographical Dictionary
Who's Who
Who's Who in America
World Almanac and Book of Facts

Exercise 4

1. Select five books at random, either from books on the library shelves or from cards in the file if the stacks are not open to you. Look through the card catalog for the author, titile, and subject cards for each book. Copy the information given on the author card in each case, and indicate how the title and the subject cards differ from the author card.

2. In *The Readers' Guide to Periodical Literature*, locate entries for five magazine articles on any one or more of the topics below. Copy the entries exactly as you find them, and then recopy them with all the abbreviations completed and all the symbols explained.

Exercise 4,
continued

Studies in minority group culture(s)
Television advertising
Rockets and missiles
Great Britain
Drug addiction
Professional football

3. See what follows the name of your state in the entries of one or two encyclopedias. Summarize the information you find.

4. Try to locate some brief facts about the life of a famous man from your state. Check both encyclopedias and biographical sources. Write a brief summary.

5. In a source such as the *World Almanac and Book of Facts*, try to find some bit of data regarding your state. Look for its record for a specified time in some achievement— miles of highway, bushels of corn, tons of wheat, and so forth. Summarize the facts.

6. In what class would you find each of these books, according to the Dewey Decimal System?
   (a) A cookbook
   (b) A history of the United States
   (c) A dictionary of the English language
   (d) A book on music
   (e) A book of poetry
   (f) A book on plants

TOPIC AND TITLE

Now that you have reevaluated your library skills, let's go back to excerpt D, on text pages 249-265, to consider some of the choices the writer might have faced and to supply possible reasons for the viewpoint he finally adopted. Remember that this theme has many formalities of presentation that our everyday applications of the research process do not include. However, at the heart it makes an *appeal to authority,* just as we do, informally, in our conversations, discussions, and arguments.

Both the topics and the title of this formal theme are very general. For many situations, such an approach would be too general. It does not sufficiently *limit* the direction of the research, nor does it provide a yardstick by which the available information can be sorted, sifted, and summarized. The writer committed himself to covering practically every available scrap of information on his subject.

However, there might be some justification for this overall approach to the topic. Subliminal perception was generally unheard of until the news of the experiment described in the opening of the paper aroused immediate curiosity on the part of the general public. The anticipated readers of this theme may never have heard of the term. A sweeping, general coverage might be in order for such an audience.

Had readers had some elementary knowledge of subliminal perception, the writer might have addressed himself to a more specific point. He might then have confined his whole study to just *one* of the areas comprising the major subdivisions of his material, as shown in his outline on text page 251. In your choices of topics, you will be wise to incline *toward* the specific and *away from* the general, unless you can see ample justification for doing otherwise.

Narrowing the Topic

You will often be asked to do research on a topic that has been suggested or assigned to you. If you have freedom within the subject area, however, many choices are still left up to you. Above all, you may limit the scope of the paper by narrowing the topic until it can be handled thoroughly in the *time* and *space* assigned. This can be done by focusing attention upon *one* aspect of the general subject. Thus, if assigned "The European Common Market," you might readily focus upon "The Problem of Currency in the European Common Market." If assigned "Professional Football," you might narrow it to a consideration of "The Growth of Professional Football" or "The Newest Professional Football League" or, even more specifically, "The Growth of the San Diego Chargers Professional Football Team." This kind of narrowing involves focusing upon just a limited segment of the larger subject. You may discover that you can write more, not less, on the limited topic.

Exercise 5

1. Supply four revised topics that might represent more specific focus of attention within each of these subject areas:
   (a) Careers for women
   (b) Famous black athletes
   (c) American communes
   (d) American colleges and universities
   (e) Nobel Prize winners
   (f) Science study for future space travelers

2. From the topics below, abstract a narrower topic from which a still narrower one can be drawn. Consider limitation by time, place, or circumstance. Try to carry this process to the third or fourth degree.

Exercise 5,
continued

EXAMPLE:

(a) Cotton — (1) International trade in cotton
           (2) U.S. international trade in cotton
           (3) U.S. imports in cotton
           (4) Imports of Middle Eastern cotton into the U.S.
           (5) Imports of Egyptian cotton into the U.S.
           (6) Imports of Egyptian long-staple cotton into the U.S.

(a) The struggle for civil rights in the U.S.
(b) The Presidents of the United States
(c) The armed forces of the United States
(d) The emancipation of women
(e) The Indians of North America
(f) Freedom of speech in the United States
(g) Asian influence in the American West

The Question Approach to a Topic

Whether or not you are assigned a topic, you may find the research process easier and more natural if you base your work on a question (which may or may not actually appear in your final title or finished paper).

Curiosity, aroused by a question, is a natural beginning for the research process. Proof lies in delving into the lives and achievements of many scientists and inventors. The pattern of experimental research called "the scientific method" also offers proof. Something starts a question gnawing at your mind. So you postulate an answer and then devise an experiment which will serve to contradict or reinforce your answer. Moreover, most of the research you may do after leaving the classroom is likely to be motivated by such curiosity — your own or that of your employer.

Is Car A safer than Car B?
What airline handles the most passenger service from the West Coast to the Orient?
Is law enforcement a promising career field?
What is the possibility of mass producing electric cars?
What caused the failure of the Apollo 13 mission?
Which countries were represented at Expo 70?
What are some of the best medical (dental, law) schools in the East (West)?
Does a person have to be a college graduate to become an officer in the armed forces?
Am I eligible for membership in the Peace Corps on the basis of my work with youth groups?

Perhaps the ring of familiarity in some of the questions above demonstrates how naturally a question arouses curiosity in a way that starts the research process in motion. Let's see what else it might do.

A question might limit a general subject quickly and meaningfully. Notice the last question above. It suggests with precision just what aspects of Peace Corps eligibility and activity will need to be considered. A researcher on this topic might find a tremendous amount of data on the Peace Corps in general. The question gives him a yardstick by which he can examine the mountain of information and select just the necessary details on which to make notes. He need only ask himself, "Does this information help supply the answer to my question?" If it does not, it may be ignored. He can skim over a great deal of material which he might otherwise read and note — only to realize later it was inappropriate.

A research question often requires a judgmental answer — a statement of opinion rather than a factual reply. Such questions always contain a high degree of speculation.

Will Antarctica ever support a permanent settlement?
What is the best way to guarantee a job for every man?
What is the best low-priced car now on the American market?
To what extent are moviemakers financially dependent on a young audience?

Even questions that may at first seem to be purely a matter of statistics might demand the exercise of judgment in interpreting the terms of the inquiry. Here is such a question: "What is the proportion of private to state-supported schools in the eastern United States?" Before you can begin to search for figures, you must decide what figures are to apply. Under "state-supported," are you going to count *district*- and *county*-supported schools? Are you going to count all levels of instruction or just "higher" education? And which states are you going to count as within the "eastern" United States?

Since the exercise of the researcher's judgment might be considered desirable (and perhaps essential) in the research process, the use of the question approach has merit in this regard. Not only does the researcher get practice in drawing conclusions from evidence, but the conclusions will give unity to the project and supply it with a meaningful purpose.

In other words, when your research project is formulated in a question, the question points a definite direction for the search to take; it keeps you from getting sidetracked in hazy heaps of data, and it demands an answer the discovery of which tells you the search is completed. It tells you where to go; it keeps you going; and it lets you know when you have arrived. And if the question demands speculation, it will exercise your power to make judgments and help you know just when and where to bring your own views into your project.

Exercise 6   *Rank from 1 to 5 the questions in each of the groups below, giving the 1 rating to that which comes closest to making the distinctions described above. Be prepared to justify your choices with logical reasoning.*

Topic	Questions
A. Photography	(a) What is the purpose, source, and result of filters?
	(b) What is the best kind of enlarger?
	(c) Why is photography the Number 1 national hobby?
	(d) How is photography used in warfare?
	(e) How big a business is amateur photography in the United States?
B. Cosmetics	(a) How misleading are cosmetic advertisements?
	(b) Are cosmetics too expensive?
	(c) How is lanolin produced?
	(d) What is the history of the use of cosmetics?
	(e) How much money do Americans spend annually on cosmetics?
C. Cities	(a) What is the future of the large city?
	(b) How can cities improve their educational facilities?
	(c) Is private or public transportation preferable in large cities?
	(d) Have city populations increased or decreased in the last ten years?
	(e) What are the ten largest cities in the world?
D. Basketball	(a) Is basketball a tall man's game?
	(b) How has the game of basketball changed in the last fifty years?
	(c) How does a winning basketball team in a school improve school spirit?
	(d) What is the average height of all the players selected for the major All-American teams in collegiate basketball in the last twenty years?
	(e) Why has basketball gained tremendous popularity?

Titles for Research Papers

It is quite common for the title of a research paper to identify the topic under discussion. This is especially true when that topic has been assigned. For example:

Sources of Pollution
Colonization of Australia
The Purchase of Alaska
American Dialects

Your choice of a title for your paper could be the determining factor in capturing the interest of your reader.

Subject Title The topics above suggest a general, descriptive, or explanatory sort of paper. However, one might do a paper on such a topic with such a title while seeking to answer a question that remains unasked, except in the mind of the researcher. He may wonder as he works, "What characteristics, if any, are common to all sources of pollution known in the United States?" "Which country has sent the greatest number of colonists to Australia?" "How was the purchase of Alaska received by the general public in 1867?" But when committed to a broad topic, questions may not easily occur to the writer.

Question Title When a question lies at the heart of the research, however, the use of the question in the title may serve at least two useful purposes: (1) it may strengthen communication, by letting the reader know just where to direct his attention within a general subject, and (2) it may arouse his curiosity in a way no subject label can. This is demonstrated in the following titles, one a subject title and the other a question title:

Mexican Jumping Beans
What Puts the Jump into Mexican Jumping Beans?

Answer (Conclusion) Title A research paper might appropriately be given any one of these titles:

Lowering the Voting Age
Should Eighteen-Year-Olds Vote?
Eighteen-Year-Olds Are Ready to Vote

The first title suggests a topic, the second a question on that topic, and the third an answer to that question. The third title focuses attention on the writer's judgments, presumably drawn at the conclusion of the paper on the basis of evidence (appeals to authority) cited in the paper. While the answer title clearly directs the reader's attention, as does the question title, it may sacrifice the appeal to reader curiosity usually contained in the question title. In addition, the answer title might even turn away readers who are strongly committed to an opposite point of view. Therefore, the answer title may be effective (a) when you are aiming for an audience that is likely to be committed in advance to the conclusions drawn, or (b) when it suggests a position which is so unique, so startling, or so opposed to the reader's view that he *must* read the entire paper to learn how that conclusion was reached.

For information on the arrangement of the title, see the comments on text page 252.

Exercise 7 *For each of the general areas listed below, devise a less general subject. Then from it construct (a) a subject title, (b) a question title, and (c) an answer (a conclusion) title.*

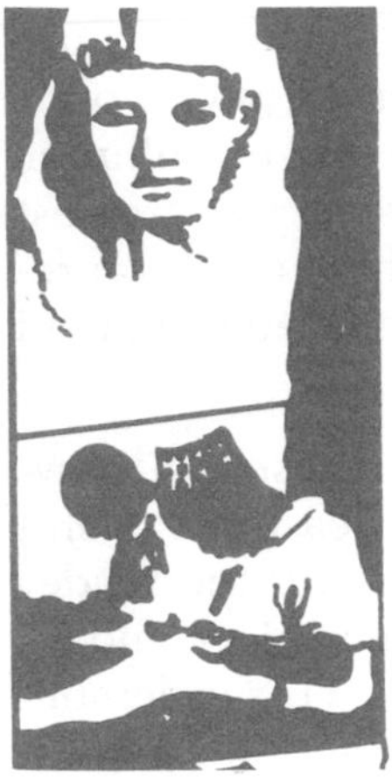

1. Mountains of the world
2. Crime
3. India
4. The agriculture of my state
5. The industry of my state
6. The parks of my city
7. Water pollution
8. Historic places in America
9. Missiles
10. Automation

THE OUTLINE

The outline for excerpt D on text page 251 is the final outline–the finished product. Such an outline develops as the research itself develops. If you know enough about your topic to construct a highly detailed outline *before* you have collected your information, it might indicate that your project may involve not research and discovery but a review of what you already know.

You will find it helpful in organizing your material if, before you begin to take notes, you make up a *rough* outline on the basis of what you do know. This working outline can grow and change with your findings, right up to the finished form of both your outline and your paper.

It stands to reason that if you have not gathered the information on a topic, your working outline cannot reflect factual distinctions but must be based on logical subdivisions of a subject field.

Imagine that the writer of excerpt D had read *only* the account of the New Jersey experiment in subliminal perception. What questions might he be asking himself about the strange device and the unusual psychological principle behind it?

(I)	**The New Jersey Experiment**
(II)	What is subliminal perception?
(III)	How does it work?
(IV)	What happens to a person when he "sees" it?
(V)	Who wants it anyway? Why?
(VI)	Who is against it? Why?
(VII)	What has actually happened to it since the New Jersey experiment?
(VIII)	What will happen to it in the future?

Compare this list of questions with the main Roman numeral entries of the finished outline for excerpt D. Do you see how each main entry suggests that *that* section of the finished paper will answer these unstated questions?

Making a tentative outline may help you find and select the detailed information you want. Moreover, it can make the job of *organizing* your material a gradual and simple task, as we shall demonstrate later.

⌐ For information on the formalities of outlining, see the comments on text page 250.

Exercise 8   *Suggest several subdivisions of each of the issues below. Your list will reflect your previous experience with the subject matter, so do not hesitate to suggest a division of the anticipated material that differs from that of a fellow student.*

1. How does being out of a job affect an unemployed person?

2. Are we Americans preserving our lakes and streams?

3. How does the food-producing (pulpwood) (manufacturing) industry affect the economy of this state?

4. A plan for improving living conditions in my neighborhood.

5. Do war heroes have a record of success as public officeholders?

6. What summer jobs are available in ____?

7. What rights do you have as a citizen of the United States if you are arrested?

8. Scholarship opportunities in the state colleges and universities.

FINDING YOUR MATERIAL

Remember: The three vital bodies of information to be found in a library are

(1) books,

(2) periodicals, and

(3) other reference works.

Be sure to explore each body of information carefully when collecting material for a research paper.

Why do you suppose that periodicals were the principal sources of information used in the preparation of the research paper produced in part on text pages 249-265? It may be assumed that since the New Jersey experiment brought the topic suddenly before the public, and the research paper was probably written shortly thereafter, few books on the subject were then available. In your own research, however, you will no doubt be able to find information in a wide range of sources. The sections that follow will help you avoid the pitfalls of amateur researching.

KEEPING TRACK OF YOUR SOURCES

Once a book, a magazine article, or another source has been found, the vital information on that source should be accurately recorded — usually on a 3 x 5 card, called a *bibliography card.*

When you are doing research for a paper, arm yourself with a set of blank cards. On top of this stack of cards, place pattern cards, similar to those shown on page 285. Each time you visit the library, even just to browse, take the cards with you. When a source proves fruitful, you will have on hand not only a blank bibliography card but also a pattern for recording the needed information in a conventional way. Once you have recorded bibliography data on a card, it will not be necessary to rewrite the information until it is put into footnote and bibliographic form in the final draft. When you follow a system, less work — not more — is the eventual result.

You will also find it helpful to give each bibliography card an identifying symbol in the lower right corner. When you begin taking notes, you can use the symbol instead of the full title to identify the source of the information on the card.

Bibliography Cards

PATTERN CARDS TYPICAL CARDS

For a Book

```
Call Number
Author (Last Name, First Name)
Title of Book
Place of Publication
Publisher
Date of Publication

                    Identifying
                    Symbol
```

```
659.1
P 5
Packard, Vance
The Hidden Persuaders
New York
David McKay Company, Inc.
1957                    HP
```

For a Magazine Article

```
Author (Last Name, First Name)
"Title of Article"
Name of Magazine
Volume (Month, Day, Year)
Pages

                    Identifying
                    Symbol
```

```
Brean, Herbert
"Hidden Sell' Technique
Is Almost Here"
Life
vol. 44 (March 31, 1958)
pp. 102-104
                    LIFE
```

For an Encyclopedia Article

```
"Title of Article"
Name of Encyclopedia
Volume and Pages




                    Identifying
                    Symbol
```

```
"Advertising"
World Book Encyclopedia
vol. 1, p. 62




                    WB-1
```

Exercise 9   *Prepare sample bibliography cards, taking from the data below whatever information is necessary and arranging it in the prescribed manner.*

1. *Newsweek*
   vol. 75
   pp. 30-40
   "Ravaged Environment"
   January 26, 1970

2. Doubleday & Company, Inc.
   Abraham S. Behrman
   1968
   Water Is Everybody's Business
   New York

3. February 7, 1970
   "How Students See the Pollution Issue"
   Business Week
   pp. 86-88

4. "From the Floor: Questions and Answers"
   December, 1969
   American Forests
   pp. 40-41
   vol. 75

5. *U.S. News & World Report*
   vol. 68
   February 2, 1970
   "Latest Moves on Pollution Control"
   p. 5

6. vol. 34
   p. 34
   Look
   "Five Who Care"
   R. Dubos
   April 21, 1970

7. *Water: The Vital Essence*
   New York
   Harper and Row, Inc.
   Peter Briggs

TAKING NOTES

Some of the original note cards used in the preparation of the research paper on subliminal perception are reproduced on page 288. By studying these cards, you should be able to make several observations about note-taking in general. In the lower right corner, there is a symbol which positively associates the note card with the symbol in the lower right corner of the bibliography card for that particular note. (If more than one article from the same magazine is cited or if more than one book by the same author is used, each article and each book would have a separate bibliography card with its own identifying symbol.) In addition to the identification of the source, the exact page number of the particular note is indicated (for footnote information that will be needed later). At the top of the card, there is a symbol indicating what part of the working outline the note *might* later fit. All the samples on page 288 are marked "I" to indicate that they were expected to apply under the first division in the working outline.

A very limited bit of information is entered on a single card. The notation may seem to be a waste of time and card space at this point, but it will be compensated for in time saved later on in the organizing process. Since you cannot predict with certainty where each piece of information will fit into your paper, putting just one bit of data on a card will give you greater freedom to shuffle material later on, when the paper begins to take shape.

Some of the information on note cards may be in the form of questions. Key phrases, unusual words or phrases, and phrases that indicate a strong personal judgment are quoted *directly,* while more verifiable information is gleaned from the sources in summary form. Statements answering such questions as *who? what? when? where?* suggest factual information that may often be summarized in your own words without distortion. But words suggesting a strong personal evaluation, a guess, a hunch, an opinion, or an attitude are often the food of controversy. It is difficult to paraphrase such nonfactual expressions without changing their tone and possibly distorting their intent.

Exercise 10

Examine the nine statements at the top of page 290. Mark F those that you think relate impersonally to who, what, when, *or* where. *Mark O those that you think incline toward private opinion or belief, guesses, personal attitude, and so forth.*

Brean, Herbert
"'Hidden Sell' Technique
   Is Almost Here"
Life
vol. 44 (March 31, 1958)
pp. 102–104
                        LIFE

Talese, Gay
"Most Hidden Hidden
   Persuasion"
The New York Times
Magazine
January 12, 1958
pp. 22, 59–60   NYT

Mannes, Marya
"Ain't Nobody Here but
   Us Commercials"
Reporter
vol. 17 (October 17, 1957)
pp. 35–37
                        REP

Time & Place   I
Demonstration of SP at Ft.
Lee (N.J.) movie house;
late summer, 1957,
"several weeks."
                        LIFE
                        104

No. of people   I
cites N.J. demonstration:
45,699 patrons

                        NYT
                        22

Nature of demonstration I
During feature (Novak,
Picnic) flashed "Hungry?
Eat Popcorn" & "Drink
Cola" alt. every 5 sec. at
1/3000 sec.   LIFE
                        104

Results   I
cites 45,000 patrons. Incr.
57.5% popcorn sales;
18.1% cola, per
Vicary
                        REP
                        35

1
2
3
4
5

What Is Subliminal Perception?

For several weeks during the late summer last year (LIFE 104), 45,699 movie fans (NYT 22) filed in and out of a theater in Ft. Lee, New Jersey, apparently as usual, watched a picture, ate popcorn, and drank soft drinks. What they didn't know, as they watched such stars as Kim Novak in Picnic, was that two advertising slogans — "Hungry? Eat Popcorn" and "Drink Cola" — were being flashed on the screen, alternately, every five seconds, for just one three-thousandth of a second. This was much too brief for the conscious mind to be aware of. (LIFE 104)

But subconsciously, the forty-five thousand movie-goers did see the slogans, and many reacted to them, according to the tester,
g researcher and psychologist.
ather startling proof to back
, popcorn sales went up 57.5%,
(REP 35) Vicary gave all the

What Is Subliminal Perception?

For several weeks, during the late summer of 1957,[1] 45,699 movie fans[2] filed in and out of a theater in Fort Lee, New Jersey. They watched the double attraction, ate popcorn, and drank soft drinks. What they did not know was that two advertising slogans, "Hungry? Eat Popcorn" and "Drink Cola," were being flashed on the screen alternately every five seconds for just one three-thousandth of a second. This exposure was much too brief to be consciously perceived by the Fort Lee patrons.[3]

But subconsciously, the 45,699 movie-goers did see the slogans, and many reacted to them — according to the tester, Mr. James M. Vicary, a New York marketing researcher and psychologist.[4] Mr. Vicary's proof: Popcorn sales went up 57.5 percent during the test, he said, while soft-drink sales picked up by 18.1 percent.[5] Vicary gave the credit for the boost to the unseen advertisement — the "phantom plug," as one critic called it, a process which

[1] Herbert Brean, "'Hidden Sell' Technique Is Almost Here," *Life,* vol. 44 (March 31, 1958), p. 104.
[2] Gay Talese, "Most Hidden Hidden Persuasion," *The New York Times Magazine* (January 12, 1958), p. 22.
[3] Brean, "'Hidden Sell' . . . ," p. 104.
[4] Ibid.
[5] Marya Mannes, "Ain't Nobody Here but Us Commercials," *The Reporter,* vol. 17 (October 17, 1957), p. 35.

Exercise 10,
continued

a. I saw an old film last week called *The Great Train Robbery.*

b. *A Raisin in the Sun* was a very exciting film, one of the best I've ever seen.

c. My brother broke out in a rash after eating dill pickles.

d. Elephants are my favorite circus animals — after lions.

e. I have come to the conclusion that the candidate opposing me is obnoxious, overbearing, loud, and spiteful.

f. I live on West 92nd Street, in a five-room apartment on the top floor of a very large building.

g. It is thought that the robber fled by a rear door and made his escape in a 1970 Ford hardtop.

h. The fire chief gave three possible causes of the blaze: spontaneous combustion, careless smoking, or arson.

i. Four men and a boy were observed leaving the garage in an old, battered pickup truck.

Exercise 11

Study an item selected by your teacher from a newspaper, a magazine, or a book. Take ten note cards, and on the first enter one bit of information that you consider the most important in the article. On a second card, list the most significant point not covered by the previous note. Continue until you have ten notes ranked in importance from most to least important. A day or so later, write a summary of the original item from your notes. Make the summary about a third as long as the original item, and be sure to put quotation marks around words and phrases whose uniqueness clearly identifies them as part of the original passage.

Exercise 12

On note cards, summarize the remarks of a strongly opinionated writer of an item furnished by your teacher. Use direct quotations for the most colorful, spectacular, or controversial expressions of the writer, but condense his other remarks in such phrases as . . . he said that . . . , according to . . . , and so forth (see pages 243-244).

Then, in a brief summary, emphasize what you felt was most significant, omitting what was least important. Above all, leave no hint in your summary of whether you agree or disagree with the opinions stated by the original writer. As a researcher, you must be objective while reporting your findings. Later you will have a chance to state your own position.

THE ROUGH DRAFT

On page 289 is a sample of the rough draft of the research paper on subliminal perception. The note-taking has ended. The working outline has been reconsidered in the light of all that the writer has learned in his research. Now the note cards must be arranged to correspond with the revised outline. Placement will be easy if each note is given a place in the working outline as that note is taken.

The advantage of having only one piece of information on a card will be obvious when you have to assign that card to a position in the order of notes. Try to be consistent within whatever conventional pattern you are asked to use. Do not, without approval or a definite reason, handle part of the technicalities according to one pattern and the rest according to another.

Finally, do not become so involved in the niceties of *form* in "dress parade" papers that you lose sight of the research process. The aim of the research process is not flawless footnotes and extensive bibliographies; it is *discovery*. It is the reaching beyond your own experience to discover authorities who will inform you and support you. These authorities will supply you with the evidence upon which you can base your own decisions and upon which you can present those decisions convincingly to all who will hear your voice and read your written words.

WORKING FROM NOTES

Now all the note cards are in an orderly stack. There has been some hard work but no wasted effort. There has been no needless running back and forth to the library to correct previous oversights. There has been no recopying of data.

Start writing. Your task is to move the discussion as smoothly as possible from one bit of researched information to the next, and from one group of notes (major divisions of the paper) to the next. Offer no new information that your research did not uncover; offer no information for which you show no source, either by associating it with a person introduced in the paper or by reference to a footnote identifying the source.

Notice that excerpt D contains three kinds of statements. First there are factual statements (*who, what, when, where*) which suggest that the observations involved have been or could be verified. Second, there are the opinions advanced by the authorities who are cited in the study. Third, there are the writer's own opinions, which enter the theme as his concluding remarks.

These three kinds of statements are clearly distinguished. With factual statements, there may be only a footnote to indicate the source. But rarely is a statement of opinion given without tying it to a speaker, or without some other acknowledgment.

On the other hand, the writer's own opinions in his concluding remarks are clearly indicated as his own, not only because they come all at once at the end but because the pronoun labels identify them. And in this respect, there is nothing ignoble about the use of the pronoun *I* as often as necessary when stating your own conclusions. You may choose to inject your opinions at intervals in the paper, but you should clearly distinguish them from researched data *or* the opinions of your authorities.

Appeals to authorities are emphasized. If, as has been stated before, the research process is an operation extending beyond the sweep of one's own experience to support received from others, then the need to make the *most* of the authorities cited is apparent. This need involves supplying identifying details that will amplify the pronouncements of the authority. References to the title a person holds may help readers accept his judgments. Notice the following:

> . . . according to Dr. Jones . . .
> . . . word has been received from General Dunn to the effect . . .
> . . . Professor John R. Jones agrees that . . .

Other identifying details, combined with each citation of the authority, may add further to the reception of his point of view.

If one of the claims to authority rests in an office held by the person cited, his position should be prominently alluded to at least once:

> John R. Mills, Director of the Highway Radiation Laboratory, is of the opinion that . . .
> Mr. Howard Brown, President of the Chamber of Commerce, said . . .

In excerpt D both the immediate source (Mr. Vicary) and a less direct source (*Life*) were cited in the text of the paper. Quotations bring both the prestige of the person *and* the prestige of the magazine to the attention of the reader. After all, if *you* are convinced by your sources, and if *you* respect their authority, your readers may share that conviction and respect. You must, however, enhance the prestige of your sources in as many ways as possible.

THE FINAL FORM

Making the final draft from this point was largely routine work for the writer of excerpt D. The title page (text page 249) was constructed to *identify* and *date* the project. The outline was typed after it had been checked for agreement with the completed rough draft. A bibliography was typed directly from only those bibliography cards describing sources actually cited in the paper. With the bibliography information on cards, the data was arranged in alphabetical order according to the author's last name. Books and periodicals used in the preparation of excerpt D were listed separately, but in a shorter bibliography they might have appeared in a single alphabetical list.

◖ For information on the correct form for a bibliography, turn back to the comments on text pages 260, 262, and 264.

The final form requires the addition of footnotes. Look at the parenthetical notes in the rough draft on page 289. Having already written the bibliography in final form, the writer can consult it and estimate from it how many lines on the page each footnote might take.

◖ For information on the correct form for footnotes, turn back to the comments on pages 252, 254, 256, and 258.

The form of the research paper is a matter of convention. Do not be surprised to learn that other ways of handling the formalities touched upon in this chapter exist and thrive. Perhaps your teacher will ask you to modify the patterns given here for preparing bibliography cards, note cards, rough drafts, footnotes, title pages, and so forth.

Exercise 13   Using the various sections of this chapter as a guide, prepare a research paper on a topic of your own choosing.

Summing Up

The research process is an appeal to authority — either to a direct source or to an indirect source. The best place to search out an indirect source is, of course, the library. You should become familiar with the kinds of books, periodicals, and reference works available to you and know how to use the card catalog.

After selecting a topic for a research paper, you will have to narrow it for proper handling and then determine your approach — by subject, by question, or by answer. Finally, after taking notes, preparing an outline, and making a bibliography, you will be ready to write your paper.

In transferring the results of your research to paper, there are certain conventions of form that should be observed — either those conventions followed in the excerpt on text pages 249-265 or those suggested by your teacher.

ဆင့် ဖြံခံပေါ် သောလှိုင်းတိုက်စားမှုအတွက် အသုံးကျစေ၏။ တိုက်စားခြင်းဆက်
လက်ဖြံခံပေါ် စဉ် လှိုင်းစားကမ်းပါးဆင့်များ ဖြံခံပေါ် လာ၏။ ဂင်းကိုကုန်းဖက်ပိုင်း
တွင် ထောင်လိုက် သို့မဟုတ် ထောင်လိုက် နီးပါးခန့်ရှိသော ကမ်းပါးထစ်ဖြင့် သတ်
မှတ်ထား၏။ လှိုင်းစားကမ်းပါးဆင့်ကို တခါတရံ လှိုင်းစားခုံမြင့်၊ လှိုင်းစားရေ
တိမ်ပိုင်း၊ လှိုင်းစားကမ်းပြင်၊ လှိုင်းစားလွင်ပြင်ဟူ၍လည်း ခေါ်ကြ၏။ ထိုလှိုင်း

Burmese စားကမ်းပါးဆင့်နှင့် ကမ်းပါးစောက်များမှ ရရှိသော အနည်အနှစ်များကို ရေအ

CREATIVE
WRITING

**A Look
Back
and
A Look
Forward**

You have learned the techniques of writing and where to look for source material. The chapters you have covered thus far lead to your next undertaking—creative writing.

Your aim in Chapter 4 will be to put words together to create a feeling of reality for your reader. You will learn how to present word pictures of actual human experiences. If you can stimulate your imagination sufficiently to arouse emotion in others, you will evoke suspense—a degree of urgency—that will grip the attention of your reader.

295

WHAT IS FICTION?

Most of the writing discussed so far in this book, and probably most of the writing in the world today, concerns *actual* human experiences. You read and write about what is happening today, what happened in the past, and what might actually happen in the future. How are things in Hong Kong this morning? What occurred long ago in Pompeii? What reaction can you expect if you mix Chemical X with Chemical Z?

Picture the range of books in a library, row after row, shelf upon shelf: current events, history, biography, life science, physical science, social science, political science—medicine, theology, law—textbooks, workbooks, handbooks—books, books, books. And most of them deal with actual human experience. Even those that speculate about the future usually do so in terms of what might actually happen.

The books on one shelf contain no specific facts such as: "The temperature in Hong Kong this morning is 71 degrees Fahrenheit." The shelf is labeled FICTION. The writers of these books have been free to take *words* and manipulate them (throw them around just for fun) without having to stick to accounts of actual happenings in the world. Some of the authors may have tried to create the illusion of the actual and the factual. The one about Hong Kong, for example, is not about Hong Kong this morning—it is about Hong Kong on the second Tuesday of this week, or last week, or never. The situations are fictional, the persons, fictitious; they have been invented by the author.

WRITING FOR YOURSELF

Just as a toddler can "paint" without rules or lessons or elaborate directions, *you* can write fiction for your own enjoyment. As the child needs only paints, brush, and water—and a brief demonstration of how to bring these elements together for his purpose—you need only some words at your command and a demonstration of how to put them together.

> It to me ready no maybe a on book to too two four New York think back rubber band green slate white paper toy watch go team go keep up fall down try

If you search the passage above for some secret-but-important message, you will have overlooked the possibility that there was no attempt made to communicate, at least not consciously. Words thrown around just for fun need not communicate anything directly, not even to the person who wrote them; those above didn't, to their writer. As long as a writer of fiction chooses to operate for his own private enjoyment, then —like the child with the paints—he is free of facts, of rules, and of making sense.

There is, however, another reward for fiction writers, one beyond private satisfaction. This secondary benefit lies in the response that the writer of fiction *may* produce in the mind of a reader of that fiction.

REALITY IN FICTION

Take another book from the fiction shelf. It reveals many things about a person, the book's main character. Yet the writer invented this character. The person in the story is not real; that is, he has never been a part of verifiable events in the actual world of time and space. But there is a curious thing about this imaginary story character: you are given so many vivid details of his personality, you are shown such an intimate view of the invented person that he seems actually to exist. Thus a fiction writer can cause you to experience a feeling for an unreal character that is stronger than your feelings for Aunt Martha, for instance, who occupies space in time, who is factual, not fictional. This is part of the magic of fiction.

WRITING REALISTIC FICTION

Since fiction making in its most natural form (for the private enjoyment of the painter or writer) has neither rules nor restraints, there is nothing to do but hand you the language or set of paints and stand back to observe the results.

Concern for the remainder of this chapter, therefore, will be focused upon the composing of fiction that is consciously made to draw a response from readers. The primary effect aimed for is a *feeling of reality* in the mind of the reader and the subsequent responses that may follow that feeling of reality.

It will be assumed that if your fiction is patterned on human experiences, making representations, not copies of actual events, and imitating the patterns, not the facts of reality, you may best evoke the feeling of reality desired.

You should practice inventing fictional people to inhabit fictional places, where they may discuss fictional subjects in fictional conversations or leap into fictional action. The ability to make such fiction and the very personal pleasure the attempt can bring are within the reach of every one of you.

Will the results be creative?

Yes, the results will be unique and original. They will reflect your individuality. They will express your imagination and your initiative. In doing all these things, they will be creative. Beyond this nothing can be promised.

Will your fiction be any good?

Will your fiction be great art?

Will your fiction be literature?

Will your fiction be read and appreciated?

Will your fiction make you rich or famous?

These judgments rest with the world, and they depend, among other things, on the strength of the emotional response your fiction produces in the readers. Can you, through fiction (unreal events, persons), cause a reader to have a stronger feeling of reality than he might have if confronted with real events? Will a reader of your fiction, for instance, feel more sadness at the passing of your fictional hero than he did on reading of five factual deaths in his morning paper?

You may measure your fiction by the strength of this feeling of reality, the emotional response in your readers. The words in the language are many and free to all; but it is a rare and wonderful accomplishment to choose a few words and arrange them so, and—through the magic of an imaginary person or place or act—have them spring to life in a reader's eyes. It is not for every writer of fiction to be Rumpelstiltskin, able to turn straw into gold. But you can do some fresh, imaginative, creative writing, nevertheless.

EXPLAINING OR DRAMATIZING?

Read the following news item:

> Nine-year-old Gary Bender, son of Mr. and Mrs. Henry Bender, 2113 Beulah Drive, was found alive and unharmed this morning after spending last night on the slopes of Turkey Peak, where the temperature dipped to 17 degrees above zero.

In these few words is quite a lot of information. For instance:

Who	Nine-year-old Gary Bender, son of Mr. and Mrs. Henry Bender, 2113 Beulah Drive
What	. . . was found alive and unharmed
When	. . . this morning after spending last night
Where	. . . on the slopes of Turkey Peak, where the temperature dipped to 17 degrees above zero

The news item tells you about Gary Bender. But what emotion, if any, did the account produce in you? Did it engage your feelings? Would it not be better to show you some details of the incident in a way that will help you feel the *who*, the *what*, the *when*, and the *where*? Instead of an explanation of what happened to Gary, let's construct a *dramatization* of what happened to him.

The boy awakened, shivering violently, just before dawn, when the eastern sky was brightening and the black lines of trees began to show clearly against the forest behind them.

He realized that the pine boughs he had pulled over him had fallen away as he slept, but he did not want to take his hands from where they burrowed into the pockets of his thin jacket. It seemed that all the remaining warmth of his body was captured in the clenched fists and the two small places where those fists pressed against his ribs. So he lay, shivering, amid the jumble of sticks and limbs and branches he had pulled together as darkness came on the night before, after he had grown hoarse from shouting and had begun to feel that he would not be found that night — if at all.

Now he lay huddled on his side, his teeth chattering and his breath condensing into brief puffs of vapor. With his chin he could feel the roughness where his breath had formed ice on his jacket collar, and he noticed the heavy frost on the grass and the pines. Down the mountain and up the slope that stood opposite Turkey Peak, he saw the patches of snow that had attracted him and thus coaxed him away from the Boy Scout camp at Cave Springs, one morning ago.

He remembered assuring himself that his tracks in the snow would guide him back to camp. He hadn't expected the sun to melt so much of the thin snow. Now he felt again the approach of tears as he recalled the awful emptiness of realizing that he was lost and alone. But the numbing cold and beginning pangs of hunger brought him out of his reverie. After all, he thought, he had come through one night, and he was almost ten years old. He drew himself tighter together and went on shivering and breathing in rapid puffs that were cut short because of his uncontrollable shaking.

As the sun's first rays began to sparkle on the frosty, timbered peaks, the boy debated exposing his warm hands enough to pull his pine-bough bedding around him again. But hunger began to overrule cold, and with the sun, his hopes began to rise. Maybe they did miss him, he thought. Maybe they were searching for him.

He forced himself to straighten out. With the first movement against new, colder points of contact, his arms and legs were shocked into reacting; he rolled to all fours and then to his feet, though his arms and legs still kept somewhat to their cramped positions.

Suddenly he had never felt so much alive, despite his various miseries. The gnawing hunger that he felt aroused him to action.

"Hey," he shouted to the woods and mountains. Then, testing to see how much voice he had left after the hoarseness of the night before, he shouted as loud as he could. "Hey!"

From down the mountain an echo seemed to come back. "Heeyy . . . !"
Then from far away came the words, "That you, Gary? Hey . . . Gary . . . ?"
The boy shook his head, once, in disbelief and then broke into a grin.
"Hey!" he shouted again.

Cramps gone, cold vanished, hunger forgotten, he sprang completely over
his hasty shelter and began streaking downhill toward the sound of his
name, yelling jubilantly as he ran.

Does the dramatization answer the questions: Who? What? When?
Where?

Which of the two accounts engages your feelings more? Which version makes you feel as though you know the boy named Gary? Which
version makes you feel that you know what happened and where? Which
account helps you feel the immediacy (the *now*) of Gary's rescue?

The approach in the second version represents an attempt to *show*
rather than *tell* who, what, when, and where. It calls for presenting
specific details that may permit the reader to recreate the experience
for himself, so that he can feel the events (respond emotionally to them)
rather than simply know (respond intellectually to) them. Earlier it was
suggested that one measure of fiction rests in how strongly it can produce
in the reader the feeling of reality, despite its being fictional. It seems
logical, therefore, that the feeling of reality—or any emotional response
in the reader—will be strengthened through a dramatization rather than
an explanation of events.

Exercise 1   *Reconstruct the accounts below so that each makes a more
direct appeal to a reader's senses. Substitute emotional certainty ("I feel it") about the subject in place of intellectual
certainty ("I know it"). In other words, try showing what is
so far only told about. Words that convey sight, sounds,
tastes, smells, and sensations (touch) will be especially effective, as well as those that convey more general human emotions—love, pity, sympathy, sadness.*

Child Treated for Rat Bite

The parents of one-year-old Angela Brown who lives at
2406 South Dakota Avenue, Apartment 704, reported to city
health authorities that they had to go out in last night's storm
at 3 a.m. to seek treatment for a rat bite on their child's hand.

Fred and Lena Brown, parents of the injured child, were
clearly shaken by the incident. They told of finding the animal in the room after they responded to the girl's cries. They
speculated that either the baby was asleep with its arm hanging from its crib, or it reached toward the rodent out of
curiosity.

Exercise 1,
continued

News Item

A local teen-ager, Howard Barnstorm, son of Mrs. Mary Barnstorm, 814 Vine Street, was injured early last night when the car he was driving left State Route 4 two miles west of town and overturned four times.

Witnesses reported that young Barnstorm appeared to go off the road as though blinded by the glare of lights from on-coming cars.

The young man, a senior at North High School, was taken by Johnstown ambulance to Community Central Hospital, where his condition was reported last night as serious but not critical.

BASIC ELEMENTS OF FICTION

Let's consider the places, persons, events, and other elements that writers often put into their fictional dramatizations of human experience. To pull one such element out of fiction and study and practice it is rather artificial because the feeling of reality so important to the effect may be shattered by analysis. The effect must be achieved by the inter-action of place, person, event, and so on. But let's start with the single element of *place* in fiction. Then in taking up new elements, let's con-sider them first in themselves and second in terms of their effect on other elements and on the piece of fiction to which they are added.

The Element of Place

Factual events are assumed to occur at a particular time in space. Accounts of the events can be pinpointed: Where? When? Likewise, in fiction, the sense of place (where) and place-in-time (when) are often essential to effectiveness (feeling of reality). *Place* furnishes the stage and the scenery on which and against which the characters may act. Vivid, specific details in descriptive passages also help to convey place in fiction.

Your fathers will not remember the old Tylor farmstead because it crum-bled to gray ruin before their time. Tramps and drifters burned the scraps of its weathered boards in their campfires, and cattle walked through the broken fences and trampled the dry weeds and the ashes of the campfires and the last of the gray boards into dust.

But your grandfathers will remember. They can still picture the Tylor place, not only at the time of its abandonment by the last surviving heir, crippled Jimmy Tylor, but as it stood in the years before the tragedy. Then its freshly painted gables brightened the morning sky; and in the glow of its lamps and lanterns after sunset, it was alive with the shadowy flashing of dancers, the quick movements of young men and women, young boys and girls, and always the sound of young voices—loud and interrupting, and mixed with laughter, and quick with the quickness of young life itself.

Descriptions such as the one above may be developed in themselves, or they may be intermingled with other elements throughout the whole presentation. The latter approach is especially noticeable in modern fiction.

The passage above contains few, if any, statistics. The feeling of time is attempted not through clocks or calendars, but through a picture of the effects of the passage of time. The feeling of place has been attempted through impressions rather than measures of height and distance, number of rooms, and so forth.

Specific images (words that make pictures) have been used in an attempt to reach the reader through his five senses (smell, touch, taste, hearing, and sight) as well as through his inner sensations (sympathy, pity, sadness, and so on).

As a writer of fiction, you have the choice of any location your mind can conceive. If you are trying to produce the feeling of reality, however, your picture of that spot must be logically consistent with the world the reader knows. There must be such things as gravity, day-and-night, birth-and-death, and change, always change. And let there be no mixing of such anachronistic elements as high-button shoes with jet airplanes.

Not only can you choose your location but also the *time* you wish to show that location. The passage above briefly shows two times at the Tylor place—past and present, or prosperity and ruin. Furthermore, you have an almost infinite choice of accompanying circumstances with which to convey the feeling of a place. Is your fiction to be dramatized in winter or summer, light or darkness, sunshine or clouds, snow or rain, bad times or prosperous times, youth or age, peace or war—or any intermediate stages of any of these?

The Element of Choice

As you can see from the discussion above, the power to choose from almost endless alternatives is the unique advantage of the fiction writer. Not only does he have three areas of choice in the places of his fiction (location, time, and background circumstances), but the range of alternatives is multiplied each time a new element is introduced. It is true that you, the writer, might make these choices automatically or unconsciously, yet you need only to pretend otherwise to realize the vast range of alternatives.

Let's say that to dramatize a fictional experience you decide to choose from among ten places, ten persons, ten courses of action, and ten ways each course of action might be resolved. A bit of multiplication will indicate that you could develop at least ten thousand different fictional combinations of these elements without introducing any new variables. When you realize that there are many other variables possible, and that your choice of a person or place or action might be from among hundreds or thousands rather than tens, the great versatility of fiction is evident. Furthermore, this flexibility makes fiction writing an excellent instrument for individual self-expression. Faced with the astronomical number of alternatives of fictional places, people, conflicts, actions, resolutions, and so forth, your choices—largely unconscious, perhaps—must certainly reflect not only who you are but what you think and feel and believe and want in life—all that makes you an individual, different—in some ways—from every other person alive. Similar astronomical alternatives must surely face the composer of music, the sculptor, the painter—the artist in any medium. Does not each express his originality in the choices he makes?

Exercise 2

1. Find a photograph or painting that engages your interest, one depicting a scene without any people. Try to capture in words the look and feel of the scene.

2. Choose a fictional location and describe it (and the feel of it) under each of two different conditions, varying either in time or in accompanying circumstances. Possibilities include the variations listed below. (Do not get sidetracked into accounts of persons or events.)

   Change in time of day
   Change in time of year
   Change in the feel of the location
   Change in weather (atmospheric conditions)
   Change in appearance—through age, calamity
   Change in what has happened or will happen

3. Through specific detail, range of sense impressions, imagery, place-in-time, try to construct with words each of the following locations. Your description should make the reader say, "I feel that such a place exists somewhere." (Do not get sidetracked into presenting persons.)

   A crowded room
   The heart of a very large city
   Inside a speeding car, train, or airplane

The Element of Persons

You can write fiction without people; you can make imaginary worlds of talking objects or three-toed Martians or what have you. But in fiction that aims at evoking the feeling of reality, there will usually be people.

You can make your fictional people seem real in a variety of ways. Generally, fictional people should look, talk, act, feel, and think in *patterns* a reader will recognize as logically consistent with actual persons. But at the same time they should differ from any pattern in enough ways to reveal personality.

Remember, too, that making fictional people seem real is no guarantee that they will be exciting and interesting to the reader. If they are colorless and dull, like some real persons, they may not engage a reader's interest, attention, or sympathy, no matter how realistically they may be drawn.

How do you become acquainted with the (real) people you meet? How do you make friends and learn to understand or develop your attitude toward them? Are they not like jigsaw puzzles to which you could always add another piece?

You actually see them—their appearance, their manners, and their mannerisms.

> He might have been over six feet tall in youth, but now, gray and bent, he stood no higher than five feet eight or nine.
> Her left hand tugged persistently at a string of colorful glass beads that graced her well-proportioned neck and shoulders.
> Poised and quiet, she stood a moment on the platform, holding the wide brimmed hat casually in her hand.

Sometimes you speculate (often wildly) on the basis of your observations and first impressions.

> He is a dumpy little man with a sneaky smile and stealthy movements.
> She walked with a self-assured stride and a bright smile, but defiance was in her eyes.

If you are perceptive, you will not jump to conclusions about people. You will "keep the book open" to add a page with each new encounter; you will visualize the jigsaw puzzle called *personality* as unfinished, never assuming that you know all about anyone. Thus the personality of those people you meet—real or fictional—may be constantly emerging.

Beyond what shows on the outside, directly, how else is the human personality revealed? Sometimes it is by what a person says.

> I grew up in a jungle of unlit streets and had no formal education.
> I like fast cars and fast music; that long-haired stuff bores me to death.

Sometimes it is revealed in what others say about a person.

> You'll never find a softer touch than Bill. He's always good for a small loan—about half the money he is carrying at the time.
>
> Good grief! Do you have to invite Mary Ann? Don't you realize that nobody will ask her to dance the whole evening?

But most of all, personality is reflected in the choices a person makes from among the alternatives open to him. These choices are often revealed in action and especially that action that resolves a conflict, solves a problem, or helps the person out of a dilemma.

But what will you look for in what a person says and does as well as in what others say about him? He may be wrong about himself, or even lying; those who speak about him are not always reliable either.

These possibilities must always be taken into consideration. What is said directly might not be as important to the picture as what is revealed indirectly—in the words and actions. Ask yourself these questions about any person—real or fictional: What makes him "tick"? What does he want—specifically, now, and what does he want from life, in general? Is he capable of thinking? If so, what does he think? What does he believe —and believe in? What things does he value—in what order and to what degree? Above all, what does he feel?

The Combination of Persons and Places

When human experience is dramatized, the elements (place, persons, and so forth) are fused into one complicated pattern, just as life itself is a confusion of times, places, people, conflicts, and resolutions before your eyes. Having tried to invent fictional places, let's now try adding a person. Later people will be brought together to produce talk and conflict, out of which may come dilemmas to be resolved by *action*. The job of combining elements will become increasingly complex, but the principle will be the same as with just person and place. The elements should not be simply tacked together; they must be logically consistent with each other, and they should interact so that the feel of a place will heighten the feeling about a person, and *vice versa*. The result might be a feeling of reality that is satisfying to both writer and reader.

Person and Place

He stood beside a sign next to the blacktop, casting practically no shadow himself, while using the sign's thin band of shade as a shield against the midday glare. Viewed first from a distance, he was not recognizable as human or even living, but only as one of several vertical black marks— exclamation marks that danced in the shimmering heat waves rising from the highway. As the mirages retreated down the constantly narrowing strip of roadway, the exclamation points stopped dancing and then turned into a number of road signs and a solitary human figure.

Behind the signs and the figure lay flat empty expanses touched here and there with a clump of wiry grass or a few weeds, exposed rocky patches, or bits of brush. These expanses stopped at various flat-topped red-clay buttes, which also jiggled and shimmered under the noon sun.

The first sign bore a shield and a highway number; the second informed its reader that he was now leaving a town which was evidenced only by an ancient stone foundation that rose no more than two feet above the otherwise barren soil.

The man stood facing the westbound vehicles, his left arm raised to shield his face, while with his right hand he made a brief gesture that was at the same time a wave, a flagging down motion, or the thumbing of a ride, as the viewer wished to interpret it.

Beside him lay a dingy gray and white paperboard suitcase held shut with a loop of string. The shoes he wore were ankle high and heavily constructed, but the seams were bursting, and the leather was scuffed to the color of his faded, khaki trousers. He wore a blue work shirt, equally faded, and streaked with perspiration, its sleeves rolled unevenly to his elbow. He was hatless, and his black hair, once crew cut, was shaggy, while his stubble of beard might have been two or three days' growth. His teeth were exposed in what might have been a smile or a squint, and his eyes were narrow, dark slits almost closed to the bright clamor of the glaring sun.

Above him the sign gave the mileage to Bernardo, Socorro, and Albuquerque, New Mexico. Beyond it another sign, a billboard, urged travelers to spend the night in the quiet luxury of the Desert Charm Motel, equipped with an olympic-size swimming pool and free television in every airconditioned room.

Exercise 3   *Without engaging him in action, picture in words each of the persons below in the places indicated. (Be sure not to lapse into an explanation of a kind of person; just remember*

that you are to dramatize one particular person in one particular place through description alone.)

An old man in a bus depot
A child on a subway
A laborer at work
A person alone on a park bench

CONVERSATION IN FICTION

When more than one person occupies a fictional place, talk usually ensues, and the dramatic effect can be heightened by conversation if it is handled well.

What is said may be related indirectly:

> He said that I should tell Rocky not to worry, so I told him I would if he would stop trying to get me to do his work, and . . .

But more often an attempt is made to reproduce the natural conversation of real persons. Since actual conversations are often dull and repetitive, the writer of fiction may wish to confine himself to reproduction of only those snatches of talk that (a) reveal significant detail or (b) dramatize persons, places, and problems that are vital to the total effect of the work.

In what he says and how he says it, a fictional character may reveal his own personality, as well as that of the person spoken to. In addition, conversation may be used to strengthen any of the other elements — place, conflict, dilemma, action, or resolution.

Before practicing conversation, you should study real people conversing. The talk of a single person may change from conversation to conversation, depending on the listener, the occasion, the formality of the situation, and so forth. Most talk is less formal than much written composition. Talk is not writing said aloud: you often talk in bits and pieces; you stop; you start over; you interrupt others; you leave statements unfinished; you repeat yourself. Your talk may reflect where you came from, how much education you have had, your social position — all this in addition to the actual messages your words are intended to convey.

See if you can sense two distinct persons and the feel of a place emerging from the following conversation by Kurt Vonnegut, Jr.*

> "It's about time this place got set on its ear," said Jim.
>
> "Is it?" said Helmholtz. "That must be so if one of our students wants to murder it."
>
> "What good is it?" said Jim.
>
> "Not much good, I guess," said Helmholtz. "It's just the best thing human beings ever managed to do." He was helpless, talking to himself. . . .
>
> "If you smashed up all the schools," said Helmholtz, "we wouldn't have any hope left."
>
> "What hope?" said Jim.
>
> "The hope that everybody will be glad he's alive," said Helmholtz. "Even you."
>
> "That's a laugh," said Jim. "All I ever got out of this dump was a hard time. So what're you gonna do?"
>
> "I have to do something, don't I?" said Helmholtz.
>
> "I don't care what you do," said Jim.
>
> "I know," said Helmholtz. "I know."

* from "The Kid Nobody Could Handle," in *Welcome to the Monkey House.*

Exercise 4

Try to reproduce a conversation that you think would be logically consistent with the personalities of the people in the places indicated below. Remember to begin a new paragraph with each change of speaker. Talk is usually quite informal; no two persons say the same things in quite the same way. (Do not try to develop any line of action, beyond mannerisms, in your speakers.)

1. Two drifters camped under a railroad bridge

2. Two women, one with small children and the other with grandchildren, in a chance conversation at a bus stop

3. A teen-age boy and girl, both shy and unable to dance, striking up a conversation while on the sidelines of a school dance

4. A teen-ager and his preschool brother or sister, discussing an object borrowed from one and mislaid by the other

Exercise 5

Copy the speeches in the balloons of some nationally known comic strip. Study the written conversation separated from the pictures and see how much or how little the speeches reflect (1) the distinctiveness of characters, (2) the personalities of characters, (3) the place, and (4) the situation.

Exercise 6

Listen, unnoticed, to an actual conversation in some public place. Try to take it down (or reproduce it later) as close to the facts as possible. Do not overlook the implications of gestures, repetitions, tone of voice, or degree of loudness in which words are uttered. Study the results in terms of the generalizations made earlier in this chapter about the nature of conversation.

Exercise 7

Write twenty lines of straight dialogue without any commentary. Read the lines aloud and then ask your classmates to tell you as many things as they can about the personalities of speakers, the place, the situation, and so forth. When an impression is advanced by one student, notice the response of the class. Was his a private reaction, or did several (a majority) of the class members see the same implication—about person, place, and so forth? Note: When you move from speaker to speaker, try not to overwork distinguishing tags

Exercise 7,

continued

(he said, she said, and so on). Wherever the distinction between speakers is clear through other means, no such tags are needed. Beyond that, it may be tiresome on the one hand to read:

> he said,
> he said,
> he said,

but it may be even more distracting to read:

> he said,
> he replied,
> he expostulated,
> he remonstrated,

or:

> he said gaily,
> he said shyly,
> he retorted smoothly,

You may be able to get by effectively with just a few simple tags, such as:

> he said, . . .
> he replied, . . .
> he answered, . . .

and the variety you can effect this way:

> he said, . . .
> the man replied, . . .
> Morgan said, . . .
> Bob answered, . . .

ACTION IN FICTION

Having practiced with fictional places, combining places with people and people with conversation, you are ready to send your fictional characters into action.

If fiction-for-your-own-amusement is your aim, then any action your mind can conceive is yours to invent, and you need neither rules nor restrictions. Your characters can walk across the ocean floors; they can rocket to Pluto for lunch; they can descend into volcanoes, all without the aid of special equipment.

Since you have thus far been trying to produce the feeling of reality, let's proceed on the assumption that the actions you invent will be logically consistent with (a) the places you have created, (b) the personalities of the figures you have invented, and (c) the general pattern of human events. In other words, your weaklings should not beat up boxing champions (without a logical explanation), your little orphan heroine should not solve all the problems of a whole country in two weeks, and lightning should not strike your villain just in the nick of time to solve all your problems. While these devices have been effective in fiction, they represent action that is not logically consistent with the general pattern of actual human experience.

Exercise 8   *Suggest three or four different sequences of events that you think might follow logically from the situations indicated below.*

1. A teen-ager is suddenly confronted by a classmate who doesn't like him.

2. Several boys go out of their neighborhood in search of excitement.

3. Three girls with differing tastes in entertainment are deciding what to do on a Saturday afternoon.

4. A sixteen-year-old boy is reporting for his first day's work in a supermarket.

5. A girl's mother has offered to teach her how to sew.

CONFLICT IN FICTION

No matter how realistically presented, fictional accounts of routine occurrences may fail to catch and hold a reader's interest. Furthermore, performance of routine actions may offer little opportunity to dramatize deeper feelings of either the fictional person or the writer of the fiction.

The remedy for this lack of reader interest might be found in observing actual human experience. Do real persons attract our attention in the performance of routine tasks?

Not very often.

But what about people with problems?

Trouble is another matter. A man may pass by unnoticed, but let him be injured or in danger, and he will be the center of attention. This kind of attention has sometimes been called *morbid curiosity*, but whatever it is called, there is the suggestion of emotional engagement between the person in trouble and the passerby. Applied to fiction writing, the implication is that people in trouble, whether fictional people or real, may engage the feelings of those who might otherwise pass by.

Let's describe the confrontation of a fictional person with his fictional problem as *conflict*, no matter what the nature of the problem, whether you picture the hero:

"in trouble"
"in a stew"
"in hot water"
"in a jam"
"in danger"
"in distress"
"between the devil and the deep blue sea"

The pattern of actual human conflict should provide innumerable ideas for fictional conflict. There are those who say you must suffer before you can become a great artist (writer, painter, sculptor, composer). Perhaps they are suggesting that to experience actual problems prepares you to invent realistic conflicts for your fictional people. If you have never been sick or hurt or very hungry or in danger, you might have trouble showing fictional people in such circumstances. "He jests at scars who never felt a wound," Shakespeare said.

Exercise 9   *Add twenty examples of human conflict similar to the situations outlined below.*

1. A lone man is held up on a dark street.

2. A parachutist has suffered a partial malfunction in the way his main parachute has opened.

3. A man is adrift on the ocean.

4. An engagement (to be married) has been terminated by one person causing suffering to the other.

5. A person has fallen from a cliff but is clinging to a bush, hoping to be rescued.

6. A soldier has been thrust into the thick of battle.

7. A child has become lost in a large gathering.

8. A pilot is faced with a forced landing.

9. An inexperienced teacher is faced with unruly students.

10. A penniless person, hitchhiking across the country, is faced with hunger.

11. A hard-working father finds his job terminated for reasons (production decline and so on) not of his making.

12. A driver is rushing an injured person to a hospital over very hazardous mountain roads.

13. A girl is without a date for a very important function.

Exercise 9,
continued

14. Parents are distraught because their ten-year-old child has run away from home.

15. A candidate faces almost certain defeat unless he changes his stated position on an issue.

16. A young man is in misery because he has been unable to persuade the most attractive and most popular girl in school to give him a date.

17. A person has awakened to discover his building ablaze.

18. A young man has acquired a dent in the family car the first day out without supervision.

19. A person in an isloated area faces danger from a wild animal.

20. A person finds himself in danger because he has been mistaken for someone else.

The Built-In Resolution of Conflicts

Just as quickly as you can give the responses, complete the following question about each of the conflicts presented in Exercise 9.

Will he (she, they), or won't he (she, they) ____?

To the degree to which you could quickly state the outcome in each case, you learn that fictional conflicts usually point toward their own *resolution*. At the same time, they present alternatives of outcome. The reader asks himself, "What will happen?" Curiosity is heightened by his subsequent speculation, amid the apparent possibilities.

External and Internal Conflicts

Among your vast powers as a writer of fiction is the power to draw up the terms of the struggle, either *inside* or *outside* (or both), of your fictional person.

In conflicts 1, 3, 5, 6, and 19 of Exercise 9, for example, you might make the issues of the conflict quite beyond the will of the person.

CONFLICT 1; Will the man come through the holdup unharmed, or will he be injured?

CONFLICT 3: Will the man be rescued from the ocean, or will he be lost?

CONFLICT 5: Will the person be rescued from the cliff, or will he fall?

CONFLICT 6: Will the soldier come through the battle, or will he be a casualty?

CONFLICT 19: Will the person prevail against the wild animal?

On the other hand, look at conflicts 10, 12, 15, and 18; see how easily you can draw up the terms of the conflict so that the person is faced with a *dilemma,* that is, he must choose between disagreeable, dis-advantageous — almost impossible — choices.

CONFLICT 10: Assuming that he has made every effort to find work or food through honest means, should he (a) go hungry or (b) get food dishonestly?

CONFLICT 12: Should the driver decide to drive slow at the risk of the in-jured person's life, or should he drive faster through danger-ous terrain at the risk of other lives, including his own?

CONFLICT 15: Should the candidate choose to accept defeat, or should he choose to change his stand?

CONFLICT 18: Should the young man admit the damage to the car and risk the consequences, or should he remain silent and hope that someone else will be blamed for the damage or that it will go unnoticed?

A dilemma that forces the fictional person to choose between an expedient course of action and one considered wrong in the eyes of society is called a *moral dilemma.* But it takes the action (or some of it) out of the arena of external events and puts it in the will of the fictional person.

Exercise 10

Restate each of the remaining conflicts described above (2, 4, 7, 8, 9, 11, 13, 14, 16, 17, and 20) in two different ways. On the one hand, describe the conflict in terms suggesting resolution through external circumstances; on the other hand, suggest a dilemma wherein the person must choose between equally disagreeable alternatives leading toward resolution of the conflict.

BEGINNING AND ENDING FICTION

You can open your fiction with the first word and close them by ceas-ing to write, but the person-in-trouble device (conflict) provides a more unified, often more satisfying, framework.

Life has a way of going on and on, from day to day, with one event leading to another. But problems do arise; conflicts do develop that must be resolved.

You can apply these observations to your fiction writing. You now realize that you can draw fictional conflicts calling for speculation on a possible resolution even while hiding the eventual developments. Presentation of conflicts, therefore, offers logical starting points for fiction—fiction whose logical end will come with the resolution of the conflict, a resolution that has been foreshadowed (only hinted at) in the terms of the conflict.

Exercise 11    *Suggest at least one specific place, time, sequence of events, and so on with which the situations (conflicts) in Exercise 9 might be begun and ended.*

SUSPENSE IN FICTION

The degree of urgency with which a reader will anticipate the resolution of a conflict is often described as *suspense*. A fiction that is strongly and obviously constructed to elicit suspense is often called a "cliff hanger," and conflict 5 above shows you why. No matter how unknown a person may be, or how indifferent you may be toward him, if he gets himself into a cliff-hanging situation where his whole existence is reduced to "either-or" terms, you must explain what happens to him. This is suspense in its most obvious terms.

However, almost any conflict confronting a person, real or fictional, about whom you care will have its own built-in suspense factor. This suspense may be strengthened if you can heighten the reader's speculation about the outcome by dropping hints from time to time. This technique is called *foretelling* or *foreshadowing*. See if you can find any evidence of it in the following passages:

> He wondered what strange and wonderful sights awaited him at the end of the hallway.

> If he had known then what he was soon to learn so painfully, he would have turned and fled as fast as his stubby legs could carry him.

> It was in the early fall, months before the tragedy, that Len McBride rode into the quiet world of Cooper's Valley.

> He had known all along what the results of his impulsive departure might be; but when the actual consequence was described to him, he was startled beyond understanding.

The prevailing characteristic of these hints is that they foretell without telling; they provoke questions while seeming to offer information.

ORDER OF EVENTS IN FICTION

The bulk of fiction is usually taken up with accounts of actions — with the presenting of a sequence of events. Yet, for that action to be meaningful, it should follow naturally out of the situation that produces it. Moreover, the alternatives of fictional action are so nearly numberless that it is almost impossible to generalize regarding them. If restricted to realistic fiction arising out of conflict, it would be possible to say that any action is successful that dramatizes the events whose presentation resolves the conflict. In other words, choose a sequence of events from among the almost limitless alternatives, and show these developments as graphically as possible. (*See* "Explaining or Dramatizing?" on page 298.)

The commonest order for the presentation of fictional events is the order in which the events occurred in the natural time sequence — chronological order. However, there are exceptions to this pattern.

You could get bogged down in chronological order and find yourself trying to tell (or show) every event in every detail. To avoid the monotony occurring under these circumstances, you may instead dramatize a limited number of scenes that will advance the action and resolve the conflict. A *scene* in this case is a unified set of actions, talk, and so on bound together by their occurrence in a single place during a limited time. Necessary bits of action outside the time or place of one of these scenes may still be worked in, if necessary.

> It had been two days since she had talked to Johnny at the airport, and she had tried to telephone him twice in the interval.

Whole scenes may be developed outside the chronological order. They usually turn back into the past and are thus called *flashbacks*.

Order of Presentation

——————→	——————→	——————→	——————→	——————→
Scene 1	Scene 2	Scene 3	Scene 4	Scene 5
——————→	——————→	←——————	←——————	——————→
May 1965	Oct 1965	| Dec 1961	Mar 1962	| Nov 1965

A flashback scene might begin like this:

> Whatever he was searching for, the riddle had first presented itself on that Sunday in December when the battleships went to the bottom of Pearl Harbor.
>
> There was roast beef for dinner and hot, rich brown gravy. He ate two helpings because Uncle John challenged him by calling him "picky" about his food . . . .

Exercise 12  *Suggest a logical resolution for two or three of the conflicts in Exercise 9 on page 311. Then summarize a sequence
of events that would produce such a resolution. Next, outline
a few scenes through which these events might be presented.
Finally, indicate the order of these scenes if you choose any
other than chronological order.*

THE ELEMENTS IN COMBINATION

Having practiced the processes considered so far, you are now ready
to combine all these elements — place, people, conflict, action, and resolution — into a work of fiction. Since your effectiveness may be measured by the feeling of reality you produce in a reader, you face a stern
task. Once these elements are put together, they interact. Therefore, if
in one element you have failed to engage a reader's feelings, your failure
may undermine the feeling of reality of the whole. If you succeed, it
will be because you have chosen well. The sense of reality will pervade
the world you construct; the reader will feel that he knows and cares
about the people you create; their problems will engulf him, and the
way they resolve those problems will intrigue and enlighten him.

Exercise 13  *In a short piece of fiction, create an imaginary place and
person appropriate to one of the conflicts described below.
Then through dramatic action resolve the conflict.*

1. Unknown to each other, two good friends file for election to the same student office in their high school.

2. A boy leaves the school dance to which he has been permitted to drive the family car. Against his parents' wishes,
   he takes his friends for a ride and hits a parked car during
   the ride. No one else sees the accident.

3. A girl returns from school to her home town, where, almost immediately, she meets a boy who asks for a date.
   Only after accepting does she learn that the boy is supposed to be the "steady" of her best friend.

4. A boy learns from others that his favorite teacher has
   mistakenly identified him as the person who streaked
   paint on the door of the school shop. The boy wants
   desperately to clear himself, but (a) he is too shy to approach the teacher, and (b) he thinks that raising the
   subject might be suggestive of guilt.

THE REWARDS OF REALISTIC FICTION

At least three benefits accrue from fiction producing a feeling of reality. First, they permit you, the writer, to exercise your individuality and convey your deepest feelings and convictions. You may do so directly through having your fictional people speak for you. More often, however, you do it by every choice you make — in time, in place, in person, in conflict, in action, and in resolution. Your most conscious choice will be in how you resolve the conflict. There are many such choices in the simplest fiction; in a long work hundreds or even thousands. You make so many of them without thinking, that is, unconsciously, that you might be unaware of a choice. Yet in all these things, you, the writer of fiction, proclaim to the world who you are, what you think and feel and want for yourself and from yourself. There is no room for pretense or affectation. While it has no factual basis, realistic fiction must be honest to human emotions; therefore, no personal pretense on the part of the writer (about himself) is likely to survive there.

The second benefit in realistic fiction is in the reader's response. If it produces in him the feeling of real experience, then — without a factual basis — it can increase his emotional experience. Such fiction may give him a "feel" for life that reading hundreds of factual accounts in his daily paper fails to provide. Who is to say, also, that there is not comfort in learning how people resolve their conflicts? These are fictional people, yes, but they seem real; they might even seem more alive than many whose names are in a telephone directory.

A third possible benefit of realistic fiction is a benefit to society as a whole, through a general plea for understanding of human problems. While the fiction writer invents, yet his commitment to the feeling of reality will keep him within a general pattern of actual human experience. His power as a transmitter of this human experience is increased by his freedom to show, to dramatize, and thereby to deal in a medium which crosses the conventional boundaries of language, custom, race, color, or creed. That medium is the *emotions* of human beings.

SOME ADDITIONAL ELEMENTS

There's no reason why you cannot please yourself and entertain your friends by writing fiction on the basis of what has been presented.

If, however, you are not satisfied just to compose fiction but feel that you must talk with others about writing fiction, then certain conventional terms are likely to make their way into the discussion. Some of them have been thus far avoided in the belief that their familiar-sound-but-sometimes-ambiguous-presence on the scene might imply that writing fiction is harder than it really is.

Some of these terms were introduced when their meaning could be clarified in context: *fiction, realistic fiction, dramatization, conflict, resolution, dilemma, suspense,* and *scene.* Others that you are almost certain to run into are: *setting, characters, plot, narrative, sketch, story, short story, novel, play* or *drama, point of view,* and *theme.*

The first three in the second group may be applied to things already considered. *Setting* may be substituted for fictional "place," especially when you mean "time" and "accompanying circumstance," or anything else that adds to the feeling of a place or a situation.

Characters are the people you invent to inhabit your fictional places. *Plot* is often associated with the action of the fiction, or a summary of the fictional events. It is sometimes called the "what happens."

The word *narrative* may be associated with any sequence of events, real or fictional, or with the relating of such a sequence. The word *story* may be similarly associated with any account of events, real or fictional.

Sketch is often used to label a fictional passage in which a feeling of reality is attempted through some uncomplicated device, such as the presentation of place, person, or uncomplicated action, either alone or in simple combination. The term is sometimes applied to a work of fiction to distinguish it from one in which *all* the elements are employed — place, person, conflict (action), and resolution.

The term *short story* is sometimes applied to any story (*see* above) that is "short." However, the term is more formally applied to a work of fiction that includes all the elements mentioned above. Because of its length, the short story must make economical use of words to create place, person, conflict, and so forth. The focus of attention may be entirely on one person, and a single line of action taken, a single conflict resolved.

An extended work of fiction is usually called a *novel* unless it is written to be presented upon a stage, in which case it is called a *play* or a *drama.* The novel may involve much more leisurely development of place. It will portray more people more penetratingly. It may offer a number of conflicts and several lines of action to resolve them.

Point of view is the term applied to the fiction writer's assumed relationship to the persons and events he creates. If he puts himself directly in the piece, he is taking the "first person" point of view.

> As the train left the Kansas City terminal, I studied the orders that had been delivered to me by the sergeant from the Ft. Leavenworth personnel office. He had reminded me not to open them before I left, an admonition I felt little inclined to obey until I pondered the nature of my mission. Then . . .

When the fiction writer assumes the attitude of one who is recording the experiences of others, he is employing the "third person" point of view.

> Newt arrived at the Kiner farm early the next Saturday morning. There was a note from Jake tacked to the barn door saying that he and his wife would be away until afternoon. GORDON PARKS

Point of view varies, also, in how much insight into events and into the minds of his fictional persons the fiction writer permits himself. He may restrict himself to only what shows on the outside, as a camera might (objective third person). He might tell his story through both the eyes and thoughts of one person (limited third person). If he chooses, however, the writer of fiction can assume an all-knowing attitude and relate thoughts and events from all times, all places, and through all minds. This position is called the *omniscient* third person point of view.

Those who talk about fiction are often more inclined than writers are to worry about something they call *theme*. At the same time, there may be considerable disagreement over just what constitutes theme in fiction.

Theme has been called "what the whole story adds up to" as well as "what the whole story means," "what the writer is trying to say," or "a statement summarizing the idea the story dramatizes." It might also be called "the writer's philosophy as reflected in the particular work," or "what the writer is trying to say without actually saying it."

In any case, the most comforting realization to a writer of fiction is that most of these things are going to be reflected in any honest attempt at complicated realistic fiction, whether or not the writer wants them to.

Do you think you could design and build a doghouse without having a great deal of your personality reflected in the finished product? Why would you make a four-foot doghouse for a six-inch dog? Why would you choose a certain size of lumber and of nails?

In every choice not ruled by some immediate necessity, is it not likely that the alternative you settled upon had something to do with who you are, what you think, and how you feel—not only about dogs but about yourself, your friends, your enemies—about life in general?

Now consider a complicated work of fiction with hundreds, perhaps thousands, of choices—many made below the threshold of your conscious awareness.

Shall this fictional person be tall or short, rich or poor, happy or unhappy, honest or dishonest? Your deepest feelings will be reflected in your choices, and in the total effect of all the choices put together in one piece of fiction.

Any attempt to generalize about the internal person (the writer and his feelings) on the basis of these external choices is likely to be the wildest kind of speculation even for the writer himself, and even worse for outsiders. He is closer than anyone to the place where the discriminations were made, but many were made without any conscious reflection on his part.

If you approach the fiction writing process honestly and invent people, places, conflicts, and resolutions, theme will take care of itself nicely. If you wish through conscious reinforcement to hammer home an attitude or a feeling, then you will give your theme searchers something tangible to go on. You might even plant statements in the fiction, even in the mouths of characters, but all this can become overdone very easily. You might do better to let theme take care of itself until you become a more practiced writer.

Exercise 14   *Invent a fictional dilemma and then outline how you would adjust that situation for presentation in (a) a brief sketch, (b) a 3000-6000-word short story, (c) a 50,000-word novel.*

ROMANTIC FICTION

Sometimes the writers of fiction invent places, people, situations, and so on that are not consistent with actual human experience in general. When such fiction, though otherwise realistic, portrays a world that reflects not so much "what is out there," as it reflects "what you wish were out there," that is, the world as you might like to have it, then that fiction is *romantic*.

The world of romantic fiction is the world of happy endings and pearly white smiles. It is a world of good people and bad, with the two always clearly distinguishable, where the bad are punished and the good win the boss's daughter and the canary-yellow convertible and the vice-presidency of the bank.

This is a world where the happy possible is made to seem probable. It is a world of make-believe, but it must be otherwise pictured as near-to-life as possible, short of destroying the fantasy that "everything is going to turn out all right in the end." Therefore, most of what has already been said about persons, places, and conflicts can still apply if invention does not come too close to reality.

The benefits of romantic fiction are obvious. For both the writer and the reader, there is suspension of reality, an entertaining escape from a world where some people have yellow teeth in spite of all the claims of the dentifrice manufacturers.

Exercise 15   *Except for a basic commitment to avoid situations that might be somber, sad, depressing, discouraging, or ugly, write as realistic a short story as possible from one of the conflicts below.*

1. Frank has just turned eighteen. He knows he is eligible for the draft, and he hasn't been accepted at college yet. He doesn't want to go in the Army.

2. Tom is sure he would be as happy as he assumes everyone else is if only he could get a date with Julia, the most popular girl in school.

3. Mary wants very much to go to the school prom, but she doesn't have a suitable dress.

4. Larry feels certain that if he could only try out for the Eager Beavers baseball team, he could win a place on the squad, but so far he has been denied permission to take part in the competition.

LYRICAL FICTION

Having considered both realistic and romantic *prose* fictions, you might give a thought, in passing, to a third field for imaginative writing, one called *lyrical* fiction. As you proceed, you will see that lyrical fiction may be either realistic or romantic in the views it reflects; otherwise, it differs radically in form from what you have discussed so far. But fiction it is, nevertheless, since it, too, attempts to produce a largely emotional response through a nonfactual use of language.

The term *lyrical* was chosen for two reasons: first, it suggests music and is therefore appropriate in considering some of the musical effects words can create. These effects may be produced quite apart from or in addition to the message conveyed by the formal meanings of the words themselves.

> E-low glub,
> E-low glub,
> E-low glub,
> Skitaway!

If you think you know the lexical message of these lines, you are in on a secret not shared by the writer because to him they are nonsense. On the other hand, if you say them aloud, you might hear something that sounds musical.

Second, by discussing lyrical fiction, you can avoid defining either the word *poetry* or the word *verse*. Whether you look on these words as synonyms, as some people do, interchanging them in many contexts, or see them as pointing toward two vastly different things, you should be able to recognize a lyrical quality in almost everything you call either poetry or verse. You should be able to study the distinctions made and apply what you learn as well to a greeting-card salutation as to the most profound statement of your most precious principles. Whether the result will be verse, poetry, both, or neither is something for the world to decide.

Several characteristics of lyrical fiction are explored below.

In order to distinguish different lyrical devices, you may deliberately use nonsense syllables, to avoid the possible distractions from the meanings of the words themselves. At other times, you may have to sacrifice significance for convenience in the message of the example. It must be remembered that once you have learned to apply these lyrical devices, you may determine the level of seriousness you wish to assume in your utterances.

RHYTHMIC EFFECTS

The human heartbeat, the breaking of waves against a shore, the sound of a drum have all been called *rhythmical*. Let's find a characteristic they share; perhaps it is *rhythm*.

Is this comparison made from one heartbeat, one drumbeat, or one wave against a shore? No, it is the awareness of many occurrences to which you could apply the word *rhythmical*. It becomes obvious at this point that the similarity lies in the fact that each of these events repeats itself. After further examination, you will discover that they do not repeat themselves in the same pattern. The drum might go tum, tum, tum, tum, tum, while the heart says something sounding like this:

> lub dup,
> lub dup,
> lub dup

They do not have the same pattern of repetition; each has its own pattern. By making yourself aware of the pattern, you may anticipate the coming repetitions. Therefore, anything that repeats itself according to a discernable pattern is rhythmical. Think of rhythm as patterned repetition.

Consider the rhythms within you. There is patterned repetition in your pulse, your heartbeat, your breathing, your eyeblink, your motions such as walking or chewing, your mannerisms, and many more. Most of these "repeat performances" go on and on without any conscious effort or even conscious awareness on your part. It is not surprising, therefore, that you respond to those things outside your nervous system that repeat themselves according to their discernible patterns. While your reaction to music is probably the most striking example of such response, yet the rhythmic effects of spoken utterances also offer a wide range for fictional experimentation.

Repetition of End Sounds

One of the most noticeable ways of arranging words to produce patterned repetition is through the final sound(s) of two or more words. This rhythmic device has been known to most of you as *rhyme*. It is usually accomplished in one of two ways: the first involves only the final sound of each utterance, while the second involves at least two syllables in each instance.

Typical of the first are repetitions like these:

hood – good	top – mop
black – slack	door – more

Typical of the second are:

cradle – ladle	eyeglass – spyglass
foreman – doorman	needless – heedless

Exercise 16   **A.** *Give several words whose pronunciations produce the same end sound or sounds as each of these words:*

night	news
beside	pray
frail	intelligent
ditch	shouting
carriage	sunning
green	eating
stone	dating

B. *Write three or more sentences whose last words rhyme.*

Repetition of Beginning Sounds

Al always ate with Anne,
with Alice and with Allison,
withal . . .

Some proof of the popularity of word patterns that repeat beginning sounds can be found in the longevity of such expressions, long after they have been frowned upon, as clichés.

> *b*lind as a *b*at
> *d*ead as a *d*oornail
> *p*retty as a *p*icture

There is, of course, the possibility that the permanence of such expressions stems from some other, less noticeable, quality.

Exercise 17   *In each blank below, add a word that will be reasonably appropriate to the sense of the passage, but limit yourself to words with a similar beginning sound as the word toward which the arrow points.*

_____ ↘ Sam laughed ↙_____ at the antics of the _____↘ pigeons as he controlled the _____↘ car through the _____↘ twists and turns of _____↘ Hardesty Boulevard. As Sam ↙_____, a _____↘ cop emerged from the evergreens to tender a ticket to the _____↘ Sam.

Repetition Through Duplication of Terms

Abraham Lincoln used the terms:

> Of the people,
> by the people,
> for the people . . .

While an unknown balladeer wrote:

> "Why dois your brand sae drap wi bluid,
> Edward, Edward,
> Why dois your brand sae drap wi bluid, . . ."

Thus repetition of sound patterns through duplication of expressions, with or without minor variations, is also employed as a rhythmic device.

> To market, to market to buy a fat pig
> Home again, home again, jiggity jig;
> To market, to market to buy a fat hog,
> Home again, home again, jiggity jog.

Repetition Through Stress

Read the following expressions aloud, about as you would say them in an appropriate situation:

> Go home!
> Here we go!
> Let me go!
> I will go in his place.

Now consider the amount of stress you put on the word *go* in each expression. Was it the same in all cases? Was it the same for the whole class on any one expression?

When you speak a syllable, you have a choice of the degree of stress you want to give it. This degree may vary with the meaning you want to convey; it may vary from one person to the other; it may vary with each time you use that syllable. With all this variation, how can there possibly be a pattern?

To recognize a pattern or to construct one, you must ignore most of the individual variations and try to decide the degree of stress a syllable is generally given compared with that given other syllables. Then if you distinguish only two extremes, one where the syllable is strongly stressed (´) and the other where it is not stressed (˘), certain patterns may emerge.

'Twas the night before Christmas, and all through the house,

To die, to sleep;

To sleep: perchance to dream: ay, there's the rub:

As a writer of fiction, you might remember this about these patterns: you may take as little or as much account of them as you wish. It might be practical to write what you wish and then consider the arrangement of stresses, changing a few words here or there to improve the rhythm of a particularly awkward passage. Or you might bear in mind that English writers in the past have inclined predominantly toward this pattern:

(˘ ´)
unless
begone
to go . . .,

Here a stressed syllable follows an unstressed syllable. As you develop an ear for these patterns, your own use of them will become increasingly subtle. Some writers distinguish these as *accented* and *unaccented* syllables.

Exercise 18   1. Select passages from books at random and, as a class, pick out the syllables you agree should be heavily stressed when the passages are read aloud. See also what agree-

Exercise 18,

continued

ment you can attain about words that would be lightly stressed or left unstressed. Do not dwell long on words where there is obvious disagreement, unless through discussion the disagreement might be resolved.

2. Write twenty polysyllabic words and mark them to indicate how you think they should be pronounced.

3. Write several sentences following one of the patterns illustrated on pages 323-325. (You may have to change the wording to bring them into line with the pattern.)

Repetition Through Line Length

Read the following lines, to see if the rhythmic pattern sounds familiar to you, even though nonsense syllables have been used instead of words:

> Ta-dum ta-dum ta-dum ta-dum
> Ta-dum ta-dum ta-dum
> Ta-dum ta-dum ta-dum ta-dum
> Ta-dum ta-dum ta-dum

Not counting rhyme, at least three other patterns of repetition are evident here. First, there is the regular alternation of stressed and unstressed syllables. Second, there is repetition of the eight-syllable (or four-unit) line, and repetition of the six-syllable (or three-unit) line. Third, there is the pattern whereby eight and six syllable lines are alternated and bundled into groups (stanzas) of four lines. This pattern, by the way, (with many possible variations) is called the *ballad* form. It has been widely used in English, in both sung and spoken utterances. Coleridge's *The Rime of the Ancient Mariner* is an example of the application of these patterns. Here are the last two stanzas:

> The Mariner, whose eye is bright,
> Whose beard with age is hoar,
> Is gone; and now the Wedding Guest
> Turned from the bridegroom's door.
>
> He went like one that hath been stunned,
> And is of sense forlorn;
> A sadder and a wiser man,
> He rose the morrow morn.

Another commonly used pattern is called the *heroic line*. For example:

> Ta-dum ta-dum ta-dum ta-dum ta-dum

The heroic line is employed in a wide variety of stanza patterns and variations in rhyme. Fourteen such lines with a particular arrangement comprise the *sonnet*. Rhymed in pairs, heroic lines become the *heroic couplet.*

> To fight abroad and be a coward still
> Is more an act of habit than of will:

Heroic lines, if not made to rhyme at all, are called *blank verse* while lines that have neither rhyme nor consistent length are called *free verse.*

Exercise 19

As a class, compose a list, from memory, of twenty or more famous poems. Then each class member might take one or more of the titles, find the poem, and note its pattern (or lack thereof) of lines—their length and grouping into stanzas as well as variations within the stanza. While you have the poem handy, see if a discernible pattern of stress is evident, and record the pattern of rhyme if there is one.

IMAGINATIVE EFFECTS

While rhythm achieved through patterned repetitions is a musical device for fiction, there is also a lyrical quality in the many imaginative uses of words which, though effective in all writing, are especially noticeable in combination with the rhythms of poetry or verse.

Freshness of Expression

There is a test of the freshness of expression in a poem, a test which your teacher may find interesting. He might mimeograph copies of what he considers (a) a very good poem and (b) a very bad one, but with about half the words blocked out in each case. You should find that the poorer poem has employed such tired expresssions that you'll have little trouble (working as a class) supplying the blocked-out words. The language of the other poem may have such freshness and spontaniety of language, however, that your best efforts will fall short of the phrasing of the original.

Imagery: Words That Make Pictures

Try to picture these expressions:

> . . . unexampled dereliction of duty . . .
> . . . expansion of expression . . .
> . . . a journalistic device . . .

Now consider these expressions in the same light:

> . . . a place to die . . .
> . . . a half-forgotten battleground . . .
> . . . a cringing puppy . . .
> . . . a green wave, cresting . . .
> . . . the smell of last year's leaves, now moldy in March

Words that play on your senses (that you can see and feel and smell and taste and hear) draw pictures for a reader's senses, too.

Figurative Expressions

> Outside, in the street, a puddle glazed with neon shimmer . . .

Sometimes you deliberately describe things, not as you know they are, but as they seem to you at the moment. You are not fabricating; you expect the reader to realize that he is getting a sense impression, not a fact.

> . . . Daylight will never come, tomorrow is frozen below the curve of the sky . . .
> . . . I was dead on my feet . . .
> . . . blinded by the blackness of your hair, benumbed by nameless powers from your eyes . . .
> . . . trapped forever in that dream of which I tell . . .
> . . . "What's to eat? I'm starving!" said the boy . . .
> . . . he carried the play when the others forgot their lines . . .
> . . . the jungle birds flapped their remnant-counter wings and fell silent . . .

Comparisons

To make clear what is vague, to picture what is difficult to describe, to encourage a reader to transfer his feeling about one thing to another for which he has no feeling, verbal comparisons are made. Your dictionary can supply you with technical distinctions between specific devices. Look up these words: *allusion, metaphor, simile, personification, analogy, allegory,* and *parable.*

> The young boxer charged from his corner like an enraged bull, heavy on his feet and head down . . .
> As soft as the puffs from the cottonwoods that drifted lazily on the April air, . . .
> Two blue-white diamonds were her eyes, beyond price, but hard and humorless and cold.
> A wind whispered, "Come away."

Words That Convey Feelings

In all fiction, the most effective words are those that attempt to transfer not *fact* but *feelings* from writer to reader. Such transfer borders on the impossible. If you doubt this, try to tell another person how beans taste to you, or try to tell a blind person what a rose looks like to you. Facts will give you little help, indeed. A broad sensitivity both to the power of words and to human feelings may be your most valuable asset.

SO YOU WANT "TO BECOME A WRITER"

If in addition to the personal satisfactions already mentioned, you want "to become a writer," here is a plan of action: Practice!

A first-class pianist often practices five hours a day. Oh, but everybody knows how to write, practically from birth. Almost every child can be taught to play "Chopsticks" on the piano, too, but that is no ticket to Carnegie Hall. Practice the patterns discussed until you know them so well that you can use them without thinking. Then forget the patterns and concentrate upon using words to produce feelings in a reader.

Develop a critical eye. While you are in school, the teacher will direct you. But once on your own, decide for yourself what is "good writing" and judge your efforts accordingly. Anticipate the response your fiction might evoke in the audience you are trying to reach. Then test the actual response against what was anticipated, and adjust your "critical eye" accordingly.

Try to convey through what is fictional a feeling for what is real, the feeling of reality. If you succeed, you may help yourself and others to understand life in the particular through the feeling of life in general.

If, however, the life you describe is tinged with the fantastic, the ideal, or the romantic, you may provide in fiction an entertaining escape from the cold realities of the day, for which readers will reward you.

Exercise 20

1. As a class, practice maintaining several patterns of nonverbal rhythm in combination. Divide into three or four groups and develop patterns of taps, ticks, and so on so that each group can maintain repetitions of one sound at one interval, while the other groups repeat other sounds at other intervals.

2. Study the following lines from Langston Hughes' *The Negro Speaks of Rivers** and in a brief paper describe the characteristics of lyrical fiction that you can find:

* Copyright 1926 by Alfred A. Knopf, Inc., renewed, 1954 by Langston Hughes. Reprinted from *Selected Poems* by Langston Hughes by permission of the publisher.

Exercise 20,
continued

I've known rivers:
I've known rivers ancient as the world and older than the
    flow of human blood in human veins.

My soul has grown deep like the rivers.

I bathed in the Euphrates when dawns were young.
I built my hut near the Congo and it lulled me to sleep.
I looked upon the Nile and raised the pyramids above it.
I heard the singing of the Mississippi when Abe Lincoln
    went down to New Orleans, and I've seen its muddy
    bosom turn all golden in the sunset.

I've known rivers:
Ancient, dusky rivers.

My soul has grown deep like the rivers.

3. In a short essay, state, as directly as possible, one of your
strongest convictions, with factual evidence to back it
up, if possible. Then try to convey the same conviction
in (a) a 30-line lyrical fiction (poem or verse) and (b) a
2000-3000-word short story.

4. The lines below represent a rhythmical collection of
new words found in a recently published dictionary. This
list is not supposed to make sense. Study these lines and
write a brief paper pointing out the various devices of
lyrical fiction it employs (as those devices are described
and illustrated above). It is assumed, of course, that after
you have practiced the distinctions shown above, you
will write some lyrical fiction—poems or verse—which
does make sense or have something to say, beyond its
musical accompaniment.

A Ballad of New Words*

stubble mulch, slop jar
string quartet, stock car
source book, sacred cow
steamer trunk, solemn vow
sudden death, smoke-filled room
sandwich board, sonic boom
silver screen, strep throat
spinner play, straw vote
shish kebab, sandy loam
scandal sheet, soldiers' home

* By permission. From *Word Study*, Copyright 1963 by G. & C. Merriam Co., Publishers of the Merriam-Webster Dictionaries.

Exercise 20,

continued

squirrel cage, sour mash
song and dance, swung dash
shelter half, swim fin
state guard, scatter pin
scrub brush, swimmer's itch
service charge, slip stitch
spirit lamp, sucking louse
section hand, solar house
surgeon general, scratch sheet
sweat pants, sliding seat
set point, strawberry roan
spoon feed, strike zone
shore dinner, striped bass
sweetie pie, sung mass
shop steward, skid row
steel band, ski tow

Summing Up

All writing is creative writing inasmuch as it permits the writer many choices of words in putting ideas on paper. To the extent that his choices allow the writer to express his individuality, his hopes, his fears, his values, that writing is creative whether he writes epic poems or television commercials. A commitment to facts, to what really happened, limits a writer's freedom to invent, to make choices, thereby limiting (but not stifling) his creative range. But a writer of fiction faces no such limitations. In each setting he invents, in every choice of character, conflict, and outcome, he proclaims to the world his uniqueness as an individual. Since he has no facts to trade in, he becomes a translator of human feelings, especially his own.

ꦲꦏꦸꦫꦠꦺꦏꦸꦭꦸ꧞ ꦠꦏꦺꦴꦠꦺꦴꦏꦲ ꦩꦥꦥꦸꦭꦸ꧀ꦲꦺꦴꦲꦺꦴꦏꦸꦮꦸꦭꦸ꧀ꦲꦺꦴꦏꦸꦮꦸ ꦩꦥꦥꦸꦭꦸ꧀ꦲꦺꦴꦤꦴꦱꦶ
ꦮꦏꦴꦠꦸꦭꦸ ꦤꦴꦱꦴꦮꦠꦴ ꦠꦴ ꦩꦥꦥꦸꦭꦸ꧀ꦲꦺꦴꦲꦺꦴ꧞2꧞ ꦲꦥꦤ꧞2ꦤꦠ ꦩꦥꦥꦸꦭꦸ꧀ꦤꦤ꧞2ꦱꦶ꧞ ꦠꦩꦠ
2ꦠ ꦩꦥꦥꦸꦭꦸ꧀ꦲꦺꦴꦥꦶꦤꦸ ꦲꦲꦩꦠ ꦩꦥꦥꦸꦭꦸ꧀ꦭꦲꦮꦸꦭꦸ꧀꧞ ꦭꦩꦥꦶꦤꦠ ꦩꦥꦥꦸꦭꦸ꧀ꦭ
ꦮꦸꦠꦴ꧞ ꦭꦴꦮꦩꦥꦶꦤꦠ ꦱꦶꦩꦥꦶꦩꦤꦴꦤꦶꦤꦴꦩꦴ ꦠꦴꦩꦩ ꦠꦴ ꦩꦥꦥꦸꦭꦸ꧀ꦱꦶꦮꦴꦤꦴꦩꦴ꧞ ꦱꦶꦮꦴꦤꦴꦠꦴ ꦠ
ꦩꦥꦥꦸꦭꦸ꧀ꦮꦸꦩꦩꦴꦥꦶꦤꦥꦶꦤꦩꦠ ꦩꦤꦥꦶ ꦏꦴꦠ ꦱꦥꦠꦱ ꦮꦸꦮꦸꦩꦴ꧟ ꦭꦴꦩꦴꦭꦩꦶ ꦱꦦꦥꦠ2ꦮꦤ ꦅꦤꦴꦮꦴ ꦏꦩꦮꦤ ꦭꦴꦤꦤ ꦠꦴ ꦮꦴ ꦭꦴꦩꦴ
ꦭꦶꦮꦴ ꦲꦭꦩꦶꦭꦶꦩꦤꦤꦩꦤꦩꦤ꧟3꧞ ꦱꦴꦱꦴꦱꦤ ꦅꦤꦥ ꦏꦩꦴꦱꦥꦼꦮꦴꦤ ꦩꦤꦴꦩꦤꦴꦮꦴꦤ ꦮꦶꦤꦴ꧀ꦩꦴꦩꦴꦩꦮ ꦩꦴꦩꦴꦩꦮ꧟ꦩꦤ꧀

New Javanese

Chapter 5

REVISING
AND
REWRITING

A Look Back and A Look Forward

In the preceding chapter, you learned how to paint word pictures of actual human experiences and how to evoke suspense.

As you study the last chapter, you will recognize the need for rewriting and revision. First of all, you must be satisfied with the structure of your sentences and paragraphs. Second, you must catch and hold your reader's interest by effective development of your topic. Third, you must try to convince your reader through a meaningful presentation. Finally, you must reread carefully for any weaknesses in the mechanics of writing. Let's begin.

A CHECK LIST FOR REVISION

The best writing results from careful revision and rewriting. Composition is a complex process, as you have discovered, and the first draft is often a rather rough expression of the ideas that occurred to you as you attempted to follow your outline. However, after a careful study of the draft, you are ready to revise and rewrite the material so that your final product will be satisfactory to you and acceptable to your reader.

A check list should be helpful in your revision. The one below is in the form of questions that you might ask yourself as you proceed with your task. There are four main points for consideration: organization, effectiveness, critical thinking, and mechanics.

ORGANIZATION
The Whole Theme
1. Is the topic clearly stated, limited, and linked with the main idea of the whole theme?
2. Is each subordinate topic related to the subject of the theme?
3. Are the subordinate ideas arranged with some relation to their importance?
4. Is there adequate transition between subordinate topics?
5. Is there evidence of repetition?

The Paragraph
1. Is there a topic sentence, and if so, is its placement one that will receive appropriate emphasis?
2. Is each paragraph developed around one main idea?
3. Is the paragraph developed according to some definite plan?
4. Does it contain any irrelevant material?
5. Are the transitions effective?
6. Is there evidence of repetition?

The Sentence
1. Are there any sentence fragments, run-together sentences, comma faults?
2. Is each sentence unified and clear?
3. Are some of the sentences too long and involved?
4. Are coordination and subordination used effectively with proper regard for coherence and emphasis?
5. Are details arranged in an orderly manner?
6. Are there any unnecessary words that might be eliminated?
7. Does variety in sentence structure indicate that you have exploited grammatical resources adequately?
8. Is there evidence of faulty parallelism?

1. Have you carefully planned the method of development of your topic in terms of what is needed?
2. Have you elaborated statements adequately with suitable illustrations, examples, details?
3. Have you moved easily between levels of generalization, avoiding a dead-level style—either high or low?
4. Is your usage both grammatical and conventional?
5. Is your choice of language both appropriate and adequate?
6. Is your attitude toward your subject consistent with the tone of your writing?
7. Have you made the most of your subject, satisfied that your reader can conclude with the comment, "This writer certainly has something to say"?

CRITICAL THINKING
1. Have you defined all ambiguous terms?
2. Have you consistently kept to the exact meanings?
3. Have you supported assertions with adequate evidence?
4. Have you been careful to avoid unqualified generalizations?
5. Do you find unrecognized assumptions in your statements?
6. Do you find any evidence of fallacious reasoning?
7. Have you used language honestly throughout?

MECHANICS
1. Are all words spelled correctly?
2. Is the punctuation appropriate and adequate?
3. Have you used abbreviations, capitalization, and compounds according to convention?
4. Are subject and verb in agreement throughout?
5. Have all pronouns unmistakable antecedents?
6. Are there any misplaced modifiers, dangling constructions, double negatives?
7. Have you been consistent in the use of the tense of verbs and in the person of pronouns?
8. Is there any adjective-adverb confusion?
9. Have you checked case of pronouns and irregular verb forms?
10. Have you divided words correctly?

ORGANIZATION

The organization of a theme requires thought and careful planning. An outline showing how you will develop your topic should be drawn for every theme you write. An outline serves as a guide and is helpful in maintaining unity and coherence in writing.

The Whole Theme

The following theme, written by a high school student, is well organized. Although you may not agree with what this writer has to say, it should be apparent to you that she has carefully developed the main idea of her topic and that each subordinate idea relates to this main idea. Furthermore, she has tried to elaborate each of the subordinate ideas at a lower level of generalization (by illustration). Her introduction prepares the reader for the discussion developed, and her conclusion encourages him to give thought to the topic.

```
                    Finding Meaning in Life
    To find meaning in our lives has been an unending quest
since the beginning of man's recorded history.  Every action
we perform has a reason or purpose, and thus we are led on in
our search for this meaning.
    Some find meaning or motivation by helping others.  An
example is the hospital nurse who finds fulfillment in
contributing to the recovery of her patients.  For when a
nurse helps a poor, aged invalid, she knows that she is giving
him the assurance that his well-being and comfort are important.
    Others find meaning in life through God, that is, in the
goodness and kindness of a Supreme Being.  In believing that
one day they will be blessed with an eternal life, they have
found something to live for and to anticipate.
    But actually the best example of meaning in our lives is
love.  Love is one of the strongest of all emotions.  The love
of a man for a woman may serve as the basis of happiness and
success.  The love of a parent for a child may provide the
basis for a whole life of achievement.  The love of a youth for
his mother may be the means of shaping his life as a man.
    The question of meaning in life is still unanswered — and it
will remain so for generations to come.  What gives meaning
and purpose to the life of one person would not answer the
needs of another.  It is an individual affair, and unless we
turn into a world of mass conformists, the quest for personal
meaning and identity will continue indefinitely.
```

In the next theme, the writer has attempted to organize her work carefully. However, there is one idea used in her development that is not closely related to the main idea. Can you pick it out and defend your criticism? The structure of her paragraphs might be improved. What do you think? What improvements could you make? Do you think the conclusion is particularly effective? How would you conclude the theme?

```
                     Emerson's Law of Compensation
     Emerson believed in the law of compensation: for every sweet
there is a sour, if one gives he will receive, and for every
evil there is a good.  This is the balance of life.
     A blind person has better hearing and an extra sensitive
touch.  In fact, it is often said that the blind have a "sixth
sense" that seems to guide them, thus enabling them to live
normal lives.  The handicapped are often talented, have brilliant
minds, or develop other parts of their body to a greater extent.
Take, for example, the man who had polio as a child and whose
legs were left completely paralyzed.  His arms and shoulders
eventually grew to twice their normal strength because he used
them so much.  A deaf-mute develops a sign language to
compensate for lack of speech.
     The idea of survival of the fittest is nature's way of
balancing the overpopulation of one species of animal.  A small
animal eats an insect, and in turn is eaten by a larger animal.
The extinction of any animal came about either because of
environmental changes or destruction by man.  When the earth
becomes overpopulated, there is usually a war or an epidemic.
In exceptionally overcrowded countries there is a shortage of
food and many children do not survive.
     Some people have more than their share of hardships.  Yet,
because of these hardships, they are more understanding.  They
can laugh at their own mistakes; they have more compassion
for others.  Their compensation is that they are more content
with life.
     If a person really believes in the law of compensation, he
will be happier because he will feel that life always has
its rewards.
```

In the organization of the two themes above, the writers gave some consideration to the matter of emphasis. In the first theme, "Finding Meaning in Life," the writer proceeded from occupation, to religion, to love. She apparently considered love to be most significant in relation to her topic. In the second, the writer illustrated her interpretation of Emerson's law of compensation by moving from the physical examples to the spiritual reward of contentment in life despite its hardships.

The Paragraph

In examining a paragraph for possible revision in organization and development, the writer must keep in mind the basic requirements of a paragraph as an integral part of the whole theme. Let's summarize these requirements:

1. Usually, the paragraph has a topic sentence. If there is no stated topic sentence, the idea expressed should be implicit in the paragraph.
2. The paragraph should be developed around a single idea. Thus the paragraph has what we call *unity*.
3. All statements in the paragraph should relate to the main idea. There should be no irrelevant details.
4. The vocabulary of the paragraph points continually toward the main idea. The use of synonyms and related terms reinforce the topic of the paragraph.
5. The paragraph should be developed according to a plan by which attention has been paid to the relative importance of material and its position. Thus the paragraph has *coherence*.
6. Attention should be given to easy and effective transition.
7. The last sentence should be particularly effective in summarizing, restating a particularly important concept, or possibly pointing forward to what is to follow in the next paragraph.

All of this, of course, sounds very familiar to you—too much so, perhaps. Let's be more specific by examining the following paragraph:

> The core of any article is the information it presents, and dredging this material calls for thorough, complete fact gathering. The good newspaper reporter's policy of getting five or ten times more material than he will use in his story is the watchword of the feature writer. If he must use every scrap and tatter of information, he knows he has not dug deeply enough. Only when he has so much material at hand that he must select and choose which details to put into his article is he ready to begin writing. An article built upon skimpy information always gives itself away by telling the editors of its shallowness; somewhere in it, the writer doesn't know enough about his subject to make precise, unequivocal statements and has to dip into generalities.*   R. M. NEAL, "Feature Articles and Editorials"

This paragraph has unity. Each sentence relates to the idea of gathering enough material to present ample information to the reader. The final sentence points to the outcome of a writer's failure to dredge deep for his facts: nothing but empty generalities. Words like *information* and *material* occur repeatedly and direct the attention of the reader to the idea being developed. The topic sentence, which opens the paragraph, states the idea clearly. The development of the idea proceeds

* From *Writers on Writing*, published by Doubleday and Company, Inc.

from what is necessary for writing a good article to the climactic statement of what will happen if the writer fails. It is a logical plan, with the emphasis on the final statement.

The next example is the opening paragraph in the book *The Silent Language* by Edward T. Hall. Although a very short paragraph, it displays perfection in form.

> Time talks. It speaks more plainly than words. The message it conveys comes through loud and clear. Because it is manipulated less consciously, it is subject to less distortion than the spoken language. It can shout the truth where words lie.

Examine this paragraph in relation to the standards listed above. In what way does it reveal excellence in form? What do you think the author is going to discuss in the first chapter?

Many writers fail to exert the effort necessary to achieve good form in paragraphs. This fact is particularly true of student writers. If a student is careless of the formal requirements of a paragraph, he is guilty of neglecting to use and exploit a quality that is of utmost importance in writing. Form or organization, whether in the whole theme or in its parts, reinforces the substance of what has been written.

Exercise 1   *The following selection consists of the opening paragraphs of a theme written by a high school student. His topic, like that of the writer whose theme is reproduced on page 336, is "Finding Meaning in Life." Discuss the limitations of this selection and then decide how you would revise it, retaining the ideas that the student has presented and developing them as you feel they deserve elaboration. Pay particular attention to the needs for an adequate introduction and the requirements of paragraph development.*

The search for meaning in life is uppermost in the minds of most of the people of our time. Everyone needs some meaning in his life. Without it life would be a never-ending pattern of dullness.

Meaning in life for some people is a goal for which they are aiming. They try to come closer to achieving their goal each day. This goal they are working toward may never be attained, but their lives will be richer and more meaningful just because of the attempt to reach it.

Many people find meaning in their lives through helping mankind. This can be done in many ways. A person can find much reward and inner satisfaction in working with others.

Exercise 2   *Discuss the following as a model paragraph. How has the writer maintained unity, coherence, and emphasis? How has his choice of words reinforced the reader's concentration of attention on the main idea? In what way has the writer planned the development of the paragraph? How has he secured easy transition?*

The book you are now reading brings you a large amount of information in compact form. It, like all books, is a comparatively recent achievement in the history of man. Originally, man could communicate with his fellows only by word of mouth. Very slowly he learned to make crude representational pictures (pictographs) on stone of things or events that he wished to record. Thousands of years later he was able to make symbols of words, called ideographs (hieroglyphics by the Egyptians), but these were complicated systems understood by only a few wise men. Then occurred a miracle in man's communication with man. A few thousand years before the Christian era, the Phoenicians, on the shores of the Mediterranean, produced what we call our alphabet. They made symbols of *sounds* and therefore found a way to reproduce speech with fewer than twenty-six simple forms. These are the basic symbols you are now reading, with such transitional changes as have occurred in the passage of these forms through Greek, Roman, and European civilizations — and from letters understood by the few, to type cast by machine and printed at incredible speed for all.* — JOSEPH BLUMENTHAL, "The Making of a Book"

The Sentence

Let us assume that you have examined the organization of your whole theme and that you have studied the form and development of the separate paragraphs. Next you will consider the structure of each sentence.

The most serious error in the sentence structure of high school students and college freshmen is the use of fragments. Run-together sentences and the comma fault are other common errors.

The recognition and use of conventional sentence structure are basic to standard written English. Let's review once more the physical characteristics of the sentence — the features by means of which it may be identified.

---

* Reprinted from *The Wonderful World of Books*, published by Houghton Mifflin Company and The New American Library of World Literature, Inc.

1. The sentence begins with a capital letter and ends with a period, a question mark, or an exclamation point.
2. The sentence has a subject and a predicate.
3. The verb in a sentence must be a finite verb.
4. The normal word order of a sentence is subject-verb-complement.
5. The sentence may be introduced by a subordinate clause, a prepositional phrase, a participial phrase, or an infinitive phrase; but none of these subordinate elements are in themselves sentences.
6. Signals of intonation identify sentence structure. The juncture at the end of a structure attended by a falling pitch and a fading of the voice or by a rising pitch and a sudden stop will help the writer to identify the sentence structure when he reads his written material aloud.

The following selection is an extract from a student theme. Look for the sentence fragments, run-together sentences, and comma faults in this material. How would you revise these structures?

Some families live in a world of fantasy. They turn the television on early in the morning and turn it off late at night. They are completely unaware of what is going on in the world on this side of the TV screen, they talk to each other only during the commercials. They neglect their duties and rarely grasp the other things life has to offer.

In my family we enjoy TV; but we enjoy many other things, too. Going for long drives, visiting relatives, dining out occasionally, even walking in the park. We eat our meals in the dining room away from the TV screen, we discuss events of the day. We often listen to records, we get tired of the "idiot box," as it is sometimes called.

Our favorite night on TV is Thursday, in our opinion, the best programs are shown that night. We especially like the family stories. Which help us to understand some of our common problems.

Now note how a few simple revisions have eliminated the faulty structures:

Some families live in a world of fantasy. They turn the television on early in the morning and turn it off late at night. They are completely unaware of what is going on in the world on this side of the TV screen. they talk to each other only during the commercials. They neglect their duties and rarely grasp the other things life has to offer.

In my family we enjoy TV; but we enjoy many other things,
                    We go   *; we visit*   *; we dine*
too. ~~Going~~ for long drives, ~~visiting~~ relatives, ~~dining~~ out
                      ⊙We
occasionally, even walking in the park, We eat our meals in
                                                    and
the dining room away from the TV screen, we discuss events of
                                          when
the day. We often listen to records, we get tired of the

"idiot box," as it is sometimes called.
                                    when,
Our favorite night on TV is Thursday, in our opinion, the best

programs are shown ~~that night~~. We especially like the family

stories, Which help us to understand some of our common

problems.

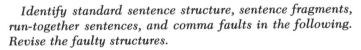

Exercise 3   *Identify standard sentence structure, sentence fragments,*
                      run-together sentences, and comma faults in the following.
                      Revise the faulty structures.

1. What to do in the event of fire?

2. When Claude arrived at the gate, he was restrained by
    fear of a huge dog that greeted him with suppressed
    growling.

3. When the wind howls around the top of the apartment
    house, and the windows rattle all night long, the long
    nights and the darkness of a frightening storm.

4. Being an honor student, Henry Fleming was able to
    finish his high school work in three years.

5. The man to watch tomorrow is that third-string quarter-
    back nobody has seen him in action.

6. I got two quarts of milk at the store isn't that what you
    said you wanted?

7. The convention will last three days, however, we hope
    to be home Sunday night.

8. There is no place like home. With all its comforts and
    conveniences and the accustomed things of daily life.

9. That you will need heavy clothing when you go to camp.

10. What a fine leader our chairman has turned out to be.

11. We enjoyed the concert the musicians were excellent.

12. The children playing and shouting in the back yard.

13. A time to think about what you will do in the future, when you will be a responsible adult and probably have a family to look after.

14. What he said when he was finally introduced and allowed to speak was very appropriate.

15. To go to Europe, to visit the great cities of the continent, this was the hope of Henry Stone as he worked day after day in the hot machine shop.

16. Then the chorus moved across the stage.

17. When the storm clouds move across the sky.

18. There will be no meeting of the Dramatic Club tomorrow.

19. To go to an auction is a lot of fun.

20. To go to the country and spend the hot summer in the mountains, what a delightful prospect.

21. "Whose woods these are, I think I know."

22. Charlotte was chosen as the leader of the group. Charlotte being the oldest girl and the most intelligent.

23. In the center of the city is an old brick building it has stained-glass windows and a high tower.

24. Older people need exercise walking is an excellent form.

25. Cleon swung at the first pitch, he hit the ball into the right-field bleachers.

Improving Sentences

The English language is very flexible. An intelligent use of its resources results in the creation of beautiful and effective sentences. Poor sentence structure, which is evidence of naïve, casual, unthinking use of the language forms, creates obscurity and confusion.

Let's examine some poorly constructed sentences. Study them carefully and try to determine what is wrong with them and how they may be improved by stating the facts clearly.

1. The buses arrived on time, and the weather was cold and the boys shivered as they hurried away from the Terminal toward Front Street.

2. My brothers upset my room at times when they play the radio or hi-fi, which belong to the whole family, but Dad keeps them in my room.

3. I've always enjoyed dressing up, so when my cousin Alma asked me to go to her graduation, I was happy to accept.

4. For instance, if Mother asks us to do something around the house while she lets the younger children go and play, we may think we are being mistreated, but if we stop to think about it, the future when we will be on our own isn't far off and perhaps Mother is just training us for that.

The first sentence lacks unity because it contains two entirely unrelated ideas. There must be some sequence of meaning or a logical relationship between the ideas in a sentence.

The buses arrived on time, and we were all happy to have arrived safely at our destination.

The ideas in the faulty sentence might better have been communicated in two separate sentences:

The buses arrived on time. The weather was cold, and the boys shivered as they hurried away from the terminal toward Front Street.

The second faulty sentence is involved; it, too, lacks unity. The writer packed too much into one sentence. The ideas might better be communicated in two sentences. The use of subordination would reinforce the logic of the sentence and of the ideas that are related in the sentence.

My brothers upset my room at times when they play the radio or hi-fi. Although these belong to the whole family, Dad keeps them in my room.

Better subordination would improve the third faulty sentence. It was written as a compound sentence expressing a coordinate (equal) relationship between the two main ideas. These ideas could be related in a more meaningful sentence by the use of an introductory subordinate clause.

Because I've always enjoyed dressing up, I was happy to accept my cousin Alma's invitation to attend her graduation.

In the fourth faulty sentence, the writer has put down on paper the same breathless kind of rambling that we sometimes hear in ordinary conversation. This sentence might be called a "runaway" sentence. It should be broken up for better communication.

When Mother asks us to work in the house after sending the younger children out to play, we may think we are being mistreated. We should remember, however, that perhaps Mother is training us for the duties of later life.

The writer achieves sentence clarity—the basis of successful communication—when he observes the requirement of sentence unity. He achieves sentence effectiveness when he makes effectual use of the devices of coordination and subordination.

Now examine three more sentences that illustrate common structural faults:

1. There is a vase on the table which belongs to my mother.
2. Harold is a boy who takes life seriously, who works very hard, and he will be a success.
3. Uncle Ralph has money in the bank, a small house in the city, and a summer home in the Adirondacks.

As you read these sentences, do you find faults in structure? The first sentence is ambiguous. Does the vase or the table belong to Mother? To avoid ambiguity, rephrase the sentence.

The vase on the table belongs to my mother.

Now look at this sentence:

There is a boy in this room who looks just like my brother.

The relative pronoun *who* (as well as the context of the sentence) shows that the subordinate clause modifies the noun *boy*. However, when the clue is not given, uncertainty of meaning results:

There is the brother of Mr. Castle who lives in Mesa.

In this sentence the relative pronoun is not a clue since it might refer either to brother or to Mr. Castle. The ambiguity of such a sentence can be avoided by recasting it.

Mr. Castle's brother lives in Mesa.

The second sentence suggested for examination is an illustration of faulty parallelism. As a rule, *and* and *but* connect like grammatical elements—two or more nouns, two or more subordinate clauses, and so forth. Here, *and* connects two adjective clauses and a NS-LV-N PATTERN. The sentence can be improved by substituting an adjective clause for the basic sentence pattern:

Harold is a boy who takes life seriously, who works very hard, and who will be a success.

The details in the third sentence are not arranged in the best order. It is generally more effective to arrange the items in a series as a climax—beginning with the least important and concluding with the most important:

Uncle Ralph has a small house in the city, a summer home in the Adirondacks, and money in the bank.

Sue overcooked the vegetables, scorched the potatoes, and burned the chops to a crisp.

Sometimes an anticlimax is used for humor:

On the ride up Mt. Washington, I lost my left ski, my handkerchief, and my composure.

Exercise 4

Discuss the structure of these sentences. Revise them for greater clarity and effectiveness.

1. Jim got up at ten o'clock and in the afternoon he went to a ball game.

2. There was no ham in the refrigerator, so Father had to take cheese in his sandwiches.

3. The books are not on the desk, in the living room, or anywhere that you would expect to find them.

4. The traffic was heavy in the late afternoon, and we drove very slowly to the Midtown Tunnel and then we had to wait for an hour because of an accident which had occurred in the tunnel just before he got there.

5. Mother has a picture on our living room wall which was painted by my father.

6. The accident was the fault of the driver of the first car, who swerved across the center line and he was killed instantly as well as two people in the second car.

7. In the distance we could see the mountains rising high above the land, the road threading its way through the valley, and the blinking lights of farmhouses.

8. He is a friend of Mr. Smith who wants to buy a new car.

9. The younger members of the family in particular have a desire to watch TV rather than doing their homework.

10. In the meantime we sang, did dishes, hiked, made preparations for lunch, and took sunbaths.

11. Upon dragging our weary bones out of bed the following morning, we were greeted by a delectable array of tasty dishes, which simply means that for the second morning in a row, we ate scrambled eggs, bacon, toast, hot chocolate, and orange juice.

12. Jim likes math so he plans to go to college and study engineering.

Exercise 4,
continued

13. Fred has been a substitute on the football team, but last Saturday he ran fifty yards for the winning touchdown.

14. The child was running across the street when he was hit by a car.

15. They wanted to find religious freedom so they came to America.

EFFECTIVENESS

In developing a topic, never lose track of your aim—to inform your reader and to catch and hold his interest. Make every effort to communicate your ideas in a way the reader will fully comprehend.

The problem of deciding how best to develop a topic is one that has to be considered seriously. For example, to describe a living room, one might begin at one side and enumerate each piece of furniture in its spatial arrangement. The result would be an inventory, not an effective piece of writing. On the other hand, one may select an overall effect and relate each part of the room to this effect, or dominant impression. The room may be furnished with Victorian pieces of furniture. The Victorian motif may serve as the unifying idea of the description.

Perhaps your topic for a theme is "High School Dropouts." Just how will you develop this topic? Well, you might search your brain for reasons behind the dropouts; you would probably come up with four or five that you have heard about or read about. Then you could develop these points in a very general way. (This is quite a common method of developing a subject by inexperienced writers.)

Or you might go to the library and search the current periodicals and newspapers for articles on the subject. These articles are usually based on careful research and provide a wealth of material, called secondary sources. They deal with different aspects of the problem by competent writers. How serious is the problem of high school dropouts? What factors contribute to it? How is it being solved in some communities? What are its social effects? You might limit your topic and decide to develop it in terms of one of these ideas.

A third method of development of the topic under discussion is the case-study method. You might go to your high school principal or guidance director and ask for information. He would not identify the individuals, of course, but he could give you valuable data about students who have left school. Many of their stories would make very interesting reading and would give primary evidence of the nature of the problem in your own community.

One of the most serious limitations of students is their failure to elaborate statements made in their themes. In proofreading your first draft, the question of elaboration and illustration is of extreme importance to the effectiveness of your material. If you have left your reader with generalities, you have accomplished little from the standpoint of effective communication.

Exercise 5   *The student theme reproduced below — once again, the topic is "Finding Meaning in Life" — illustrates the fault described above. Read the theme. Then reexamine it in light of the questions that follow it.*

Finding Meaning in Life

The search for meaning in life is uppermost in the minds of everyone. We all need some meaning in life. Without meaning, life would be a never-ending pattern of dullness.

For some people meaning in life is a goal. Each day they try to come closer to achieving their goal. They may never reach it, but their lives will be richer and more meaningful just because of the attempt.

Many people find meaning in life through helping mankind. A person can find much reward and inner satisfaction in working for others. Missionaries sacrifice the comforts of civilization to help backward people. Yet missionaries are usually the most contented people in the world.

Meaning in life can be found in the things around us. Nature itself has deep meaning that can be transmitted to anyone who looks for it. People should take time out from the hurried world of today just to relax. Then, while relaxing, they should take a good look at the things around them. It takes only a few moments to realize how beautiful nature is and what deep meanings it can hold for everyone.

Meaning in life is essential to inner peace. Meaning can be found in many ways, usually through everyday occurrences that are not recognized as having this deeper meaning. Mankind will have to keep on searching, even if it seems that peace will never come. Life becomes so much richer and fuller through the searching that has been done and will continue to be done.

Exercise 5, continued

1. Does the writer remain at a high level of generalization, or does she illustrate her ideas with examples?

2. How might the writer have taken her first idea—that of a goal in life—and built it into an effective discussion of how people have found meaning in life by working toward a goal?

CRITICAL THINKING

You check your themes for weakness in reasoning, in judgment, in the careless and dishonest use of language. You are concerned with the validity of your conclusions. You want your material to be convincing as well as clear to your reader. Just what are you looking for as you read what you have written? Review the list once more.

1. Undefined terms
2. Inconsistencies of meaning
3. Unsupported assertions
4. Unqualified generalizations
5. Hidden or unrecognized assumptions
6. Unwarranted conclusions
7. Fallacies of one kind or another

In order to provide some concrete examples for discussion, let's examine some excerpts from themes written by high school students.

```
My philosophy of life is to live a happy beneficial life.
One should strive with all his might toward a goal of a happy
life.  Each person should leave behind him some beneficial
thought or deed that his friends and family could remember his
doing or saying.
    One has great power within himself to build his own life.
He can set his own goal.  It is terrifying to think how many
people abuse this power.  They permit false pride, jealousy,
hatred, love, and almost every other emotion in life to prevent
them from leading a happy life.
    Many times society has an important role in determining a
man's way of life.  As a member of society, one has to conform
to certain rules and standards.  Many times these are rules and
standards just opposite to his own personal beliefs.  He is,
therefore, classified as a nonconformist, troublemaker, or just
someone who goes around breaking rules.
```

List some observations and criticisms related to the use of critical thinking by the writer of the selection above. For example:

1. Definitions needed
    philosophy of life, goal, beneficial thought, great power, false pride,
    jealousy, hatred, society, standards, nonconformist
   These terms are highly abstract and need explanation on lower levels
   of generalization.
2. Assertions
    "Each person should leave . . . ."
    "One has great power . . . ."
    ". . . how many people abuse this power."
    "They permit . . . ."
    "Many times society has . . . ."
    "As a member of society, one has to conform . . . ."
    "Many times . . . ."
3. Unwarranted conclusion
    "He is, therefore, classified as . . . ."
4. Hidden assumption
    People should have a goal in life in order to achieve happiness.

The selection consists of a series of unsupported assertions, and the
writer made no attempt to elaborate them. The reader is left with a
sense of confusion because of the extreme vagueness of the writing and
the impression that the writer lacks the knowledge necessary for handling the subject. This kind of writing is common when high school
students tackle highly abstract subjects.

You, as a student of writing, should study this material and decide
how you could improve it and make it more meaningful. What are your
ideas on this subject and how could you communicate them in a concrete way?

Now examine another selection from a class theme.

    Time passed. The colonists came to America. They built their
own homes, raised their own food, and prepared all the
necessities of life. Yet take a look at today's woman, who
does not know any more about preparing food than to open a can
and pour its contents into the skillet.
    The world has progressed. But is this good? Modern man can
no longer tell the time by the sun or recite the names of the
stars. He can no longer chop trees, clear fields, and catch
wild animals for food. We live in a day and age of convenience.
    Modern man has become lazy. He has lost his determination to
be great. Today he is content to be just average. Today we
even face the problem that modern man has forgotten how to think!
    Yes, the world has progressed. But the skills and ideals of
mankind have deteriorated. And so will the world some day.
For modern man will no longer have the strength to hold it
together.

What kind of thinking is illustrated in this selection? What kind of reasoning prompts the statement about "today's woman"? What is the unrecognized assumption underlying the condemnation of "modern man"? In four words the student asserts, "The world has progressed." Does this satisfy you as a valid statement? Would you like to know how it has progressed? Perhaps the writer is trying to contrast the scientific progress of civilized man with his presumed physical weakness. Don't you think that the contrast would be more effective if some concrete examples were provided?

Exercise 6

1. List all of the unsupported assertions in the selection on page 349.

2. Are there any unwarranted conclusions?

3. Are there unqualified generalizations?

4. Read the following selection from a theme written by a high school student. Discuss it from the standpoint of the essentials of critical thinking.

Television, that great mass medium, has come into our lives with many and varied results. These results are best shown by their effect on the family group, or unit of culture.

The first point we should examine is the effect it has on the cultural aspects of the family. Television is a great force for entertainment—it brings into the home first-rate movies, sports programs, quiz shows, and dramas. It also has the advantage of being inexpensive and handy. Despite this fact, how many people actually take advantage of it for their own betterment? If the finer programs and educational series were considered as a starting point for discussion or watched for information rather than only entertainment, television would be a truly cultural asset. But people regard it only as entertainment, to be watched and then forgotten. They want to be able to sit down and be entertained, not instructed or encouraged to think. The younger members of the family in particular show a preference for watching TV rather than for doing their homework. In this case television is a marked disadvantage.

Another aspect to be considered is the unity of the family. Heated debates over what program to watch can hardly be conducive to family peace   The

Exercise 6,
continued

family, normally drawn closer through conversation
at the dinner table, when watching TV at this time,
is split into staring entities, nibbling untasted
TV dinners. And the programs being watched will
not be a source of later discussion so that they
might redeem themselves. The family, when split,
grows into several distinct and separate beings.
The constant noise and humming of the TV can
drive people insane. This one-eyed monster has
invaded our privacy of mind, insulted our intelli-
gence, and flaunted our sense of the decent and
proper. Television, despite its possibilities for
good, is detrimental both to the culture and
structure of the American family.

MECHANICS

Proofreading in the minds of many students means checking a paper
for misspelled words, errors in punctuation, subject-verb agreement,
pronoun reference, misplaced modifiers — all the elements of careful
composition which we think of as the mechanics of English. Of all the
requirements of written communication, these matters are of secondary
importance. Naturally, it is necessary to spell correctly, punctuate effectively, and so on, but these are matters of convention. The major elements of written communication are what you have to say, how you
have said it, and how well you have established the validity of your
statements.

Apart from relative importance, however, errors in mechanics are
usually symptomatic of other weaknesses in writing. Also, the weight
of public opinion is heavily directed against the writer who makes mistakes in the basic conventions of English composition. Getting and holding jobs may depend on one's spelling and punctuation. Even reputation
and respectability may suffer because of errors in the mechanics of
English. It is unwise to underestimate the importance of conventions
in our lives in organized society.

Therefore, let's direct attention to review material that will help to
retain your sensitivity to the misspelled word, the missing comma, the
dangling participle, the lonely pronoun without an antecedent, and the
double negative.

Exercise 7   *Correct the errors in mechanics and sentence structure*
found in the theme on the next page.

Exercise 7,
continued

Saving Money

There are several ways of getting money, you can work hard for it which is the most lodgical idea. Or you could borrow it which is not very lodgical. And there's always everyone's dream of inheriting a couple million dollars. No matter how you get your money it is always good to save a little for a rainy day, or just save for your old age.

If you save while your still young you can almost have enough money to retire on when you get old. There's veryus ways of saving money when your young, the best way is to give it to your parent's for safe keeping to make sure it gets to the bank. In most elementary schools they have savings stamps. You could always by stamps and filla book, when the books full you can get yourself a United States Savings bond. If you don't get much money you can always just save pennys, nickles, or dimes in a piggy bank. When you have some lose change just drop it in. You'd be surprised how it adds up.

If you have a good job and make good money you can afford to save a little each week for the kids or something for your house or family needs. If your single and like to have a good time you can save half of what you make and put the other half in whatever you want to, a good time, a better place to live, a new car. Or save a third for one of thooo things and a third just for saving it and the other third to live off of. But never blow a whole pay check at once on a good time or something that won't show any use a day from the time you got it. And don't become a miser thats worse than anything, there you become greedy want everything but not putting out for hardly anything. Just remember a penny saved is a penny erned.

Exercise 8

Punctuate the following sentences and correct errors in spelling, capitalization, and abbreviations:

1. Mr cummings has moved to waco Texas where he is going to open a branch office of hoca pola ice cream inc

2. The great steamer titanic a magnificent tribute to opulence lies in the mud of the Atlantic where each year it slips farther and farther into the darkness of the centuries

Exercise 8,

continued

3. jefferson long a black man from the state of georgia was the first negro to be elected to the united states house of representatives.

4. charles brownell d d s is my dentist.

5. after earning a phi beta kappa key from new york university countee cullen entered harvard and received his master of arts degree in 1926.

6. the city streets were litered with trash and papers a matter which was of great concern to the mayor as well as to all the city's inhabitants.

7. kurt vonnegut jr. the author of slaughterhouse-five has also written several other novels and many short stories most of which are availible in paperback form.

8. Strongfellow the gorilla is in his cage on the truck

9. When the winter snows melt and the spring rains come grandpa is always susceptable to rheumatism

10. The demonstrators chanted the question when are we going to be granted the freedoms of other people

11. Upon registering at the new school Louise was confronted with many problems buying books finding classrooms putting her room in order and making friends

12. The long hours past Clarence had few answers for the many difficult questions on the entrance test

13. The opening of school for the new semester an event which always creates an atmosphere of excitement will be marked this year by a change in the administration Mr. Sparks will be the new principle

14. The annual hike of the boy scouts to the camping area on the Tennesee River always ends with the same question when do we eat

15. We visited the old city of Jamestown it was founded you remember in 1607 and took many interesting photographs

16. They travelled from Albuquerque New Mexico to Phoenix Arizona on the atcheson topeka and santa fe railroad

17. Frances remarked I find it very difficult to read Yeats poetry its the symbolism that I find hard to understand

18. Pete Olson the all American guard from Missisippi saved the game in the last five minutes of play with a dropkick.

Exercise 8,
continued

19. The Rev Thompson who lives on the west side of town will award the prize to the student who writes the best essay.

20. We will attend the Brahms concert which will begin at 8 oclock.

Exercise 9

Identify the errors in the following sentences. Revise the sentences in which you find errors.

1. Looking through the microscope the bacteria appeared like wiggling corkscrews.

2. Father won't object to our plans because he don't like arguments.

3. Nobody likes to have their name posted on the failure list after grades come out.

4. There goes Ray Burke with his umbrella walking down Lenox Avenue.

5. Tom said he don't know the answer to the question.

6. I saw Jimmy's brother driving his car past the high school.

7. Anna Mae forgot her lines just where the heroine faints for the third time.

8. Jack looked real good when he returned from camp this summer.

9. He don't hardly need no blankets on this camping trip to the desert.

10. The newspaper and the mail has been delivered to your home every morning.

11. Mrs. Bob Smith with all the little Smiths have left for the mountains.

12. All of my children do not like spinach.

13. Most all the hay has been cut.

14. There is a rake, a hoe, a shovel, and a pick in the shed.

15. There was an epidemic of measles in the town which caused the School Board to order the schools to be closed.

16. The teacher asked Rosa and I to take the leading parts in the Senior Play.

Exercise 9,
continued

17. Preserved in heavy syrup, we enjoyed Aunt Matilda's delicious canned pears.

18. One must be cautious in making such decisions about buying an expensive fur because you never can tell if it is genuine.

19. Henry is one of those fellows who likes to play dominoes.

20. Buddy feels badly about his failure to make the first team.

21. Neither the coach nor the members of the team was allowed to return to the field.

22. Every student has an obligation to be loyal to their school.

23. Mr. Finch is the new employer who you will be working for.

24. Everyone is working hard to improve their grades.

25. The meat was boiled tenderly in the iron kettle.

Summing Up

From the final chapter of this text you have learned the necessity for careful revision of a first draft, based on an outline to guide the development of your topic. If each subordinate idea clearly relates to the main idea, you achieve unity and coherence, requisite to any written material. To avoid confusion, you must, of course, be conscious of the structure of not only each paragraph but of each sentence.

The second requisite of a theme is effectiveness. Try to create a dominant impression, make reference to authoritive sources to support your views, and maintain consistency in the tone of your writing.

Logic is the third requisite of a theme. Avoid ambiguous terms, unsupported assertions, unqualified generalities, and fallacious reasoning.

Finally, proofread each theme for errors in the mechanics of English — spelling, punctuation, agreement, modifiers, verb forms, and pronoun antecedents. Be certain that you have made no mistakes in the basic conventions of English composition.

Supplementary Tests

A NOTE ON THE SUPPLEMENTARY TESTS.   The test questions that follow cover the various phases of grammar and composition studied in this book.

Part I

1. Name a few of the early Greek and Roman grammarians and describe their contributions to the study of language.

2. How do you account for the influence of Latin grammar in shaping the directions for the study of English grammar?

3. Describe the basic issue involved between the descriptive and prescriptive grammarians.

4. Discuss the similarities and differences between the older traditional grammar and the modern structural grammar.

5. What is meant by historical linguistics? Discuss the importance of this study to the modern student of language. What elements of interest in this subject might be found for the high school student?

6. Describe six physical characteristics of the English sentence. Use illustrations for clarification.

7. Discuss the importance of word order in English.

8. Describe and illustrate seven basic sentence patterns.

9. How are basic sentences expanded? Illustrate.

10. What is meant by a noun cluster? a verb cluster? Illustrate.

11. Develop sentences showing how single-word and word-group modifiers are built about a noun headword; a verb headword; an adjective headword; an adverb headword.

12. Name and illustrate three different kinds of subordinate clauses.

13. List and illustrate the different functions of the adverb clause.

14. List and illustrate the different functions of the noun clause.

15. What subordinators are used as connectives for the adjective clause? Write illustrative sentences.

16. Explain and illustrate the meaning of *immediate constituents*.

17. Explain what is meant by form classes. Discuss the formal characteristics of each. Illustrate.

18. Name and illustrate with sentences four different kinds of noun complements.

19. Write sentences to illustrate as many different functions of the noun as you can.

20. Write sentences to illustrate four different facts about forming the possessive of nouns.

21. Distinguish between regular and irregular verbs. Give illustrations of five-part, four-part, and three-part irregular verbs. List all inflected forms of each verb.

22. Write sentences to illustrate the ways in which each form of a five-part irregular verb may be used; a four-part irregular verb; a three-part irregular verb.

23. List and illustrate the different functions of the adjective.

24. List and illustrate the different functions of the adverb.

25. Distinguish between *grammar* and *usage*.

26. What is meant by standard written English?

27. Discuss the meaning of "correct English."

28. Explain how the knowledge of the inflected forms of nouns and verbs will be of help in standard usage; of adjectives and adverbs.

29. Illustrate all the areas of agreement between subject and verb. What factors create a problem in usage for the writer?

30. What is meant by archaic and obsolete language? Under what conditions is archaic language used?

31. What is meant by nonstandard English? substandard English? slang? What determines, in the final analysis, one's choice of language forms?

32. Explain in detail how the student may use his knowledge of grammar in improving his themes; his paragraphs; his sentences.

33. Discuss the importance to the writer of knowing how words communicate. Illustrate.

34. Summarize the uses of the comma, the semicolon, quotation marks, the colon, the apostrophe, italics.

35. Develop a table of symbols, either pronunciation or phonemic, of the forty-four common sounds of English.

36. List all the common spellings of each of the sounds of English.

37. Develop word lists of each spelling of at least five of the English sounds.

Part II

1. Summarize a few of the reasons why a writer must provide some sort of definition of the significant terms he uses.

2. What characterizes an effective definition of terms to be included in a theme?

3. Write a paragraph in which you clarify the following generalization through sentences containing terms on lower levels of abstraction:

> The exchange of goods between our country and Country X should be changed to conform with a sound fiscal policy.

4. List three important steps in the process of problem solving.

5. Identify four of the six logical fallacies discussed in Chapter 1, "Critical Thinking."

6. Very briefly, describe each of the fallacies you identified in item 5, above.

7. Supply an illustration or example of each of the fallacies you identified and described in items 5 and 6, above.

8. Rewrite the following passage, retaining as much of the essential message as possible, while reducing the word count to approximately half that of the original:

> As we proceeded up the Amazon River, we were fortunate enough to catch fresh fish to eat at each evening meal and to take a bit of game from the adjacent forest every few days to supplement our otherwise meatless diet. On the other hand, securing ourselves for the night was more of a problem than we had anticipated. In addition to the mosquitoes, which we had expected (although not in the size and numbers we found them), there were many other species of flying insects that either threatened our comfort or at least disturbed our sleep with their high-pitched droning. Furthermore, the boat was not as unapproachable as we had pictured her; crocodiles were as yet no trouble to us, but we had to take turns standing watch at night against other prowling beasts and reptiles that might have had an eye for boarding while we were tied up for the night.

9. Rewrite the foregoing passage (item 8, original), retaining as much of the essential message as possible, while reducing the word count to approximately a fourth that of the original.

10. List five occasions where, in day-to-day living, we make appeals to authority—thus demonstrating how the research process touches our lives.

11. List three questions that one might ask himself in order to evaluate a writer's claim to authority.

12. Identify the three main classes of library material described in Chapter 3, "The Research Process."

13. Through what device are the books in a library usually made available to readers? magazine articles?

14. List at least three of the steps one would probably take in preparing a research paper. Indicate the order in which these steps would be taken.

15. Summarize the information that might logically appear on an effective bibliography card (specify book, magazine, and so forth), and indicate at least in part the function of the various bits of information in the overall research process.

16. Write a brief definition of the word *fiction* that could apply equally well to a novel, to a narrative poem, to a painting, and to a piece of sculpture.

17. Summarize in a sentence or two some advantages in the use of dialogue, where appropriate, over conveying the same information in a more expository way.

18. Explain very briefly and then offer an example of "dilemma" in a fictional character (or "fictional character in a dilemma").

19. In Chapter 5, "Revising and Rewriting," are listed several basic requirements of the paragraph as an integral part of the whole theme. Identify four of these requirements, putting them in your own words, if you wish.

20. Identify the sentence fragments and run-together sentences in the following passage:

> *The Ox-Bow Incident* is a story about the men of a community who take the law into their own hands. These men ride out in search of suspected cattle rustlers and murderers they decide to catch and punish the guilty parties. Without benefit of a jury trial. Two of the riders are not from that community they still join in. Because they do not want any finger of suspicion to be pointed at them. Gil and Croft are the names of the two outsiders the latter is also the narrator of this story. Which of the two is less anxious to go is never quite clear. But it is evident that neither Croft nor Gil really wants to be mixed up in it such an ignoble undertaking it is. Yet worse comes to worse the men do what they set out to do, and they return to their homes. Mistaken all around.

21. Revise and rewrite the following passage, strengthening, if possible, the terminology, the structure, and the meaning:

I feel that the main object to having an athletic banquet is to show the community appreciates what the football or baseball team is doing for them. The players after working hard all throughout the season being about ready to have somebody else do the work for a change. Its nice when civic leaders take the trouble to let the poor athletes know that everybody hasn't forgotten them just because the season is over. One of the biggest thrills a player like myself can receive is when he's called forward to be handed over a plaque or award which tells everybody that he was the best. Its true the food at an athletic banquet is not usually so hot, but when it is someone like O. J. Simpson, Bill Bradley, or some other sports great of the day up at the front table to give a talk, you do not mind very much. So I am strong in favor of athletic banquets and would not like to see them not have one this year.

The Language of Grammar

Since word power will prove a valuable asset throughout your life, you should strive to acquire a vocabulary of words on which to draw in both speaking and writing. This section lists in alphabetical order the terms essential for grammatical expression of your ideas. You should find both the explanations and the illustrations helpful.

Absolute Structure

The term *absolute structure* describes a sentence element that apparently does not have a specific function within the sentence.

<u>Our vacation plans having been completed</u>, we went shopping for suitable clothes.

Active Voice

The term *active voice* describes the form of a verb in a N-V-N or N-V-N-N PATTERN in which the subject performs the action communicated by the verb. Active voice is contrasted to the passive voice in which the subject is usually the receiver of the action.

Adjective

The term *adjective* describes a word class. Adjectives can be identified in communication by their form and their function.

Some adjectives have characteristic suffixes: care-*less*, attent*ive*, caut*ious*. Adjectives may be inflected by adding -*er* and -*est* to show degrees of comparison: *young, younger, youngest.* Words called *intensifiers* are frequently used with adjectives: *very* young, *really* pleasant, *more* beautiful. The intensifiers *more* and *most* and *less* and *least* are used to show the degree of comparison of some adjectives of two syllables and of all adjectives of three or more syllables.

Adjectives function in the sentence as modifiers, linking-verb complements, and objective complements.

The temperamental youngster stamped her foot.
She was temperamental as a child.
Her mother considered her temperamental.

Adjective Clause

The *adjective clause* is one of three kinds of subject-predicate word groups, sometimes called *subordinate clauses.* The adjective clause modifies a noun or a noun substitute. It follows the noun which it modifies. Adjective clauses are introduced by the connectives *who, whose, whom, which, that,* or *when.*

The player <u>who is leaving the field</u> has been injured.
The car <u>that I like best</u> is that convertible.

Adjective Suffix

The term *adjective suffix* describes certain derivational suffixes that are characteristic of the word class called the *adjective*.

-ful	respectful	-ous	furious
-able	laughable	-en	wooden
-ive	collective	-ent	provident

Adverb

The term *adverb* describes a word class. Many words belonging to this class are characterized by suffixes such as *-ly, -ward, -time, -long: happily, sideward, sometime, headlong.* Some adverbs are marked with the prefix *a-: abroad, away, ahead.* There are also several miscellaneous adverbs such as *soon, tomorrow, then, still, north.* Semantically, adverbs answer to *where, when, why, how,* and sometimes *how much.*

Adverbs function usually as modifiers of verbs and of predicate adjectives. However, adverbs also modify other adverbs, nouns, and sometimes the whole sentence.

Don drives carefully.
This new novel is terribly exciting.
The officials said the new plan was exceptionally well received.
The captain turned his ship ten miles northward.
Noisily, the crowd surged up the street.

Adverbs also function as linking-verb complements.

The sale was yesterday.

Adverb Clause

The *adverb clause* is a subject-predicate word group, sometimes known as a *subordinate clause.* An adverb clause usually modifies a verb or a predicate adjective, but it may modify an adverb.

The crowds hurried <u>when it began to rain.</u>
Workers were happy <u>because they had a holiday.</u>
The victim recovered sooner <u>than the doctor predicted.</u>

Sometimes an adverb clause introduces a sentence. In this position, the clause usually modifies the whole sentence.

> Since our car was garaged for repairs, we postponed our trip.

Adverb Prefix

The prefix *a-* is called the adverb prefix. It signals such adverbs as *away, aboard, abroad, apart,* and *aground.*

Adverb Suffix

The term *adverb suffix* describes certain derivational suffixes that are characteristic of the word class called the *adverb.*

-ly	greatly	-where	everywhere
-time	sometime	-side	outside
-way	anyway	-long	sidelong

Affixation

The process by which a prefix or a suffix is attached to a root or to a root word is called *affixation.* Suffixes are used primarily as signals of function: *-ion* is a signal that *action* functions as a noun; *-ate* is a signal that *activate* functions as a verb. Prefixes, however, have a lexical function: they change the meaning of the root or the root word to which they are attached. *Postpaid,* for example, means something quite different from *prepaid.*

Agreement

The bound relationship that exists between subject and verb under certain conditions is called *agreement.* Agreement is expressed by concurrent changes in the form of the subject and the verb. A singular subject is followed by the singular form of the verb. A plural subject is followed by the plain form of the verb.

> That student learns easily.
> Most students learn eventually.

The determiners *this* and *that* may also be considered in relation to agreement since they, too, change form to *these* and *those* when modifying plural nouns.

Analytic Language

An *analytic language* is one that depends on word order, position, and function words rather than on inflectional changes as determiners of function or meaning. English is an analytic language. The term *analytic* is contrasted with *synthetic*, which refers to a language that depends largely on inflection as a signal of function. Latin is a synthetic language.

Antecedent

The *antecedent* is a word or group of words replaced and referred to by a pronoun. In context, the antecedent precedes the pronoun.

Tom put away his books.
The huge yellow-and-black butterfly spread its wings and flew away.

Apostrophe

An *apostrophe* is a mark of punctuation used to indicate the possessive of nouns.

Some of Poe's stories are gloomy.
Did you go to the sale of men's suits?
Many of the students' themes are good.

The apostrophe is also used to indicate a contraction in a word or a group of words and to show certain plurals.

Why doesn't Joe wear a necktie?
Be at the station at one o'clock.
Sam is careless about his *I*'s and his *l*'s.

Appositive (*See also* Close Appositive, Loose Appositive.)

Technically, *apposition* is a side-by-side relationship. An appositive relationship exists ordinarily between nouns or between a noun and a noun clause.

William Penn, founder of Pennsylvania, was granted a charter by Charles II in 1681.
The fact that William Penn lived in Philadelphia is well known.

Auxiliary

The *auxiliary* is commonly called a "helping verb." It serves two main functions. As a function word it serves as a verb marker or signal. In the verb phrase, it serves to communicate shades of meaning in time, attitude, feeling, and condition. Combinations of auxiliaries in a verb phrase give flexibility and lend fine shades of meaning to the English language.

> The students did work hard last year.
> They will work harder next year.
> Perhaps they could have worked harder last Monday.

Basic Sentence Elements

Two *basic elements* of the English sentence are the subject and the predicate.

> The car / stopped.

The keyword in the subject is a noun or a noun substitute; the keyword in the predicate is a verb. When a verb does not communicate of itself all that the writer or speaker wishes to say, a noun or a noun substitute or an adjective is used in the predicate as a complement.

> The driver / waved his hand.
> His whistle / was shrill.

The three basic elements of the English sentence, then, are the subject, the predicate, and the complement.

Basic Sentence Patterns

The basic sentence elements communicate meaning in seven basic patterns.

1. N-V
2. N-V-N
3. N-V-N-N
4. N-LV-N
5. N-LV-ADJ
6. The Inverted Sentence
7. The Question

Each of these patterns is described in this glossary under its own entry.

Case Form

Case describes the inflected forms appropriate to certain functions of personal pronouns and of those subordinators known as relative pronouns.

SUBJECT CASE FORM (SUBJECT FUNCTION)
He should refer to the dictionary.
They are going to the beach.
Sam is the one who planned the trip.

OBJECT CASE FORM (OBJECT FUNCTION)
Sue took him to the supermarket.
Dad gave me a watch for my birthday.
The man to whom he referred is an authority on Michelangelo.

POSSESSIVE CASE FORM (MODIFYING FUNCTION)
Your new hairdo is becoming.
Whose book this is I don't know.

Clause (*See* Subject-Predicate Word Group.)

Close Appositive (*See also* Appositive.)

A *close appositive* is one which has a restrictive, or identifying, relationship to the word with which it is in apposition.

his pal Bill
the merchant Woolworth
the industrialist Carnegie

This type of appositive may be contrasted with the nonrestrictive, or descriptive, relationship of the loose appositive.

Comma Fault

The term *comma fault* describes the unconventional use of a comma instead of a semicolon between two basic sentence patterns that are not joined by a coordinator.

Bob was ill, he's better now.

July 4 is a holiday, therefore, let's celebrate.

Comparative Degree (*See* Comparison of Adjectives and Adverbs.)

Comparison of Adjectives and Adverbs

Comparison is the grammatical device of affixing -*er* or -*est* to a modifier or of putting the intensifiers *more* and *most* or *less* and *least* before a modifier in order to show a different degree of the quality or characteristic indicated by the modifier.

Adjectives (and adverbs) have three degrees of comparison. An adjective in its simplest, or plain form, is in the positive degree: *old.* An adjective used to compare two persons or things is in the comparative degree: *older.* An adjective used to compare more than two persons or things is in the superlative degree: *oldest.* Some adjectives of two syllables and all of three or more syllables are compared by using *more* and *most* or *less* and *least.*

A few adjectives have different words for the comparative and superlative degrees: *good, better, best.* All adverbs ending in -*ly* are compared by using *more* and *most* or *less* and *least.*

Complement

The *complement* is one of the three basic sentence elements. Verbs in certain contexts do not communicate by themselves all that the speaker or writer wishes to say. Such verbs require a noun, an adjective, or another word to complete the sense of the predicate. The complement is usually a direct object, an indirect object, a linking-verb complement, or an objective complement.

> Ford introduced the assembly line.
> Admirers gave the candidates their loyalty.
> The Boy Scouts are patriotic.
> Hemingway was a successful novelist.
> Mr. Turner named the bank trustee of his estate.

Complete Subject

The *complete subject* refers to the word group consisting of the subject noun (or noun substitute) and its modifiers.

> Anyone who thinks that our differences of opinion can be reconciled without further investigation / is mistaken.

The complete subject includes everything to the left of the slash mark.

Complex Sentence

A *complex sentence* is one that includes one or more subordinate clauses. Subordinate clauses are classified as adjective clauses, adverb clauses, and noun clauses.

My friends who have visited Hawaii recommend the trip by sea.
We missed our appointment because the train was late.
What the guide showed us was unbelievable.

Compound Grapheme (*See* Grapheme.)

Compound Phoneme (*See* Phoneme.)

Compound Predicate

The term *compound predicate* describes two or more predicates joined by a coordinator.

Our athletes fought hard and won all the contests except one.

Compound Sentence

A *compound sentence* is one which contains two or more basic sentence patterns joined by a connective. In some compound sentences, a semicolon substitutes for the connective.

The day was bright, and the travelers made an early start.
The guide was charming; he showed us through the entire estate.

Compound Subject

The term *compound subject* describes two or more subjects joined by a coordinator.

The policemen and the firemen paraded.

Compound-Complex Sentence

A *compound-complex* sentence is a compound sentence which contains one or more subordinate clauses.

When Congress again meets, many more laws will be introduced, and a large percentage of them will probably be passed.

Conjunction (*See also* Connective.)

A *conjunction* is a connective. Conjunctions that join coordinate elements are called *coordinators*. Conjunctions that include subordinate clauses within a basic sentence pattern are called *subordinators*.

> Christmas is celebrated throughout the world, but Thanksgiving is an American holiday.
> Thanksgiving is celebrated only by Americans, while Christmas is universally celebrated.

Conjunctive Adverb

Adverbs that function as connectives between coordinate clauses are called *conjunctive adverbs*.

> Christmas is celebrated throughout the world; however, Thanksgiving is a holiday sacred to Americans.

Connective

A *connective* is a function word that (1) makes a word group or a subject-predicate word group part of a basic sentence pattern and (2) joins two or more basic sentence patterns into a compound sentence. Connectives include prepositions, coordinators, subordinators, and conjunctive adverbs.

Consonant

A *consonant* is a speech sound that is uttered with a complete or partial stoppage of the breath. Consonants are represented in English by all the letters of the alphabet except *a, e, i, o, u, w, y,* and *h*. The last three are sometimes called *semivowels*. The first five are vowels.

Contraction

A *contraction* is a shortening of a word or of a combination of words by the omission of one or more letters.

> Let's meet for lunch tomorrow.
> I can't wait until next Saturday.

Conventions of Punctuation

The term *conventions of punctuation* describes those standards of punctuated English that are a matter of custom and not of syntax.

Coordinate Adjectives

Two adjectives that modify the same word and have equal semantic value as modifiers are called *coordinate adjectives*. They are separated by a comma.

a shrewd, ambitious politician
a fantastic, spellbinding story

Coordination

Coordination is the grammatical process of joining two or more basic sentence patterns either with or without connectives.

The curtain rose, and the actors appeared.

Coordinator

A *coordinator* is a connective ordinarily used to join two coordinate clauses in a compound sentence, two nouns or noun substitutes in a compound subject, two verbs in a compound predicate, and so forth.

The grades were presented, and then the class was dismissed.
Larry and Tom passed the English course with flying colors.
They grinned and gave three cheers.

Cumulative Adjectives

Sometimes an adjective has a very close relationship to the noun it modifies. When a modifier is placed before this combination, it actually serves as a modifier of both the first adjective and the noun. Such modifiers are called *cumulative adjectives*. There is no comma between cumulative adjectives, nor can the position of cumulative adjectives be interchanged.

a poor old hermit
a heavy woolen coat
a soft low voice

Dangling Modifier

A *dangling modifier* is one which apparently is not related closely enough to any word in a sentence to be qualified by its modification. For this reason, a construction of this kind will cause ambiguity.

> <u>Being loaded with bricks,</u> the boy could not push the wheelbarrow.

Determiner

A *determiner* is a function word that serves as a noun-marker. A determiner always precedes the noun and any single-word modifier or combination of single-word modifiers that comes before the noun.

> an actress
> a talented actress

Diphthong

A *diphthong* is a compound phoneme $(\backslash \dot{o}i \backslash)$ in which two simple phonemes $(\backslash \dot{o} \backslash + \backslash i \backslash)$ are blended so completely that they may be considered one sound. The compound phonemes $\backslash a\dot{u} \backslash$ and $\backslash \bar{i} \backslash$ $(\backslash a \backslash + \backslash \dot{u} \backslash$ and $\backslash \ddot{a} \backslash + \backslash i \backslash)$ are also diphthongs.

Direct Object (*See also* Complement; Inner Complement.)

In a N-V-N PATTERN, the complement is a *direct object* and the verb is a transitive verb.

> The President signed the bill.

Double-Bar Juncture

Double-bar juncture $(\diagup \| \diagup)$ is a terminal juncture accompanied by a rising pitch.

> Will you go with me next week?
> 2   3
> Will you go with me next week ‖

Double-Cross Juncture

Double-cross juncture $(\diagup \# \diagup)$ is a terminal juncture accompanied by a falling pitch.

> I may go alone.
> 2   3   1
> I may go alone #

Feminine Gender (*See* Gender.)

First Person (*See* Person.)

Five-Part Irregular Verb

There are approximately fifty verbs remaining in the English language that are inflected with five forms — the plain form, the singular form, the past form, the present participle, and the past participle.

PLAIN	SINGULAR	PAST	PRESENT PARTICIPLE	PAST PARTICIPLE
do	does	did	doing	done
see	sees	saw	seeing	seen

Five-part verbs have a special form (the past participle) which is used with certain auxiliaries and with combinations of these auxiliaries.

Joe has done all his homework.
It has been done since last Friday.

Almost all other verbs, both regular and irregular, use the past form in the function illustrated above.

Form

Morphology, a branch of the study of grammar (structure), deals with form — form of words, affixes, stems. When we speak of characteristics of form, we think of the inflected forms of verbs, nouns, pronouns; we think of the characteristic suffixes that mark nouns, adjectives, adverbs, verbs. Form is contrasted with function which relates to position, or syntax. Function determines meaning, and form usually serves as a signal of function.

Jean is writing a letter of application.

The verb is *writing*. Its function, or syntax, is that of predicate verb in a N-V-N PATTERN. We identify *writing* as a verb because of its position between the subject and the complement. However, its form (the *-ing* inflectional suffix) serves to reinforce its position and to signal its function.

Four-Part Irregular Verb

There are approximately sixty four-part irregular verbs in English. These verbs do not have a special form for the past participle as do the five-part irregular verbs. The past form is used in those contexts in which the past participle of a five-part verb would be used.

PLAIN	SINGULAR	PAST	PRESENT PARTICIPLE
keep	keeps	kept	keeping
lay	lays	laid	laying
spend	spends	spent	spending

The storekeeper kept a variety of articles.
He had always kept many items.

Function

The term *function* describes the way in which a word or a word group communicates within a sentence. The various functions include subject, predicate, complement, modifier, appositive. Position — reinforced by signals of form and by certain function words — is the most important determinant of function.

Many visitors have crowded the auditorium.

The position of *visitors* before the verb is the normal position of the subject noun. The determiner *Many* is a noun-marker and tends to reinforce the factor of position. The position of the verb between the subject and the complement is the most important signal of predication. Here, position is reinforced by the *-ed* inflectional verb suffix and by the function word *have* which is also a verb-marker. The position of *auditorium* after the verb is the normal position of the complement.

Function Word

The term *function word* describes those words which have no lexical meaning but which give pattern or structure to communication. Words belonging to this word class include connectives, pronouns, auxiliaries, determiners, and particles.

Jerry and Herb are daydreamers.
Will they fail English?
Most of the students are working hard.
The class seems to be making progress.
English is not easy for some students.

Functional Shift

The term *functional shift* describes the grammatical device whereby a given word may be used in a variety of functions.

NOUN	I have a dollar in change.
MODIFIER	Ask the man at the change booth.
VERB	Will you change this bill, please?

Gender

Gender relates in a general way to sex. In English only the personal pronouns in the third-person singular are inflected for gender.

MASCULINE	he	him	his
FEMININE	she	her	hers
NEUTER	it	its	

Gerund

When an *-ing* verbal functions as a noun, it is called a *gerund.*

Fighting among the boys is being discouraged.
Tourists enjoy riding the cable cars.
Improve your theme by revising it.

Gerund Phrase

When a gerund takes a complement or has a modifier, the word group formed is a verbal phrase, or—more specifically—a *gerund phrase.*

Jerry likes tinkering with his ham radio.

Grammar

The word *grammar* is a popular term, not a technical term. It is a term with a number of different meanings. In modern terminology, *grammar* refers to the structure of language or to a description of that structure. As developed in *Modern Grammar and Composition,* grammar is the study of the form and function in communication of the words and word groups that make up sentences. It includes a study of the structure of the words themselves and of the patterns of sound that make up the words. It includes the study of the relation of sound to spelling and of intonation to punctuation.

English is not a static system of language. Twentieth century English is different from nineteenth century English, and nineteenth century English is in turn different from the language of Shakespeare. In the same way, the English of Chaucer's time is difficult for many to understand, and the language of Beowulf, although called "Old English," seems like a foreign tongue to us. It is important to remember, then, that grammar is a description of language as we observe it now, not as it was observed one hundred years ago, two hundred years ago, or several centuries ago.

To many people, grammar is nothing more than a study of what is to be preferred or avoided in inflection and syntax. Although *Modern Grammar and Composition* sets up guidelines for clear and effective communication, its emphasis is on understanding the structure of the English language.

Grapheme

The *grapheme* is the basic unit of the written language. The twenty-six letters of the alphabet are the principal graphemes of English. A single letter that represents a sound is a simple grapheme; two or more letters that represent a sound are a compound grapheme. The *f* in *fake* is a simple grapheme. The *gh* in *laugh* is a compound grapheme. Both the *f* and the *gh* represent the phoneme \f\, one of the basic sounds of our language.

Headword

The *headword* is the nucleus around which clusters of modifiers are built. The headword may be a noun, a verb, an adjective, an adverb, a function word, or a verbal. A noun cluster refers to a noun headword and its modifiers, a verb cluster to a verb headword and its modifiers; and so forth.

The unchecked gaiety of the partygoers disturbed the neighborhood.

Headword	gaiety
Modifiers	unchecked
	of the partygoers

The deer leaped gracefully away into the woods.

Headword	leaped
Modifiers	gracefully
	away
	into the woods

Immediate Constituents

The *immediate constituents* are the largest functioning parts in a structure.

The animals   performed beautifully.

This sentence has two immediate constituents: the subject *The animals* and the predicate *performed beautifully*. The subject in turn has two immediate constituents: the determiner *The* and the subject noun *animals*. The subject noun consists of two immediate constituents: the morphemes *animal* and *-s*, an inflectional ending. The predicate has two immediate constituents: the verb *performed* and the adverb *beautifully*. *Performed* and *beautifully* each have two immediate constituents.

Indirect Object (*See also* Complement; Inner Complement.)

When the outer complement in a N-V-N-N PATTERN is a direct object, the inner complement is an *indirect object*.

The President gave the Boy Scout a medal.

Infinitive

The *infinitive* is the plain form of the verb—or the past or past participle form plus auxiliary—introduced by the function word *to*. The infinitive is a verbal that functions in the sentence as a subject, as a complement, as a modifier, or as an appositive.

To laugh at the wrong time can be embarrassing.
Do you like to dream
To have finished on time would have been impossible.
It will be great to see you again.

Infinitive Phrase

When an infinitive takes a complement or has a modifier, the word group formed is a verbal phrase, or—more specifically—an *infinitive phrase*.

Ted's ambition <u>to write the great American novel</u> is waning.

Inflection

Inflection refers to the changes in form that a word undergoes in order to mark certain grammatical distinctions.

Noun:

SINGULAR	PLURAL	POSSESSIVE
girl	girls	girl's
woman	women	woman's

Verb:

PLAIN	SINGULAR	PAST	PRESENT PARTICIPLE	PAST PARTICIPLE
swim	swims	swam	swimming	swum
talk	talks	talked	talking	

Pronoun:

PERSON		NUMBER	
First	I	*Singular*	I
Second	you	*Plural*	we
Third	he		

GENDER		CASE	
Masculine	he	*Subject*	I
Feminine	she	*Possessive*	my, mine
Neuter	it	*Object*	me

Inner Complement

In the N-V-N-N PATTERN, there are two complements, an *inner complement* and an outer complement. These terms describe the position of the complements. In general, two main sentence types conform to this pattern.

Miss Clark lent Sally her dictionary.

In this sentence, the outer complement is a direct object and the inner complement is an indirect object.

The class elected Joe president.

In this sentence, the outer complement is an objective complement and the inner complement is a direct object.

Intensifier

In modern grammar, words like *very, rather, more, most, less, least* are called *intensifiers,* not adverbs. Intensifiers are function words with little lexical meaning. They are used with adjectives and with adverbs.

very clever	rather anxious
most amusing	less stormily

Intonation

Intonation describes the changes in pitch, stress, and juncture which make up the communication pattern of spoken English. This pattern is unique to English; other languages have their own patterns. Intonation helps us respond to questions and statements. A shift in stress sometimes indicates a change in the function of a word.

Intransitive Verb

The verb form used in the N-V PATTERN is an *intransitive verb*. It does not have a complement.

I read all through the night.

A verb may be intransitive in one sentence and transitive in another.

The orchestra played until after midnight.
The orchestra played one hit after another.

Inverted Sentence

The normal order of the basic sentence elements is: SUBJECT-VERB-COMPLEMENT.

When the position of subject and verb is changed in any way, we describe the change as "inverted order." If the sentence communicates a statement, we think of the sentence as an *inverted sentence*, one of the seven basic sentence patterns.

There goes the bookmobile
Here is the book I borrowed.

The preceding sentences illustrate the most common types of inversion. However, inverted sentences are not necessarily limited to these types.

> From behind the curtain stepped the clown.

Inverted Word Order

When a sentence is written with the normal positions of the subject and verb wholly or partly changed, we speak of the word order as inverted. *Inverted word order* occurs in the inverted sentence, described above, and in the question.

> How soon are you going?
> When will you return?

Irregular Verb

The *irregular verbs* are those whose pattern of inflection differs from that of the regular verb.

	PLAIN	SINGULAR	PAST	PRESENT PARTICIPLE
REGULAR VERB	ask	asks	asked	asking
IRREGULAR VERB	bend	bends	bent	bending

There are five-part, four-part, and three-part irregular verbs. The most irregular verb is *to be*; it has eight different forms: *be, am, is, are, was, were, being,* and *been.*

Five-Part Irregular Verb

PLAIN	SINGULAR	PAST	PRESENT PARTICIPLE	PAST PARTICIPLE
grow	grows	grew	growing	grown

Four-Part Irregular Verb

mean	means	meant	meaning

Three-Part Irregular Verb

cost	costs	costing

Juncture

As we speak, we separate our words and word groups with minute pauses. These pauses vary in length and in accompanying pitch. Linguists identify four basic types of separation, or *juncture*: plus juncture $(/+/)$, single-bar juncture $(/\ |\ /)$, double-bar juncture

$(\diagup \parallel \diagup)$, and double-cross juncture $(\diagup \# \diagup)$. The first type is an internal juncture (between words); the last three are terminal junctures (between word groups).

Language

For many thousands of years, human beings have communicated by means of sounds. These sounds are characteristic of the community and are developed in unique patterns. The patterns are interwoven with changes in pitch, stress, and juncture and are usually accompanied by other noticeable behavior characteristics. *Language* is the name given to the patterned sound system used in communication.

Lexical Meaning

Lexical meaning refers to the definition of a word within the vocabulary of a language—as distinguished from grammatical meaning, which varies from one inflectional form to another. The lexical meaning of the verb *play* is found in the dictionary; the grammatical meaning is defined in terms of number (*we play* as distinguished from *he plays*), of tense (*he played* as distinguished from *he plays*), and so forth.

Linguistics

Linguistics is the name given to the scientific study of language. A linguist, then, is a scholar engaged in this study.

In the past, the term *linguist* was used to refer to a person who had a mastery of a number of languages. While the term is still used for this meaning, discriminating speakers and writers now use the word "polyglot" to describe one who speaks and writes several languages fluently.

Linking Verb

A *linking verb* is one which couples or connects the subject and the complement. When the complement is a noun, it has the same referent as the subject. When the complement is an adjective, the adjective describes the subject. The linking verbs include *to be, seem, appear, become, taste, smell, sound,* and others.

> The first prize was a gold medal.
> Barbara seems excited.

Linking-Verb Complement

The term *linking-verb complement* applies to a noun or an adjective complement following such verbs as *to be, seem, appear, become,* and other linking verbs.

> Our destination was a cabin in the mountains.
> The climb became steep.

A noun that functions as a linking-verb complement is a predicate noun; an adjective in this function is a predicate adjective.

Loose Appositive (*See also* Appositive.)

A *loose appositive* is one which has a nonrestrictive, or descriptive, relationship to the word with which it is in apposition. Loose appositives are set off with commas.

> The bride's dream a honeymoon in Paris, might be realized.

This type of appositive may be contrasted with the identifying, or restrictive, relationship of the close appositive.

Masculine Gender (*See* Gender.)

Modifier

A *modifier* may be a word or a word group. A modifier qualifies, limits, or restricts the meaning of the headword which it modifies; it makes communication more exact, more precise. In a sense, a modifier is attached in meaning to its headword and with the headword makes up a cluster.

> Ships sailed.
> Navy ships sailed proudly through the choppy waves of the treacherous channel.

Headword	ships
Modifier	Navy
Headword	sailed
Modifiers	proudly
	through the choppy waves of the treacherous channel
Headword	waves
Modifiers	choppy
	of the treacherous channel
Headword	channel
Modifier	treacherous

Morpheme

Morpheme describes the smallest significant unit of grammatical form. A morpheme contains no smaller meaningful units, and the term refers to such parts as prefixes, suffixes, simple words that are words in themselves, and simple words that make up compounds.

repay	(re + pay)
paying	(pay + ing)
pay	(pay)
payroll	(pay + roll)

Neuter Gender

The personal pronoun *it* is the neuter form of the third-person, singular pronoun. The word *it* designates neither masculine nor feminine and is the only neuter form in English.

Nonrestrictive

Nonrestrictive refers to a modifier that describes but does not identify the word it modifies. Nonrestrictive modifiers are set off by commas.

John H. Glenn, Jr., who was a Marine Corps test pilot, was the first American to orbit the earth.

Noun

The term *noun* describes a word class. Nouns may be identified in communication by certain signals of form and signals of function.

Nouns are inflected to form the plural, usually by adding *s* or *es*. There are other plural inflections, such as the changes in form from *man* to *men* and *alumnus* to *alumni*. Nouns are inflected to form the possessive by adding *'s* to the singular form or, if the singular form ends in *s*, by adding an apostrophe. If the plural form ends in *s*, an apostrophe is added to form the plural possessive; if the plural form does not end in *s*, an *'s* is added.

Nouns function in the sentence as subjects, as complements, as appositives, and as objects of a preposition. A noun may also function as a noun-modifier.

Many nouns terminate in characteristic suffixes: *addition, baker, abandonment, kingdom.*

Noun Adjunct

When a noun functions as a noun-modifier, it is called a *noun adjunct*.

> Whose dance band do you like best?
> Protect your textbooks with book covers.

Noun Clause

The *noun clause* is a subject-predicate word group, or subordinate clause. A noun clause has the same function as a noun: subject, complement, appositive, object of a preposition.

> What a test pilot does is incomprehensible to me.
> Test pilots know what they are doing.
> Paul's contention that space travel is for the birds is debatable.
> We hope to visit San Francisco about which most tourists are glowingly enthusiastic.

Noun Cluster

When a number of modifiers cluster about a noun, the word group that results is known as a *noun cluster*, or a noun-headed word group.

> Advertisements picture expensive, modernistic homes with beautiful landscaping.

Headword	homes
Modifiers	expensive
	modernistic
	with beautiful landscaping

Noun Suffix

The term *noun suffix* describes certain derivational suffixes that are characteristic of the word class called the *noun.*

N-V Pattern

The N-V PATTERN (NOUN-VERB) is one of the seven basic sentence patterns.

> N   V
> Waves splashed over the beach.
> N   V
> Crowds of people sang all through the night.

N-V-N Pattern

The N-V-N PATTERN (NOUN-VERB-NOUN) is one of the seven basic sentence patterns. In this pattern, the noun that comes after the verb is the direct object.

> N   V   N
> Fire destroyed all the buildings at the Chicago World's Fair.
> N   V   N
> Workers won raises in salary.

N-V-N-N Pattern

The N-V-N-N PATTERN (NOUN-VERB-NOUN-NOUN) is one of the seven basic sentence patterns. Both nouns that fall after the verb are complements. When the outer complement is a direct object, the inner complement is an indirect object.

> N   V   N   N
> The critics gave the play rave notices.
> N   V   N   N
> Larry lent Tom his golf clubs.

When the inner complement in a N-V-N-N PATTERN is the direct object, the outer complement is an objective complement.

> N   V   N   N
> The committee called Williams an outstanding dramatist.

N-LV-N Pattern

In the N-LV-N PATTERN (NOUN-LINKING VERB-NOUN), one of the seven basic sentence patterns, the noun after the verb — sometimes referred to as the predicate noun — is a linking-verb complement.

N LV   N
That ship is an aircraft carrier.

N-LV-ADJ Pattern

In the N-LV-ADJ PATTERN (NOUN-LINKING VERB-ADJECTIVE), one of the seven basic sentence patterns, the adjective after the verb — sometimes referred to as the predicate adjective — is the linking-verb complement.

N   LV   ADJ
Family programs are popular on TV.

Number

Nouns, personal pronouns, and verbs are inflected for *number* to show plural or singular meaning.

Object of a Preposition

A prepositional phrase has the pattern:

PREPOSITION — DETERMINER — NOUN
under   the   fence

A pronoun may be substituted for the noun, and the determiner may be omitted.

under it

The noun or the pronoun in this pattern is said to be the *object of the preposition.*

Object Case Form

The *object case form* is the form taken by the personal pronoun when it functions as a direct object, an indirect object, the object of a preposition, or the subject of an infinitive.

Aunt Sue saw me at the movies.
Dad had given me my allowance.
Dad was properly thanked by me.
Dad asked me to wash the car.

When the subordinator *who* has an object function in its subject-predicate word group, it takes the objective case form *whom*.

> The president of our bank is a man whom we admire.
> Sam and Joe are friends on whom we depend.

Objective Complement (*See also* Complement; Inner Complement.)

When the inner complement in a N-V-N-N PATTERN is a direct object, the outer complement is an *objective complement*. The objective complement relates to the direct object and is complementary to it.

> The class elected Ellen secretary.

Outer Complement (*See* Inner Complement.)

Parallel Structure

The term *parallel structure* describes the use of the same grammatical structure to express two or more closely related ideas.

> Awards were given for the outstanding actor, the best director, and the most colorful photography.

Participial Phrase

When a participle takes a complement or has a modifier, the word group formed is a verbal phrase, or — more specifically — a *participial phrase*.

> Floods causing untold damage left many homeless.

Participle

When an *-ing, -ed,* or *-en* verbal functions like an adjective, it is called a *participle*. The participle functions in the attributive or predicate position or as an objective complement.

> The winning athletes were acclaimed.
> Those runners look well trained.
> The mechanic declared the car broken beyond repair.

Particle

A *particle* is a function word that cannot be placed definitely in the other function word categories: connectives, pronouns, determiners, auxiliaries. Although particles are indeterminate in nature, they are useful in communication. They include the noun substitutes *anybody, nobody, somebody, anything*; the negatives *no* and *not*; the emotional words *indeed* and *oh*; and the salutations *hello* and *good-bye*. Words also known as intensifiers are included in this category.

Parts of Speech

In traditional grammar the word classes are referred to as the *parts of speech*. The parts of speech include nouns, verbs, adjectives, adverbs, pronouns, conjunctions, prepositions, and interjections. The word classes include nouns, verbs, adjectives, adverbs, and function words. Function words include the pronouns, conjunctions, prepositions, and interjections of traditional grammar.

Passive Voice (*See* Active Voice.)

Past Form of the Verb

The past form of a regular verb is formed by adding *-ed* to the plain form, frequently with a slight spelling adjustment.

PLAIN	PAST
jump	jumped
play	played

The past form of irregular verbs is formed in a number of different ways.

PLAIN	PAST
fly	flew
see	saw
eat	ate
write	wrote

Three-part irregular verbs do not have a special past form. The plain form is used.

PLAIN	PAST
set	set
cost	cost
burst	burst

Past Participle Form of the Verb

Only five-part irregular verbs have a special form for the past participle.

PLAIN	PAST PARTICIPLE
go	gone
speak	spoken

The past participle form is used with certain auxiliaries.

The players have gone to the dugout.
The coach has spoken to them.

Regular verbs and four-part irregular verbs use the past form in contexts requiring the past participle.

The musicians had played all night.
George has sold his car.

Three-part irregular verbs use the plain form as a past form and therefore repeat this form in contexts requiring a past participle.

His decision had cost him the election.
Mother has cut the cake into six pieces.

Past Tense

Past tense is the verb form that refers to past time. All regular verbs have an inflected past form. All five-part and four-part irregular verbs have an inflected past form. Three-part irregular verbs use the plain form to communicate past time.

PLAIN	PAST
walk	walked
write	wrote
fight	fought
burst	burst

Person

Only personal pronouns are inflected to show *person*. First person relates to the person speaking, second person to the person spoken to, and third person to the person spoken about.

FIRST PERSON	I, me, my, mine, we, us, our, ours
SECOND PERSON	you, your, yours
THIRD PERSON	he, him, his, she, her, hers, they, them, their, theirs, it, its

Personal Pronoun

A *personal pronoun* is a function word that serves as a noun substitute. The personal pronoun has meaning only in relation to its antecedent (the word for which it substitutes). Personal pronouns are useful in communication since they eliminate repetition and unnecessary wordage.

> The President signed the bill last evening. He used a number of pens for distribution to the people influential in its passage.

Phoneme

Phoneme describes one of the smallest units of significant sound. The \b\ sound in *bin* and the \p\ sound in *pin* are simple phonemes. Phonemes are represented in writing by graphemes, or letters. A compound phoneme is a phoneme in which two simple phonemes are blended so completely that they are considered one sound. The diphthong \aü\, which is a combination of \a\ + \ü\ is a compound phoneme.

Pitch

Pitch is one of the vocal effects of intonation. As the voice rises from low through normal and high to very high, we can recognize four levels of pitch. These levels are designated as pitch phonemes and are numbered /1/, /2/, /3/, and /4/ from low to high. Pitch communicates emotion and lack of emotion; it also serves to signal the difference between a statement and a question.

> 2   3   1
> I sold my typewriter.

Plain Form of the Verb

The *plain form of the verb* is sometimes known as the infinitive form. The plain form is used in the present tense with a plural subject and with the personal pronouns *I* and *you*. The plain form is also used with such auxiliaries as *can, may, might, must, should, could, shall,* and *will.*

Dad likes to walk.
Most people walk too little.
I walk for exercise.
Everyone should walk a mile or so a day.

Plus Juncture

Plus juncture describes the separations between words. It is represented by the phonemic symbol ╱+╱.

Position (*See* Function.)

Positive Degree (*See* Comparison of Adjectives and Adverbs.)

Possessive Case Form

The *possessive case form* is the inflected form appropriate to the modifying function of the noun and pronoun. The possessive of the noun is marked by an apostrophe or by an apostrophe and *s*.

Personal pronouns and the subordinator *who* are inflected for possessive case.

Where is my ruler?
Whose book is that in your hand?

Predicate (*See also* Complete Subject.)

The *predicate* consists of the verb and its modifiers with a complement, if there is one. The predicate communicates the active or dynamic quality of experience.

The racing cars / streaked across Daytona Beach.

The predicate includes everything to the right of the slash mark.

Predicate Adjective (*See also* Complement.)

The linking-verb complement in the N-LV-ADJ PATTERN is sometimes referred to as the *predicate adjective*.

Skywriting is fascinating.
The clock seems slow.

Predicate Noun (*See also* Complement.)

The linking-verb complement in the N-LV-N PATTERN is sometimes referred to as the *predicate noun*.

The Nobel Prize is a coveted award.

Predicate Verb

> The term *predicate verb* specifies the verb form contained within the complete predicate.
>
> The tennis match was played at Forest Hills.

Prefixes and Combining Forms

> *Prefixes* and *combining forms* (starred in the list below) are attached to the beginning of a word or a root. Most prefixes and all combining forms change the meaning but not the word class of the words to which they are attached.

PREFIX OR COMBINING FORM	ORIGIN	MEANINGS
a-	English	on, in, at, toward, in a certain manner
ab-	Latin	from, away from, off
ad-	Latin	to, toward
ambi-	Latin	both
ante-	Latin	before, in front of
anti-	Greek	against, opposed to, contrary to
arch-	Greek	chief, outstanding
*auto-	Greek	self
be-	English	on, around, excessively, make or cause to be
bi-	Latin	two, twice
*bi-, bio-	Greek	life
cata-	Greek	down
*chron-, chrono-	Greek	time
circum-	Latin	around
co-	Latin	with, together, joint
com-, con-	Latin	with, together
contra-	Latin	against
counter-	English	contrary, opposite of
de-	Latin	down from, opposite of, remove from

PREFIX OR COMBINING FORM	ORIGIN	MEANINGS
*di-	Greek	twice, double
di-, dia-	Greek	through, across
dis-	Latin	not, opposite of
en-, em-	Latin	put into or on, cause to be
epi-	Greek	upon, over
*eu-	Greek	well, good
ex-	Latin	out of, former
extra-	Latin	outside, beyond
*fore-	English	front, beforehand
*heter-, hetero-	Greek	other, different
*hom-, homo-	Greek	alike, similar
hyper-	Greek	over, beyond, excessively
hypo-	Greek	under, below normal
in-, il-, im-, ir-	Latin	not
in-, il-, im-, ir-	Latin	in, into, within, toward, put into
inter-	Latin	between, among
intra-	Latin	within
intro-	Latin	inward, within
*mal-	Latin	bad, badly
*meta-, met-	Greek	after, beyond, change
*micr-, micro-	Greek	very small, magnifying
mis-	English	bad, badly, wrong, wrongly, opposite of
*mono-, mon-	Greek	one, single, alone
*ne-, neo-	Greek	new, recent
*neur-, neuro-	Greek	nerve
non-	Latin	not, opposite of, absence of
ob-, op-	Latin	in the way, against
out-	English	in a manner that goes beyond
*over-	English	excessively
*pan-	Greek	all, all of a group

PREFIX OR COMBINING FORM	ORIGIN	MEANINGS
para-	Greek	beside, alongside of
per-	Latin	through, throughout, thoroughly
peri-	Greek	all around, enclosing
*phil-, philo-	Greek	loving, attracted to
*phon-, phono-	Greek	sound, voice, speech
*phot-, photo-	Greek	light, photographic
*poly-	Greek	many, much
post-	Latin	after, later, behind
pre-	Latin	before, in advance, in front of
pro-	Latin	for, in favor of, forward
*pseud-, pseudo-	Greek	false
re-	Latin	again, back
retro-	Latin	backward, back
*self-	English	of, by, for, or to oneself or itself
semi-	Latin	half of
sub-	Latin	under, secondary
super-, sur-	Latin	over, above, in addition to, surpassing
syn-, sym-	Greek	with, together
*tele-	Greek	at a distance
trans-	Latin	across, through
*tri-	Latin, Greek	three, thrice
ultra-	Latin	beyond, excessively
un-	English	not, opposite of

Preposition

A *preposition* is a connective which joins a certain type phrase to the headword which it modifies. A preposition is a function word and has little lexical meaning except in the context of a sentence.

> The chickens were jumping over the fence, squeezing under the wire, and circling around the posts.

Prepositional Phrase

A *prepositional phrase* is a word-group modifier that is included within a basic sentence pattern by means of a preposition.

> Around a bend in the narrow road, a tire blew out with a loud noise.

Present Participle Form of the Verb

The *present participle form of the verb* is the *-ing* form. It functions as a finite verb only when it is used with some form of *to be* as an auxiliary.

> The ball carrier was running in the wrong direction.

As a verbal, the present participle form functions as a modifier and as a noun.

> The teacher heard us whispering in the corridor. Speaking too frankly was a mistake.

Present Tense

The term *present tense* refers to present time. Unlike the past tense, there is no special verb form for the present tense. There are many ways to communicate present time in English. For example, we use the plain form with a plural subject and the singular form with a singular subject.

> The bands play all evening.
> The band plays all evening.

Present time is also communicated by means of auxiliaries used with the present participle form or with the plain form.

> The band is playing.
> The band can play.

Principal Parts of the Verb

The three verb forms from which all the other forms of a verb can be derived are considered the *principal parts*. These forms are the plain form, the past form, and the past participle form.

Pronoun (*See also* Personal Pronoun, Subordinator.)

A *pronoun* is a noun substitute. In modern grammar, we speak of personal pronouns and of relative pronouns (subordinators).

Proper Nouns

Proper nouns are special classes of nouns that are capitalized in English.

Punctuation

Punctuation is the process of using graphic symbols to separate written English into meaningful units of syntax. The graphic symbols include the period, the question mark, the exclamation point, the comma, the semicolon, the colon, the dash, quotation marks, dashes, parentheses, brackets, and others.

Question

The *question* is one of the seven basic sentence patterns. Questions are signaled by an inversion of the subject-predicate word order, by the use of auxiliaries, by the use of certain function words, and by a rising pitch.

> Have you any money?
> Do you like football?
> Where are you going?
> You are going to Boston?
> 2   3
> You are going to Boston ‖

Reference of Pronouns

A pronoun is a substitute word, a word that gets its exact meaning from the word or words to which it refers — its antecedent. If the reference of a pronoun is not clear, communication becomes ineffective.

> The captain of the ship spoke to his crew.
> The men told of their grievances.
> Senators agreed upon an amendment and proposed it to the President.

Reflexive Pronouns

The *-self* pronouns are commonly called *reflexive pronouns.*

SINGULAR	PLURAL
myself	ourselves
yourself	yourselves
himself	
herself	themselves
itself	

A reflexive pronoun may be used as a substitute word or as an intensifier.

Sue is one who thinks for herself.
She herself will make the decision.

Regular Verb

Regular verbs have four inflected forms. The past form is developed by adding the suffix *-ed* to the plain form. The present participle is formed by adding the suffix *-ing* to the plain form. Most English verbs are regular verbs. There are approximately 150 irregular verbs in our language, and more than 5,000 regular verbs.

PLAIN	SINGULAR	PAST	PRESENT PARTICIPLE
deliver	delivers	delivered	delivering

Relative Pronoun (*See* Subordinator.)

Restrictive

Restrictive describes a modifier that identifies rather than defines the word it modifies.

Mr. Walker is a man who cannot be influenced.

Run-Together Sentence

When two or more basic sentence patterns are written as one sentence without a coordinator or a semicolon, the result is an error known as the *run-together sentence.*

A new play opened on Broadway instantly it received acclaim.
Correction: A new play opened on Broadway. Instantly it received acclaim. *Or:* A new play opened on Broadway; instantly it received acclaim.

Second Person (*See* Person.)

Segmental Phonemes

Linguistic analysis has indicated thirty-three basic vowel and consonant sounds that form the segments of the stream of spoken English. These are the phonemes —called *segmental phonemes* in contrast to the supra-segmental phonemes of intonation (pitch, stress, and juncture). The first column below lists the phonemic symbols for the basic sounds of English. The second column includes a word with one of the spellings of the sound indicated. This word is a clue to the sound but is not the only graphemic representation of that sound.

PHONEME	SOUND
/b/	the sound of *b* in *bill*
/č/	the sound of *ch* in *church*
/d/	the sound of *d* in *duck*
/f/	the sound of *f* in *fill*
/g/	the sound of *g* in *girl*
/h/	the sound of *h* in *hand*
/ǰ/	the sound of *j* in *jack*
/k/	the sound of *k* in *kite*
/l/	the sound of *l* in *like*
/m/	the sound of *m* in *money*
/n/	the sound of *n* in *nest*
/ŋ/	the sound of *ng* in *sing*
/p/	the sound of *p* in *pool*
/r/	the sound of *r* in *rope*
/s/	the sound of *s* in *sack*
/š/	the sound of *sh* in *shine*
/ð/	the sound of *th* in *that*
/θ/	the sound of *th* in *thick*
/t/	the sound of *t* in *tan*
/v/	the sound of *v* in *vest*
/w/	the sound of *w* in *want*
/y/	the sound of *y* in *year*
/z/	the sound of *z* in *zip*
/ž/	the sound of *z* in *azure*
/ə/	the sound of *u* in *but*
/a/	the sound of *o* in *pot*
/æ/	the sound of *a* in *mat*
/e/	the sound of *e* in *pen*
/i/	the sound of *i* in *pin*

PHONEME	SOUND
/i/	the vowel sound in an unstressed syllable such as in *rotten, alone,* or *cotton*
/o/	the sound of *o* in *bone*
/ɔ/	the sound of *au* in *caught*
/u/	the sound of *u* in *put*

PHONEME COMBINATION	SOUND
/ey/	the sound of *a* in *cake*
/iy/	the sound of *e* in *he*
/ay/	the sound of *i* in *mile*
/uw/	the sound of *u* in *plume*
/aw/	the sound of *ou* in *house*
/iw/	the sound of *u* in *mule*
/ɔy/	the sound of *oy* in *toy*
/eh/	the sound of *a* in *bare*
/əh/	the sound of *i* in *third*
/ks/	the sound of *x* in *fox*
/gz/	the sound of *x* in *exist*

Sentence

A *sentence* is an utterance. In written English, the form of the sentence is standardized. It begins with a capital letter and ends with a mark of terminal punctuation—a period, a question mark, an exclamation point. It has a subject and a finite predicate verb. The normal word order is subject, verb, complement. A subject-predicate word group beginning with a signal of subordination is not of itself a sentence. The written sentence, when it is read aloud, follows the characteristic intonation patterns of English. It terminates with a falling pitch with a fading-off of the voice, or with a rising pitch with a stopping of the voice.

Sentence Fragment

When a word group that does not have the characteristics of a sentence is unintentionally written as a sentence, the error that results is known as a *sentence fragment*.

> Last evening I caught a repeat on TV. Bored with books and magazines.
> *Correction:* Bored with books and magazines, I caught a repeat on TV last evening.

Sentence-Modifier

A word or a word group which precedes the subject of a sentence is usually considered a *sentence-modifier.*

Suddenly, the moon appeared.
As a consequence, we went for a moonlight sail.

Single-Bar Juncture

Single-bar juncture ($\diagup$ | $\diagup$) is a terminal juncture. It separates word groups or units of syntax. It is not accompanied by a change in pitch.

Hurricanes | strike in late summer.
One hurricane | a particularly destructive one | caused many deaths.

Singular Form of the Verb

The form of the verb used with a singular subject in the present tense is called the *singular form.*

Hal dances divinely.

Standard English

Standard English is the conventional language of writing. It is the kind of language found in newspapers, with the exception of special columns and some sports stories. It is the kind of language found in most magazine articles and published reports. It is the kind of language found in textbooks and taught in schools. Most speeches are written in Standard English. Standard English is well established in the speech and writing of the educated and is readily recognized wherever English is spoken and understood.

Stress

Stress is one of the vocal effects of intonation. It refers to loudness or softness but usually communicates emphasis. According to linguists, there are four degrees of stress. The four stress phonemes are primary, secondary, tertiary, and weak indicated by the symbols $\diagup\,'\diagup$, $\diagup\,\hat{}\,\diagup$, $\diagup\,\grave{}\,\diagup$, and $\diagup\,\smallsmile\,\diagup$.

prêdícămènt

Subject Noun

The *subject noun* is the headword of the word group making up the complete subject.

Many popular songs / are based on old ones.
The wind in the highlands / blew steadily from the north.

Subject-Predicate Structure

The basic structure of English is the *subject-predicate structure.* We automatically respond to this structure which is basic to communication and which has been part of our experience since we first learned to talk. Subject-predicate structure occurs in the sentence, in subordinate clauses, and in the two or more patterns that make up a compound sentence.

The noun-verb relationship is the basis of subject-predicate structure. Either the noun or the verb may be expanded indefinitely by modifiers. The verb may have a complement. A pronoun or a word group may substitute for the subject noun. The basic structure of the sentence, however, remains actor-action, noun-verb, subject-predicate.

The Peruvian earthquake / caused much damage.

Subject-Predicate Word Group (*See* Subordinate Clause.)

Subordinate Clause

In the process of subordination, a subject-predicate word group that is included within the basic sentence pattern is called a *subordinate clause.* Subordinate clauses function as modifiers (adjective clause, adverb clause) and as nouns (noun clause).

Subordination

Subordination is the process of including a subject-predicate word group within a basic sentence pattern. The connectives used are called subordinators. The subject-predicate word group, or subordinate clause, functions either as a modifier (adjective clause, adverb clause) or as a noun (noun clause).

Trees that are known as evergreens belong to the pine family.
We often confuse the names of evergreens although they are easy to identify.
What makes it easy are their needles and cones.

Subordinator

A *subordinator* is a connective used to include a subordinate clause within a basic sentence pattern.

unless	when	as
because	where	while
if	since	whether
until	although	how

Because the traffic was light, we arrived early.
Let's go to the beach if it doesn't rain.

Substitution

The term *substitution* describes the grammatical device of using certain words such as personal pronouns, subordinators, reflexive pronouns, and determiners in place of other words. Effective substitution contributes to economy and flexibility in communication.

Suffix

A *suffix* is an affix attached to the end of a word or of a root. The noun, verb, adjective, and adverb suffixes signal these word classes. Some suffixes are signals of inflection. Other suffixes serve as word builders in the extension of vocabulary.

Superlative Degree (*See* Comparison of Adjectives and Adverbs.)

Suprasegmental Phonemes

The *suprasegmental phonemes* are the vocal effects of intonation: the phonemes of pitch, stress, and juncture that accompany, or are super-added to, the segmental phonemes of spoken English. The segmental phonemes are the vowel and consonant sounds that form the segments of the stream of speech.

| PITCH | /1/, /2/, /3/, /4/ | (low, medium, high, very high) |

STRESS / ´/, / ˆ/, / `/, / ˘/   (primary, secondary, tertiary, weak)

JUNCTURE /+/, / | /, / ‖ /, /#/   (plus, single-bar, double-bar, double-cross)

Syntax

Syntax refers to the way words are put together to form word groups, subject-predicate word groups, and sentences. Syntax also applies to the study of these language patterns as they relate to meaning.

Tense

Tense is a grammatical concept growing out of the inflection of verbs to show time. In English, only the past form of a verb is inflected for tense. In the case of three-part irregular verbs, there is no inflection for tense. A variety of meanings related to time can be communicated by combinations of auxiliaries with the verb.

Third Person (*See* Person.)

Three-Part Irregular Verb

The *three-part irregular verb* has three forms: the plain form, the singular form, and the present participle.

PLAIN	SINGULAR	PRESENT PARTICIPLE
bet	bets	betting
set	sets	setting

Transitional Adverb

A *transitional adverb* is an adverb that establishes a relationship between two sentences.

You have certainly heard of the legendary giant Paul Bunyan. Furthermore, you must know about his blue ox Babe.

Transitive Verb (*See also* **Intransitive Verb.**)

> A verb that takes a direct object (N-V-N and N-V-N-N PATTERNS) is considered *transitive*, because the action named by the verb goes across from the subject to the object.
>
> > The officer addressed his troops.
>
> In the passive construction, the action named by the verb passes over to the subject; such verbs are also considered transitive.
>
> > His troops were addressed by the officer.

Usage

> *Usage* refers to the way in which words and word groups are actually used in a language. Conventional usage depends largely on the appropriate choice of language in terms of time, place, and degree of formality. Thus in writing we usually avoid language which is obsolete, dialectal, or colloquial. Grammatical usage depends on the correct choice of language. Thus in writing we avoid the use of a pronoun that has an uncertain antecedent, of a verb form that does not agree with the subject in number, of a verb form incorrectly used with an auxiliary, and so forth.

Verb

> The *verb* is the heart of a sentence. It is the chief actor in the drama of communication. Its position in the sentence is fixed and its identification is reinforced by its inflectional forms, by certain characteristic suffixes, and by function words called auxiliaries.
>
> > New York's 1969 snowfall caused many deaths.
> > Cars and trains stalled.
> > Weathermen were amazed by its force.

Verb Cluster

> When a number of modifiers cluster about a noun, the word group that results is known as a *verb cluster*, or a verb-headed word group.

Commuters rushed madly to hotels when they learned of the stalled trains.

Headword	rushed
Modifiers	madly
	to hotels
	when they learned of the stalled trains

Verb Phrase

A *verb phrase* refers to the main verb and its auxiliaries.

The game had been postponed.

Verbal

The term *verbal* describes a word whose function has shifted from that of a verb to that of a noun or a modifier. There are three kinds of verbals: the infinitive, the gerund, and the participle. The infinitive functions as a noun or as an adjective or adverb. The gerund functions as a noun. The participle functions as an adjective.

Verbal Phrase

When a verbal takes a complement or has a modifier, the word group formed is called a *verbal phrase*. There are three kinds of verbal phrases: the infinitive phrase, the gerund phrase, and the participial phrase.

Vowel

The *vowels* are speech sounds made with a clear passage of air through the mouth. In English the letters of the alphabet that represent vowels are *a, e, i, o,* and *u.* Linguists include *h, y,* and *w* as semivowels.

Word Classes

Word classes, in modern grammar, include nouns, verbs, adjectives, adverbs, and function words. The noun, verb, adjective, and adverb word classes, or form classes, include about 93 per cent of all of the different words in the English language. When new words are added, they are either nouns, verbs, adjectives, or adverbs. These are the words that have lexical meaning, as contrasted with function words, words that have little meaning out of context.

Word Group

A *word group* is a phrase, a group of words that does not contain a subject and a verb, as distinguished from subject-predicate word groups.

Word-Group Modifier

A *word-group modifier* is a word group that functions as an adjective or an adverb. The most common type of word-group modifier is the prepositional phrase.

Word Order (*See also* Inverted Sentence.)

Word order is the single most important determiner of meaning in the English language. The normal order of sentence elements is subject, verb, and complement. When this order is changed, meaning is changed or nonsense results. The position of modifiers is largely fixed in English and is also an important factor of meaning. English is called an analytic language since it does not depend on inflections for determining meaning as is the case in a synthetic language such as Latin. Rather, it is position, reinforced by certain function words and sometimes by inflection, which largely determines meaning in English.

Navy beat Army.
Army beat Navy.

The committee considered the worthy students.
The committee considered the students worthy.

The History of English

Questions in Modern Grammar and Composition begins with a chapter called "A Brief History of Grammar." "The History of English" has been designed to give impetus to the various studies described in the Chapter 1 Summary (pages 34-35).

In the section that follows, you will investigate some of the forces and influences at work during the Modern English period (1500 to the present). In particular, you will observe how the trend toward change and the trend toward conformity have affected the form and the structure of the English spoken today.

FOUR CENTURIES OF MODERN ENGLISH

If a line from William Shakespeare has ever baffled you, imagine how baffled a man of Shakespeare's time would be if he were to read a twentieth-century newspaper. We speak of *satellites* in *parking orbit, DNA, vitamins, jumbo jets, lasers, dehydrated foods, antihistamines* — strange words to an Elizabethan eye. Strange words even to your grandmother's childhood.

Language changes constantly, as the people who speak it change and as the world of each speaker changes. In what is called the Modern English period (about 1500 A.D. to the present), the English language has undergone its most extensive changes in vocabulary. For this reason more than any other, the man of 1600 might have more trouble understanding us than we would him.

An Elizabethan man would notice other differences, however. He would use some of the same words we do, but he would pronounce them differently. In other instances, the same basic words would take different forms or would have different meanings. In four hundred years, the spelling of many words has altered. But what a person from Shakespeare's time might find most surprising about Modern English is the manner in which we have become self-conscious about our language. Forces have been at work throughout the Modern English period to bring conformity to the language — to standardize, to establish patterns of form and structure.

During the past four hundred years, the English-speaking community has extended to lands around the world. The number of people who speak English as their natural language has increased from a few million to over 300 million. During this period of expansion, it is remarkable that there have been so few fundamental changes, and that — for the most part — modern readers are usually able to understand Shakespeare without too much difficulty:

> Be not afeard; the isle is full of noises,
> Sounds and sweet airs, that give delight and hurt not.
> From *The Tempest*

Our ability to understand lines that were written some four centuries ago is all the more remarkable when we consider that two centuries before Shakespeare, English looked like this:

> How dorste ye seyn for shame unto your love,
> That anything might make you aferd?
> Have ye no mannes herte, and han a berd?
> CHAUCER

And that a few centuries earlier, it looked like this:

> þgyt him asetton segen g(yl) denne
> heah ofer heafod, leton holm beran,
> geafon on garsecg; him wæs geomor sefa,
> murnende mōd.   BEOWULF

THE TREND TOWARD CHANGE

Although the literature of the sixteenth century is intelligible today, the English language has undergone many changes during the Modern English period. On the pages that follow, you will consider some of these changes.

Changes in Pronunciation

With the introduction of the printing press into England in 1476, English spelling became fairly stabilized. At the same time, however, the sound patterns of English were in the process of a remarkable change. Briefly, all the long vowels generally came to be pronounced with a greater elevation of the tongue. The vowel sounds that couldn't be raised without becoming consonants became diphthongs. The effects of the shift are most evident in a comparison of Chaucer's pronunciations (Middle English) with those of Shakespeare (early Modern English). Linguists refer to these changes in pronunciation as the "Great Vowel Shift."

Since the early Modern English period, other changes in pronunciation have occurred. Shakespeare, for example, did not rhyme *sea* with *glee*—as we do today—nor *heap* with *keep*, nor *speak* with *seek*. However, Shakespeare did rhyme words that are not compatible in twentieth-century Modern English. In the following list, he rhymed the words on the left with those on the right:

alone	gone, one, anon
are	care, compare, prepare, rare
blood	brood, good
come	doom
everywhere	near, clear, year, appear
fiend	friend, end
forth	worth
herd	beard
is	amiss, his, this
last	taste
moan	foregone, gone, upon

near	there, were, everywhere
none	stone
past	waste, haste
tongue	song
was	glass, pass
word	afford

Changes in Form and Structure

A few lines from Shakespeare's *Richard III* will indicate the direction of some of the grammatical changes that occurred in the Modern English period:

> Gloucester: The fitter for the King of Heaven, that hath him.
> Anne: He is in Heaven, where thou shalt never come.
> Gloucester: Let him thank me that holp to send him thither.

The use of *holp* where a modern writer would use *helped* is an example of several verbs whose inflections have changed from irregular (strong) to regular (weak) since the early Modern English period. In other verb forms, an -*s* now substitutes for -*eth* or -*th*, as in *hath (has)* in the passage above or as in these verbs found elsewhere in Shakespeare: *fitteth (fits), maketh (makes), draweth (draws), doth (does), seemeth (seems), thrusteth (thrusts).*

The word *thou* is rarely used today, although *thee* is retained in some religious communities as a form of address. This particular linguistic change within early Modern English is evident in Shakespeare's plays in which he varies from one usage to another: *thou-you, thy-your, thee-you.* Words that followed *thou* also changed in form: *thou shalt* and *thou art* became *you shall* and *you are.*

Other changes in form include the substitution of *spoke* for *spake* and of *eyes* for *eyne* (more often *eyen*). Most early Modern English plurals ending in -*n (kneen, shoon)* later gave way to the -*s* inflection *(knees, shoes).*

A form added to English during the Modern English period is the possessive *its.* This form gradually took hold as English nouns lost their inflections for gender.

Present-day Modern English has lost expressions and patterns which were conventional in Shakespeare's time but which sound unfamiliar today. For example, we speak of *daybreak* or the *break of day*, while the nurse in *Romeo and Juliet* says, "The *day is broke,* . . ." Again, Shakespeare writes, "The juice of it on sleeping eyelids laid / will make or man or woman madly dote. . . ." Today we would substitute *either* for the first *or*, or would omit the connective.

Exercise 1

A. *From a selection of Shakespeare's sonnets, make a list of ten words that apparently rhymed in Shakespeare's day but do not rhyme today. Do you believe that we enjoy Shakespeare's poetry any less because of these changes in vowel sounds? Contrast the effect of these unrhymed pairs with deliberately unrhymed verse.*

B. *In the course of four hundred years, Modern English has lost certain expressions and structures that were common in Shakespeare's time. What are the modern equivalents of these quotations from Shakespeare?*

1. Saw you the king today, my lord?

2. What means this scene of rude impatience?

3. He speaks home, madam.

4. Not all the water in the rough, rude sea can wash the balm off from an annointed king.

5. Here stand I.

Changes in Spelling

Some English spelling has been simplified during the Modern English period, and the tendency toward regularity and conformity continues. In manuscripts from the early Modern English period, we find a final *e* that is no longer evident in English spelling:

againe	doe	kinde
beene	finde	soone

The final *k* in certain words has also been gradually eliminated:

Asiatick   domestick   musick   publick

A study of sixteenth-century manuscripts also shows that each writer tended to spell differently, and within a writer's works the same words are often spelled in a variety of ways. Names were not an exception:

Shakespeare	Shackspeare	Shagspere	Shake-Speare
Shakspere	Shackspere	Shake-speare	

Exercise 2

Many attempts have been made to simplify English spelling. Research and report on one of these attempts. In your report, include arguments for and against simplified spelling.

THE TREND TOWARD CONFORMITY

Many influences account for the standardization of English during the Modern English period. On the pages that follow, you will consider some of these influences.

Introduction of Printing

William Caxton (1421–1491) is credited with introducing into England the process of printing with movable type—a process which had its beginnings a few years earlier in Germany.

The year was 1476; the place, London. The impact of this event on our lives today can hardly be exaggerated. Before the widespread use of the printing press, every copy of every book was a handwritten manuscript, laboriously copied and reproduced. The copier frequently varied from the original by making deletions and additions, altering spellings, and changing words. Printed copies were, of course, identical and consequently brought increasing conformity to spelling and usage in written English. Later, as children learned to read from books, conformity in speech also increased.

By the time some of Shakespeare's plays got into print, there were several different versions circulating in manuscript form. Once in print, his works have survived the centuries. But the early printed versions varied according to their manuscript sources. Thus, scholars today are still doing detective work to decide which parts of which versions include the text as Shakespeare actually wrote it. Imagine how tangled this web would be, if—instead of ten or twenty-five years in this fluid state—Shakespeare's plays had been reproduced by hand copying for three hundred years. Over the centuries, printing has brought increasing uniformity to our language.

The Rising Prestige of London

It is only natural that the language habits of educated Londoners should become the model on which Modern English would base a good part of its standardization. Even before London became a center for printing books in English, it was the hub of a growing and shifting population. Furthermore, commerce made the city a trade and communication center. Great universities in the area added to its intellectual influence. The presence of the King and his court further enhanced the prestige of London. These and other factors contributed to the establishment of the language of London, England, as the standard for spoken and written English.

Further Uniformity Through Study

Uniformity in Modern English owes much to the deliberate study of the language which accident and the ages had given to native speakers of English. As the result of this study, standards of English were proclaimed. As schools were provided for more and more children in the early Modern English period, conformity in language habits was further encouraged. Even a uniform pronunciation was taught.

Englishmen became increasingly self-conscious about their language. They published books expounding their views on spelling, grammar and related subjects. Although their books were sometimes based on assumptions that have since been challenged, the early grammarians contributed to the fixing of many of the standards still in use today.

Famous Lexicographers

The fact that a quarter of a billion people in the English-speaking community share a language that is fairly uniform is due largely to the influence of the dictionary makers, or lexicographers. Samuel Johnson, a famous Englishman of letters, published in 1755 *A Dictionary of the English Language*. Despite its defects, Dr. Johnson's dictionary set standards for spelling and presented a more comprehensive listing of the English vocabulary than had been done previously.

In the United States, the name Noah Webster comes immediately to mind when dictionaries are mentioned. In 1806, Webster published his *Compendious Dictionary of the English Language*, which was revised in 1828 under the title *An American Dictionary of the English Language*.

One of the largest and most comprehensive dictionaries in English is *A New English Dictionary on Historical Principles*, popularly known as the *Oxford English Dictionary* (OED). This encyclopedic compilation lists all known English words and word combinations and gives historical, dated instances of their use. The OED was begun under the direction of Sir James Murray in 1884 and continued under Sir William Craigie until it was finished in 1928. Sir William also directed the preparation of *A Dictionary of American English*.

In the United States, meanwhile, dictionary makers continued in the tradition of Noah Webster. In 1889, the *Century Dictionary* appeared. In 1893 Funk and Wagnalls *New Standard* was well known.

In 1843, the Merriam brothers — owners of a printing office and bookstore in Springfield, Massachusetts — arranged to revise and print the 1841 edition of Webster's *American Dictionary*. Since that time, in a series of unabridged, college, and school dictionaries, Merriam-Webster has recorded the English language as it is spoken and written by the majority of its American users. The publication of *Webster's Third New*

International Dictionary in 1961 stirred up a flurry of editorial comment on the role of the lexicographer. For a collection of these comments, see the bibliography entry for James Sledd's *Dictionaries and That Dictionary* at the end of this section of your textbook.

Exercise 3

Research and report on one or more of the following:

1. What is a printing press with movable type? How did its introduction into England affect the English language?

2. What would the Bible be like today if it had never circulated except in handwritten copies?

3. Name five dialect areas within the United States. Name two within fifty miles of where you live. What do these dialects sound like? Why have they developed or persisted?

4. Why did London become the capital of England?

5. Find five words that have different spellings in the United States and England. List five common objects that have different names in the United States and England.

6. Lexicographers recognize that all living languages change constantly. Find five words whose meanings have changed within your lifetime or the lifetime of your parents.

THE EXPANDING VOCABULARY OF MODERN ENGLISH

While many of the words we use today have been in the language for over a thousand years, many more have not. A number of words and meanings have come into our language during the Modern English period. Since 1500, borrowings from other languages have enriched the English language. In recent times especially, innovations have kept the English lexicon sufficiently stocked to talk and write about the exciting and constantly changing world in which we live.

French Borrowings

One of the best-known language scholars of the twentieth century, Albert C. Baugh, has estimated that 10,000 French words came into the English language during the Middle English period—the time after the Norman Conquest when English was spoken by the lower classes and French by the ruling class. Modern English has continued to enrich the language with French borrowings.

caress	duel	moustache	tomato
comrade	entrance	pioneer	trophy
dessert	essay	shock	vogue
detail	explore	ticket	volunteer

French also served as a clearing house for importing Latin, Italian, and Spanish words into early Modern English.

Latin and Greek Borrowings

The influence of Latin and Greek borrowings on the English lexicon can hardly be overemphasized. The revival of interest in the classics during the Modern English period led to the widespread use of Latin and Greek terms that soon found a permanent place in the English language. Imagine English, if you can, without such words as these:

abject	denunciation	insinuate
acme	dissipate	*insomnia
*acumen	drama	logic
agile	erupt	monosyllable
allusion	exact	music
*arbiter	exaggerate	obstruction
*area	exasperate	paradox
*arena	excursion	parenthesis
astronomy	exert	pneumonia
atmosphere	expensive	*pollen
autograph	explain	pretext
capsule	external	prologue
climax	extinguish	rhetoric
comprehensible	fact	scene
congratulatory	frivolous	submerged
crisis	frugal	thermometer
criterion	*genius	*virus

* See exercise 4B.

Borrowings from Other Languages

The cultural leadership of Italy during the early Modern English period is evident in many of the Italian loanwords that came into English during the Renaissance:

algebra	design	portico
balcony	granite	stanza
cameo	grotto	stucco
carnival	piazza	violin

England's rivalry with Spain and Portugal for prominence on the seas and in newly discovered lands brought many new words into the lexicon.

alligator	canyon	hurricane
apricot	corral	mesa
banana	desperado	potato
cannibal	embargo	tobacco

Exercise 4

A. *From the list of loanwords from Latin and Greek, choose several that are associated with the theater. Are these words derived from Latin or Greek? (See the bibliography at the end of this section for sources that will help you with this assignment.) What does the origin of these words tell you about the culture of the people from whom they originated?*

B. *Several loanwords in the list referred to in part A are starred. Look these words up in the* Oxford English Dictionary *and give the date of entry into the English lexicon. Report to the class any other interesting facts you discover about these words.*

THE AMERICAN INFLUENCE

With the settlement of the American Colonies, a new intermingling of languages occurred. The English that resulted was never to be the same as the Elizabethan English that came with the first settlers.

The Dutch settled New York (calling it New Amsterdam) and gave Dutch place names to nearby geographical features such as the *Catskill* Mountains and the *Schuylkill* River. They also contributed common words such as *boss, cookie, stoop,* and *sleigh.* French settlers in the south of the new country introduced *bayou, bureau, caribou* (a French adaptation of an Indian word), and *chowder.* The Spanish influence on the southwest United States contributed such words as *canyon* and *mesa.*

When the settlers spread westward through the American continent, they encountered unfamiliar animals, plants, and objects. To describe their new environment, the settlers appropriated terms used by the American Indian tribes:

chipmunk	moose	raccoon
hominy	opossum	skunk
moccasin	pone	succotash

Perhaps the greatest gift the Indians made to the English language in America are the place names still used for cities, states, rivers, and mountains. Nearly half the states have Indian names. Among the rivers are the *Allegheny, Chippewa, Mohawk, Monongahela, Missouri,* and the *Mississippi*. Cities, too, remind the modern American of the Indians: *Sioux Falls, Ogallala, Wichita, Yakima.*

Exercise 5   Research and report on the Indian words that are used as place names in your community. Give the tribe from which each name originated and tell what the word means in its language of origin.

CHANGING WORDS FOR A CHANGING WORLD

When a man's environment changes, he needs words to describe and discuss the change. He may borrow words from another language, he may devise a new word from bits and pieces of other words, or he may give a new meaning to an old word.

Many new words are derived from proper names. *Graham crackers, diesel engines,* and *macadam roads* are called by the names of their inventors or originators. Some common words derived from names that are not quite so obvious are *boycott, dahlia, gardenia, grog, guillotine, lynch, sandwich, saxophone, shrapnel,* and *silhouette.*

Perhaps the most common of all devices by which man stretches his vocabulary to fit a changing environment is the use of an old word to fit a new situation. For example, what was once designated as a place for treatment and storage of feed for livestock (a *silo*) now designates a storage chamber for ballistic missiles.

From whatever source he finds most appropriate, man discovers words to fit the new world constantly taking shape around him. The earliest English settlers on this continent encountered many things with which they had no previous experience and for which they had no names. But they soon found words, such as *bluff* and *foothill*, to describe surface features; *clearing* and *underbrush*, to describe certain conditions; *hickory, locust,* and *pecan* to describe trees heretofore unknown to them. Their world (and the English language) also gained *squash, sweet potatoes, popcorn, log cabins, backwoodsmen, mud hens, garter snakes,* and *bullfrogs.*

If the eighteenth- and nineteenth-century American found his life (and vocabulary) changing on the frontier, the twentieth-century American has found his changing on the battlefield. Among terms acquired in World War I are *barrage* and *camouflage*. World War II planted or enlarged the meaning of the following words:

airdrop	frogman	radar
booby trap	jeep	underground
dehydrated food	landing craft	walkie-talkie

Later conflicts gave the English language the terms *cold* and *hot wars; jets, helicopters, brainwashing,* and *airlifts,* are recent adaptations and compounds. An example of the substitution of a new meaning for an old one is the use of the words *hawks* and *doves* to designate people willing to go to war if necessary and those willing to go to great lengths to avoid war. These terms, originally used in the period of American expansion before the War of 1812, were recently revived.

There have been other battlefields in the twentieth century and other frontiers. Two generations ago, today's meanings for *tranquilizer* and *antibiotic* did not exist. The invention of radio and television gave English the words *audio, video, telecast, transistor,* and such slang expressions as *boob tube* and *idiot cards.* Other words adopted in the electronic and atomic age are *computer, microwaves, sonar, radar, fallout,* and *radioactive.* Advances in aviation added to the vocabulary with words such as *sonic barriers* and *sonic booms.*

When men finally left earth for space, they coined a new vocabulary that became widely familiar within a few years:

aerospace	debriefing	satellite
astronaut	orbit	space station
blast off	propellant gun	splashdown
cosmonaut	reentry	tracking station

Some strictly technical terms—*blast off*, for example—entered everyday slang with a different meaning which may eventually become part of standard English.

Exercise 6

A. *Below is a stanza from* The Faerie Queene *by Edmund Spenser, who died in 1599. The language is understandable, with some study, but there are spellings, word forms, and idiomatic expressions that have since passed from Modern English. Rewrite the stanza in current standard English.*

The Messenger approaching to him spake;
But his waste wordes retourned to him in vaine:
So sound he slept, that nought mought him awake.
Then rudely he him thrust, and pusht with paine,
Whereat he gan to stretch; but he againe
Shooke him so hard, that forced him to speake.
As one then in a dreame, whose dryer braine
Is tost with troubled sights and fancies weake,
He mumbled soft, but would not all his silence
    breake.

B. *For each of the following categories, list ten words that came into the English lexicon in the twentieth century.*

Exercise 6,   Indicate, if possible, the source of each word you list.

continued   Food   Entertainment   The Peace Movement
               Sports   Literature   Technology

C. With what category do you think the next great wave of new words to enter the English lexicon will be associated? Be prepared to defend your answer. (Categories should not be limited to those cited in part B.)

SUGGESTED SOURCE MATERIAL

The following source material will be of use to you in preparing some of the reports called for in "The History of English." Two essential sources for any study of the Modern English period are the *Oxford English Dictionary* and *A Dictionary of American English*, published in several volumes. If these dictionaries are not available in your school or community libraries, ask your librarian for help in locating a nearby library that includes the OED and the DAE in its reference collection.

Barnett, Lincoln, *The Treasure of Our Tongue*, New York, Alfred A. Knopf, Inc., 1965.

Baugh, Albert C., *A History of the English Language*, New York, Appleton-Century-Crofts, Inc., 1957.

Bryant, Margaret M., *Modern English and Its Heritage*, New York, Macmillan Co., 1962.

Francis, W. Nelson, *The English Language*, New York, W. W. Norton & Co., Inc., 1965.

Partridge, Eric, *Origins, A Short Etymological Dictionary of Modern English*, New York, Macmillan Co., 1959.

Pyles, Thomas, *Words and Ways of American English*, New York, Random House, Inc., 1952.

Sledd, James, *Dictionaries and That Dictionary*, Chicago, Scott, Foresman and Company, 1962.

INDEX